THE EURO
THE POLITICS OF THE NEW GLOBAL CURRENCY

DAVID MARSH

YALE UNIVERSITY PRESS
NEW HAVEN AND LONDON

For my mother and father, Marguerite and Dennis

For information about this and other Yale University Press publications, please contact:

U.S. Office: sales.press@yale.edu   yalebooks.com
Europe Office: sales@yaleup.co.uk   www.yaleup.co.uk

Set in Minion by IDSUK (DataConnection) Ltd.
Printed in Great Britain by Hobbs the Printers Ltd, Totton, Hampshire

Library of Congress Cataloging-in-Publication Data

Marsh, David, 1952–
    The euro: the politics of the new global currency / David Marsh.
      p. cm.
    Includes bibliographical references and index.
    ISBN 978-0-300-12730-0 (ci : alk. paper)
    1. Money—European Union countries—History. 2. Euro—History. 3. Monetary policy—European Union countries—History. I. Title.
    HG930.5.M269 2009
    332.4'94—dc22
    2008047960

A catalogue record for this book is available from the British Library.

ISBN 978-0-300-16400-8 (pbk)

FSC
Mixed Sources
Product group from well-managed
forests and other controlled sources

Cert no. SA-COC-001530
www.fsc.org
© 1996 Forest Stewardship Council

The paper used for the text pages of this book is FSC certified. FSC (The Forest Stewardship Council) is an international network to promote responsible management of the world's forests.

10 9 8 7 6 5 4 3 2 1

2013 2012 2011 2010

CONTENTS

LIST OF ILLUSTRATIONS

PREFACE

If you are going to make a bet with the chancellor of Germany, especially one who is reputed to get his own way, then better make it on a subject where you're likely to win. That was my thought at the European summit conference at Maastricht in the Netherlands which set down the road map for Economic and Monetary Union. Helmut Kohl said in his larger-than-life fashion at a late-night press conference in December 1991 that Britain would join by 1997, since the City would push the British government towards the Euro. I argued that this would not be the case, and after some verbal sparring about what Kohl said was the English love of betting (in fact, the last time I had had a flutter was on the Grand National at the age of twelve), we agreed a wager: six bottles of English against six bottles of German wine. Following a gentle reminder, the chancellor invited me to his office to share a glass with him and generously paid out the full bet in 1997.

The story of the Euro goes back a lot further than that. One of the challenges (and delights) involved in writing this book has been to trace back the tides of history into hundreds of tributaries and eddying currents that collectively flow into the European single currency. I have tried hard to write this from an international rather than a purely British viewpoint, to see the larger political and historical as well as the purely economic and financial issues, and to piece together the complicated subject matter in a way that is reasonably accessible for readers who do not care much about abstruse monetary questions. This is a historical account that blends into a chronicling of contemporary events, for there are clear links between the attempts to quell the power of the financial markets through the European single currency and the unfolding saga of the international credit crisis and ensuing recession that erupted and deepened while I was writing this book. Ambitiously, I have attempted to show how these diverse strands join up.

I could not have undertaken this work without the help of many people to whom I owe a great deal. Before I decided to embark upon the book, in summer 2006, I sought the advice of Manfred Körber and Helmut Schlesinger, respectively former head of the press and public affairs department at both the Bundesbank and the European Central Bank, and former president of the Bundesbank – the latter distinguished but frequently extremely controversial. I wanted to gauge the support that I might glean from former Bundesbank people who had helped me in the past but might tire of satisfying my curiosity, particularly after they had retired and were hoping for some peace and quiet. Both replied that they would be pleased to help, and they subsequently lived up to this promise on several occasions. In June 2006 I visited the Bundesbank archives department – which had been extremely helpful in 1991 when I was researching *The Bundesbank: The Bank that Rules Europe*, which appeared in 1992. The same people who had assisted me fifteen years ago – Rolf Herget, Gerd-Christian Wannovius and Karin Fitzner – were even more enthusiastic, cheerful and constructive than they had been before. In my Bundesbank book, I had dug up material about the strong links between the Reichsbank and the Bundesbank, including the Nazi past of many of the Bundesbank's leading officials in the post-war years. This did not always cause unmitigated pleasure in Germany, and if anyone had indicated that this might hamper me in accessing documentation on the Euro, then I would probably have concluded that what already appeared a massively daunting task would have become plainly impossible – and would have turned to another hobby such as learning to play the piano or improving my tennis service.

Instead, these initially positive responses set me off on a voyage of discovery. All this made me realise anew how fortunate I had been to be able to maintain contact, in a variety of ways, with some of the leading players in the complex and contorted Euro story. I was able to track them all down and speak to them in a highly concentrated way between February 2007 and July 2008 – exploring their reminiscences of what had happened in the past, discussing their views on the present and the future, and checking these statements with other people's testimony and published and archival records. The personalities whom I saw were on the whole politicians and officials, many of whom were still serving in official duties running countries, businesses, departments or central banks. I supplemented these insights with many relevant documents from archives in Europe and the US, many of which have not previously been published, as well as my own first-hand knowledge of events and accounts in books and other forms of media. Only in a handful of cases did such conversations prove to be impracticable. The reasons varied: work pressures, shyness, obstructiveness, old age, illness and (in one instance, I am sorry to say) mortality.

I have used caution in trying to assemble an accurate account. Politicians' and officials' statements about past episodes can be, and normally are, inaccurate, incomplete and/or partial. Even the most powerful and best-connected people can only be in one place at one time. An ancillary reason for care in constructing a chronicle of the past is that intelligent, informed and experienced individuals often depart from meetings with different views about what went on. They may hear, and repeat later, what they want to hear, rather than what is actually said. At the time of the meeting, imprecision often abounds – particularly when individuals split off into pairs or smaller groups to speak about more important matters by themselves, and where linguistic problems are evident. Where participants spread confusion about their real thoughts and intentions, either through guile or incompetence, the result will be still less satisfactory. The least gratifying outcome is when interlocutors tell each other messages they want to project in a form that they believe others wish to hear in a language that few command at a meeting that everyone wishes speedily to finish. In view of the interlocking nature of the financial, monetary, political and strategic issues, my attempt to weave together the threads from various sources can only be a work in progress. Even when records are officially available, following the expiry of the usual thirty-year rule, piecing together the different national and international strands is problematic. Still more so is the effort to discern the truth regarding more recent events, such as the foreign exchange market turmoil of 1992–93. With respect to the epic Battle of the Franc that erupted in September 1992 and dragged on for almost another year, with enormous consequences for Franco-German relations and the road map towards EMU, the challenge is especially arduous. I have been lucky enough to have gained access to key French records for part of this account; the German records have been less readily available, although several participants have been kind enough to answer my questions to help check the veracity of the French rendering.

Irrespective of these caveats, I would like wholeheartedly to thank the following people who generously gave their time for long, detailed conversations, some on more than one occasion. (I hope I will be forgiven for leaving out, for the sake of simplicity, peerages, knighthoods, professorships, doctorates and other titles.) Most of them are quoted in different parts of the book. In nearly all cases they agreed to speak 'on the record', and subsequently authorised a set of agreed quotes, from which I have drawn the interview statements, which therefore stand as an authentic historical record. From Austria, I spoke with Gertrude Tumpel-Gugerell; from Belgium, Alexandre Lamfalussy; from Cyprus, Athanasios Orphanides; from France, Edmond Alphandéry, Marc-Antoine Autheman, Edouard Balladur, Michel Camdessus, Jean-Philippe Cotis, Jean-Pierre Chevènement, Jacques Delors, Valéry Giscard d'Estaing, Bertrand Dumont, Frédéric Gonand, Henri Guaino, Hervé Hannoun, Laurent Fabius, André Gauron, Elisabeth Guigou, Jacques de Larosière, Jean Lemierre, Philippe Lagayette, Christian Noyer, Dominique Moisi, Michel Pébereau, Jean Peyrelevade, Michel Rocard, Michel Sapin, Yves-Thibault de Silguy, Jean-Claude Trichet, Hubert Védrine; from Germany, Rolf Breuer, Hans Eichel, Wilfried Guth, Gert Haller, Hansgeorg Hauser, Hans-Dietrich Genscher, Wolfgang Ischinger, Otmar Issing, Hans-Helmut Kotz, Manfred Lahnstein, Thomas Mirow, Klaus-Peter Müller, Wilhelm Nölling, Bernd Pfaffenbach, Karl Otto Pöhl, Peter-Wilhelm Schlüter, Gerhard Schröder, Wilhelm Schönfelder, Helmut Schmidt, Jürgen Stark, Peer Steinbrück, Hans Tietmeyer, Dietrich von Kyaw, Hans-Friedrich von Ploetz, Hermann von Richthofen, Kurt Viermetz, Theo Waigel, Axel Weber, Manfred Weber, Ernst Welteke; from Italy, Giuliano Amato, Lorenzo Bini Smaghi, Lamberto Dini, Romano Prodi, Tommaso Padoa-Schioppa, Alessandro Profumo, Fabrizio Saccomanni and by correspondence Piero Barucci and Antonio Fazio; from Greece, Lucas Papademos; from Ireland, John Hurley, Tony Grimes, Tom O'Connell; from the Netherlands, Wim Kok, Ruud Lubbers, Nout Wellink, Onno Ruding, André Szász, Jan van der Tas; from Malta, Michael Bonello; from Spain, José Manuel González-Páramo, Miguel Ángel Fernández Ordóñez (by correspondence); from the UK, Bill Allen, Alan Budd, Terry Burns, Kenneth Clarke, Andrew Crockett, Eddie George, Denis Healey, Nicholas Henderson, Sarah Hogg, Geoffrey Howe, Douglas Hurd, Norman Lamont, Nigel Lawson, Richard Lambert, Robin Leigh-Pemberton, Anthony Loehnis, Denis MacShane, John Major, Gus O'Donnell, David Simon, Adair Turner, Stephen Wall, Peter Walker, Douglas Wass, Stewart Wood; from the US, Tom Connors, Donald Kohn, Robert Kimmitt, John Lipsky, Paul Volcker.

I owe a debt of gratitude to the following people in archives for their painstaking help: at the Bank of England, Sarah Millard, Jenny Ulph, Ben White, Jeanette Sherry, Kath Begley, Sue Jenkins, John Keyworth; at the Banque de France, Frédérik Grélard, Fabrice Reuze, Odile Bouttie, Josiane Cueille, Christian Lebrument, Daniel Quinet; at the Bank for International Settlements, Edward Atkinson, Piet Clement; at the Bundesarchiv Koblenz, Michael Hollmann, Claudia Zenkel-Oertel; at the Centre des archives économiques et financiers, Economics and Finance Ministry (France), Aurélie Outtrabady, Cécile Vaniet; at the Historisches Archiv, Deutsche Bundesbank (in addition to those mentioned above), Harald Pohl, Michael Müller; at the European Central Bank, Stuart Orr; at the Foreign and Commonwealth Office (UK), Patrick Salmon, Isabelle Tombs; at the Politisches Archiv, Foreign Office (Germany), Johannes von Boeselager; at the New York Federal Reserve Bank, Joe Komljenovich, Marja Vitti; at the Institut François Mitterrand, Georges Saunier; at the Schleswig Holstein Parliament Archives, Joachim Koehler. I am grateful to Klaus Rieke, brother of the former head of the Bundesbank's international department, the late Wolfgang Rieke, for making available his brother's collection of central banking photographs through the Bundesbank's archives department.

I would like to thank the following acquaintances and friends for reading parts of the manuscript, providing comments, recommending improvements and pointing out errors: Iain Begg, Bob Bischof (who read through several drafts), Stephen Collins, Anthony Evans, Nicholas Henderson, Peter Hoeller, Harold James, Antoine Jeancourt-Galignani, Norman Lamont, Dieter Lindenlaub, Michael Maclay, Peter Norman, Willie Paterson, Herbert Quelle, Helmut Schlesinger, Michael Stürmer, André Szász, Peter von der Heydt, Jan von Haeften, Kurt Viermetz, Douglas Wass. Holger Schmieding (as on three previous occasions) provided detailed and relevant comments and corrections that helped me surmount significant hurdles. Wilhelm Nölling, as in the past, performed sterling service. Any remaining errors of fact or judgement are completely my responsibility.

For proving the inspiration behind the original theme of 'Blood and Gold', I am grateful to Fritz Stern; for advice, assistance, discussion and encouragement of the most diverse kind, I thank Éric Aeschimann, Marco Annunziata, Elisabeth Ardaillon, Ralph Atkins, Tony Barber, Dave and Gayle Beek, Geoffrey Bell, Paul Betts, Nick Bray, Christian Burckhardt, Ewen and Donald Cameron Watt, Forrest Capie, Chris Collins, Robert Deane, Darrell Delamaide, Tom Eijsbouts, Jennie and Stewart Fleming, Frederick Forsyth, Francesco Giordano, Veronika Hass, Ulrich Hoppe, Jackson Janes, Bill Keegan, Jürgen Krönig, Desmond Lachman, John Makin, Andreas Meyer-Schwickerath, Carlo Monticelli, Janis Motivans, Gilles Noblet, Gabriele Pandolfi, John Plender, John Redwood, Andrew Riley, Alessandro Roselli, Tanel Ross, Regina Schuller, Philip Short, George Soros, Gabor Steingart, Gillian Tett, John Thornhill, Gianni Toniolo, Ted Truman, Peter Underwood, John Williamson, Philip Ziegler. I thank my colleagues at London & Oxford for their tolerance and zeal: Paul Newton was kind enough to support the project from the beginning, Jamie Bulgin,

Wiebke Räber and Ramona Mitschke provided essential assistance of all kinds; Freddy Hopson, Mark Leclercq and Dimitri Hatzis gave practical and philosophical advice. Arthur Goodhart was instrumental in starting and developing the book. Robert Baldock and Phoebe Clapham at Yale University Press provided immensely valuable support and guidance, including during the skilfully handled editing process. My brother Peter was extremely helpful at several important stages, and the book would not have been possible without my wife Veronika and daughters Saskia and Sabrina.

David Marsh
Wimbledon, September 2008

As I write this towards the end of 2009, the world is slowly recovering from the international financial upheavals and the savage economic slowdown that followed. By common consent, the Euro has had a good crisis. The European Central Bank – like other leading central banks around the world – has followed an appropriate course in cutting interest rates and injecting liquidity into the banking markets, and has emerged with its authority enhanced. And yet the real test for the resilience of the Euro will come when recovery gets under way and the ECB starts to raise interest rates. Additionally, if the Euro area starts to look increasingly like another, larger and more complex, version of the old D-Mark zone, then some countries which fought long and hard for monetary union, such as France, may become more openly disappointed with what they have achieved.

On the wider stage, the Euro has its part to play in the epic economic and political tussle between the US and China, respectively the world's largest debtor and creditor. The world's economic convulsions have accelerated a power shift. The rise of Asia and the other important emerging economies continues unabated. President Barack Obama, taking office in January 2009 with a message of hope for America and the rest of the world, has not made much difference to the underlying downwards trend of the dollar and the uncertainties over the US currency's longer-term international status.

One sad note. Of the many people who helped me with the writing of the book, six have unfortunately died since its completion. I would like to record their names, reaffirming my gratitude: Christian Burckhardt, Eddie George, Wilfried Guth, Nicholas Henderson, Peter von der Heydt, Jan van der Tas.

David Marsh
Wimbledon, November 2009

INTRODUCTION: THE STORY OF THE EURO

The Euro, probably more than any other currency, represents the mutual confidence at the heart of our community. It is the first currency that has not only severed its link to gold, but also its link to the nation-state.

Wim Duisenberg, President, European Central Bank, 2002[1]

The Euro, according to its supporters – and they abound in their millions, within and beyond Europe – is one of the Old Continent's brightest and grandest success stories. The supranational money at the heart of Economic and Monetary Union (EMU) launched in 1999 has become the second most important international currency after the US dollar – and one day could supersede it. The European single currency, with a unified monetary and interest rate policy across the sixteen-country EMU area, is breaking down barriers between people, companies and markets – a central component of post-Cold War Europe following the fall of the Berlin Wall and the reunification of Germany. During the international financial convulsions of 2007–08 the single currency protected Europe from still worse fall-out from the credit crisis that started in the US and then spread to the whole world.

The Euro's advocates extol how it enhances economic performance and social integration across a continent that not long ago was beset by Eurosclerosis and divided into Communist and capitalist blocs. The independent European Central Bank (ECB), running the Euro from Frankfurt in Germany, has become an institution of world-wide renown. The Euro area makes up one-fifth of the global economy and a population of 320 million – in economic size, roughly equivalent to the US. EMU's members include three of the world's top seven economies – Germany, France and Italy[2] – as well as the Netherlands, Belgium and Luxembourg, the three other founders of the original six-nation European Economic Community that started in 1958. The success of the Euro lies in its diversity, its devotees say: the other ten Euro adherents, with highly disparate pedigrees, all joined what is now the twenty-seven-state European Union (EU) over the past three and a half decades. Ireland, Cyprus and Malta were formerly under British dominion. Slovenia and Slovakia were Communist countries up to the end of the Cold War. Austria and Finland were neutral. Greece, Portugal and Spain (in 2008, the world's ninth largest economy) were dictatorships up to the 1970s.[3]

Confirming its long-held ambivalence over European integration, Britain has decided – resolutely, maybe obdurately – to remain outside EMU. Two of the other top ten economies in the European Union – Sweden and Poland – remain, too, on the sidelines, although for different reasons; formerly Communist Poland is one of the Central and Eastern Europe states that are candidates to join in the second decade of the twenty-first century. If the Euro performs well, all the non-adherents, including Britain and the other long-time EU member that has chosen non-Euro status, Denmark, will be under growing pressure to join. Indeed, in many ways, the Euro knows no boundaries. Vast numbers of people outside the Euro area have high regard for the solidity and sheer convenience of the European monetary unit. In cash terms during 2008 there were 15 to 20 per cent more Euros in world-wide circulation than dollars.[4] In Asia, Latin America and the Middle East, the Euro supplies a template for a wide range of regional monetary unions that may be established in coming years.

Underlining its international influence, the European Central Bank's authority is second only to that of the Federal Reserve Board in Washington, repository of the no-longer-so-mighty dollar. The ECB's achievements in supplying vast quantities of much-needed liquidity to international banks in the wake of the sub-prime mortgage crisis that erupted in the US in August 2007 earned the respect of many previous critics. As the world grappled with the fall-out of the credit upheaval, as well as the interlinked challenges of an explosion in oil prices and a substantial economic slowdown, the ECB appeared, to many, as a safe harbour in a storm. According to a widely-held notion, the world has moved to a new tri-currency system in which America, Europe and China parley over power; the monetary future of the globe is in the hands of a triumvirate of central banks in Washington, Frankfurt and Beijing.

Yet the rosy assessment of the Euro does not provide anything like the full picture. According to another much more negative yet still plausible view,

EMU is a flawed project and the consequences will haunt Europeans for years to come. Introduced above all for political reasons, the Euro, it is claimed, has failed to bring about sufficient economic convergence among its disparate members. The incongruous membership, the Euro's critics say, is too diverse and lacks the necessary economic flexibility to prosper as a single currency area.[5] Especially in the wake of the post-2007 downturn, which by late 2008 left Europe facing the worst recession since the Second World War, the perils of running a single monetary policy for a group of countries at different stages of development are growing steadily more visible. A prime aim of the decades-long struggle towards monetary union has been to shield Europe from US financial vicissitudes. However, according to the Euro-sceptical viewpoint, the single currency has made Europe more vulnerable to international monetary turmoil, by extending the global links between Europe's now-widened capital markets and the US – and also by exacerbating unhelpful sources of rigidity in the continent's economic management. The rise in the Euro's popularity among investors and banks reflects far less Europe's innate financial attractiveness, far more the profligacy of US politicians presiding over a steady decline in the dollar, progressively weighed down in the 2000s by America's deteriorating finances, with both the internal budget deficit and the current account deficit running at around 5 per cent of GDP in 2008.[6] Even the astonishing rise in circulation of cross-border Euros is a negative factor, on this view, since it partly reflects the tendency of international criminals to hold their illegitimate gains in large-denomination Euro banknotes, which are seen as more convenient and secure than dollars.

The negative interpretation of the Euro's speedily-won status is that pride goes before a fall. Rather than catalysing European renewal, the Euro is holding back Europe's efforts to repair its position in a world where economic dynamism is migrating to America and Asia. Still worse, emerging divisions threaten the fifty-year-old process of post-Second World War European unification. EMU economies – although growing together in many ways – display wide and sometimes increasing imbalances. At the heart of the matter is Germany, Europe's strongest economy, which by 2008 had substantially (though not wholly) recovered from the trials of reunification eighteen years previously. Fixed European exchange rates provide disproportionate support for Germany's export-orientated economy by making its industrial sales extremely competitive throughout most of Europe, increasing Germany's export surplus to record levels, and deflecting its attention from the necessary task of stimulating domestic demand – an outcome that would help both itself and its neighbours.

Ironically, one of the reasons why so much of Europe favoured the single currency plan when Germany was reunified was to counter Germany's forecast resurgence. Merging the previously dominant D-Mark with more fragile currencies was forecast to bring a more healthy European equilibrium. That argument was turned on its head in 2006–07. Less competitive countries such as Italy, Spain and Portugal – which can no longer devalue their way out of trouble – needed greatly to improve their economic performances against a newly energised Germany. Although the whole of Europe was weakened by the after-shocks of the US mortgage crisis, Germany seems likely to fare better in coming years than economies that had previously been stimulated by lower interest rates, such as Spain, Ireland and Greece – hard hit when borrowing conditions started to deteriorate in 2007. Britain, which relied on heavy consumer borrowing and a buoyant banking climate for its sixteen-year phase of continuous growth after 1992, has also been badly affected by the credit crunch. However, in the light of the Euro's track record so far, the UK would be well advised not to see EMU membership as a solution to these ills, but to maintain a highly cautious line over membership in the coming decade.

The arresting truth about the Euro is that extreme judgements on its track record and prospects, both positive and negative, can be defended with equal robustness. It is too early to say whether the ten year-old experiment will end in success or failure. The Euro has brought, and will continue to bring, substantial benefits – economic, political and social – to people and states within and outside EMU. Equally, the Euro has exposed shortcomings in economic policy among member countries that – because they can no longer be rectified by devaluation – need to be corrected by painful longer-term adjustments, through lower wage rises, increased working hours and job losses in uncompetitive businesses and sectors. For the broad mass of the European electorate, the Euro's introduction has coincided with a period when the notion of 'Europe' – in stark contrast with most of the previous post-war era – has become a byword for unpopular economic restructuring and belt-tightening.

All this adds up to an extreme set of challenges for the single currency and the political structures behind it. In view of the overarching hopes and expectations that have been invested in the Euro, mere survival is not enough. EMU must provide a genuine route for European countries to improve their economic performances, in a century that will see increasing strength from China, India and other fast-growing developing economies. If that is not the case, the gap between the more and less successful members of monetary union will widen further. And the Euro will face the danger of fragmentation, with either strong or weak countries separating from the system and reintroducing – despite all the costs and upheaval – some form of national currency management more suited to their economic requirements.

One reason for the fascination of the Euro – and the welter of contradictory opinions and forecasts that surround it – is that it marks a comprehensive break with the past. In the 4,000 years since money was invented as a means of exchange, a unit of account and a store of value, monetary policy has always been the stuff of sages, the arena of experts; currency management has seldom formed the vanguard of high politics. The coins of nations provide a guide to the march of events and the fluctuations of statehood, but they are no pioneering force. The members of that most mysterious of communities, the fraternity of central bankers, are called upon for counsel during upheaval, or to restore equilibrium when political and military turmoil wreaks economic disorder. But, in normal circumstances, they work behind the scenes, in response to change. They are followers of transition; they do not fashion it.

The Euro put an end to all that.

An avowedly historical approach to the Euro, such as this book takes, is necessary because the project has been so long in gestation – a chronicle that extends back well beyond the fall of the Berlin Wall, the formation of the European Community, and even the First World War. In a honeycomb of documents in state archives, and in the complex testimony of scores of politicians and officials who accompanied the single currency's journey, lie the secrets behind decades of intricate political infighting that led to the Euro's birth. Yet the fusion of European currencies decided in December 1991 by European leaders at Maastricht in the Netherlands, and launched eight years later for a founding group of eleven European Union countries, was not – in contrast to many past monetary reconfigurations – a product of military upheaval or social insurgency. Money no longer fought a rearguard action behind the lines; it marched to the fore, the spearhead of the new Europe. The new currency and the European Central Bank behind it were themselves the agents for forceful change.

The motivations of the Maastricht treaty were manifold; the diversity of objectives beguiling. A European money would bridge the past, the present and the future, healing social wounds, strengthening political bonds, and reviving economic fortunes. Maastricht brought to a new plane all the international monetary stabilisation efforts put into effect in Europe over hundreds of years. Most of them had ended in failure; all the more reason why the leap forward decided in the Netherlands was prepared with devotional care.

One great aim of EMU was to take further the process of European integration and recovery started after the Second World War with the 1947 European aid programme of US Secretary of State George Marshall. Despite many false starts, interruptions and setbacks, the economic building blocks of the Continent – coal, steel, industry, trade and finance – were progressively fused together. In a process which Britain supported but decided not to join, European cooperation continued with the establishment of the European Payments Union (EPU) in 1950[7] and the European Coal and Steel Community (ECSC) in 1951. The 1957 Treaty of Rome, signed by the founder members of the European Community, pledged to drive Europe on to 'ever closer union' as a means of rebuilding peace and prosperity.[8] The six-nation customs union of the European Economic Community was merged in 1967 with the two other European Communities – the ECSC and the European Atomic Energy Community (for developing nuclear power) – under a single executive body, the European Commission. The European Community (as it became known) took a further leap towards liberalised trade in 1986 when governments decided on a free-trade European Single Market that was then progressively implemented up to 1993. 'A single currency for a single market' became Maastricht's clarion call.

The currency market principles underlying the Maastricht decision marked an important ideological divide among the industrial countries that take the lion's share of the global economy. For the US, Britain, Japan and many other economies (including most of the British Commonwealth as well as many developing nations), floating exchange rates had become the norm during the previous two decades, although nearly always combined with certain amounts of currency management through exchange rate pegging, mainly against the dollar. This had been the case since the 1971–73 break-up of the post-war system of fixed exchange rates established at the monetary conference of Bretton Woods in the US in 1944. Under floating, the free flow of funds on financial markets allowed currencies largely to find their own level, steered only sporadically by central banks' foreign exchange intervention. Supporters of the system believed that floating, although sometimes inconvenient, was the best way of tailoring exchange rates to individual countries' economic circumstances, allowing maximum leeway for growth, trade and investment.

Continental Europe, led by France and Germany, had joined the general move to floating with greater or lesser degrees of reluctance, and held a generally negative view about the consequences of the new system. According to prevalent strands of opinion in these countries, fully floating rates represented an invitation to speculation and distortion that was inimical to sound economic management and rising welfare. To avoid these outcomes, floating needed to be actively managed by governments and central banks, and, if possible and under the right conditions, replaced by fixed exchange rates.

For the architects of Maastricht, the decisive lesson of the past, seen most ruinously in the 1920s and 1930s, was that fluctuating currencies produced economic and political disruption. Since the Second World War, Europe had participated in a series of attempts to stabilise exchange rates, at a global and at a regional level; the failures of successive exchange rate regimes had contributed since the 1970s, it was believed, to economic stagnation, rising inflation and persistent unemployment. The founder members of the European Community formed the core membership of two semi-fixed exchange rate arrangements that started in 1972 and 1979 respectively: the Currency 'Snake' and the European Monetary System (EMS). Crucially, the UK was the only member of the then nine-nation European Community that decided in 1978 against joining the Exchange Rate Mechanism (ERM) of the EMS. The extraordinary story of Britain's long flirtation with the ERM, its delayed entry in 1990 and departure (under disastrous circumstances) in 1992 provides important reasons why the UK did not join EMU and, in 2008, continued to look at the Euro with a jaundiced eye.

Both the Snake and the EMS/ERM were conceived as zones of European currency stability to protect the continent from the perils of floating exchange rates. But, as controls over flows of international capital were progressively eased from the 1980s onwards, leading to enormous increases in the mobility of funds, both European monetary arrangements were prone to frequent, increasingly politicised, currency upsets. Additionally, both the Snake and the EMS became ever more dominated by the D-Mark as the 'anchor currency', in line with the growing strength of Germany's economy and that of its legendarily independent central bank, the Bundesbank. In a world where fixed exchange rate systems were becoming ever more vulnerable to marauding flows of international capital, a succession of currency strains confirmed European governments' view that the EMS was not, and could never become, a permanent recipe for stability. Stemming from these past experiences, the edict of Maastricht was radical: to eradicate once and for all European exchange rate oscillations, by eliminating national currencies and fusing them into a common money for the common good.

The Snake and EMS/ERM experiences provided backing for the economic theory of the so-called 'Impossible Trinity' that gained ground during the 1980s, according to which countries could not simultaneously maintain fixed exchange rates, capital mobility and autonomous monetary policies.[9] By the late 1980s, many European countries, either voluntarily, or with varying degrees of unwillingness, had effectively given up monetary autonomy to the Germans. So the formation of a European Central Bank – in which the Bundesbank's power would (or so it was believed) be heavily diluted – gradually became an aim that could attract even countries like France that held strong traditional reservations about sacrificing national sovereignty.

The progenitors of the Maastricht treaty – led by France and Italy, as well as smaller countries such as Belgium and the Netherlands, but including, too, most of Germany's leading politicians – foresaw a variety of benefits. Stabilising Europe's internal contours would ward off past strife and propel the continent to greater cohesion. Subsuming Germany's D-Mark into a new European monetary order would consolidate the renascent German nation within a stable Europe. The Germans, made prosperous by peace, would forever forswear war. Ending European exchange rate fluctuations would provide the means for increasing growth, investment and employment. The Euro was called upon to improve the continent's prowess in competition with the emerging economies ranging from China and India to Russia, Brazil and Indonesia. The Germans believed that the European Central Bank, modelled – of course – on the Bundesbank, would quell inflation and secure political and social progress. The French, in particular, wanted a globally strong European money to counter the international pre-eminence of the American dollar. The whole of Europe saw the Euro as striking a blow for the continent's self-sufficiency and esteem in international politics and economics. Never before had a new currency been so replete with hope, so desirous of success in so many fields.

The results of the political deal-making that led to the Euro have in some ways confirmed original expectations, and in other ways confounded them. As expected, the European Central Bank's 'one-size-fits-all' monetary policy – under which interest rate-setting is unified across the EMU area, but fiscal and general economic policies remain in the hands of separate governments – has produced interest rates that have been too low for the good of domestic economics in some fast-growing states (such as Spain and Ireland), too high in countries beset by economic weakness (for example, Germany in the early 2000s). On the other hand, the rivalry between the Euro and the dollar was more potent than many expected, as the result of the US currency's long decline from 2003 to 2008.

The greater economic security and absence of foreign exchange market pressures afforded by fixed currencies and stable interest rates led to both positive and negative results. Positive consequences include a more propitious environment for companies, both large and small, expanding their businesses across Europe. The negative outcomes include a slackening of economic reforms in EMU members like Italy, Portugal and Greece, which had earlier been spurred into necessary adjustment either by the need to qualify for EMU, or by periodic foreign exchange crises – and (in the absence of such immediate pressures) saw their economic structures and performances decline relative to other nations. Measured against the world's largest economy, the US, Europe's performance as a whole has stalled since the heyday of post-war reconstruction in the 1950s and 1960s.[10] The first decade of EMU made little difference to relative output per capita across the Euro area – above all because of poor growth in Germany, France and Italy.[11]

Some of the old puzzles of previous decades persist, but in different forms. The way that Europe reacts to increased world-wide competition caused by globalisation – the breaking down of barriers for international movements of people, goods and capital – is a crucial issue. Starry-eyed hopes in some quarters that the Euro would protect the continent from competition from newly resurgent developing countries, or from financial crises with their roots overseas (such as the 2007 US mortgage upheaval), have been dashed. Perversely, but inevitably, ordinary people across Europe appear to blame the Euro both for unfavourable developments that EMU has helped accelerate – such as restructuring of uncompetitive businesses across the Single Market – and for more general consequences of globalisation where the Euro does not have a crucial influence.[12] The advent of the single currency and the ECB has given voters – and, to a certain extent, governments too – a convenient scapegoat. A Europe-wide opinion poll in January 2007 – six months before the onset of the credit crisis – indicated that more than two-thirds of French, Italian and Spanish citizens, and more than half of the Germans, believed the Euro had a 'negative impact' on their national economies.[13]

Regular opinion polls for the European Commission among people throughout the EU show widespread hostility to globalisation as a threat to jobs and livelihoods.[14] Antagonism has been greatest in France and Greece and lowest in Denmark, Sweden (both non-members of the Euro) and the Netherlands.[15] Governments' failure to win electorates' support for policies of economic and social reform were exemplified by the rejection of the European Union's constitutional treaties in referendums in the Netherlands and France in 2005 and in Ireland in 2008. In all these cases widespread, although often ill-defined, dissatisfaction with the overall make-up of European policies greatly contributed to the 'No' votes.

At the crux of the popular malaise is the uneasy co-existence between the fixing of European currencies, on the one hand, and almost untrammelled capital mobility, on the other. Ease of capital transactions across geographical regions and legal jurisdictions provided one of the reasons for three decades of speculative upheavals from the late 1960s onwards that, in turn, provided important reasons for EMU. The freedom with which international investors, companies and financial institutions can deploy capital across and within national borders frequently incites public suspicion and resentment. Yet the liberalism of an integrated European financial market is one of the essential conditions within the Euro area required to provide the economic flexibility and financial lubrication to offset the rigidity of permanently fixed exchange rates. This is a devilish bargain, a conundrum that many EMU politicians have not yet been able adequately to explain to themselves, let alone to their electorates.

The most important set of difficulties running across Europe concerns the relationship between France and Germany, the two biggest economies in the Euro area – making up half of EMU GDP. The two countries, the mainspring of European cooperation over fifty years, supplied the vital political ingredients for the enactment of the single currency, even though they frequently displayed distrust and divergence over the essential building blocks of monetary cooperation. In recent years the Franco-German partnership has displayed renewed fissures, as a result of new German assertiveness after reunification as well as disappointment in France over its fading role in guiding Europe's affairs.

Curiously, Germany's weight in the overall European economy was lower in 2008 than it was before unification, reflecting Germany's lacklustre economic growth during much of the past quarter century, as well as the impressive catching-up by a number of countries – including Britain, Spain, Portugal, Ireland and Greece – that were well behind Germany in the 1970s and 1980s.[16] Despite these trends, evidence has grown that Germany has ended up with a controlling presence at the high table of European politics and economics. During the long campaign towards the Euro, as a result of the sheer persistence and occasional brutality of German economic officialdom, led by the Bundesbank, other countries have ended up accepting a German-style monetary system for EMU.[17] The D-Mark's influence lives on beyond its demise – producing impatience and frustration in some other countries, above all France.

During the crucial bargaining phase in 1989–93, a period that includes the fall of the Berlin Wall as well as a massive, drawn-out European currency crisis, Germany succeeded in further toughening its conditions for monetary union. The historical record, as set out by this book, demonstrates that Germany did not give up the D-Mark as part of a bargain for German unification, which would have happened anyway whether or not it was accompanied by a political process that included EMU. German unity lent extra impetus to the decades-long quest for a single currency, but led to no significant German concessions on the make-up of the new monetary order. This awkward truth – displayed most palpably and dramatically by the monumental 1992–93 Battle of the Franc, the full story of which this book tells for the first time – has left an abiding legacy for Franco-German relations.

Successive pairs of French presidents and German chancellors have all placed their mark, in different ways, on the evolution of EMU. Charles de Gaulle and Konrad Adenauer, followed by Georges Pompidou and Willy Brandt, helped lay the foundations. Valéry Giscard d'Estaing and Helmut Schmidt, and then François Mitterrand and Helmut Kohl, played crucial roles in the 1970s, 1980s and 1990s in the events leading to the birth of the single currency. Two further tandems, Jacques Chirac and Gerhard Schröder and, in the 2000s, Nicolas Sarkozy and Angela Merkel, became leading actors – sometimes squabbling, frequently cajoling, yet more often than not finding accord – in the Euro's later progress.

It is, of course, over-simplistic to see the Euro's path solely as a Franco-German enterprise. Many other European countries, too, took on important parts in the endeavour, while the role of the US – both as an original inspirer of European unity and then, later, all too often as a negative role model during frequent bouts of dollar instability – cannot be ignored. Yet, as former Italian finance minister Tommaso Padoa-Schioppa, one of the leading figures behind European monetary cooperation in the last twenty-five years, puts it:

Germany and France have played the most important roles in European integration. This was because the UK opposed the project in the early years in the 1950s, and because three wars in the previous 75 years were basically France-German wars. Between the early 1970s and the late 1990s, the D-Mark replaced the dollar as the anchor of European currencies. The D-Mark experience became the transition to the European single currency.[18]

That transition is continuing still; its shape, purpose and ultimate destination are matters of conjecture and controversy. Despite its patchwork of different laws, customs, languages and cultures, Europe during the past thirty years has become a continent of greater, and more equal, opportunity. Accompanying the liberalisation of the world of money, improvements in communications and transport have opened up the continent to the spread of ideas, influence and investment in a way that was impossible in the immediate post-war decades. Ability to carry out transactions in different countries without the costly inefficiencies of changing currencies is an important, though not necessarily crucial, element in stimulating productive, wealth-creating exchanges. Cross-border trade and investment within the Euro area has intensified since the start of EMU, although this partly reflects factors that would have led to the same effect even in the absence of the single currency.[19]

The fundamental quandary for governments is that citizens everywhere are seeking solutions for uncertainties caused by world-wide economic and social change – ranging from energy security, health and education to employment protection and retirement provision. Yet in the vital field of money, EMU politicians have formally abdicated responsibility, on the grounds that the supranational, technocratic and non-elected European Central Bank will produce a better outcome than any state or combination of states have achieved so far. A series of questions requires answers. Are the positive results of EMU in some important areas outweighed by the negative consequences in others? Is the balance of reward within EMU tilting unduly towards the largest entity, Germany – now under growing pressure to show economic solidarity with weaker members of the currency bloc? Will the near-unprecedented financial strains of autumn 2008 force Euro members to demonstrate more unity of purpose – or will a revival of beggar-thy-neighbour policies push EMU inexorably towards fragmentation or break-up? Europe has the wherewithal to turn the strains of EMU into an unambiguous success story. Yet too often the continent has failed to realise its potential. The tortuous chronicle of the Euro contains exacting lessons that Europe must heed if it is to surmount rather than stumble over the hurdles that lie ahead.

1

BLOOD AND GOLD

A continental currency, with a dual metallic and fiduciary base, resting on all Europe as its capital and driven by the activity of 200 million men: this one currency would replace and bring down all the absurd varieties of money that exist today, with their effigies of princes, those symbols of misery.

Victor Hugo, 1855[1]

A currency for Europe is a design long in its pedigree, enrapturing in its endeavour. The dream of a common unit of money to invigorate and unify disparate peoples, and imbue national economies with wealth and dynamism, has sporadically captured attention throughout centuries of political thought. Because European monetary union attempts to fuse a potentially highly unstable combination of politics and economics, realising it has been an elusive aim. But because its accomplishment is believed to bring such rich rewards, the would-be builders of the single currency have proved extraordinarily persistent.

Over the ages, monetary and political union have been constant bedfellows. The borders of money and state are normally synonymous. In the past a re-ordering of currencies formed the natural sequel to the redrawing of national boundaries. The examples are wide-ranging: the unification of the Netherlands, Italy and Germany in the nineteenth century; the collapse of the Russian, Ottoman, Austrian and German empires during and after the First World War; the demise of the Soviet Union in 1991 (which saw the rise of 15 separate currencies in newly-independent states after the break-up of the rouble area).

Evidently, some areas of political or military dominion have been too large, diverse or unstable to accommodate a standard currency. The Persian Empire in the time before Christ had no uniform coinage. It took centuries for a uniform currency to spread across the Roman Empire. In more recent times geographical constraints determined that the pound sterling was not in issue throughout the British Empire. Had Germany finished victorious in the Second World War, the Third Reich's monetary planners advocated that conquered states' individual currencies would have continued in existence, at least for a transitional period, although they would eventually have been part of a monetary union beneath the dominant Reichsmark.[2]

As such examples demonstrate, not all political unions automatically involve a monetary union, but uniform money has generally been the hallmark of political homogeneity.[3] Karl Helfferich, the German economist and later finance minister,[4] described the essential interaction:

> The right of minting coins was, from the earliest days, so closely connected in the public mind with the power of the State that it was always regarded as an essential attribute of sovereignty, and the history of this exercise of power reflects the general lines of development of State authority itself . . . After the conquest of Italy by the Romans, the provincial States were only allowed to coin money of small denominations; large denominations were coined exclusively by Rome. In Germany, so long as under the Franks a strong central power existed, the King alone had the right of coinage.[5]

The greatest of the Frankish kings, and the ancestor of the rulers who gave rise to modern France and Germany, was Charlemagne. He established a new currency standard in the eighth century, the *livre carolinienne*, based upon a pound of silver.[6] In tenth century England the Anglo-Saxon King Athelstan decreed, 'There is to be one coinage over all the king's dominion.'[7] The Byzantine Empire, successor to the Romans from the fourth to the tenth centuries, introduced uniform gold coinage that was accepted across the known world, from Britain and Scandinavia through to China and India.[8] The succession of political and monetary linkages continued into modern times. The US became a fully-fledged monetary union only after its Civil War.

The search for the monetary equivalent of the Holy Grail has frequently been tinged with idealistic fervour, often co-existing with a strong dose of political and economic self-interest. George Podiebrad, a fifteenth-century king of Bohemia, suggested a European Federation that would issue a common currency to be used by a European armed force raised to fight the Turks.[9] Napoleon I advocated a common European money to advance trade – under French leadership.[10] Nineteenth-century philosopher and political economist

John Stuart Mill believed that the march of human progress through 'political improvement' would eventually encourage the adoption of one world currency.[11] French poet and dramatist Victor Hugo bracketed together a single European currency with his vision of a United States of Europe in benevolent co-existence with the United States of America. These two 'immense groupings' would 'extend each other the hand across the seas, exchanging their products, their commerce, their industry, their arts, their genius, opening up the globe, colonising the deserts, improving creation under the gaze of the Creator.'[12]

The concept of a united Europe was close to the hearts of the rebuilders of Europe after the devastation of the Second World War. Winston Churchill, in a 1946 speech propounding a 'United States of Europe', supplied a thread of rhetoric subsequently woven by European politicians into a multiplicity of benevolent but often misguided aspirations. The speech was frequently misunderstood, for Churchill had no intention that his own country should join the club.[13] Nor, in the course of time, did any other front-line European statesman sign up seriously to the concept of a political union for Europe akin to that of the US.[14] After the Second World War, Jacques Rueff, a one-time wartime Banque de France official who became a distinguished adviser to President Charles de Gaulle, famously said money would pave the way for European integration: '*L'Europe se fera par la monnaie ou ne se fera pas*' – 'Europe shall be made through the currency, or it shall not be made'.[15] Rueff's declaration demonstrated support for common principles of monetary stability rather than early advocacy of a single currency – but as a rallying cry it was destined to echo down subsequent decades.

Legacy of the Gold Standard

Maastricht and the monetary unification of Europe build on the residues of the nineteenth-century Gold Standard, first put into operation by Britain in 1821. The Gold Standard underpinned economic and social stability by setting fixed currency conversion rates for world trade and investment, linked to the strength and solidity of gold. Notes and coins were backed by and convertible into specific weights of the precious metal. John Maynard Keynes, although renowned for declaring gold as a 'barbarous relic', described the metal's age-old appeal as an instrument of stability and trust: 'Dr [Sigmund] Freud relates that there are peculiar reasons, deep in our sub-consciousness, why gold in particular should satisfy strong instincts and serve as a symbol. The magical properties, with which Egyptian priestcraft anciently imbued the yellow metal, it has never altogether lost.'[16]

The Gold Standard built on that magic. Linking the separate currencies of the great trading nations of the world – led by Britain, France, Germany and the US – the gold bloc worked as a common currency system.[17] As world trade and investment grew following the Industrial Revolution, the Age of Gold was a period of stable prices, liberalised international trade and technological and industrial innovation. By demanding uniform orthodox policies, it imposed a political as well as a monetary order. The system was operated by central banks which cooperated across national boundaries and were in many cases privately-owned institutions. Although imbued with the trappings of internationalism, they were subject to strong elements of state authority;[18] they were jealously protective of their national policies, their inbred cultures and their independence: less often from their governments, more frequently from each other.

Gold was the world's arbiter, bringing in automatic adjustment for countries which over-extended themselves by importing more than they exported and thus suffering balance of payments deficits. When that happened, gold left the deficit country to finance the payments imbalance against nations with surpluses. The money supply in the deficit country fell, causing deflation and lowering domestic demand. This eventually restored trade competitiveness and rectified the gold outflow problem. The opposite happened in surplus countries. Here, imports of bullion increased the money supply, stoked up demand, generated inflation, lowered competitiveness and thus, over time, eliminated the cause of the inflows. The rules of the Gold Standard required deficit countries to take monetary policy action to induce investors to forgo the attractiveness of holding gold, and instead maintain balances in currency. In a response to a gold shortage, central banks raised their discount rates – the rate of interest charged to member banks in the domestic money system. This achieved the dual result of attracting foreign liquid funds and damping domestic demand – thus strengthening international competitiveness and redressing the problem that led to the gold outflow. As a corollary, the Gold Standard required that countries with payment surpluses should reduce interest rates to stave off an inflow of gold, resulting in a renewed supply of the metal flowing back towards the deficit countries.[19]

Co-existing for a while with the Gold Standard were several experiments aimed at building a comprehensive monetary union and containing elements of political as well as economic harmonisation. An ambitious scheme with potentially wide international repercussions, Latin Monetary Union, comprising France, Italy, Belgium, Switzerland and (later) Greece, started in 1865 and lasted until 1927. This was a bimetallic scheme, based initially on silver and then also on gold, allowing interchangeable, common silver and gold coins to circulate in all member countries, based on a fixed conversion price of 15 to 1 between the two metals. Latin Monetary Union made members' currencies legal tender across national boundaries, with the aim of 'remedying the disadvantages resulting from the diversity of their currencies for communications and transactions between the populations of member states'. Latin Monetary Union was regarded by many, including its originator, a bombastic French parliamentarian, as the first step towards World Union.[20] The system relied on coordination among member nations' central banks. However, it petered out when the political will to support it ebbed away. Central banks abandoned common rules and instead followed go-it-alone monetary policies. The *coup de grace* came when impecunious governments in France and Italy resorted to issuing paper money that was not convertible to gold or silver.

Another example of a union that ultimately unravelled because of the lack of common monetary and political instruments was the Scandinavian monetary union linking Denmark, Sweden and Norway. Built around the three countries' different forms of taler currency, it lasted from 1873 to 1920, after members abandoned unity and gave priority to their own monetary policies.

Like the diverse monetary unions that it helped to spawn, the Gold Standard generated an aura of enduring stability – but it turned out to be an illusion. The Gold Standard maintained monetary equilibrium among its members. But the adjustment mechanism demanded a high price, in the form of sometimes rapid fluctuations in output and employment. At times of crisis, the requirement to obey international monetary rules was always likely to take second place to governmental self-interest.

The Maastricht conference brought to a head a long search for a common denominator for European money that would be less arbitrary and more secure than gold. The bond sealed at Maastricht was however essentially political rather than monetary, and it was between Germany and France. These two countries lie at the heart of the reconstruction of Europe. Yet theirs is a delicate and fraught relationship, caused by centuries of rivalries, altercations and conflicts. Long-standing French anxieties about German dominance have their genesis in a nineteenth-century war that established Germany not only as a mighty military foe but also, for the first time, as a repository of financial power. In contrast to Britain and France, which had developed into unitary states hundreds of years earlier, Germany was a latecomer to nationhood.

For hundreds of years up to 1871, Germany had been a confusion of weak, factionalised states sprawled across the political, cultural and military fault-lines of the Holy Roman Empire and then, from 1815, the German

Confederation. The fusion of these diverse subcomponents of a nation-state, and the development of modern German money and banking, took place at the same time. The first significant steps towards constructing German union out of the previous fragmentation came with the creation of the Zollverein (Customs Union) in 1834. Under Prussian leadership, this removed all internal tariffs and created a single market among its eighteen member states. The Zollverein created a loose form of unified currency, the Vereinstaler, in 1838 – bringing together an assortment of currencies that formed the dowry of the German Empire. In the mid-nineteenth century, Germany displayed a monetary muddle of the most chaotic kind. Ludwig Bamberger, a leading member of the German Reichstag (parliament) and an expert on finance and economics, led the quest for a new German currency as part of the momentum towards national unity. In 1870 he described to the Reichstag the bewildering proliferation of coins collected from the pockets of peasants in one small Rhenish town.

> The sum of 15,834 guilders consisted of double talers, crown talers, pieces of $2\frac{1}{2}$ gulden, of 2 gulden, 1 gulden, $\frac{1}{2}$ gulden, $\frac{1}{3}$, $\frac{1}{6}$ and $\frac{1}{12}$ Imperial taler, 5 franc pieces, 2 franc pieces, 1 franc pieces; then we have gold coins such as pistoles, double and single Friedrichsdor, half-sovereigns, Russian Imperials, dollars, Napoleons, Dutch Wilhelmsdor, Austrian and Württemberg ducats, Hessian 10-guilder pieces and last of all a piece of Danish gold.[21]

The Franco-Prussian War, the catalyst for Germany's political and monetary unification, was sparked by the stratagems of Prussian prime minister Otto von Bismarck, combined with a foolhardy over-estimation of France's military strength by the French parliament and army. France unwisely declared war on Prussia in July 1870 over a symbolic dispute concerning the Spanish succession.[22] After a lightning campaign by the Prussian army, French forces were besieged at Metz and defeated at Sedan in Eastern France in September. Emperor Louis Napoleon and 100,000 soldiers were taken prisoner. France's fate was sealed when a revolutionary government gained power in Paris, ruling out any question that a foreign government would send military assistance.

In the wake of the triumph, Bismarck orchestrated agreement by the previously recalcitrant southern German states for the King of Prussia to become German Emperor. With near-caricatural disregard for French sensitivities, Bismarck organised the proclamation in January 1871 at Louis XIV's gilded Palace of Versailles. On the fields outside sprawled the camp of the German army laying siege to Paris. Soon afterwards, Bismarck started negotiations on war reparations with Louis-Adolphe Thiers, the conservative Republican who became president of France under the still-provisional Third Republic. In a forerunner to manifold Franco-German monetary disagreements a century later, Thiers declared that German demands were an 'indignity'.[23] Bismarck replied archly, 'The tribute, so burdensome in appearance, will be paid by you without you being aware of it.'[24] Gerson von Bleichröder, Bismarck's assiduous and many-sided banking adviser, was at Versailles to assist with the financial technicalities. He wrote to Prussian Crown Prince Friedrich-Wilhelm: 'Count Bismarck would seem to have conducted himself during the negotiations with monstrous brusquerie and intentional rudeness.'[25]

These tactics had the desired effect. Thiers agreed to pay an indemnity of FFr5 billion and to cede Alsace and Lorraine.[26] The funds were to be transferred in three large tranches up to March 1874. The payments had the flavour of a ransom. Only when France paid the debt would Germany withdraw its troops from Eastern France. Germany's feat in masterminding a large pay-off from its brief conflict did not endear it to the rest of Europe. The London *Economist* proclaimed: 'To extract huge sums of money as the consequence of victory suggests a belief that money may next time be the object as well as the accidental reward of battle.'[27] The reparations – although settled with alacrity and skill by the French authorities – became one more festering wound in the resentment-ridden matrix of Franco-German politics.

Forerunner of the Bundesbank

With the unification of Germany's factional states and the birth of the German Empire came a freshly-forged currency: the Mark backed by gold. As the Bundesbank later laconically described, chaotic diversity gave way to a new order:

> In 1871 twenty-five associated states established the German Empire, comprising seven currency areas, in which 119 forms of gold, silver and token coin were circulating ... Paper money was made up of 56 different note issues of state paper currency as well as 117 types of banknotes from 33 note-issuing banks. The anachronistic system of generalised notes and coins was replaced within a few years by a modern single money system. War reparations from defeated France enabled the changeover from various silver currencies to the Empire-wide decimalised gold-backed currency, the Mark. From 1876 the Mark was legal tender for the whole Empire.[28]

The gold backing was a novelty. Silver had previously been the metal backing currencies in issue in Germany and much of Europe.[29] Germany joined the UK with a currency 'as good as gold'. In 1875 the new German state established in Berlin the forerunner of the Bundesbank, the Reichsbank, to operate the new currency. Already, there were signs of the tension among different European money centres that, a century ahead, emerged as a driving force for monetary union. Suddenly the long-established Bank of England and Banque de France, founded in 1694 and 1800 respectively, had a competitor. All the more important were French efforts to ensure that the reparations payments to Germany were paid smoothly and on time. Thiers' government was anxious to settle most of the bill in foreign currency, raising the funds through converting into foreign exchange the proceeds of several well-managed and heavily-oversubscribed bond issues.[30] In paying reparations, France sought to avoid large physical movements of gold and silver. This would have emphasised France's painful position as the vanquished party, and also could have caused great monetary perturbations. Only a small part of the total French reparations – FFr273 million – was discharged in gold, with a similar quantity in silver. Instead, France assembled a sophisticated international banking syndicate which purchased letters of credit and bills of exchange payable by German debtors throughout Europe. France redeemed a large part of its German war debts using paper that had originally been issued by the Germans themselves.[31] Germany converted these payments into gold on the London market, providing the reserves for the formal backing of the Gold Mark.

France's new rival was in the ascendant. The French government, however, extracted modest consolation by paying its war debts ahead of schedule. France preserved its gold reserves, and the Banque de France enhanced its reputation for monetary management. The extraordinary allegiance between the French state and gold, and the high standing, at home and abroad, of the Banque de France, continued unabated for many years – a rock in the stormy sea of French monetary fluctuations. In 1875, the Budget Commission of the French parliament announced that the reparations episode had not damaged France's financial stability: 'The continued movement of French savings will succeed in re-establishing our gold stocks . . . The operation of the 5 billions testifies to the prudence but also to the audacity with which it has been conducted.'[32]

Despite the successful reparations payments, the emergence of a greatly strengthened Germany set off a vast train of repercussions. Victor Hugo's well-known plea for a United States of Europe, shortly after the end of the

Franco-Prussian war, was no altruistic espousal of European beliefs. Rather, Hugo cried aloud his pain at the loss of Alsace and Lorraine – and his desire to win them back:

> Let Germany feel happy and proud, with two provinces more and her liberty less. But we, we pity her; we pity her enlargement which contains such abasement . . . We shall see France arise again, we shall see her retrieve Lorraine, take back Alsace. But will that be all? No . . . Seize Trier, Mainz, Cologne, Koblenz, the whole of the left bank of the Rhine. And we shall hear France cry out: It's my turn, Germany, here I am! Am I your enemy? No! I am your sister. I have taken back everything and I give you everything, on one condition, that we shall act as one people, as one family, as one Republic. I shall demolish my fortresses, you will demolish yours. My revenge is fraternity! No more frontiers! The Rhine for everyone! Let us be the same Republic, let us be the United States of Europe![33]

The German Empire consolidated its position in the centre of Europe. Unbridled population growth, accompanied by surging migration from the countryside to the urban centres, fuelled rapid industrialisation. The Germans became the youngest and most dynamic nation in Europe,[34] contrasting with the stagnation of France's population after the Napoleonic Wars at the beginning of the century. However, the German economic upsurge precipitated by victory over the French was a bumpy ride. The financial markets succumbed to over-heating.[35] Germany witnessed some of the negative effects of the Gold Standard. Even before the formal establishment of the Reichsbank in 1875, some of the gold purchased by the Prussian State Bank with the proceeds of the French reparations flowed back to London, forcing a rise in the Prussian discount rate to 6 per cent.

Such fluctuations added to the concerns of Bismarck's adviser Bleichröder over the introduction of an exclusive Gold Standard, as opposed to bimetallism in which gold shared its monetary role with silver, and coins struck in the two metals were interchangeable. He believed the Gold Standard would lead to destabilising fluctuations in the cost of credit as Germany reacted to the gold outflow by raising interest rates.[36] In a piquant foretaste of the interdependence of modern European financial markets, Bleichröder warned Bismarck of the dangers of dependence on the British bullion market. If the Bank of England raised interest rates to keep gold in London, the Germans would have to follow suit. But 'our industry,' he noted, 'unlike England's, is not sustained by great capital, but needs a steady flow of bank credit. Even now, our industry is no longer capable of successfully competing with foreign producers, because wages and money rates are too high.'[37]

Bleichröder's self-doubt was indicative of the times. For Germany, the final quarter of the nineteenth century saw boom, bust and renewed expansion.[38] Even when it was growing fast, Germany was demonstrably insecure. The Banque de France – with a near-unblemished track record of monetary rectitude – was a financial role model for the Germans.[39] The Reichsbank had to maintain a consistently higher discount rate than the Banque de France in order to preserve inflows of foreign capital.[40] Buoyed by gold reserves that had scarcely suffered from the war, France was conspicuously better equipped to handle its international payments than Germany.[41] This was a state of affairs that the coming conflict put cruelly on display.

Crisis Management

The outbreak of the First World War in August 1914 led to the first exercise in central banking crisis management of the modern age. The catastrophe provided an inkling of the self-feeding effects of a breakdown in political and financial cooperation. This was the yardstick against which all monetary coordination efforts for the rest of the twentieth century and beyond were ultimately judged. The war-time death toll totalled ten million. The list of casualties included sound money. France, Germany and Britain acted immediately to protect their bullion reserves against panic buying of gold by severing the convertibility of paper money into metal.[42] Reflecting on the lesson of Prussian seizure of its offices in eastern France during the Franco-Prussian War four decades earlier, the Banque de France swiftly transported its stocks of gold and securities into the provinces – well beyond the reach of German armies.[43] After the ominous initial German military successes in the east, the Banque de France followed the French government by transferring its official headquarters to Bordeaux in the south-west.[44]

One by one, European nations followed the lead of the Big Three nations and departed from the Gold Standard. A new age of monetary dissoluteness began. The combatants financed the war through massive increases in the volume of paper, either through money in circulation or through short- and longer-term government debts, uncovered by gold or by taxation. Since all the principal countries expected the bill to be covered by the losers, stopping the war was impracticable; inflation was the inevitable result. No country believed more fervently than Germany that its superior policies would bring victory and financial compensation. As Karl Helfferich, the monetary theorist turned finance minister, told the Reichstag in 1915: 'The lead weight of billions has been earned by the instigators of this war; they will have to drag it for decades, not we.'[45]

After the unexpected collapse of German morale in August 1918, the Armistice was signed in November. The peace treaty enacted at the Palace of Versailles in 1919 turned the tables on the new Weimar Republic. The Treaty took away German territory in the west and east, placed massive restrictions on Germany's industrial and military infrastructure and paved the way for war crimes charges against leading Germans. The victors sent Berlin a reparations bill of 132 billion Marks, to be paid with dollars stemming from a series of punitive bond issues.[46] Faced with instalments totalling 750 million Marks falling due in early 1922, Rudolf Havenstein, the hapless president of the Reichsbank, wrote a long-winded begging letter to Montagu Norman, Governor of the Bank of England asking for help to acquire a credit of 550 million Gold Marks (£30 million) from the London market.[47] Norman was unforthcoming. 'I have consulted with those best competent to form an opinion . . . Such advances cannot be obtained in this country.'[48] Having failed to quieten its adversaries with either armaments or monetary advances, Germany turned to the printing presses. The result of an astronomical leap in money in circulation was the Great Inflation in 1922–23, when cash was carted in wheelbarrows.

The Weimar government slowed reparations payments to a trickle, as it was forced by civil unrest to channel scarce budgetary resources into public works programmes to boost the hard-pressed economy and curb political disarray. In a bid to force the Germans to pay up, French and Belgian troops occupied the Rhineland in January 1923. The occupation sparked renewed German demands for a moratorium, and a new campaign of civil disobedience.With the largest gold reserves in Europe, France was the fiercest guardian of monetary probity. Former President Raymond Poincaré, prime minister and foreign minister after the war, was exasperated by German intransigence. In August 1923 he issued a striking indictment of German waywardness, spiced with an improbable litany of reprobation. Never before, and never since, could France so utterly command the economic and moral high ground over its large, troublesome eastern neighbour.

To support its request [for a moratorium] Germany has been invoking the disarray of its finances, the decline of its currency, its economic distress. But it has done nothing to restore budgetary order. Since peace was established, it has followed a policy of waste and dilapidation . . . To meet its expenses,

Germany has had recourse to a great inflation. It has realised no reforms. Germany made no effort to stop the aggravation of its financial, economic and monetary situation. It is obstinate in its abuse . . . The indefinite depreciation of the Mark, the incessant increase in the cost of living, the economic and financial disorder are such that this can lead Germany, from one day to the next, into catastrophes of the most lamentable kind.[49]

Poincaré's statement coincided with a lugubrious prediction from the Reichsbank that 'enormous demand' for banknotes would cause 'a considerable new inflation'.[50] The printing presses were churning out 60,000 billion Marks a day in new bank notes. Currency in circulation, 120 billion Marks in 1921, reached 497,000,000 trillion in December 1923. The so-called Autonomy Law of 1922, passed at the request of Britain and France, making the Reichsbank formally independent of the Reich government,[51] had no effect on quelling progressive currency instability. The official index of consumer prices rose nearly 2 billion-fold in 1923. The Mark was put out of its misery towards the close of 1923 with the introduction of a new currency, the Rentenmark, valued at one trillion Marks and pegged to the dollar. Germany's travails did not, however, come to an end – a graphic illustration of Keynes's thesis that 'There is no subtler, no surer way of overturning the existing basis of society than to debauch the currency'.[52] Hjalmar Schacht, a former statistics chief of the Dresdner Bank, later known as 'Hitler's Magician',[53] took over the reins of the Reichsbank and implemented a Mark stabilisation plan.[54] For a few years, the Weimar Republic appeared to be on the road to salvation. But the stage was prepared for a fresh and more thoroughgoing overturning of the European order.

Gold Alliance

International unrest and agitation in the years before the Second World War brought volatility into the staid world of central banking. During the 1920s, the pre-war members of the Gold Standard progressively re-joined the system, starting with Britain in 1925, only to leave again in the early 1930s. France and Germany remained firmly wedded to monetary rectitude based on gold. During two years of financial market disorder started by the Wall Street crash of October 1929, Schacht resigned from the Reichsbank in March 1930 in protest against the reparations burdens heaped on Germany by Versailles.[55] After facing great economic strains caused by an over-valued pound, Britain departed from the Gold Standard in September 1931 – a move much criticised by the Reichsbank and the Banque de France since it set off a cycle of currency devaluations that worsened French and German competitiveness problems.

Adolf Hitler became German chancellor in January 1933. Schacht – who had campaigned ceaselessly for the Führer to take power – regained the Reichsbank presidency in March 1933. Schacht placed himself firmly in the gold camp at an international monetary stabilisation conference in London in June–July 1933.[56] When the US government made known its opposition to a general return to the Gold Standard, the governments of France, Italy, Switzerland, Belgium, the Netherlands and Poland established a Gold Bloc of European nations linked by their formal commitment to the central role of gold. Governor of the Banque de France Clément Moret wrote to Schacht: 'To my mind, in the present chaos nothing is more important than to maintain monetary stability in those countries that remain faithful to the Gold Standard . . . It is infinitely precious to receive from you a new testimony of the perfect concord that exists between the monetary ideas of the Reich government and those of my Government.'[57]

The stern defence of the Franc's gold parity, and the much-heralded private sector character of the Banque de France, crumbled in 1936 with the arrival in power of the Socialist Popular Front under prime minister Léon Blum. Germany's move to send its army into the Rhineland, in contravention of the Versailles Treaty, provoked a fresh speculative assault on the Franc. The Blum government agonised over whether to take the Anglo-American route towards a lowering of the Franc's gold parity, or to introduce German-style exchange controls.[58] Blum eventually broke with Germany and abandoned the 'strong Franc' policy by deciding to devalue in September 1936 under a tripartite agreement with the US and Britain. Further government action clipped the wings of the central bank. The denizens of Gallic capitalism who made up the private sector shareholders of the Banque de France were known in popular mythology as the 'Two Hundred Families'.[59] The Popular Front reduced their power considerably and ended the Central Bank's autonomy.[60] On the other side of the Rhine, Hitler's government in 1937 took full control of the Reichsbank. Schacht welcomed the decision – perhaps not believing fully in his words – as removing 'the last traces of Versailles',[61] and providing 'the best possible guarantee for maintaining monetary stability'.[62]

German Monetary Rule

The legacy of the Fall of France in 1940 was to be deeply etched into French and German minds, including those of monetary policy-makers. The four years in which the Banque de France was under German control formed part of a legacy that dogged Franco-German ties long after the Second World War.

The Banque de France began preparations in 1938 for the conflict that most feared was inevitable. The September Munich agreement allowing Germany to subsume the Sudetenland in northern and western Czechoslovakia triggered Banque de France action to safeguard its reserves from potential Germanic depredations. Governor Pierre Fournier started to transfer the bank's 2,430 tonnes of gold away from the path of any future Wehrmacht advance.[63] The shift towards instability quickened in January 1939 when Schacht was dismissed after the Reichsbank directorate signed a letter to Hitler protesting about rising inflationary pressures.[64] 'Germany is on a road that leads fatally to catastrophe,' proclaimed a leading Parisian newspaper.[65] After war was declared in September 1939, France shipped 400 tonnes of gold to Nova Scotia in Canada and to Turkey. As German armies launched a swift incursion into Belgium and France on 10 May 1940, Fournier ordered all remaining gold to be transported overseas.[66] The French government transferred its headquarters first to Tours on the Loire and then to Bordeaux. The Banque de France followed suit.

Paris succumbed to German monetary rule on the evening of 15 June. Henry de Bletterie, the sprightly veteran Comptroller left in charge of the Banque de France, had spent the previous night incinerating the central bank's stocks of Franc banknotes. When German troops arrived in early evening at the central bank's building close to the Paris stock market, he told them that Governor Fournier had escaped to the provinces.

German soldier: 'Do you have gold, currency, foreign securities, banknotes, how much?'

De Bletterie: 'We have nothing left here, no gold, currency or foreign securities. We have just 200,000 to 300,000 Francs worth of banknotes.'

German soldier: 'Where are the valuables that are no longer here?'

De Bletterie: 'Far away, in unoccupied France.'[67]

The Germans, not pleased with this explanation, briefly threatened de Bletterie with prison.[68] The next day – Sunday, 16 June – German officers returned to the bank and in a military ceremony hauled down the *tricolore*.[69] On the same day, British prime minister Winston Churchill put forward a belatedly unrealistic offer to his French opposite number Paul Reynaud for a full-scale Union between the two countries.[70] In the evening, Reynaud resigned. Marshal Philippe

Pétain, the First World War veteran entrusted with salvaging the vestiges of France's honour at its hour of doom, formed a government of surrender. The remaining 726 tonnes of Banque de France bullion held in the Brittany naval port of Brest and surrounding areas was embarked on a hastily-assembled fleet of large and small boats on the evening of 18 June, under a hail of German bombs and machine-gun fire. The final gold shipments left Brest harbour for Dakar in French West Africa only hours before the German army entered the city. After the armistice on 22 June, France was divided into two zones, north and south, the latter 'Free Zone' escaping – for 2½ years – full German overlordship.[71]

Carl-Anton Schaefer, a versatile German banker who had been president of the Danzig Central Bank and then a senior Reichsbank official overseeing German-occupied Poland, took over the monetary reins in Paris. He was appointed as Commissioner of the Banque de France,[72] becoming known universally within the Central Bank as 'Monsieur le Président'.[73] The Reichsbank's top man in Paris spent four surreal years in an atmosphere of war-time austerity shot through by the petty controversy of mutual antagonism. Relations between Schaefer and his Banque de France subordinates were strained but correct.[74] Schaefer's recommendations and instructions – on matters ranging from banking statistics and raw materials for coins and note issues to confiscations of foreign securities, repressive measures against Jewish enterprises and disposal of blood-stained Reichsmark notes found on the bodies of dead German soldiers – were written in German; his interlocutors invariably answered in French.[75]

The French pressed for sole control over provision of banknotes for Paris and surrounding regions. They argued against sharing currency management with the Reichskreditkasse, the German war-time agency that supplied German troops with occupation currency.[76] The Banque de France protested against the unrealistically low exchange rate set by the German authorities for the Franc against the Reichsmark.[77] The French maintained this would unjustifiably raise the level of French war indemnities paid to the Germans, enable German troops to buy up French produce at distorted low prices and would cause inflation.[78] The Vichy government pointed out that punitive war indemnities to Nazi Germany were being largely financed by direct recourse to the Banque de France. 'Money in circulation is growing at an exceptionally dangerous pace . . . This is exerting considerable impetus on prices.'[79]

The Germans made several efforts to capture France's gold reserves that had been sent overseas, much of it taken to Dakar.[80] Later in the conflict the occupation regime became more rigorous. The Germans stepped up repressive measures against the Jews, including members of the Banque de France's staff.[81] Occupation costs were raised to FFr500 million a day in December 1942.[82] The Commissioner's exchanges with the Banque de France took on a petulant tone. Schaefer criticised an official Banque de France report in January 1943 that made 'political allusions' about occupation costs.[83] Shortly after the Allies' D-Day landings in northern France in June 1944, Schaefer made one last attempt to gain access to the Banque de France's bullion stocks.[84] The Reichsbank man failed. France lost its honour, but it kept its gold.

In the unforgiving times after the Liberation of France in August 1944, the Banque de France's humiliation brought inevitable recriminations about collaboration between French functionaries and their German rulers. Under the post-1944 French government, the two war-time Banque de France governors Pierre Fournier and Yves Bréat de Boisanger[85] were stripped of their functions, though later rehabilitated. Schaefer was imprisoned by the French authorities until 1948,[86] accused of assisting illegal export of German assets through clandestine banking operations in Monaco.[87] Several years after his release, the Banque de France's former ruler ended up in innocuous respectability in northern Germany, as finance minister and deputy prime minister in the Schleswig-Holstein state government.[88]

Schaefer's fluctuating fortunes provide a piquant symbol of Franco-German financial vicissitudes during a century marked by blood and gold. A generation of French policy-makers scarred by Second World War occupation included several of President de Gaulle's future key economic advisers.[89] Jacques Rueff was deputy governor of the Banque de France until January 1941, when he was forced to resign under France's Nazi-inspired anti-Semitic legislation. He became de Gaulle's most celebrated monetary adviser, and a firm advocate of gold-backed money. Maurice Couve de Murville, who worked closely with Rueff, later became French foreign minister for ten years (and briefly finance minister and prime minister).[90] Jacques Brunet and Wilfrid Baumgartner, both key wartime monetary functionaries, were post-war Banque de France governors.[91] These men understandably harboured no initial enthusiasm for post-war Franco-German monetary rapprochement. Its utility, maybe even its necessity, became apparent only later.

Advent of the Dollar

As war still raged in Europe and Asia, a month before the Liberation of Paris, forty-five Allied nations convened in Bretton Woods in New Hampshire to set an international monetary framework for the coming peace. US Treasury Secretary Henry Morgenthau declared at the conference opening:

All of us have seen the great economic tragedies of our time. We saw the world-wide depression of the 1930s. We saw currency disorders develop and spread from land to land … We saw unemployment and wretchedness: idle tools, wasted wealth. We saw their victims fall prey, in places, to demagogues and dictators. We saw bewilderment and bitterness become the breeders of fascism, and, finally, of war.[92]

Bretton Woods enshrined the US dollar as the fulcrum of a system of globally fixed exchange rates. The once-pivotal role of the pound sterling in international trade and investment passed to the currency of Britain's former dominion, confirmed as the world's leading monetary power. The conference revived elements of the Gold Standard. Bretton Woods established stable parities for international currencies, tied this time to both the dollar and gold. In contrast to the amorphous self-regulation at the heart of the Gold Standard, the Bretton Woods regime was policed by the new institution set up by the conference, the International Monetary Fund (IMF) – established along with the International Bank for Reconstruction and Development (later known as the World Bank) to drive post-war reconstruction and development. Behind both bodies stood the US Treasury, custodian of the world's largest gold stocks, befitting the one combatant nation that had emerged from the Second World War with its economic strength and dynamism enhanced.

The new monetary guardians were designed to ensure permanent protection from the beggar-my-neighbour competitive devaluations that had depressed world trade during the 1930s and contributed to European and global upheaval. Each country established a legal gold valuation for its currency, registered with the IMF. From this flowed the sets of currency parities that individual countries were obliged to keep in place, defined principally vis-à-vis the main reserve currency, the dollar. The rates were held in place through intervention on the foreign exchanges, using the monetary reserves of their Central Banks, mainly in dollars. Member countries' commitment to supply foreign currencies at small fluctuation limits around central exchange rates was equivalent to the fixed rates for gold under the Gold Standard.

Bretton Woods brought the world of currencies long-craved stability and predictability. This was an essential feature of the European revival. Yet, like the Gold Standard, Bretton Woods produced disadvantages as well as benefits. Countries whose economic performances failed to adapt smoothly to the disciplines of fixed exchange rates faced painful periods of disruptive adjustment through higher unemployment and low growth. In extreme cases, they could be forced to devalue their currencies, with potentially serious political and social repercussions. There was another drawback. The Bretton Woods system failed to distribute equitably the burdens and privileges of membership. The leading country in the arrangement, the US, was able to finance its increasing payments deficits by issuing dollars as international reserve assets to foreign central banks. This automatic funding mechanism allowed America to escape some of the disciplines borne by other countries in the Bretton Woods system. In the post-war years, this disparity was destined to become an ever-growing source of international tension – and to spur the Europeans towards greater monetary independence from the US.

AT THE EPICENTRE

Shall we be caught between a hostile (or at least less and less friendly) America and a boastful but powerful 'Empire of Charlemagne' – now under French, but later bound to come under German control?

Harold Macmillan, British prime minister, 1960[1]

The quarter of a century after the Second World War saw a rebuilding of the European monetary landscape that was as wide-ranging as had been the calamities and disorder of the 1920s and 1930s. At the epicentre was the Federal Republic of Germany, the western rump of a defeated, devastated and dismembered nation, established under the tutelage of America, Britain and France. Bretton Woods brought a special irony. Ultimately, the greatest European beneficiary of the financial concordat emanating from the ravages of war was the country that bore the main responsibility for its outbreak: Germany. Yet in the immediate aftermath of the fighting, there was little indication that the Germans would ever rise again. Allied monetary representatives returned from Germany stunned by the destruction. William Gavin, a Bank of England official, described a visit to the one-time industrial heartland of the Ruhr in May–June 1945:

I have seen the London Docks and other heavily razed towns where one drives three, five or perhaps even eight minutes without seeing a habitable dwelling. In the Ruhr I motored three hours through destruction that, with the exception of little islands between the towns, was complete. Cologne, Duisburg, Düsseldorf, just chaos, and worst of all perhaps Essen. Bulldozers have cleared a route through the main roads of the shattered towns. Across pavements and most side-streets sprawls the ponderous debris, masses of masonry, twisted tramlines and overturned trams, boilers, baths, cisterns, great pieces of roof that have slid down intact, with other pieces perched aloft caught up by some shattered wall, but ready to slide down at any moment. There are very few people about, no one searching the ruins. Perhaps they have gathered all they hope to find. One wonders how many bodies lie beneath the rubble.[2]

Two years later, Donald MacDonald, another Bank of England official, visited shattered Berlin. The situation was not much better: 'The Reichsbank is destroyed. The Schloss gone. The Tiergarten a mass of weeds and blackberry bushes. Nothing has been done to set things to right . . . If it is desired to destroy Germany, then there is no need whatever for any change in the present set-up.'[3] In a symbol of the diminished status of defeated and occupied Germany, the old Reichsbank building in Frankfurt was placed under the control of the American authorities. It became the depository for the recovery of assets that the Nazis had plundered from all corners of Europe.[4]

Cold War antagonism with the Soviet Union imposed new priorities on the US and Britain. As Germany moved towards formal division between the Communist East and the capitalist West, initial Allied hesitation on whether to rebuild or run down West Germany's industrial fabric gave way to pragmatic insistence on renewal. Under the Marshall Plan, American arms that had battered Germany into submission gave way to a surge of dollars to revive it. The West German state set up in 1949 was embedded into a system of European integration and revival. The driving force for reconciliation came not just from France, Germany and Italy but from many smaller countries too. Governments were determined to place Europe on a common political and economic footing that would render impossible a repetition of the First and Second World Wars. Britain, politically upgraded yet economically shattered by victory in 1945, stood aside from the rebuilding of Europe. The UK's aspirations for a future outside the European Community suffered successive setbacks, notably from the opprobrium caused by misguided intervention in the Middle East in the 1956 Suez crisis, which include a spectacular breakdown in monetary cooperation with the US.[5] Worsening economic misfortunes, too, exacted a progressive toll. By the time the UK joined the European Community sixteen years after the signing of the Treaty of Rome, sheer passage of time rendered well-nigh impossible any attempt by the British to portray themselves as equal partners to France or Germany.

Reflecting the central role of these two countries, a central tenet of European reconstruction was an equitable balance between French agrarian and West German industrial interests, enshrined in economic mechanisms put into place from the 1950s onwards. Under the Community's inter-locking political and financial arrangements, French farmers gained regulated prices and incomes from the Common Agricultural Policy (CAP), formally set up in 1962, while German manufacturers were supported by a lowering of tariffs and wider opportunities for cross-border trade. Subsidised farm prices, introduced to counter widespread food shortages in the 1950s, resulted in many negative economic effects, particularly through encouraging over-production and consequent costly agricultural surpluses. But the CAP turned out to provide a highly propitious matching of Franco-German interests. West Germany learned how to balance its own political and economic requirements with those of the countries around it. The Germans became expert at crafting a liberalised foreign trade environment to support fast-growing exports of manufactured goods. The process provided the Europeans with guiding principles that supported further stages of integration stretching into the twenty-first century.

Path to Prosperity

A principal theme was money. The birth of the D-Mark in 1948 played a supreme role in setting war-shattered Germany on a path towards respectability and prosperity. The new German currency became both instrument and symbol of recovery. The 1950s and 1960s were a time of slowly increasing monetary tension. This stemmed first from the inflationary effects of the Korean War and then from US payments imbalances and capital outflows resulting from the American military build-up in Vietnam.[6] Distributing the fruits of Europe's rapid re-industrialisation created built-in tensions among the members of the nascent European Community. With a vigour that bordered on sanctimoniousness, Germany broadcast its determination not to fall prey to the recurring problems that had dogged the country since Bismarck's unification. Economic instability – rooted in unstable money – was the demon that needed to be ousted. The institution fated to carry out the task was the new West German Central Bank. The Bank deutscher Länder was a hybrid organisation combining structural checks and balances imposed on defeated Germany by the victor powers (above all, the US) with traditions of the 1875 Reichsbank. It was established in March 1948, three months before the D-Mark. The bank evolved into its better-known successor, the Bundesbank, in 1957 – an institution that soon emerged as a fundamental pillar of the West German state and of European central banking.

When it started in 1948, the Bank deutscher Länder's reserves of foreign exchange and foreign confidence were nil. The fledgling central bank was made independent of government partly because, when it was established, there *was* no German government.[7] The US and Britain intended the bank to have more influence on interest rates than the Reichsbank, part of a general policy to devolve post-war German political and economic power. The occupying powers decreed that the new bank 'will not be subject to domination by the state . . . It will therefore be possible to avoid many of the undesirable monetary and credit policies followed by the German central banks in the past.'[8] The Bank deutscher Länder had little initial sway over financial policy-making. US and British representatives from an occupation body called the Allied Bank Commission were in formal, though half-hearted, control.[9] From the beginning of the Federal Republic, the Bank deutscher Länder (and later the Bundesbank) had control of interest rates, but decisions on exchange rates were made by the Bonn government and its Allied overseers. In April 1948 the decision to set an exchange rate of 3.33 Reichsmarks to the dollar – compared with the nominal wartime exchange rate of RM2.50 – was made by the Allies without any consultation with the Germans. The central bank was only scantily involved in the landmark currency reform of June 1948 when the Reichsmark was replaced by the D-Mark to eliminate the inflationary currency overhang created by reckless war financing.[10] This wiped out the savings of many Germans, yet set the country on the trajectory to recovery. When the newly-established D-Mark was devalued by 20 per cent in 1949 in the wake of the 30 per cent devaluation of the British pound, the decision was taken by the Allies, not the Germans.[11] In ensuing decades, however, the division of responsibility for the 'internal stability' of the D-Mark set by the Bundesbank's interest rate policy, and the 'external stability' governed by the Government's stance on the exchange rate, was to become increasingly blurred.

The Bank deutscher Länder was owned by western Germany's state central banks (*Landeszentralbanken*) established across the western occupied zones of Germany. The structure embodied two tiers of decision-making. The highly decentralised model of the US Federal Reserve was modified as a result of the British authorities' desire for a centralised set-up (similar to the Reichsbank and the Bank of England) to meet the high credit demands of the British occupation zone in northern Germany, particularly badly affected by war damage. A Council run by the Land central bank presidents set policy, which was implemented by a smaller Directorate in charge of day-to-day operations. Directorate officials took part in Council meetings, but (with the exception of the president) did not have a vote until the Directorate was strengthened in

1957. The dual system combining Land presidents and a centralised Directorate proved long-lasting. The Bundesbank–Bank deutscher Länder arrangement combining principles of the Federal Reserve, Bank of England and Reichsbank provided the template for the European Central Bank when it was established in 1998.[12]

The centrepiece of the Bundesbank's inheritance was its desire to prevent any repetition of the economic waywardness that, in the 1920s and 1930s, had promoted the rise of Hitler. The most striking reflection of that objective was the independence from government, eventually enshrined in the Bundesbank Law of 1957. The missionary fervour of the Bundesbank, passed on through three post-war generations, became a permanent factor in international monetary diplomacy. Many of the Bundesbank's leading staff had worked in the Reichsbank, and not a few of them had been members of the Nazi party. Far more significant than the continuity with the past was, however, one spectacular contrast. The Reichsbank looked back at a chronicle of repeated failure. The Bundesbank – despite sporadic setbacks – laid down a gradually-improving record of success. The Bundesbank's credo was effective because it worked. Germany emerged as the quintessentially hard currency country.

Conflict and Controversy

Recovering from the Third Reich experience of dictatorship and debauchment, West German politicians took time to adjust to an independent central bank and a strengthening currency. Konrad Adenauer, the crustily avuncular former mayor of Cologne, became West Germany's first chancellor. Like most seasoned politicians, he disliked interference with his economic policies. Aged 73 when he took office in 1949, 'der Alte' (the old man) soon showed his disapproval of the Bank deutscher Länder's predilection for raising interest rates. Many of the early conflicts between the Bank deutscher Länder and the Adenauer government presaged tussles faced half a century later by the European Central Bank.

The bank was under the control of two men with extensive experience of ruinous pre-war monetary conditions. Karl Bernard, president of the Council, and titular head of the bank, was a former Reich Economics Ministry official who had been forced out of the civil service in 1935 because his Greek-born wife was half-Jewish. Wilhelm Vocke, president of the Directorate, was a man of austere tastes. Dubbed by Adenauer 'an over-cooled ice-box',[13] Vocke quickly established himself as the main source of power within the bank. A former directorate member of the Reichsbank, he was known, at least to the British, to harbour 'deflationary inclinations'.[14] Vocke took zealously to his post-war duties, proclaiming, 'Our task is to defend and secure with all means the trust which the D-Mark and the Bank deutscher Länder have been able to achieve.'[15] Vocke and Bernard made extensive use of the Bank deutscher Länder's independence. They courted frequent disputes with Adenauer's administration as the bank pushed through monetary policy tightening in 1950–52 to counter price increases precipitated by the Korean War.[16] The Bonn government put forward proposals, later abandoned, to place the central bank under state control.[17]

West Germany's success in the first post-war decade enhanced its international monetary influence. In 1955 the Bank deutscher Länder suggested making a $100 million loan to the Banque de France to assuage French payments difficulties. The Bank for International Settlements – the Basle-based central bankers' bank set up in 1930 to handle Germany's post-First World War debts – proposed that it handle the loan, to avoid political sensitivities about the fledgling central bank's growing international activities.[18] In conversations with its neighbours on new treaty arrangements for the European Economic Community, Bonn made plain its desire to place stable money at the heart of Europe's economic governance.[19] Controversy arose when Bernard told Adenauer that the Bank deutscher Länder had 'equal rights' with the government over economic policy-making[20] and Vocke warned that the bank would need to tighten money as a result of 'serious errors' threatening D-Mark stability.[21] After the bank raised interest rates sharply twice in two months, Adenauer protested that it was 'an organ responsible to no one, neither to parliament nor to any government . . . The guillotine falls on the man in the street.'[22]

In September 1956 Adenauer unsuccessfully proposed that the Bank deutscher Länder's successor, the Bundesbank, should be set up in his home base in the Rhineland, Cologne, to make it easier to influence.[23] The suggestion provided a foretaste of wrangles between Germany and France over the site of the European Central Bank in the early 1990s. When the Bundesbank was established in 1957, the government recovered some measure of control by gaining the right, hitherto vested in the Land central banks, to choose the Directorate. But the institution retained its home in Frankfurt and its independence. This set a long-lived pattern that was destined to outlast the D-Mark.

The Battle over D-Mark Revaluation

The Bonn government's working relationship with the central bank improved immeasurably after Karl Blessing became president of the newly-formed

Bundesbank in 1958.[24] Blessing, a bespectacled technocrat with conservative political leanings, had been on the Reichsbank Directorate with Vocke in the late 1930s[25] and quickly struck up a mutually supportive relationship with Adenauer on matters such as wage negotiations and indexation of pensions.[26] The Bundesbank–Bonn interaction delivered results. Under the fixed exchange rate Bretton Woods system, lower inflation in Germany compared with its trade partners produced a significant devaluation of the D-Mark in 'real' (inflation-adjusted) terms, after allowing for price differences with other countries. This led to high trade surpluses and dynamic export-led growth.[27] One striking consequence was a rapid recovery in West German gold reserves, legally owned by the Bundesbank. Ever since the formation of the Reichsbank in 1875, French bullion reserves had eclipsed Germany's. As late as 1950, reflecting the ruin of war, the Bank deutscher Länder still had no gold. But, as the Federal Republic amassed considerable export surpluses, by 1956 its gold reserves outstripped those of France.[28]

Fast economic recovery and low inflation in West Germany, combined with the exchange rate stability of Bretton Woods, set the scene for political turbulence over changes to the world-wide system of fixed currencies. A growing debate on a possible D-Mark revaluation centred on whether the Bundesbank should give priority to the D-Mark's external stability, reflected in the exchange rate, or internal stability, expressed as the inflation rate. The Bundesbank believed that the 'real' (inflation-adjusted) D-Mark devaluation produced imported inflation by encouraging exports and making imports more expensive – lowering competition within Germany and stoking up price rises. Otmar Emminger, the Directorate member responsible for international monetary affairs, led what was at first a lonely campaign for D-Mark revaluation.[29] This gradually built up into pressure that ultimately was to shake Bretton Woods to its foundations. Emminger, a gifted but peppery economist, believed relatively high German interest rates, rising international inflation and an undervalued D-Mark exposed Germany to destabilising inflows of hot money. The solution, Emminger recommended, was not to raise interest rates but instead to agree a higher D-Mark exchange rate to counter speculative capital flows and cheapen imports. Effectively, this would be akin to altering a currency's parity under the Gold Standard – an experience which, as the 1930s had shown, could set off massive world-wide repercussions.

Emminger's views collided with the Bundesbank's 1950s doctrine that economic overheating was mainly a domestic phenomenon, caused particularly by the construction sector. In a long letter in August 1959 the Bundesbank Directorate warned Adenauer of 'monetary policy dangers' resulting from

6 per cent economic growth, but it stopped short of proposing exchange rate changes.[30] Blessing told Adenauer in March 1960 that the economy faced 'excessive demand', creating the threat of 'drastic credit policy measures', with 'undesirable effects on the social structure of the economy'.[31] The famously impatient Emminger told Bundesbank colleagues in January 1960 that West Germany's growing payments surplus was caused by the 'sick man' of the world economy, the US, and called for a major shake-up of Bretton Woods through a 7.7 per cent D-Mark appreciation.[32] At first, Emminger's recommendation fell on deaf ears. Instead, the Bundesbank raised its leading interest rates for lending to banks – the discount and Lombard rates – by a full percentage point. But the anti-inflationary effect was countered by the US simultaneously lowering its own lending rates.[33] As a split developed with and within the government over growing inflation, cigar-chomping economics minister Ludwig Erhard, at the height of his power as the father of the German 'economic miracle', drove the campaign for monetary rigour.[34] In November 1960 the Bundesbank abandoned its attempt to constrain inflation through interest rate increases. It cut rates by one percentage point, followed by a further reduction in January 1961. Finance minister Franz Etzel joined Erhard in favouring revaluation.[35] But Adenauer, backed by Blessing and influential industrial and banking advisers,[36] continued to resist.[37] President John Kennedy's refusal to devalue the dollar heightened belief of an imminent German revaluation. The decisive moment came in February 1961 when Erhard persuaded Adenauer to change his mind and back revaluation.[38] The economics minister's moment of triumph was an important step in the process under which he eventually dislodged Adenauer (by this time aged 87) as West German chancellor in 1963. As the 5 per cent D-Mark revaluation (matched by a similar revaluation of the Dutch guilder) was formally sealed, a chastened Blessing considered resignation, saying: 'For a central bank, the exchange rate parity is sacrosanct.'[39]

The revaluation episode was a landmark in the history of Bretton Woods and in European monetary thinking. In understanding how to harness the counter-inflationary power of a rising currency, the Bundesbank learned a lesson that was set to dominate recurring currency skirmishes.

The Stirrings of Monetary Union

The 1961 revaluation of the D-Mark and Dutch guilder set alarm bells ringing in the European Commission – and created the first stirrings of a political move towards Economic and Monetary Union. This was an early sign of a persistent ideological gap over money between the Germans and the Dutch on the one hand, and France and Belgium on the other. (Italy tended to back the German line in some areas, and sided with the French in others. Luxembourg, which was linked to Belgium via currency union between the Belgian and Luxembourg Franc, played a relatively minor role. Initially, this was aligned to Belgium, but as the importance of Luxembourg as a banking and financial centre grew in coming years, the Grand Duchy became progressively more allied to the German monetary cause.) The 1961 changes in European currency parities risked distorting the farm support prices in the Common Agricultural Policy that entered into force in 1962, threatening the entire political balance of Europe. In a memorandum in October 1962, the Commission argued for a permanent fixing of EEC exchange rates. Robert Marjolin, the French member of the EEC's executive body, the European Commission, proclaimed that currency disturbances undermined the Common Market. In October 1964 he told EEC central bank governors to prepare for monetary unification.[40] In January 1965 Marjolin declared that monetary union was 'an inevitable obligation'.[41]

Not everyone agreed. Arguing that currency flexibility was necessary to defeat inflation, the Bundesbank treated the Commission's suggestions with disdain. So did the Dutch central bank, the Nederlandsche Bank, which by joining in the 1961 D-Mark revaluation was confirmed as the Bundesbank's closest European ally. This was the beginning of a long schism between different monetary factions, setting the tone for decades of infighting. The D-Mark revaluation had pointed the way for the 'hard currency' countries (led by the Germans) to escape imported inflation. But it had also raised the old threat of disruptive currency movements that had disfigured the world economy in the 1930s.

Europe's financial experts were deeply divided. The so-called Economists group was led by the German and Dutch governments and central banks, with some support from the Italians.[42] They believed countries had to run convergent economic policies before they could permanently fix exchange rates. As a condition for monetary union – which could lead ultimately to a single currency – countries would first have to enact very similar policies and achieve similar results on prices and wages, taxes and budgets, internal competition and foreign trade. Monetary union would come at the end of a long journey. Balance of payments deficits, according to the Economists, were a sign of excessively expansionist policies in weaker countries, requiring strict corrective action. No country with a strong and persistent trade deficit, on this basis, would be fit to join a monetary union.

The opposing group of Monetarists* were mainly found within the French, Belgian and Luxembourg administrations, with widespread support in the European Commission. Monetarists believed that the way to convergence lay through a common approach to monetary issues. Monetarists agreed that balance of payments deficits were a sign of financial disequilibrium. But they believed that responsibility lay equally with surplus and deficit countries, both of which had to take action. The Monetarists backed early steps to fix exchange rates, as a prelude to full monetary union later. A prerequisite was that stronger currency countries with balance of payments surpluses would pledge to support weaker nations through currency intervention and pooling of foreign exchange reserves. Enacting such monetary policies, the Monetarists believed, would provide governments with the right tools to produce the convergence in budgets, growth and incomes that was both the goal of, and an essential support for, monetary union. The divergence between the French-led Monetarists and the German-influenced Economists hinged on a crucial issue: whether money should be the instrument, or the objective, of economic convergence. Behind the theoretical-sounding language lay a persistent Franco-German gap in economic culture and philosophy that persisted for half a century.[43]

Marius Holtrop, long-serving post-war president of both the Nederlandsche Bank and the Bank for International Settlements, was firmly in the Economists' camp. Shortly after the war, he had alluded to a common European currency subsuming the guilder.[44] But the right conditions had to be in place – and this could take decades. In July 1964, exuding an air of stern Calvinist authority, Holtrop attacked 'sometimes exaggerated or false tendencies in favour of European monetary union'.[45] Bundesbank President Blessing thought similarly. He argued that monetary union required 'a common trade policy, a common finance and budget policy, a common economic policy, a common social and wage policy – a common policy all round'.[46] Blessing cannily hoped that the UK, which in the early 1960s was clamouring to join the Common Market, would support his sceptical approach. In October 1962 Blessing sent a secret letter to Lord Cromer, governor of the Bank of England, enclosing a copy of Marjolin's proposals on monetary union, recording 'the Governors [have come] to the conclusion that Marjolin's ideas go too far and move too fast and that nothing should be laid down that would prejudice the British position'.[47]

---

* The Monetarists are not to be confused with the followers of the late Chicago economics professor Milton Friedman who believe in the essential influence of the money supply as the principal determinant of inflation.

In October 1964 Blessing and Holtrop widened their criticism. Holtrop told European central bankers, in Marjolin's presence, that the Commission's monetary union plans were 'theoretical'. Blessing informed the same meeting that monetary union had to be part of political union, requiring 'transfer of national sovereignty'.[48] Blessing told the new West German chancellor, Ludwig Erhard, that additional European currency rules were 'neither desirable nor practically realisable'. Monetary union would impede the essential flexibility of the Bundesbank's stance on inflation: 'The Central Bank has to gear its policy simultaneously to internal and external stability . . . We would find it totally intolerable if the Central Bank was asked to concentrate solely on maintaining external stability.'[49]

Skirmishes over Gold

While Europe's financiers argued over economic and monetary differences, the trans-Atlantic financial relationship was heading towards breakdown. Fissures started to appear in the Bretton Woods edifice as a result of a growing dispute over the gold price, set at $35 per ounce as the centrepiece of the post-war gold–dollar standard. The episode was of crucial importance for the Germans, who had to choose whether to support the US or France in an esca-lating monetary confrontation. During the early 1960s, US payments imbal-ances grew steadily. American debts to foreign central banks and other official holders of dollars began to exceed the value of the US government's gold stock. Dollar owners doubted whether, at the fixed gold price, American reserves were sufficient to maintain convertibility. France had accumulated large dollar reserves during a run of payments surpluses following two devaluations of the Franc in 1957 and 1958. President de Gaulle's staunchest advisers included monetary traditionalists, led by Jacques Rueff and Maurice Couve de Murville, who believed America was undermining the link with gold that was the fundament of international money. De Gaulle discerned that, by converting France's excess dollar reserves into bullion, he could support the international status of gold and simultaneously mount a political and economic strike against American monetary leadership.[50]

The separately unfolding fate of sterling was of pivotal importance for the dollar. The two Anglo-Saxon currencies were joint pillars of the Bretton Woods system but sterling was undermined by the physical and economic burdens of six years of war, as well as the strains of coping with the aftermath. The effort to manage sterling's gradual decline from international monetary predominance was one of Washington's key priorities. Both sterling and the dollar came under attack from worsening international payments imbalances. Their destinies were inextricably linked. As Milton Gilbert, the BIS economic adviser, put it: 'Whenever sterling might be devalued, confidence in the dollar price of gold could be expected to evaporate.'[51]

British prime minister Harold Macmillan found himself squarely in de Gaulle's sights, caught in the middle of a Franco-American currency dispute. Macmillan recognised that 'for the first time since the Napoleonic era, the major continental powers are united in a positive economic grouping.'[52] Prompted by dawning recognition of Britain's own frailty after the 1956 Suez *débacle*, Macmillan launched Britain's campaign to join the Common Market. De Gaulle believed the British move heralded the arrival of American domination in Europe. He seized on sterling's shortcomings as an excuse to oppose, and eventually block, the application on the grounds that the UK was too financially weak to join the EEC Six.[53] De Gaulle delighted in the prime minister's duress. Shortly before he vetoed the UK's membership, he described Macmillan to his ministers as 'this poor man, to whom I had nothing to give'.[54]

The travails of the Anglo-Saxon currencies were exacerbated by a rapid build-up of swirling stocks of offshore dollars on the Eurodollar market.[55] Eurodollar expansion increased the volume of under-regulated financial instruments available for currency transactions by international companies and investment firms – and heightened American vulnerability to financial attack. De Gaulle and his advisers maintained that fixed exchange rates linked to gold represented the sole way to drive home to the Americans and everyone else the need for discipline in monetary affairs. At first without great publicity, and then with an ever-greater show of strength, the Paris government converted surplus dollars into gold, stoking pressures for increases in US interest rates. Between 1958 and 1966 France acquired on average about 400 tonnes of gold annually, regaining its traditional ascendancy over Germany's official gold holdings in 1965. De Gaulle told Per Jacobsson, managing director of the International Monetary Fund, that – since Napoleon's founding of the Banque de France – France had played a strong role in world affairs only when its currency had been in order.[56] Yet de Gaulle's gold aggression involved high risks, and ended up rebounding against France's own interests. The Bretton Woods gold–dollar system depended on central banks keeping the US currency in their reserves on the basis that – at the official price of $35 – the dollar was 'as good as gold'. De Gaulle challenged that tenet. By undermining a cornerstone of Bretton Woods, the French president helped accelerate the progressive collapse of the world monetary system that ultimately contributed to his own downfall.

Alarmed by rises in the London gold price to $40 per ounce in 1960, the world's leading central banks – under considerable pressure from the US – decided a joint response. They combined forces from 1961 onwards to sell gold to maintain the $35 parity. The Gold Pool was initiated by the US government as a measure of straightforward self-interest. Britain, Germany and (with increasing reluctance) France lined up with varying degrees of support, reflecting the main industrial countries' desire to stabilise the value of the dollars in their reserves. The system worked moderately well at the outset. But after several years of gold price stability, in January 1965 the compromises behind the scheme started to unravel. The Banque de France announced its intention to convert into gold all new dollar inflows, as well as part of its existing currency stocks.[57] President de Gaulle intensified his admonitions of US fiscal laxity by launching a project for world monetary reform.[58] His grand aim was to strengthen the role of gold – 'which has no nationality, which is eternally and universally accepted' – and eliminate the reserve currency status of the dollar and sterling.[59] De Gaulle's finance minister, the youthfully imperious Valéry Giscard d'Estaing, reiterated the message.[60] Giscard complained of America's 'exorbitant privilege' in issuing depreciating dollars as a means of funding massive foreign investment from which it derived a large surplus.[61] According to French philosopher Raymond Aron:

> The *de facto* equivalence which gradually became established between gold and the dollar scandalised General de Gaulle, because it set the seal of approval on a kind of special entitlement for the US to mint money. They paid their foreign debts with their own currency, then when the dollar was devalued, holders of foreign reserves had to take the consequences.[62]

Other Europeans shared the French point of view. Having progressed to the centre of the capitalist system, the Americans appeared determined to undermine it by operating the international currency regime in a way that all too transparently aimed to serve their own interests. In June 1965 Giscard put forward a detailed plan for a 'collective reserve unit' (CRU) that would be linked to gold and composed in fixed proportions of the currencies of the main industrialised countries.[63] This was the new composite currency that was later born, with considerable European support, as the Special Drawing Right issued by the International Monetary Fund.[64]

De Gaulle's gold doctrine presented the German authorities with a serious dilemma. The Bundesbank was a very large holder of dollars and, since the 1950s, had been the owner of the world's most important stock of monetary gold after the US.[65] Germany's Cold War alliance with America was its most important international relationship. It paid billions of D-Marks every year to maintain US troops and military hardware on its soil.[66] The Federal Republic had a crucial interest in doing nothing to destabilise America's position as the fulcrum of Bretton Woods.[67]

De Gaulle's anti-dollar campaign coincided with rising international tension over Vietnam. The US military build-up strengthened fears about rising American inflation. At the same time as France intensified the gold pressure, the Bundesbank increased its discount rate in January 1965 for the first time since 1960. In July 1965 the Bundesbank told Chancellor Erhard of 'growing concern' about rising government spending. Further discount rate rises followed in August 1965 and the following May. Erhard was ejected in October 1966 after the Bundesbank precipitated West Germany's first post-war recession, and replaced by Kurt-George Kiesinger in a Grand Coalition between the Christian Democrats and Social Democrats.[68] Blessing said later he had used 'brute force to put things in order'.[69]

On the gold market, the simmering dispute between France and the US came to a head. For both foreign and monetary policy reasons, Blessing confirmed to William McChesney Martin, chairman of the Federal Reserve Board, that the Bundesbank would not follow the French in converting official dollar holdings into bullion.[70] The step prompted controversy. The governor of the Belgian central bank complained that it established a precedent that the Americans might extend to other countries.[71] Blessing himself indicated later that the letter was a mistake, since it relaxed pressure on the US to comply with anti-inflation disciplines.[72] The move was fundamentally a device to save America from undue foreign policy discomfiture. Germany's gold stance did not stop the Banque de France from officially withdrawing from the Gold Pool shortly after the Six-Day War in the Middle East in June 1967 pushed up world-wide demand for bullion.[73] Nor did it mark more than a pause in the count-down to the collapse of Bretton Woods. Yet the Blessing letter of support for the US was of supreme symbolic significance.[74] The Germans signalled that, in the fight for monetary stability, their primary allegiance lay with the Americans, not with the French.

Sterling in Crisis

The British tended to regard de Gaulle as a wearisome bully. But behind the French president's bluster lay a certain self-doubt. Chancellor Kiesinger was privy to a first-hand confession of France's inner fragility.

General de Gaulle once told me that his country had become terribly run down in the last 150 years, 'damaged' was the word he used. He saw his task as bringing about a turnaround, as far as he could. For this, he needed a period of calm, and he would let no one disturb this . . . As France went through a process of renewal, the General would like to see other European states grouped around it, forming a type of confederation under French leadership. But he could realise this aim only if he kept Britain out.[75]

Whatever the psychology behind his actions, de Gaulle maintained the anti-British barrage throughout the 1960s. Prime minister Harold Wilson, who took over when Labour replaced the Conservatives in 1964, was the next British leader to face the French president's monetary onslaught. James Callaghan, Wilson's first Chancellor of the Exchequer, wrote later, 'His announced dual ambition was to end the role of sterling as a reserve currency and, more important, to bring down the mighty dollar.'[76] By selling dollars against gold, France attacked the pound, too, taking aim at the sterling-denominated reserves held in London by countries from the Commonwealth and elsewhere – the so-called 'sterling balances'.[77]

When he took office, Wilson decided, misguidedly, to maintain sterling's Bretton Woods parity unchanged, in spite of a record trade deficit caused by low international competitiveness and domestic economic overheating.[78] This marked the start of a decade of international monetary tension that eventually ended internationally fixed currencies and inaugurated floating exchange rates. To begin with, Britain's allies rallied around in providing monetary support to avoid the sterling devaluation that most believed would be inimical to world trade and investment. In November 1964, a month after Labour's narrow election victory, the Group of Ten most important industrial nations, linking the US, Canada, Japan and the leading countries of Europe, agreed a $3 billion support package. The Bundesbank provided the largest contribution of any individual country after the US. Backed up by standby credit lines from the International Monetary Fund, this was at the time the biggest-ever international central banking credit operation – paving the way for massive similar support packages that were a persistent feature of international monetary arrangements into the late 1990s.[79] Labour started a three-year struggle, using 'quite fantastic manoeuvring', to stave off devaluation.[80] International efforts to shore up the British currency through central banking support packages were punctuated by constant harassment from France's gold policies and conversion of sterling balances into dollars.[81] De Gaulle's government enlisted the French national broadcasting organisation in a disinformation campaign to undermine sterling.[82] Chancellor Erhard declined to make a statement supporting sterling, on the grounds of 'the strong belief in German circles that sterling ought to be devalued'.[83] This was a turning point in the three-year British campaign against devaluation that ended in November 1967, when – after last-minute brinkmanship in Washington and at the BIS[84] – the pound was finally devalued by 14.3 per cent. The decision was formally made at a Cabinet meeting on 16 November, yet not announced until two days later. This caused an additional $1.5 billion in UK reserve losses[85] – a foretaste of the much larger drain caused by delay in Britain leaving the European Exchange Rate Mechanism in September 1992. The Bundesbank's Emminger gave an unsentimental verdict: the devaluation was caused by 'the inability of the British economy to compete'.[86]

The pound's devaluation precipitated fresh sales of the dollar and a flight into gold. Wilson's Chancellor of the Exchequer Callaghan compared the consequences to 'those of a climber on the mountainside who dislodges a stone, which in turn sets off the avalanche that engulfs the valley below'.[87] The pound came under further strain as the expected improvement in Britain's balance of payments failed to materialise and overseas sterling holders remained restive. 'We were staring over the precipice into the abyss,' admitted Roy Jenkins, Callaghan's successor as chancellor.[88] 'Sterling had got into the position in which, when you have a history of weakness in a currency, almost any event put[s] it under pressure . . . Once you've been knocked down into a ditch several times, it's very difficult to get up without another car coming along and knocking you into another ditch.'

In March 1968 sterling's trials brought the Gold Pool to an end. On 8 March 1968 the Gold Pool lost 100 tonnes of gold, compared with five tonnes on a normal day, as international investors stepped up sales of dollars for gold at the undervalued official bullion price, resulting in a cumulative $3.7 billion of losses.[89] 'We central bankers are behaving like a rabbit that has been hypnotised by a snake,' complained Jelle Zijlstra, president of the Nederlandsche Bank and of the BIS.[90] Central bankers flew secretly to Washington for the final weekend agreement to end the Gold Pool.[91] Sterling was eventually stabilised. Partly this reflected a second Sterling Group Arrangement, negotiated between February and September 1968 as a formal $2 billion safety net for the sterling balances.[92] Sterling slowly began to strengthen in response to the delayed effect of the 1967 devaluation in increasing UK exports. Paul Volcker, who in 1969 was US Treasury under-secretary for international monetary affairs, witnessed the turning tide when he visited Chancellor of the Exchequer Jenkins in September 1969.

This was a crisis atmosphere. The British were losing reserves. The last thing we wanted was another sterling devaluation. Jenkins withstood the pressure. I saw him at his country house at the weekend. He slyly mentioned that the next set of monthly British trade figures would show a small surplus, showing that the effects of the 1967 sterling devaluation were starting at last to work through. After that, the atmosphere of urgency and the pressure on sterling eased off.[93]

The rebuilding of confidence in sterling ended de Gaulle's monetary glory. The events of 1968–69 formed the first act in thirty years of currency attrition centred on the D-Mark and Franc that ended in 1999 with Economic and Monetary Union. After the stabilisation of the pound, the foreign exchange markets sensed a new victim. The Franc had become clearly overvalued against the D-Mark as the result of high French production costs. Social unrest that erupted with the student revolts of May 1968 triggered an intense bout of Franc selling. The Banque de France was forced to apply for emergency foreign exchange assistance from the Federal Reserve and other central banks. Having been an accomplice in de Gaulle's attacks on the dollar, the Banque de France in 1968 suddenly found itself under enormous speculative pressure.

As capital flowed back into the D-Mark, the Bundesbank showed it had learned its lesson from the 1961 revaluation. It came out in favour of an upward shift in the German currency,[94] and recommended this to Karl Schiller, economics minister in the Grand Coalition government. Schiller was a former economics professor who brought into the greyness of German politics a touch of showmanship – as well as a penchant for petulant mood swings. He had yet to undergo his later policy conversion towards accepting appreciation of the D-Mark, and, backed by Kiesinger, rejected the Bundesbank suggestion.[95] At a BIS meeting the Bundesbank and Banque de France agreed to recommend to their governments a simultaneous D-Mark revaluation and Franc devaluation.[96] But despite furious pressure from the French, Americans and British, the Germans refused.[97] Instead, Bonn decided on a package of border taxes to make imports cheaper and exports more expensive, claiming that this was a more flexible method of countering currency inflows.[98]

The German announcement came on the eve of a spectacularly fruitless meeting of central bank governors and finance ministers from the Group of Ten in Bonn on 20–22 November. The Germans maintained their refusal to revalue and instead put the onus on the French to decide a devaluation. In what the British labelled an 'inept' performance,[99] and the Americans called 'a disaster',[100] Schiller, chairman of the meeting, allowed it to ramble on for two days. The sole conclusion was a new $2 billion central banking aid package for France.[101] German policy won support from the populace. Protesters picketed the Economics Ministry's barrack-like conference building with placards proclaiming 'Save Our Mark'.[102] The Bundesbank increased the pressure, sending a pro-revaluation telegram to Bonn which was promptly leaked to the press,[103] but Kiesinger and his Ministers remained obdurate.[104] Manoeuvred into a corner by the Germans, French finance minister François-Xavier Ortoli reluctantly agreed a 10 per cent Franc devaluation, only to be blocked by de Gaulle, who regarded a strong currency as a sign of virility.[105] Instead of devaluing, France reintroduced tough exchange controls. The US administration hoped that France's rejection of unilateral action would provide a respite for the dollar. Ironically for a leader who had fought so hard against American monetary supremacy, de Gaulle received a congratulatory telegram from President Johnson as a modest prize for repulsing Germany's devaluation demands.[106]

Shortly after the Bonn conference the European Commission attempted to turn the setback into a springboard for a common currency. However, the Bundesbank and other central banks opposed the idea. The Bundesbank contradicted the Commission's opinion that pooling Community foreign exchange reserves, as a means of marshalling common ammunition against speculation, could have prevented the crisis. Blessing stated that such actions required member states to give up sovereignty in other areas, 'for which they are evidently not ready'.[107] A few days later, in Basle, Raymond Barre, successor to Robert Marjolin as France's European Commissioner, unveiled plans for a 'permanent mechanism for monetary cooperation' at the Community level. This was a more pragmatic version of Marjolin's 1962 ideas. But the three governors most traditionally hostile to government interference – Guido Carli from the Banca d'Italia, Jelle Zijlstra from the Nederlandsche Bank, and Karl Blessing from the Bundesbank – rejected any changes.[108]

In the aftermath of the Bonn *débacle*, pressure redoubled on the Franc. The French discovered the unstoppable momentum of a currency in decline. De Gaulle told the West German ambassador on New Year's Day 1969 that France and Germany no longer saw 'eye to eye' on European and other international issues. Germany had a different attitude on monetary questions, de Gaulle stated, because it was a more industrialised country.[109] De Gaulle's lofty standing on the French and European political scene started to look dangerously like isolation. In March 1969, a month before he resigned after the unfavourable outcome of a referendum on regional policies, the French president told

Chancellor Kiesinger, 'France has a certain hesitancy and caution regarding Germany's economic strength, as it does not wish to be inundated by German industry.'[110] He continued:

> Germany has been a large industrialised country for a long time. As a result, with its entrepreneurs, its population and its infrastructure it is best equipped for production, trade and especially export. That is the nature of Germany, that is the German reality. France went into the phase of large-scale industrialisation much later. It has been an agricultural country for much longer, with far fewer large cities and large corporations. In France there is nothing to compare with the enormous complex of the Ruhr or the former Silesia ... In industry and trade Germany is in the lead.

De Gaulle's successor Georges Pompidou launched a much more pragmatic policy towards the Americans and France's long-suffering European allies. The change of leadership convinced currency markets that long-delayed parity changes were only a matter of time. As capital flowed into Germany in expectation of a D-Mark revaluation, Schiller made a momentous policy shift. In May, with the explicit support of the Bundesbank, Schiller proposed to the Cabinet a 6.25 per cent D-Mark revaluation.[111] Kiesinger maintained his refusal 'finally, unequivocally and eternally' to revalue the currency.[112] Events moved more quickly on the other side of the Rhine. Two months after Pompidou took power, his finance minister Giscard d'Estaing – who had regained his old job in the new political line-up – carried out a 11.1 per cent devaluation of the Franc in August. This was the first of three progressively more humiliating currency decisions inaugurated by Giscard during the seven years to 1976 (the first two as finance minister, the last one as president) – an essential part of Giscard's experience driving him towards monetary union.

The long-overdue step of the August Franc devaluation was implemented quietly and without drama – but it increased expectations that a D-Mark revaluation might follow soon afterwards.[113] The D-Mark's future became a central issue in the September 1969 West German general election, which resulted in Kiesinger's ousting and a change of coalition in favour of the Social Democrats (SPD) and Free Democrats.[114] Following fresh capital inflows into the D-Mark and a brief period of floating, the new Bonn government under SPD Chancellor Willy Brandt decided a 9.3 per cent revaluation of the D-Mark against the dollar on 24 October. Through its victory over Kiesinger, the Bundesbank emerged with its reputation further strengthened. Kiesinger later rued his blocking of revaluation as his 'biggest error'.[115]

The manoeuvring confirmed the Bundesbank as the toughest monetary institution on the international scene, in charge of an economy that had re-emerged as Europe's powerhouse. German gold reserves (3,540 tonnes in 1970) once again comfortably outstripped those of France – and were three times Britain's. For the French it was distressingly evident who was in charge. De Gaulle's former foreign minister Michel Debré wrote: 'In November 1968 the strength of the Mark permitted Germany for the first time to speak with a very loud voice. This strength ensured it of the economic supremacy that made it the master of Europe for a very long time.'[116] American central banking economists too had little doubt about the new balance of forces. In an internal memorandum, the New York Federal Reserve Bank's foreign research division calculated that the combination of D-Mark revaluation and Franc devaluation had given France a 20 per cent cost advantage against Germany. But, if the exchange rate changes were to produce a positive effect, the French needed to bring their economy under control. 'The Franc may thus remain vulnerable to speculative attacks and devaluation rumours for some time.'[117] The sobering American assessment turned out to be correct. In a decade-long wrangle with the great powers of international finance, France had played for the highest of stakes. It finished, incontrovertibly, on the losing side.

Widening and Deepening

Emerging in 1969 from de Gaulle's baleful shadow, President Pompidou struck out on a new European path. As Maurice Couve de Murville, the pernickety economic diplomat who had been the General's foreign minister and prime minister, put it: 'He wanted to show he wasn't like de Gaulle.'[118] Pompidou was a former school-teacher who had worked for the Rothschild bank in the 1950s. As de Gaulle's prime minister he was responsible for the peaceful resolution of the May 1968 student unrest. Pompidou could read balance sheets and saw that Europe's was turning against him: the result of a stirring of German power.

At a meeting of European leaders at The Hague in December 1969, Pompidou declared that the Common Market should win 'control of its own destiny'.[119] Just over a month after the watershed of the D-Mark's October revaluation, the Community agreed a new strategy of widening and deepening European integration. Abandoning de Gaulle's anti-British blockade, Pompidou reshaped Europe's political map by launching the EEC's first expansion, designed to bring in Britain, Ireland, Denmark and Norway – the first of a series of six membership extensions up to the twenty-first century. At the same time, the EEC Six set about constructing a detailed blueprint for

Economic and Monetary Union.[120] In the wake of the Hague summit, the Community asked Luxembourg prime minister and finance minister Pierre Werner to convene a committee of European experts to map the monetary way forward. All these policies were part of a framework to protect Europe's interests against perceived American indifference or even hostility. And they were an effort to find a counterbalance for Germany's economic and industrial strength. At the Hague summit, Brandt made plain that he understood Pompidou's reasons for widening the Common Market: 'Those who fear that the economic strength of the Federal Republic could upset the balance within the Community should favour enlargement for this very reason.'[121]

America's departure from monetary rectitude provided the Europeans with a powerful stimulus to improve their own cooperation and reduce dependence on the US. In the early 1970s Germany was the target of a cascade of speculative international capital from the dollar area. Under the stewardship of its sharp-tongued economics and finance minister Karl Schiller, Germany was engaged in near-constant brinkmanship over the future of the world monetary system. The brilliant yet unpredictable Schiller orchestrated Germany's efforts to transfer to other Common Market currencies some of the burdens of the D-Mark's near-uninterrupted appreciation against the dollar. France and the UK were highly reluctant to follow the D-Mark upwards for fear of damaging their exports. On this issue, Schiller clashed repeatedly with his French counterpart Giscard d'Estaing. Franco-German monetary understanding improved after Schmidt took over from Schiller in 1972, but Germany's relationship with the US was no easier. America wanted the Germans to shoulder the disagreeable effects of dollar adjustment by agreeing to revalue the D-Mark – if necessary, in league with its Community partners – and leave the dollar's parity against gold unchanged.

US monetary policy became known as 'benign neglect'. Many Europeans saw it as a malign attempt to export American economic problems to the rest of the world. A straight-talking renegade Democrat and former governor of Texas, John Connally, took a central role. Nixon named him Treasury Secretary in summer 1971. He became notorious for what the fastidious Federal Reserve chairman Arthur Burns called his 'brutal techniques'.[122] The Treasury Secretary trumpeted to America's foreign counterparties, 'The dollar may be our currency, but it's your problem.'[123] This was the politer version of a more savagely authentic Connally *bon mot*: 'Foreigners are out to screw us. Our job is to screw them first.'[124] The dollar's slide threatened international recession by disrupting trading and investment relationships around the world. The effect went well beyond the realm of economics. The mismanagement of the dollar provoked, and was nurtured by, wider European–American suspicions and antagonism. As the seasoned monetary practitioner Charles Coombs at the Federal Reserve Bank of New York put it, 'Washington planning became increasingly dominated by political considerations, much like French policy under de Gaulle.'[125]

Shifting political priorities in the US had a sizeable impact on Europe. Pompidou, Brandt and Heath each concluded that this was the time for fine-tuning separate diplomatic overtures into a single European theme. The Ostpolitik of Willy Brandt's Social Democrat-led government was a crucial element in the European force field. Brandt, a quixotic and visionary leader, had joined the Socialist party as a young man and fled Nazi Germany in 1933 to live in Norway. Born (to an unmarried mother) as Herbert Frahm, he adopted the pseudonym Willy Brandt to avoid detection by Nazi agents, When the Berlin Wall was built in 1961, he attained world-wide celebrity as the city's mayor. Brandt's febrile intellect did not easily lend itself to systematic government. He favoured phrases of quizzical self-description: 'I believe in diversity, and hence in doubt.'[126] Brandt's aim, using myriad detours and byways, was to overcome the post-Second World War division of Europe by normalising West Germany's ties with the Soviet Union and Communist Europe. The plan unnerved not only the French, but also the US administration – in particular, German-born Henry Kissinger, Nixon's all-encompassing, all-seeing, all-suspecting Assistant for National Security Affairs and later Secretary of State. Kissinger realised – as did French President Mitterrand two decades later – that Germany would fulfil its aim of reunification with East Germany only if the Soviet Union suffered grave weakness. In the meantime, Kissinger believed, the West Germans would use their industrial strength to build 'selective détente' with the Soviet Union that would disadvantage the US.[127]

Into this freshly-formed European political landscape strode a self-confident and intensely pro-European British prime minister. Edward Heath displaced Harold Wilson at the general election in June 1970, shortly after the negotiating process for the EMU plan under Luxembourg prime minister Pierre Werner got under way. Heath had convincingly combined Conservatism and Europeanism since his youth. His love of music and politics took him to Germany in the 1930s where he met Nazi functionaries such as Heinrich Himmler ('soft, wet, flabby handshake') and Josef Goebbels ('his pinched face white and sweating – the personification of evil').[128] Heath had headed the team negotiating Macmillan's abortive attempt to join the European Community in the early 1960s. A few days after de Gaulle's anti-British veto in 1963, he declared defiantly that the British were not going to 'turn our backs' on the Continent.[129]

Seven years later, with de Gaulle replaced by Pompidou, Heath pressed ahead with a renewal of European membership negotiations. Britain was suddenly in demand. The French regarded the British as a counterweight to Germany's growing strength; the Germans believed that a tie-up with the UK would show France that Bonn's attentions were not universally geared to the East. There was plenty of emotional complexity in the *ménage à trois*, as well as confusion about the third partner's exact place in the domestic arrangements. As part of a strategy to ensure favourable treatment from its new partners, Britain declared itself in favour of the Werner Plan for fixing Community currencies.

Walking a Tightrope

In 1970–71, by agreeing to a substantial deepening of European integration through the EMU plan, Pompidou was walking a tightrope. Germany's demands for tightly-coordinated European economic policy required much more supranational decision-making than the French were prepared to concede. Equally, France's desire for speedy moves towards currency fixing and reserve-pooling collided with a dawning German belief that more currency flexibility was required. The Bundesbank progressively realised that a higher D-Mark, by lowering import prices, could ward off imported inflation. Franco-German contradictions came to the surface soon after the Hague summit. The traditional Economists versus Monetarists wrangle – on whether economic convergence or monetary alignment should take precedence – became painfully apparent. Brandt told the Bundestag that monetary union had to be based on stability.[130] Brandt took his cue from Schiller, who had enlarged his role by combining the Economics and Finance Ministries. Expounding the policy that Germany was destined to repeat for a quarter of a century, Schiller announced that monetary union would happen only once European economies had converged.[131]

The Bundesbank and the Bonn government showed steely resolution. At the central bank, Karl Klasen, the languidly autocratic former chief of the Deutsche Bank, took over as Blessing's successor in January 1970. Unusually for a top banker Klasen was a Social Democrat. Repeatedly in ill-health, he maintained a bedroom for afternoon naps on the executive twelfth floor and lounged in armchairs at internal meetings. Klasen scorned colleagues who read the fine-print of research papers, but he maintained Blessing's strictures on European money. Shortly after the Werner Committee was established, the Bundesbank president labelled as 'premature' and 'very dangerous' preparations for sharing out European currency reserves (where Germany accounted for the dominant share) for use in intervention operations.[132]

The Germans held sway over EMU deliberations. Johann Schöllhorn, State Secretary in the Economics Ministry, Bonn's senior representative on the Werner Group, told Klasen in April 1970 that the committee's first meeting 'confirmed all our fears. With the exception of my Dutch colleague, all other members have made clear, more or less bluntly, that they give priority to automatic monetary mechanisms, especially the pooling of reserves.'[133] Schöllhorn sent committee members a schoolmasterly paper underlining that economic union had to precede monetary union.[134] Hans Tietmeyer, the future Bundesbank president, who was Schöllhorn's deputy on the Committee, was equally uncompromising. He emphasised the need for 'harmonisation or unification of economic policy' and a 'central autonomous organ' to enact future policy, made up of heads of member central banks.[135] This was an early indication of German persistence that central banking independence had to be at the heart of EMU. There were many other differences. Klasen told central bank governors that the EMU process could achieve 'liberation from dependence on the dollar' only if the new system were to be anchored 'on one Community currency' – the D-Mark.[136] Brandt himself brushed aside a Belgian attempt to accelerate reserves pooling.[137] Klasen advised European central bankers to imitate the Bundesbank by publicly criticising their governments' policies. For Bernard Clappier, Governor of the Banque de France, this went too far. He warned Klasen against 'perfectionism in proposing too much too early'.[138]

The result of the deliberations of Pierre Werner's monetary union committee was published in October 1970. Festooned with opaque language and studded with half-hearted compromises, the report proposed a three-stage plan to create Economic and Monetary Union within a decade. The plan foresaw eventual transfer of key policy responsibilities – including budgetary and monetary affairs – from national parliaments, governments and central banks to Community institutions, which would be under the surveillance of a reformed European Parliament. The first stage of the process was relatively clear-cut: reduction of permitted currency fluctuations, guidelines for economic policy, and co-ordination of budgetary policy. So was the final stage: irrevocable fixing of exchange rates, convergence of economic policies and establishment of a Community system of central banks. The Werner Report was explicit on the need for political union. What was far less clear was how the Community would accomplish it. European central banks reacted unenthusiastically. Paolo Baffi, governor of the Banca d'Italia, said differences in Community wage levels would undermine the move towards EMU.[139] Klasen objected to European

Commission proposals for interfering with national central banks during the first stage of EMU.[140]

Some of the most incisive commentaries came from the UK, which though not yet in the Community was following intently the progress of the EMU discussions. There was general confidence in Whitehall that Britain would join the EEC by 1973. The Treasury and Bank of England assumed that Britain would be part of the first preparatory stage of a decade-long progression to EMU. Both institutions subjected the Community plans to intense scrutiny. A Treasury paper argued that the Werner Report was a highly theoretical exercise that took little account of political realities.[141] An internal Bank of England document, while sympathising with this overall judgment, recognised the political nature of the process: 'Apart from the overtly federalist vision of a united Europe the object [of the EMU plan] was to create a Europe that could stand up to the economic might of the US and thus command for itself a more powerful voice in world affairs . . . A major objective is to develop a role for European currencies with which to oppose the monetary dominance of the US dollar.'[142] Another Bank of England paper voiced arguments that would echo around the Community for the next thirty years: 'The plan for EMU has revolutionary long-term implications, both economic and political. It could imply the creation of a European federal state, with a single currency. All the basic instruments of national economic management (fiscal, monetary, incomes and regional policies) would ultimately be handed over to the central federal authorities.'[143]

Germany hardened its anti-inflation line on EMU. Willy Brandt, while embodying neither expertise nor enthusiasm for monetary issues, confirmed Germany's uncompromising views. In his memoirs, Brandt claimed that diehard German officials frustrated his aim of creating monetary union with Pompidou.[144] In fact, far from disagreeing with the Economics Ministry and the Bundesbank, Brandt stiffened their habitual stringency. When the Werner Report was published in October 1970, the Chancellor ordered Schiller to apply orthodoxy with unwavering force: 'We should be careful to stamp our hallmark on future work to implement the Werner report in Europe. This offers the best guarantee that, throughout the Community, our monetary policy views prevail in the widest possible fashion.'[145]

In the months after the Werner Report was published, multiple cracks emerged in the monetary union plan. Schiller told the Bundestag and the Bundesbank that monetary and economic coordination would run in parallel.[146] Yet Pompidou pointedly excluded any form of agreement over wide-ranging abdication of national sovereignty. The French president was taken aback by opposition from Gaullist parliamentarians.[147] He declared that France would concentrate on establishing the first stage of EMU, and further institutional decisions would have to wait. Pompidou showed his pragmatic streak in conversations with the UK over the perpetually thorny issue of the sterling balances. Giscard – who stayed on as finance minister under Pompidou's presidency – visited the UK in November 1970 to discuss European monetary cooperation. His host was Heath's Chancellor of the Exchequer Anthony Barber, an opportunistic politician with a predilection for tax cuts that caused the disastrously short-lived 'Barber Boom' later in Heath's premiership. Barber declared to Giscard that Britain was willing to 'join in any arrangements for linking the currencies of the Community more closely together' and 'would be willing to move as far and as fast as the rest of the Community'.[148] Told by his British hosts that the Werner Plan's longer-term goals on political integration 'frightened some people in the UK', Giscard said that 'they frightened some people in France too'.[149] At a European summit in November 1970, the Germans criticised lack of progress towards political union.[150] Just before Christmas the Bundesbank's Emminger wrote to Schöllhorn and revealed the full extent of Franco-German suspicion:

> One has to assume that the French will try everything to conclude negotiations on monetary union as quickly as possible . . . There are several reasons for this. First, there are always enough people in France who want to use a European currency bloc as a battering ram against the dollar. Second, the French want to put shackles as quickly on possible on to what they see as our sinister German monetary policy. They don't want Germany, with its superior stability policy, to dance out of line . . . Third, the idea of joint use of monetary reserves, or at least improved access to mutual balance of payments assistance, plays a role in French thinking. All this will lead in practice to a monetary harmonisation of inflation.[151]

In January 1971, Brandt and Pompidou met in Paris to try to repair EMU divergences. The threat to European monetary stability caused by an alarming increase in American capital outflows gave the Europeans a forceful reason to seek harmony. Over the previous year the Federal Reserve had switched to a policy of cheap money.[152] For the Bundesbank, inflows of capital into Germany represented a potent source of inflation. The Bundesbank attempted to stem the tide with progressive cuts in interest rates,[153] but with each step the Federal Reserve cut its own rates further. With Paris newspapers full of suspicions that Germany was back-pedalling on EMU, Brandt and Pompidou used their Elysée Palace encounter to trade mutual reassurances. They each declared that monetary union could take place 'in 10 or 12 years'.[154] Brandt rejected as 'completely false' French press reports that his government 'wanted to set such steep conditions for Economic and Monetary Union that nothing will come of it, so as to free Germany's hand in Eastern Europe'.[155]

Pompidou went to great lengths to acquiesce with German conditions,[156] declaring that, at times of crisis, Germany could be relieved of its obligations to intervene to support weaker currencies. Yet for Pompidou the key sticking point was the German request for France to give up economic sovereignty and permit supranational control of its economy. Brandt advanced the Bundesbank's special sensitivities on inflation and independence as the reason why Germany could not waver from its orthodox negotiating line.[157] This was the same position as that taken by Kohl twenty years later. Following the Paris talks, Germany's Johann Schöllhorn concluded that the French were 'not prepared to agree [the] Werner concept'.[158] Backed by Brandt, Schiller proposed a 'clause of limitations' for EMU. If no progress was made in economic convergence within four years, the monetary provisions of the first stage of EMU would be suspended and the Community would return to the *status quo ante*.[159] German caution appeared vindicated by fresh opposition to the Werner Plan from leading French politicians. Arch-Gaullist Michel Debré said monetary union 'would mean that Europe was one nation. That is not our approach.'[160] When European governments formally adopted the Werner Plan in March 1971, they avoided a firm timetable for monetary union – in contrast to the original ten-year timetable. They agreed that, during the three-to-five year first stage, Common Market currencies would fluctuate within narrower limits than against the dollar.[161] The Community would bring in a currency support mechanism providing medium-term financial assistance, bolstered by a European Monetary Cooperation Fund. Both sets of arrangements faced considerable setbacks before they could take effect.

Looming Points of Conflict

Beset by pressure from Paris and Washington, as well as by sporadic foreign exchange market disarray emanating from the UK, Germany struggled hard to steer a mid-course between looming points of conflict. Between March 1971, when EEC governments decided the first stage of EMU, and March 1973, when the Bretton Woods system ended, Europe endured two years of disorder. The Bundesbank and the Bonn government suffered violent disagreements over currency policies, the US intensified dollar unilateralism, and European discord worsened over UK and French fears of being locked to an over-strong D-Mark. Before the 'narrower bands' of the Werner Plan could be implemented, a wave of speculation forced the German authorities to float the D-Mark. The decision was taken in May 1971 after an intricate dispute between the Bundesbank, the Bonn government and Common Market partners over a possible joint EEC float against the dollar. France feared that linking the Franc to the strong D-Mark would weaken its own export competitiveness. Giscard pleaded for a unilateral D-Mark revaluation – an idea immediately rejected by Schiller.[162] Germany's failure to win a multilateral approach on the dollar, and its reluctant decision to carry out unilateral floating, was a resounding defeat for German monetary diplomacy. The French government declared that EMU plans – including the move towards narrower margins – would be put on hold until Germany returned to a fixed parity.[163]

The US sensed that the Europeans' squabbles heralded a forthcoming assault on the dollar. New York Federal Reserve foreign exchange chief Charles Coombs concluded that European countries were preparing for the US to close the gold window through which central banks could convert dollar reserves into bullion. Coombs wrote in an internal note that a flood of dollar selling by private investors could unleash $15 or $20 billion within a few days, sparking 'a mass exodus of foreign funds [that] could easily trigger a virtual collapse of the New York stock market'.[164] Coombs realised that European efforts to forge monetary integration represented insurance against dollar risks. A worsening of America's balance of payments deficit[165] and a US Congressional report presenting dollar over-valuation as an 'inescapable conclusion'[166] were harbingers of crisis. The German government and the Bundesbank stoked tensions by seeking the return of $500 million worth of gold sold to the US a year earlier.[167]

On 11 August 1971, New York Federal Reserve president Alfred Hayes wrote to Federal Reserve chairman Arthur Burns: 'Confidence in the dollar has now become so badly eroded as to threaten a breakdown of the entire international financial system within a matter of weeks if not days.' Hayes blamed the German government, and above all Karl Schiller, for 'allowing German industrial firms to engage in massive dollar borrowings in the Eurodollar market, thereby widening still further the spread between Eurodollar and US interest rates and sucking huge amounts of short-term capital funds out of the US'.[168] The British authorities, too, appeared to press for gold conversion. Coombs was 'absolutely crestfallen . . . If the British, who had founded the system with us, were going to take gold for their dollars, it was clear the game was over.'[169]

President Nixon's announcement suspending the dollar's convertibility into gold – billed as 'the most significant economic action since World

War II'[170] – came on 15 August. The move was part of a wide-ranging array of measures dubbed the 'New Economic Program' including tax cuts, a ninety-day freeze on wages and prices, and a temporary 10 per cent surcharge on imports 'to ensure that American products will not be at a disadvantage because of unfair exchange rates'. The decision was made in great secrecy.[171] When Fed Chairman Burns told Connally that America's trading partners might retaliate, the Treasury Secretary's response was typically forthright. 'Let 'em. What can they do?'[172]

Paul Volcker, embarking on a notable career as the US administration's international monetary trouble-shooter, flew promptly to London and Paris, where finance minister Giscard reaffirmed France's resistance to floating and warned that central banks would be reluctant to hold dollars.[173] The mood soon lurched towards confrontation. Federal Reserve Chairman Burns warned Nixon of rising unemployment and economic slowdown outside the US, with 'far-reaching implications for the kind of monetary and trade settlement that we can work out with the outside world'.[174] The Bundesbank's Emminger threatened to cut Bundesbank interest rates to weaken the D-Mark unless the US agreed new currency parities and removed the import surcharge.[175] The US embassy in Paris told Washington of French pressure for retaliatory trade action and 'incalculable consequences for our political interests in Europe'.[176] These uncompromising messages provided the impetus for the Americans slowly to consider action that had previously been unthinkable: to devalue the dollar against gold.

In late November Heath proposed to Brandt and Pompidou a three-point plan to resolve the monetary impasse. This included new exchange rates and a change in the dollar price of gold; elimination of the US import surcharge; and an 'orderly reduction in the use of national currencies as international reserve assets through their gradual conversion into an acceptable form of international asset'. This last proposal, Heath wrote, in a notable tilt towards long-standing French views, 'must bring to an end the asymmetry in the system which has enabled the US to finance large deficits'.[177]

In December 1971 finance ministers and central bankers convening at the Smithsonian Institution in Washington reached agreement on a series of parity changes that restored – temporarily – fixed rates for the dollar. The breakthrough came during a meeting between Nixon and Pompidou in the Azores a few days earlier, at which the Americans agreed to increase the official gold price from $35 to $38 dollars per ounce.[178] The Smithsonian agreement devalued the dollar by about 10 per cent against the main world currencies, with larger changes against the yen and the D-Mark and smaller ones for the French Franc and sterling.[179] Nixon dubbed the accord 'the most significant monetary agreement in the history of the world'.[180] The agreement contained many positive aspects, providing a competitive fillip to American exports that promised a significant improvement in the US current account deficit. But flows of international capital, far more important than the transactions generated by traded goods and services, were becoming the main influence on world currency movements. The Smithsonian deal provided no more than transitory calm on the path to a storm.

Early in 1972 the US government returned to the policies of benign neglect, engineering a further cut in interest rates to boost the economy. Capital inflows accelerated into Germany, prompting the Bundesbank to lower interest rates, and Bonn enacted capital controls to prevent German companies from borrowing abroad. Pompidou complained about America's failure to enact key elements of the Azores and Smithsonian agreements.[181] Brandt and Pompidou met again in Paris to restore momentum towards EMU, relaunching the plan for narrower exchange rate fluctuation margins that had been shelved in 1971.[182] The Community set up a new regional system for controlled floating, called the Snake. Each pair of Community currencies could oscillate either side of a 2.25 per cent margin – half of what was allowed under the Smithsonian Agreement.[183] Plotted on a graph, the new path of European currencies resembled a serpent writhing inside the Bretton Woods fluctuation 'tunnel'. The currency arrangement set up in April 1972 was dubbed the 'Snake in the Tunnel'.

The prospective EEC members UK, Ireland and Denmark joined the Snake a week later.[184] Britain's commitment soon foundered. The Bundesbank started to raise interest rates.[185] A wave of international selling of the pound forced Britain out of the Snake in June 1972 after the Treasury and Bank of England suffered reserves losses of $2.6 billion in a week through forced intervention sales to prop up sterling.[186] (At the high point of the ERM crisis in September 1992, the UK suffered a reserve loss of $30 billion in one day.) Britain's ejection was the delayed result of a miscalculation in the Smithsonian Agreement that had left sterling over-valued against European partners.[187] The attack on sterling set off further upwards pressure on the D-Mark, and at the end of June the Bundesbank backed a German government plan for a further tightening of capital market controls.[188] Complaining that this countered free market principles, Schiller urged a joint float of Community currencies against the dollar. He was rebuffed and resigned from the Cabinet, replaced as finance and economics minister by Helmut Schmidt, the previous defence minister.

On the other side of the Atlantic, too, a whiff of turmoil hung in the air. A bungled burglary on 17 June at the Democratic National Committee headquarters at the Watergate hotel complex in Washington started a count-down that led eventually to Richard Nixon's resignation two years later. On 23 June, in a White House conversation with his chief of staff H.R. 'Bob' Haldeman, Nixon authorised a cover-up of the Republicans' involvement in the break-in. As the world discovered later, tape-recorders revolved inconspicuously in the background. An excerpt from the transcript of the conversation, later renowned as the 'smoking gun tape', revealed the president's insouciance towards the vicissitudes of the European Snake.

Haldeman:	'Did you get the report that the British floated the pound?'
Nixon:	'No, I don't think so.'
Haldeman:	'They did.'
Nixon:	'That's devaluation?'
Haldeman:	'Yeah. [Presidential Assistant Peter] Flanigan's got a report on it here.'
Nixon:	'I don't care about it. Nothing we can do about it.'
Haldeman:	'You want a rundown?'
Nixon:	'No, I don't.'
Haldeman:	'He argues it shows the wisdom of our refusal to consider convertibility until we get a new monetary system.'
Nixon:	'Good. I think he's right. It's too complicated for me to get into.'
Haldeman:	'[Federal Reserve Board Chairman Arthur] Burns expects a 5 per cent devaluation against the dollar.'
Nixon:	'Yeah, OK. Fine.'
Haldeman:	'Burns is concerned about speculation about the lira.'
Nixon:	'Well, I don't give a shit about the lira.'[189]

The US showed little interest in defending the Smithsonian agreement.[190] Britain's departure from the Snake was a blow to France. Pompidou meanwhile complained that the floating of the pound put monetary union 'into the waiting room.'[191] Brandt stepped up the efforts to find common ground with the British[192] and stressed a common Anglo-German line on monetary and economic convergence.[193] The British government worried that absence from the monetary scheme could result in last-minute exclusion from the Community,[194] but on 1 January 1973 the UK, Denmark and Ireland entered what officially became known as the European Community. France voiced irritation that the UK had not chosen accession to bring sterling back into the Snake.[195] The French and Germans made clear that the floating pound was 'a major problem'.[196]

Confusion and Acrimony

The stakes rose dramatically in February 1973 as dollar selling intensified in the wake of Bundesbank interest rate increases.[197] The indomitable Volcker traveled 31,000 miles in a helter-skelter series of intercontinental shuttle flights for currency negotiations with Europe and Japan, culminating in an agreement on a further 10 per cent devaluation of the dollar against gold, from $38 per ounce to $42.22. At the same time, the Japanese government allowed the yen to float – producing a yen revaluation of 5 per cent.[198] These complex negotiations were accompanied by confusion and acrimony on whether or not the D-Mark would be floated.[199]

Meanwhile Germany and the UK embarked on a convoluted exercise to build a monetary framework to protect Europe from a fully floating dollar. The idea was to allow the Snake to depart from the 'dollar tunnel' and float freely, but to keep European exchange rates stable against each other. The British, mindful of their 1972 Snake ejection, said they would rejoin a European currency bloc only if it gained access to large-scale unconditional credits, while France – trying to avoid D-Mark domination – said it would join a floating Snake only if the UK participated too.[200] Schmidt proposed substantial assistance for the UK as a means of cajoling both Britain and France into a joint float. However, he failed to inform the Bundesbank. At a BIS meeting in Basle, Emminger – who was temporarily in change of the Bundesbank since Klasen was in hospital – professed ignorance of Schmidt's offer and brushed aside any question of special help for the UK. Failure to agree a European initiative exposed the D-Mark to a fresh torrent of speculative funds. The dam burst on 1 March 1973, when the Bundesbank was forced to make $2.7 billion obligatory dollar purchases as the US currency sank to its lowest permitted point within the Bretton Woods system. This was the largest daily currency intervention ever undertaken. Emminger travelled to Bonn and won Brandt's approval for a suspension of intervention commitments and a closure of the foreign exchanges. This was the end of Bretton Woods.

As chance would have it, Edward Heath had chosen 1 March for an evening of talks with Brandt in Bonn, to be followed by further bilateral governmental sessions the next day. For Heath, a lover of music and architecture, the visit to Bonn was a prelude to the high point of his German trip: a weekend of roaming around baroque Bavarian churches and monasteries.[201] Instead, when the British prime minister arrived on the Rhine, he was plunged into an atmosphere of operatic melodrama. Heath's southern German excursion was cancelled; the closest he got to an epic setting was a helicopter view of Cologne Cathedral.[202]

Brandt greeted Heath by telling him he had expected that the dollar devaluation agreed in February would provide a breathing space of six to eight months. In fact it had lasted three weeks. During the next twenty-four hours Britain came tantalisingly close to joining the other Common Market countries in a joint currency bloc to protect Europe from foreign exchange unrest. At a dinner with Brandt in Gymnich Castle near Bonn, Heath compared Europe's monetary predicament with the Fall of France.

> There are times when political leaders have to take big decisions on a political basis. We are in such a case in relation to monetary affairs. Before very long the Community will be faced with the sort of situation with which we were faced in June 1940 when Sir Winston Churchill offered the French common citizenship with the British. There is a time when political leaders come to the point of taking great decisions and making a great leap. We are near, if not at, that point in relation to European monetary affairs.[203]

The pivotal German monetary player at the Heath–Brandt talks was Karl Otto Pöhl, State Secretary and the deputy to Helmut Schmidt at the Bonn finance ministry.[204] Pöhl was a quick-thinking, fast-learning economics official, a member of Brandt's Social Democratic Party. After a poverty-stricken early life during economic depression and war, he had started his career as a freelance sports reporter and then enjoyed a meteoric rise in Bonn. The March 1973 episode prefigured twenty years of eminence in which, as president of the Bundesbank, he became a dominant figure in international finance. On the night of the collapse of Bretton Woods, in conversations with Brandt, Heath and Derek Mitchell, the UK Treasury's top international official, Pöhl took the lead. He almost succeeded in rewriting the international monetary agenda when Mitchell suggested that a 'substantial acceleration' of the Werner Plan might be needed.[205] Pöhl responded positively, reiterating Germany's strong interest in bringing the UK into a Community currency bloc[206] with harmonisation of monetary, interest rate and fiscal policies.[207] Mitchell reminded the Germans that the Bundesbank had been 'less than enthusiastic' about sharing its reserves to defend weak currencies. Ironically in view of his later position as an arch-defender of the Bundesbank's independence, Pöhl declared imperiously that, if necessary, the Bundesbank would be overruled.[208]

Mitchell wrote a secret late night brief for his political masters, a sceptical mandarin's summary of the implications of rejoining the Snake. He pointed out the problems of pegging sterling against Community currencies when the dollar was floating: 'We would be liable to drop out or need massive support to keep us in. The Governor of the Bank of England [O'Brien] has told the Treasury that he is deeply opposed to the whole idea of a common float because of the obligations which we would inevitably incur.' Mitchell then tackled the thorny longer-term issues raised by the European proposals.

> What we are talking about is pooling of reserves which in its complete form would take us at one move to full EMU. Full EMU would deprive member countries of many of the policy instruments needed to influence their economic performances and (particularly in the case of the exchange rate) to rectify imbalances that arise between them . . . In an EMU, equilibrium could only then be restored by inflation in the 'high performance' countries and unemployment and stagnation in the 'low performance' countries, unless central provision is made for the imbalances to be offset by massive and speedy resource transfers.[209]

These strategic questions were left unanswered. Instead, in their final round of talks the following day, the two sides tackled more immediate matters. With a politician's desire to bring the money markets to heel, Heath asked Pöhl how control could be exerted over the Eurodollar market. Pöhl replied grandly: 'By creating a European Central Bank.'[210] Heath reiterated Britain's interest in joint floating but said Britain would need substantial credit support 'without payment of interest and without fixed repayment arrangements'.[211] Pöhl stated reassuringly, 'In a joint float every member would have to support the other . . . The Germans would be prepared to do anything they could.'[212] Pöhl overplayed his hand. British conditions for participation in a joint float turned out to be too extreme for the Germans – especially for the Bundesbank.[213] At a Brussels crisis session of Community finance ministers on 4 March Anthony Barber laid down conditions for British participation in a floating Snake that included 'unconditional mutual financial support without limits of amount, without guarantees, without specific obligations to repay'. The message was backed by a telegram from Heath to Brandt on 6 March that effectively asked Germany for a blank cheque.[214] Brandt replied that the British proposal 'might well prove to be a dangerous factor in accelerating the inflationary processes in the European Community'.[215] He rejected the British suggestion of unlimited, unconditional credit as 'too far reaching'.[216]

A second Brussels meeting of finance ministers dashed any lingering British hopes that the Community would refrain from a joint float if Britain stayed out.[217] The meeting decided that the Community float would start the following week, excluding Italy, the UK and Ireland.[218]

When the post-Bretton Woods era started with the reopening of exchange markets on 19 March after a two-week closure, the Snake was no longer moving in the Tunnel. Fixed exchange rates against the dollar were no more; the Tunnel had disappeared. The UK Treasury concluded that the weight of hot money pouring across the foreign exchanges had proved triumphant. 'The flows are bigger and faster each time.'[219] The vision of a wide-ranging European float had come to naught. The beginning of generalised floating left Europe with a *de facto* D-Mark bloc. European governments mouthed sporadic platitudes about returning to the plan for monetary union.[220] But such statements were near-meaningless. The Bundesbank's floating currency policy was victorious. The European Community was becalmed and rudderless. On the day that the foreign exchanges re-opened, Pompidou warned that, as long as monetary union plans remained unfulfilled, Europe would be 'blocked'.[221]

Opportunity for Assertiveness

The breakdown of Bretton Woods created a new opportunity for monetary assertiveness in Europe, which the Bundesbank exploited. Two years of wrangling over the dollar had proved a costly distraction from the Bundesbank's prime focus. With prices rising at an annual 7.5 per cent in early 1973, Germany had lost its low inflation edge. Higher domestic costs and the relentless appreciation of the D-Mark had sharply lowered Germany's export competitiveness. Freed from the destabilising obligation to absorb excess world dollars, the Bundesbank could concentrate on increasing interest rates and reining in excess liquidity. It shifted to a new method of damping inflation through direct control of the central bank money stock – a step with considerable implications in later years for European monetary control.[222] In summer 1973 the Bundesbank stepped decisively on the monetary brakes,[223] and proposed a dramatic programme of spending cuts, tax freezes and general economic restrictions.[224] The aim, Klasen wrote to Brandt, was to 'crush the inflation mentality' with 'an overall package that must surprise [the electorate] with its harshness and radicalism'.[225] The package outlined by the Bonn government two days later had the desired effect of curbing Germany's economic overheating. It led to further upward pressure on the D-Mark – resulting in a 5.5 per cent revaluation within the Snake in June[226] – and dashed Edward Heath's hopes that Britain could rejoin the European Snake.[227] The British prime minister sent an unusually critical letter to Brandt at the end of July complaining about the 'crisis overtones' of the Bundesbank's credit tightening.[228]

By autumn 1973, on the eve of the sharp rise in international oil prices, Germany had established a comprehensive anti-inflation lead over France, Italy and the UK. The Bundesbank warned the UK not to return to the Snake in view of the potential for currency instability.[229] The Germans were growing worried, too, about France. In a gloomy summary of Europe's prospects, presented to Brandt, Heath and Bank of England governor Gordon Richardson in October 1973, Pöhl revealed that the Bundesbank had spent DM5 billion in September defending the Franc.[230] France had lost 10 per cent of its reserves within a week. 'This situation could easily recur. The alternative to heavy intervention and losses would be the destruction of the Snake. . . . The objectives of France and Germany in economic policy are not the same. The French are much more concerned with the expansion of their economy. Germany is much more concerned with the fight against inflation.'[231]

Pompidou and Heath did their best to lift each other's spirits. They agreed in November on the need for 'further and more rapid progress towards EMU'.[232] Yet Pöhl's forecast proved correct. As pressure grew on its foreign exchange reserves, France could no longer keep up with the D-Mark. During the previous decade, France had constantly castigated flexible exchange rates, and pleaded for the disciplines of fixed parities. In January 1974 the policy changed. Finance minister Giscard declared that France was withdrawing from the Snake,[233] turning down a $3 billion German credit offer to maintain the Franc in the currency mechanism.[234] Shortly before the official announcement, Giscard visited Pompidou in his modest village home north of Paris to seek the president's views.

Pompidou: 'And what will happen if we let the Franc float?'

Giscard: 'Certainly not much. We will maintain our parity against all other currencies. But the gap with the D-Mark will increase and, as a result of the price increases of German products on our market, that will strengthen inflationary tendencies.'

Pompidou: 'Can we stop this?'

Giscard: 'For a certain time, but that will become very expensive for us. And ultimately we will not be able to prevent the Franc and the D-Mark from drifting away from each other.'

Pompidou: 'Then we have no other choice. We will not waste our last reserves, simply to delay an event that is evidently unavoidable. We must leave the currency snake . . . At the last summit conference, I noticed that [the Germans] do not have much understanding for our situation. As soon as one comes to

them with monetary questions, they react completely egoisti-
cally. They like to exploit their superiority.'[235]

Giscard blamed competition from the floating Italian and British currencies
for the Franc's departure. He turned to a traditional rallying cry, employed
many times during tussles with the Germans: France's first priority was to
'*protéger l'encaisse*' – to protect its reserves. Giscard admitted that the withdrawal would bring a 'parenthesis' to monetary union. In fact, France's departure from the Snake marked the burial of the Werner Plan. There were no
more optimistic communiqués on monetary affairs. This was the end of the
road, too, for the embattled group of British, French and German leaders who
had struggled for four years to reconcile irreconcilable positions on EMU. In
the spring of 1974 the Heath, Pompidou and Brandt trio suddenly unravelled,
ejected from office, respectively, by election, death and espionage.[236] Patching
up a framework for European money was an unenviable task left to their
successors.

TYRANNY OF THE MARK

The French made a very honourable effort to cling to the D-Mark. They didn't like to play second fiddle to the Germans, yet they didn't have the power, the authority or the currency to do otherwise. They learned over a period of years a rather ironic lesson: that in order to stand up to the Germans, you had to be subservient to them – by following their lead in key questions of monetary affairs.
Paul Volcker, former Chairman, US Federal Reserve Board, 2007[1]

Helmut Schmidt and Valéry Giscard d'Estaing were self-confident, internationally-renowned finance ministers when – within eleven days of each other – they became leaders of West Germany and France in May 1974.[2] The new chancellor and president were men who understood money, with all its codes, charms, whims and temptations. During their respective eight- and seven-year periods in office, Schmidt and Giscard elevated Franco-German monetary cooperation – enshrined in the semi-fixed rate European Monetary System that they constructed in 1979 – to a central instrument for balancing the exigencies of politics, economics and history. They faced different, yet interlocking, requirements. The sensitivities stemming from his country's bellicose past caused Schmidt to play down Germany's growing economic might by emphasising currency cooperation – a goal also supported by Bonn's desire to safeguard German exports by holding down the rising D-Mark. Similar considerations prompted Giscard, with Schmidt's compliance, to assume the role of catalyst and promoter in a new European monetary framework – even though France's inferior economic performance, especially its considerable lag in fighting inflation, in fact made it the junior partner.

The two leaders professed the common aim, at a wider European level that superseded national borders, to regain monetary stability forfeited through a century of war and disruption. According to Giscard, the road to a European money was part of a journey that had been abandoned when the Gold Standard ended: 'During the second half of the nineteenth century, up to the 1914 war, France enjoyed continuously successful economic growth and a steady build-up of its engineering industry, with a currency that was totally stable. With their roots in a rural economy and their cultural leaning towards the fundamental values of savings and thrift, the French as a nation cannot cope with an inflationary economy and a weak currency. They thrive on stable money.'[3] Schmidt, too, affirmed a link between the goal of EMU and the Gold Standard: 'We had a currency union up to 1914 in Western Europe – the Gold Standard. From a historical point of view, I would draw a direct parallel.'[4]

Intertwined with a yearning for old certainties was a firmly-held desire to counter the newer exercise of German power. 'Why do I talk so much about Germany?', Giscard asked rhetorically in 1978. 'Because it would not be a good idea for Europe to be dominated by one country. I want France to ensure that there are in Europe at least two countries of comparable influence, Germany and France.'[5] Later, more than a decade after he left office, Giscard was more adamant still: 'We need an organised Europe to escape German domination.'[6]

For Schmidt, constructing the European Monetary System as a stepping stone to EMU was a key condition for strengthening the political fabric of the European Community. 'The two core countries, France and Germany, will endure as the backbone of the Community only if they are not members of two different monetary areas; only if they are members of a common monetary area can this core of political stability be maintained.'[7] Mindful of past catastrophes, Schmidt believed EMU would prevent Germany first taking a controlling position, and then falling into fateful isolation: 'Without a common currency, the D-Mark would over time play the leading role and the German banks and insurance companies would accomplish market-dominating position well beyond our borders, producing irritation and envy among others – and with malign political consequences for us [Germans].'[8]

Both men grew up in the troubled inter-war years. Schmidt was born in 1918 in Hamburg, six weeks after the end of the First World War. He came from a humble middle-class background; his mother and father were teachers and his grandfather was a dockyard worker. Giscard was born eight years later in Germany, in Koblenz on the Rhine, where his civil servant father served during the 1920s in the Franco-Belgian military administration occupying the German Rhineland after the First World War.[9] Schmidt wrote later of his astonishment at visiting the castle that was the aristocratic Giscard's home.[10] Both Schmidt and Giscard saw military experience in the Second World War, although Schmidt's – first on the eastern front and then in the German Air Ministry – was far more extensive. As a sixteen-year-old, Giscard took part in the Liberation of Paris in 1944. After Germany surrendered Schmidt became a prisoner of war of the British army in northern Germany for three months in 1945.

Throughout his career, Schmidt was oppressed by the weight of the past. Only when he had passed his sixtieth birthday, in the early 1980s, did he reveal publicly that his grandfather had been Jewish. His ancestry, had it been uncovered during the Third Reich, could have landed Schmidt's father in a concentration camp.[11] He peppered his statements and speeches with lugubrious allusions to the burden of the Nazi history and the legacy of national division. He deflected British prime minister James Callaghan's pleas for help in rescuing sterling in 1976 by pointing out that Germany 'still had not found its identity' and could act only in concert with the European Community 'because it alone provided a safe haven for the German psychology'.[12] One of Schmidt's constant themes was that Germany needed its neighbours, above all France, to accomplish its wider goals: 'After Hitler, Auschwitz and the Potsdam agreement [dividing defeated Germany into zones of occupation] the German political class cannot be considered for [European] leadership.'[13] Grim thoughts of past conflict frequently intruded into Giscard's and Schmidt's discussions, for instance when they met for political exchanges in a Michelin-starred restaurant in Alsace in eastern France in 1977 – the first time post-war French and German leaders had met in a region that had changed hands twice since 1870. This was an opportunity for rural ceremony, with the village band playing in the background. Giscard wrote later: 'Helmut stepped out of his car, wearing his Hamburg seaman's cap. We listened to the music, shook hands. Amid all this I could not forget the war, the battles, the cruelty. It was as though we were in a stage setting that had been quickly set up to hide the ruins, the rubble, the corpses.'[14]

The memory of Auschwitz, Schmidt pointed out, persisted long after reunification. Speaking in 2007, close to his ninetieth birthday, firmly ensconced as Europe's eldest statesman, Schmidt said Germany's history was one of the reasons restricting German banks' ability to forge alliances elsewhere in the continent, particularly in France. 'The past is too present: the bloody past is too much present.'[15]

European Manoeuvrings

In 1974 Schmidt attained the chancellorship, and Giscard the presidency, in unexpected circumstances. Willy Brandt resigned as chancellor as a result of the unmasking of one of his key Chancellery advisers as an East German spy. Schmidt, who had earned a glowing reputation as defence and then finance minister, was the Social Democratic Party's natural choice to succeed him. Giscard had a similar pedigree, having served nine years as a precocious finance minister under de Gaulle and his successor Georges Pompidou. When Pompidou died suddenly in April 1974,[16] Giscard – a leading member of the pro-European, liberal wing of the French conservatives, with a strained relationship with the right-wing Gaullist mainstream – was chosen as the Right's unity candidate against the Socialist leader François Mitterrand. Giscard defeated his rival in the May 1974 poll and took the presidency at the youthful age of forty-eight.

Schmidt and Giscard faced severe economic problems after the collapse of the Bretton Woods system the previous year and the sharp rise in oil prices. Neither man ever gave the impression that he would be anything but equal to the tasks. The two leaders could be acerbic and difficult;[17] this is one reason why they got on so well. A British Foreign Office official gave this pithy description of Giscard as French finance minister in 1970: 'Giscard's achievements, ambitions and possibilities are almost too good to be true. From the start it was clear he was going to the top. . . . Giscard's greatest personal assets are his intelligence, energy, originality and practical ability and experience; and his greatest shortcomings are lack of popular appeal due to his arrogance, cold manner and the silver spoon he allows too obviously to stick out of his mouth.'[18] Schmidt and Giscard were permanent rivals in arriving late for European finance ministers' meetings. According to Dutch central banker André Szász, 'Observing this lack of consideration meeting after meeting, I sometimes could not help feeling that their manners left something to be desired. Giscard has a haughty, languid, quasi-aristocratic air. Schmidt had a bluntness that, combined with a sharp voice and an abrupt manner of speech, earned him the nickname "Schmidt the Lip" (*Schmidt Schnautze*).'[19] Sir Nicholas Henderson, Britain's ambassador to Bonn, painted a somewhat graceless picture of Schmidt at an official Bonn dinner in 1973:

> By 8.15, which was the time for dinner, everybody had arrived except Helmut Schmidt . . . He eventually arrived after we were all in the dining room. He made no apology for being late. He may have thought we were lucky to have him here

at all; to the Prime Minister he gave initially, I believe, an impression of aggressiveness ... He entered carrying, as his custom, a large leather bag, the sort of elaborate affair you can buy at Asprey's for carrying shaving equipment, but which for him contained pipes, cigarettes, tobacco, lighter and matches. He placed it on the table in front of him as he sat down and immediately lit a cigarette. He chain smoked throughout the evening.[20]

The third principal leader on the European stage in 1974 was British prime minister Harold Wilson, who regained power at the helm of a minority government in March.[21] The three men were bonded by a common dislike of the bureaucracy and endless official parleying that appeared natural concomitants of the European Community; they preferred intimate meetings among like-minded men of vision.[22] Schmidt, according to his confidant and protégé Karl Otto Pöhl, 'disliked Brussels and all its works and was preoccupied with the budgetary problems that membership had created'.[23] Schmidt claimed an instinctive dislike for central banking and finance ministry experts whom he classified witheringly as 'technicians'.[24] However, the record shows that he heeded their advice much more frequently than he cared to admit. The intensely technocratic Wilson, too, affected disdain for the 'experts' – even though he was one of them. Additionally, he was intensely suspicious of Europe's ability to interfere with British economic policy, calling an early referendum on UK membership of the Common Market.[25]

In France, Giscard – though deeply unsentimental about the Brussels political machinery – was on the other side of the European argument. He was frequently torn between his own pro-European leanings and his need to maintain favour with the French Gaullists who were suspicious of Germany's re-acquired economic muscle and jealously opposed giving up power to European institutions. Giscard's 1974 withdrawal of the Franc from the Snake was one of his few policies to draw Gaullist acclaim.

The effects of the oil price rise drove the three leaders together. Consultations between Wilson and Schmidt in June 1974 were overshadowed by what Schmidt called 'the opening phase of a major economic crisis' with 'enormous inflation taking place which was unparalleled in time of peace'.[26] In spite of uncertainty over British Common Market membership, Wilson pledged support for further Community deepening.[27] Schmidt told Wilson the future lay in a 'triangular relationship' between Britain, France and Germany.[28] In practice, in the months after Wilson's return to power, the UK's contribution to Community affairs was negligible.[29] After a visit to London on a European trip in June 1974, New York

Federal Reserve president Alfred Hayes reported: 'Much of the low ebb of business reflected political fears. In the eyes of the City, several of the senior Ministers were regarded as sinister threats, with plans for nationalisation and socialisation.'[30]

Profiting from his friendship with Bundesbank president Karl Klasen, Schmidt forged a close relationship with the Central Bank – and used this as an instrument to build up German monetary influence throughout Europe. The Chancellor's watchword was monetary orthodoxy: 'We cannot defend the hard D-Mark with soft measures.'[31] The alliance with the Bundesbank centred both on the fight against international inflation – which had risen to 24 per cent in Italy, 16 per cent in the UK, 12 per cent in the US and France and 7 per cent in Germany – and on credit assistance for weaker European countries. Schmidt focused attention on Italy, realising that shoring up the country's balance of payments was crucial to preventing a further lira decline that could damage European trade in general and German exports in particular. During the summer of 1974 Schmidt drew on his close relationship with Klasen to mastermind a $2 billion German credit for Italy from the Bundesbank's reserves, secured against part of Italy's official gold holdings.[32] Klasen's influence ensured that Schmidt won Bundesbank acceptance for the transaction without the time-consuming necessity of seeking approval from the Central Bank Council.[33] Schmidt's ability to engineer such bilateral agreements – on terms that were more amenable to the government than multilateral arrangements proposed by the European Commission – gave him enhanced international status and a taste for further European monetary deal-making.[34]

But, even for Schmidt, there were limits to his alignment with the Bundesbank, shown when he tested the bank's independence on interest rates – and met an uncompromising rebuff. Early in 1974 the Bundesbank injected liquidity into the German banking system by loosening restrictions on minimum reserves, but kept its discount and Lombard rates unchanged at the high 1973 levels. In a blatant attempt to bring down interest rates before important regional elections in October, Schmidt wrote a highly unusual personal letter to Klasen in July 1974, warning that Germany's economy was slowing down. 'I would like to see credit policy providing stronger support for the economy and for business sentiment.'[35] Schmidt's letter was ineffective. This was an occasion where Klasen, even if he had wanted to, could make no decisions on his own; he was dependent on the rest of the Council. The Bundesbank waited until October 1974 to reduce interest rates, for the first time since the beginning of 1972.[36] The cut took place just a few days before state elections in Bavaria and Hesse. In both cases Schmidt's Social Democratic Party suffered sharp falls in its share of the vote.

While the Bundesbank maintained its tough monetary line, France sought to repair the damage wrought by its departure from the Snake. The French government saw in the growing importance of the D-Mark a problem similar to the long-running dollar challenge during the Bretton Woods era. Schmidt was pessimistic about French prospects for returning to the European currency fold.[37] The Snake had shrunk from a major European Community policy instrument to an informal mechanism among central banks. In a particular snub to French sensitivities, the working language for European monetary consultations was no longer French, but English.[38] In September 1974 Giscard's finance minister Jean-Pierre Fourcade proposed a 'European monetary relaunch' involving a basket of Community currencies as a new unit of account to counterbalance the D-Mark.[39] The Fourcade Plan coincided with early conversations between Schmidt and Giscard on how to turn the existing loose European apparatus for monetary cooperation into a European Central Bank.[40]

The Fourcade plan for 'greater symmetry' (the French code word for reduced German influence) in the Snake was spelled out to the European Monetary Committee by a senior official in the French Treasury, Jean-Yves Haberer.[41] A man of mordant intelligence and a penchant for conspiracy, he became notorious in the 1990s for his controversial stewardship of two large French banks, Paribas and Crédit Lyonnais. The vague ideas behind the *relance monétaire européenne* – 'a sort of waiting room or convalescence station' pending a more formal rate-fixing system later on – were designed to remain secret from the foreign exchange markets. This was a world away from de Gaulle's overbearing rallying calls for monetary reform – testament to muted French monetary self-confidence and the constraints imposed on Giscard's European cooperation by the restive Gaullist party.[42] France's European partners rejected the plan, partly because it would involve an unwarranted extension of credit facilities.[43]

Instead, Switzerland and Germany proposed a separate initiative for the Swiss Franc to join the Snake, as a hard currency substitute for the Franc – a move the French were desperate to forestall.[44] Jacques de Larosière, director of the French Treasury, spelled out for his political masters France's fears of isolation, and concluded that the best way to stymie a German–Swiss deal was to revive momentum for EMU.[45] However, in a prescient forecast of the outcome when the single currency was eventually introduced thirty years later, de Larosière balanced his findings with a brilliant analysis of the risks that could stem from elimination of currency adjustments:

The evolution of the exchange rate of the European currency compared with other world currencies will affect the competitiveness of member states' products in different ways. If, globally, the Community has an interest in fixing its rate of exchange at a certain rate, the interest of each member state taken in isolation could be different . . . The creation of a European currency in no way causes the disappearance of the notion of the commercial balance and the balance of payments between member states. Some of these balances could be in permanent disequilibrium, as a result of divergent evolutions in productivity and prices.

France's desire to regain the centre stage of European money won the upper hand. The Paris government announced in July 1975 it was returning to the Snake to 'strengthen the mechanisms of Economic and Monetary Union' and restore a 'fixed order' to world currencies.[46] The Franc rejoined at the same parity at which it had left the Snake the previous year, dashing German hopes that Paris would devalue by 5 per cent to produce an adequate safety margin.[47] In Washington, European representatives on the IMF Executive Board voiced scepticism about the terms of the Franc's return – sparking a formal French complaint.[48] But in March 1976, France lost a quarter of its reserves in a week's heavy intervention to protect the Franc, and Giscard was forced to announce, for the second time, that France was leaving the Snake.[49] At a highly-charged meeting of Snake members in Brussels on 14 March, German finance minister Hans Apel put the blame squarely on the Franc's over-valuation against the D-Mark.[50] Dutch finance minister Wim Duisenberg – the future Nederlandsche Bank and European Central Bank president – gave a hint of the straightforwardness that was to become his hallmark (and the cause of considerable misfortune) when he took over at the ECB. Duisenberg backed Apel's line and told Fourcade bluntly that France had no choice but to adjust the Franc's value because it had failed to get a grip on inflation.[51]

Although Apel was more compliant to Fourcade at the Brussels meeting than some of his Snake colleagues, Giscard remarked to Schmidt afterwards that the Germans had shown less willingness to compromise than expected.[52] One reason why Germany was reluctant to assist France, the French government suspected, was because heavy intervention to support the Franc would have depressed the D-Mark against the dollar and compromised Germany's anti-inflation objectives.[53] Relations cooled further during a public row between Schmidt and Giscard's prime minister Chirac after the German chancellor openly criticised Gaullist policies.[54] Giscard appointed a new prime minister, Raymond Barre, to replace Chirac in August 1976. Barre launched a fresh economic stabilisation plan, but Bonn remained sceptical. Giscard's 'fight to win back internal and external stability' was 'late, perhaps too late', reported Germany's ambassador in Paris.[55] A few days later, Giscard and Barre sent a joint message to Schmidt saying that the legacy of the Bretton Woods breakdown was casting a dark shadow over the Community.[56]

With Europe's economic future stalled by Franco-German squabbles, the stage was set for an attempted revival of Anglo-German *entente*. Prime minister Harold Wilson resigned unexpectedly in March 1976 and was replaced by a politician of genial cunning, previous Chancellor of the Exchequer and Foreign Secretary James Callaghan, a one-time trade union official and war-time naval officer. Callaghan, a battle-scarred veteran of the 1967 devaluation, was plunged immediately into a fresh upheaval over the weakness of sterling.[57] The pound's plight was a natural reason for intensive conversations with Helmut Schmidt, with whom Callaghan, as Foreign Secretary, had already developed a warm relationship.[58] During 1976 Schmidt and Callaghan acted out an elaborate piece of theatre. The plot centred on Callaghan's hopes of a bilateral German solution to the recurring threat to Britain's monetary reserves posed by the risk of withdrawals of foreign central banks' large sterling balances held in London.[59] Callaghan hoped Germany would contribute to a sterling 'safety net', a credit facility to be covered by the Bundesbank's monetary reserves,[60] as a prelude to a large International Monetary Fund loan. Schmidt held out the prospect of substantial German assistance, similar to that provided to Italy, but foresaw prophetically: 'I will get into deep trouble with my central bank when we come to such a decision.'[61]

Hectic personal discussions between Schmidt and Callaghan in October 1976 yielded little beyond verbal German support for the pound.[62] Schmidt suggested a partial drawing on Germany's reserves to provide roughly half a $10 billion loan to the UK,[63] but both Karl Otto Pöhl at the finance ministry and the Bundesbank were against the idea.[64] Pöhl stressed the 'helplessness' of the German government when faced with resistance by the Bundesbank. Schmidt concluded the episode by sending Callaghan a letter steeped in economic orthodoxy, plainly guided by the Bundesbank. 'The decisive basis for the stabilisation of the British economic situation cannot be provided from outside but must be achieved by Great Britain itself.'[65] Callaghan was disappointed, but hardly surprised.[66] Callaghan hardened his position on European exchange rate cooperation. Britain reached agreement on an IMF loan and on a safety net for the sterling balances.[67] Relations between Schmidt and Callaghan remained courteous. But the vision of a special German–British monetary relationship was unattainable.

Lengthening the Stride

While international aid for sterling was being finalised, a former UK Chancellor of the Exchequer was preparing to travel to Brussels to play a key role along with Giscard and Schmidt in building the European Monetary System. Roy Jenkins, a full-blooded pro-European[68] who had fallen out with the Labour party over its anti-Community stance in the early 1970s,[69] moved to the centre of European policy-making, as the first British president of the European Commission. Memories of sterling's travails during Jenkins' 1960s tenure as Chancellor of the Exchequer buttressed his desire for currency stability. He saw a direct link between Europe's economic problems and the imperfections of floating exchange rates. Jenkins took over in Brussels in January 1977 from another former finance minister, French Gaullist Francois-Xavier Ortoli, who stayed on as European Commissioner for monetary affairs. Stating 'the member states have recently gone too much their own way', Jenkins immediately set about instilling a new spirit. His views were in line with a general spirit of malaise after a series of setbacks to monetary cooperation.[70] In view of the floating of sterling, the Franc and the lira, the Banque de France complained in February 1977: 'The Community character of the Snake has been weakened. It has now become virtually a Mark zone.'[71]

Jenkins told the European Parliament that many pressing Community problems in areas such as agriculture were due to 'the lack of an approach to Economic and Monetary Union'.[72] Other members of the Commission, however, believed Jenkins' evolving views were over-ambitious and impractical. His predecessor Ortoli called the British politician's ideas 'politically absurd'.[73] Yet Jenkins pressed on and, in October 1977, issued a metaphor-studded call for monetary unity: 'Monetary union could help establish a new era of price stability in Europe and achieve a decisive break with the present chronic inflationary disorder. . . . We must change the way we have been looking at monetary union. . . . Let us think of a long-jumper. He starts with a rapid succession of steps, lengthens his stride, increases his momentum, and then makes his leap. The creation of a monetary union would be a leap of this kind.'[74]

European finance ministers were sceptical. But Jenkins' initiative chimed with the political mood in Bonn and Paris.[75] Schmidt and Giscard – for different reasons – were spurring on the Community's previously faltering monetary efforts. Schmidt was driven by frustration with slow European growth and with the monetary and fiscal policies of the new US president, Jimmy Carter, a man with his roots deep in America's agricultural South. Schmidt referred to him disdainfully as 'the peanut farmer' or 'Jimmy the

Carter'.[76] According to Dutch central banker André Szász, 'Schmidt was concerned about Carter whom he considered a dangerous nitwit. Whenever they were worried about the Americans, the Germans looked to the French.'[77]

The French authorities were growing increasingly restive about the Germans' monetary power, all too evident after a series of devaluations of Snake currencies between October 1976 and August 1977.[78] Prime minister Raymond Barre put pressure on the Bundesbank to cut interest rates at a Franco-German ministerial meeting session in June 1977,[79] arguing this would help the Paris government's electoral fortunes.[80] Bonn's ambassador to France, pointing to rising political difficulties with Paris, wrote of French sensitivities because 'it feels increasingly inferior to Germany'.[81]

In December, European government leaders re-launched efforts towards monetary union by asking Community finance ministers to make a 'thorough study' of the latest Commission proposals.[82] However, the underlying tensions between Germany and France were as deep as ever. The Banque de France's foreign department in February 1978 listed a long series of factors complicating France's aim of returning to the Snake and blamed 'the tyranny of the Mark' for Germany's undue influence over European money.[83] The Bundesbank was initially sceptical about the Schmidt and Giscard currency plans, but – especially in the second half of 1978 – there was ample coordination between the central bank and the government. And, at the defining moments, the Bundesbank ensured that the finished product bore its inimitable hallmark.

Two men with a vital role in maintaining the central bank's grip were veterans of the 1970s upheavals. Otmar Emminger took over as president when Klasen retired in June 1977. The government appointed Karl Otto Pöhl to join the bank as Emminger's deputy at the same time. Pöhl had built up a close rapport with Schmidt during four and a half years at the Finance Ministry. Schmidt saw Pöhl as 'a different type of man . . . He had a broader framework than Emminger and [chief economist Helmut] Schlesinger. He had one great advantage over these people: he came from the outside, and that means his yardsticks, his standards had not been set by the wallpaper within the Bundesbank.'[84] However, once ensconced in Frankfurt, Pöhl started to display the Bundesbank's legendary independence. He said later: 'Schmidt may have had the view that, once I was on the Bundesbank Council, I would serve him by being respectful of the Government. That turned out not to be the case.'[85] Years later, Schmidt confirmed with wry understatement his disappointment at Pöhl's transition: 'He had been more critical [of the Bundesbank] before he became deputy president than afterwards.'

At the beginning of 1978 both Emminger and Pöhl were well aware of the far-reaching nature of Schmidt's monetary proposals. Emminger took part in a top-level meeting in Bonn with Schmidt on 1 March 1978 to discuss the chancellor's ideas for reducing the importance of the dollar in world reserves by establishing a European reserve currency.[86] Schmidt's aims, according to an internal note from Emminger, were broad-based: to shield European Community members from the 'dollar calamity', extend the status of the fledgling European composite currency known as the European Unit of Account, and take further steps towards Economic and Monetary Union.[87] Pöhl recorded in a subsequent letter to Schmidt that his new Bundesbank colleagues were 'critical and sceptical' of his ideas.[88] Exchange rate flexibility, Pöhl wrote, had protected Germany from the need to carry out destabilising currency intervention and from the severe inflation that hit Britain, Italy and France. However, Pöhl comforted the chancellor with his view that the tide had since started to turn. During the 1970s, Pöhl recounted, Germany's interests had switched towards wishing to hold down an excessive rise of the D-Mark – lending important impetus to Schmidt's and Giscard's EMS concept:

If the D-Mark's high valuation of the D-Mark against the dollar continues, then this might not only endanger our economic recovery but also give rise to structural changes (transfer of production facilities abroad) that could lead to permanent massive unemployment. We must therefore have an urgent interest in sharing the pressure of revaluation on as many shoulders as possible.

Schmidt delayed deliberations on a Franco-German monetary blueprint until Giscard surmounted an important political hurdle – the French parliamentary elections in March 1978. Before this, Schmidt was anxious not to publicise news of his plans, fearing 'the old rebuke' from France's Left and Right that the president 'was delivering up France to Germanic economic might'.[89] Conditions moved into place when Giscard and prime minister Raymond Barre achieved an unexpected victory over the Socialist and Communist parties.[90] Ten days later in Frankfurt, Emminger and Pöhl met Bernard Clappier, the governor of the Banque de France, at Giscard's and Schmidt's request, to push the plans forward.[91] This meeting helped pave the way for Franco-German proposals that were launched at the European Copenhagen summit the following week, including plans for reserve-pooling through a new institution to be called the European Monetary Fund, enhancement of the European Unit of Account and a joint European policy on the dollar.[92]

Britain showed strong doubts at British–German talks at Chequers on 23 April.[93] Callaghan told Schmidt the new mechanism would depress the D-Mark and strengthen the pound, arguing, 'That would help Germany, not Britain.' Callaghan recalled the UK's abrupt exit from the Snake six years previously; Schmidt countered that Britain had 'capitulated' too quickly.[94] Gordon Richardson, governor of the Bank of England, emphasised the fundamental lesson of that episode. Repeating the point made by Heath and Barber in 1973, the governor said Britain would consider participating in the new scheme only if the Germans provided substantial credit facilities through pooled currency reserves. Callaghan's Chancellor of the Exchequer, Denis Healey, later claimed that a crucial reason for Britain's hostility to the EMS was because Manfred Lahnstein, Pöhl's successor as State Secretary at the Bonn finance ministry, told him over a glass of beer 'the key principle of German economic policy was to persuade the French and Italians to pay to lower the value of the D-Mark so as to make Germany more competitive.'[95]

As Britain's reluctance to join became increasingly apparent, Germany mounted a campaign to win EMS adherents elsewhere. Lahnstein undertook clandestine missions to persuade Ireland and Italy to sign up. He recalled:

Before 1979, the monetary policy of the Bank of Ireland was run by the Bank of England. I went to see prime minister Jack Lynch – I remember he spoke like a man from Boston – and the director general of the Treasury, and I said: 'You want to be an independent country and you don't even have your own currency?' They had no practice at that. The question was whether the Irish punt would rise too much against sterling. The most vociferous critics of Irish membership were Irish mushroom producers exporting to Liverpool. In the end, the promise of eventual financial assistance for Ireland through the enhanced Community regional spending tipped the balance.[96]

The Irish move to enter the EMS was part of the country's gradual shift to emancipate itself from the effects of British rule and promote integration with the rest of Europe. As John Hurley, governor of the Central Bank of Ireland, put it thirty years later: 'We had moved away from protectionism in the 1950s towards a more externally-oriented model of economic development. The move to join the Euro was part of a continuum over 40 or 50 years, very different from the earlier part of the century – a reconnection to the rest of Europe, recognising our previous cultural, trading and monastic links.'[97]

In Rome, Lahnstein met greater resistance. Italy faced a familiar dilemma: Paolo Baffi, governor of the Banca d'Italia, and Giulio Andreotti, the prime minister, were doubtful about joining, on the grounds that Italy's high inflation rate would quickly cause it to become uncompetitive, whereas Filippo Maria Pandolfi, the Treasury Minister, was convinced that Italy should join to import Germany's anti-inflation discipline and stability. Lahnstein worked out the conditions for Italian membership bilaterally with Pandolfi, including a 6 per cent fluctuation band for the lira to soften the impact of Italy's higher inflation rate.

The ECU is Born

Schmidt took extremely seriously the concerns of countries like Britain about the need for sufficient ammunition to head off attacks on weaker currencies. This produced a counter-reaction from the Bundesbank. Alarmed by reports from Schmidt's key monetary aide Horst Schulmann about wide Franco-German commitments for EMS intervention, Emminger wrote to Schmidt at the end of June, querying the planned use of the Bundesbank reserves in the putative European Monetary Fund.[98] At the Bundesbank Council the next day, Pöhl attacked the idea of setting up a 'second Snake' with softer conditions for the UK and Italy.[99] He condemned as 'technically impossible' France's recommendation that intervention obligations for the new system would be based on the rates of individual currencies against a weighted average of European currencies (the so-called 'currency basket' that had already been a centrepiece of the ill-fated Fourcade proposals in 1974). The 'currency basket' proposal would change the balance of European monetary power by forcing the Bundesbank into intervention to lower the D-Mark before weaker central banks were obliged to defend their own currencies. At the same meeting Emminger said that a proposed joint intervention policy against the dollar could 'take D-Mark creation fully out of our hands'.

The waspish Bundesbank response helped ensure that the next meeting of European leaders, at Bremen at the beginning of July, took no binding decisions on the EMS. However, the summit set guidelines towards a final accord, backing a crucial aspect of the French 'currency basket' approach by agreeing that the European Unit of Account – renamed the European Currency Unit or ECU – should be 'at the centre of the system'.[100] In particular, the EMS would create ECUs – initially as a technical unit for use in financing central bank intervention operations, later perhaps as a proper currency – through the workings of the proposed European Monetary Fund. For Giscard this was as an elegant means of reminding the Germans of an epoch when France had held monetary sway over the rest of Europe. The ECU designation revived memories of the Ecu, a medieval French gold coin in circulation under Louis XIV.[101]

After the Bremen meeting, battle lines hardened between French-inspired supporters of an ECU-based system and Bundesbank-led campaigners bidding to uphold the Snake's hard-line anti-inflation features. This was a new and more sophisticated version of the traditional Economist versus Monetarist argument over the balance between technical measures and economic adjustment as the key to convergence. The Bundesbank and the Nederlandsche Bank regarded the ECU as a suspect instrument of so-called 'symmetry' that would put undue pressure on the surplus countries and lower constraints on the weaker currencies.[102] The showdown came when Giscard and Schmidt met in Aachen with their key officials in September. Schmidt rejected the Giscard ECU-based proposals and agreed the Bundesbank line: to transfer to the new system most of the main features of the Snake. This was a seminal moment in the history of the EMS, which set the tone for twenty years of political debates about monetary union. Pöhl and Emminger played crucial roles in changing Schmidt's mind, although, according to Pöhl, it was the latter who earned the chancellor's wrath.[103]

Emminger was against one of the central proposals of the European Monetary System – the idea that all countries in the system would be able to intervene with the ECU in their own currency, and pay back debts in their own currency – that would have amounted to a community of inflation. Emminger's view was that debts had to be repaid in hard currency, either in dollars, D-Marks or gold. In addition, in an emergency, the Bundesbank had the right to suspend intervention obligations. This was eventually enshrined in the agreements. I had to fight for the Bundesbank's position at the Aachen meeting. I was absolutely hoarse, I couldn't speak any more. Thank God, Schmidt's anger was directed against Emminger and not me, even though I was in total agreement with Emminger on this point.[104]

While Europe sought to find protection from the dollar's volatility, America was at last starting to act to counter the basic reasons for the currency's decline. On 1 November 1978 the Carter administration unveiled a dollar support package including $30 billion in borrowings from foreign central banks, the IMF and the capital markets and an increase in the Federal Reserve discount rate by 1 percentage point.[105] Against this turbulent international background, the complex balance of EMS risk and reward remained an immense preoccupation for the French. Jean-Yves Haberer took over as director of the French

Treasury in 1978 when Jacques de Larosière moved to Washington as managing director of the IMF. In the wake of the American monetary package, Haberer penned a long analytical note that outlined doubled-edged French fears over the EMS. France's top monetary diplomat wrote that a wider system with more currencies pegged to the D-Mark was needed to strengthen the Franc's position against 'the strong currencies of the present Snake' and 'dilute the hegemony of the D-Mark'. On the other hand, if France continued with a relatively high inflation rate, and unless the EMS contained procedures for occasional 'de-dramatised' exchange rate adjustments, France could be constrained into 'defending artificial parities' that 'suffocate exports and economic growth' and 'imbue the system with a permanent deflationary bias [that could] even imperil its existence'.[106]

Haberer's note signalled strong antagonism towards Britain and the US – showing how de Gaulle's anti-Anglo-Americanism lived on a decade after his demise. Haberer called for France to take action to 'isolate' the British, who, with 'their backs to the wall', would be the only Community member not to join the EMS. 'They know that this self-induced demonstration of [British] weakness cannot fail to lead the foreign exchange markets to anticipate a fall in sterling, which would pose problems during an electoral period.' Haberer added that the American government 'will be tempted to seek at least a post-ponement of the European Monetary System ... The recently-announced economic and monetary measures by President Carter will certainly not be adequate in restoring confidence in the future of the dollar.'

As the French government was plotting to use the EMS preparations to discomfort Britain, manoeuvrings between the Bundesbank and Bonn gathered pace in the run-up to a crucial Brussels heads of government meeting in December 1978. On 16 November the Bundesbank Council sent Schmidt its approval of key elements of the prospective EMS agreement coupled with a list of points for further clarification, including the need to safeguard the Bundesbank's 'autonomy' and its desire to be freed from the obligation to intervene with unlimited support for weaker currencies at times of monetary crisis.[107] Schmidt sent Emminger a telex message signalling agreement on all the outstanding issues apart from the intervention exemption.[108] On 30 November Schmidt attended a lengthy Bundesbank Council meeting to clinch agreement on the EMS details – the first visit to the Bundesbank by a head of government.

After he left office in 1982 Schmidt spread the view that he broke the Bundesbank's resistance to the EMS by threatening to persuade the German parliament to remove its independence.[109] The story seems greatly exaggerated, if not wholly untrue. As André Szász, the Nederlandsche Bank director, put it, 'Schmidt encouraged rumours that the Bonn government would change the Bundesbank Law unless the Bundesbank agreed, but this was nonsense. In the end, the Bundesbank got its way, but all the bargaining took place behind closed doors.'[110] The Bundesbank's hitherto secret 73-page verbatim transcript of the proceedings[111] – which Emminger sent to Schmidt the next day[112] – demonstrates extensive harmony between the chancellor and the Bundesbank on nearly all aspects of the EMS.[113] Schmidt went out of his way to praise 'the extraordinary utility [the Government has drawn] in the last weeks and months from the arguments of the autonomous Bundesbank and its Council'.[114] Consensus between the central bank and government provided benefits for both sides, further embellishing the Bundesbank's reputation and giving Schmidt vital ammunition for clinching EMS negotiations at home and abroad.

Schmidt's secret speech to the Council was one of the longest and most impassioned presentations ever made at a central banking policy session. He declared that the EMS was far more than a currency bloc:

A purely German initiative [for the EMS] would have been completely out of the question. Clearly, it was only feasible as a joint effort of France and Germany, with the explicit backing of the Benelux countries – and that of the Danes, too. Any attempt by Germany to go it alone in this field would trigger visceral fears in other countries of being steamrollered, and so provoke instant and widespread opposition . . . German foreign policy cannot operate successfully without a functioning Common Market and a European Community that can punch its weight both economically and politically. German foreign policy rests on two key pillars: the European Community and the North Atlantic alliance . . . The entire strategy that we have pursued over the last 10 years – vis-à-vis the Soviet Union and Eastern Europe, that we have pursued to shore up Berlin, the 'city of German destiny' – would have been impossible without these two pillars underpinning us. We are vulnerable on two fronts and will remain so until well into the next century. We are vulnerable, first, because of Berlin and because of the open flank in the East, because of the division of our nation, symbolised by Berlin's insular position. And we are vulnerable, second, because of Auschwitz. The more successful we are in the fields of foreign, economic, social and defence policy, the longer it will take for Auschwitz to fade from the fore of collective consciousness.[115]

Schmidt told the Bundesbank that launching the EMS would be impossible without his close ties to Giscard. He cast strong doubts – which later turned out to be fully justified – on the economic credentials of French opposition leader François Mitterrand.[116]

> Giscard and I have been united on this point [the EMS] for a long, long time. I can tell you discreetly: With Mr Mitterrand, I would not have dreamed of making such a proposal. Our proposals reflect France's confidence in the continuity of the German government; and also our trust in the French government, represented by the two personalities Giscard d'Estaing and Raymond Barre. Without this, the risk would be too great. Certainly, the President [Giscard] will stand for re-election in 1981. It appears as if he has a good chance of being voted in for a further seven years.

Lively exchanges with Council members focused on the key issue of whether, at times of crisis, the Bundesbank could be freed from the constraint of making unlimited intervention purchases of weaker currencies that would inflate the German money supply. Schmidt pointed out, to Emminger's evident satisfaction, that – in relation to this crucial point – he had annotated the Bundesbank president's letter of 16 November with an 'r' to indicate '*richtig*' ('right' in German) or, as he said, 'factual agreement'.[117] Uncannily foreshadowing political controversy with the French and Italian governments that exploded in September 1992, Schmidt told the Council that the sensitivity of what later became known as the 'Emminger letter' made formal written undertakings impossible.

> Let us imagine that this appeared in a French or Italian newspaper tomorrow. The editorials would criticise their own governments for believing such a shallow promise from the Germans. A [German] government promises to intervene to uphold certain rules of the game, but then writes in an internal paper that it intends to act differently at times of emergency.[118]

Schmidt reminded the Council of the past precedent – during the switch to floating rates in March 1973 – for giving the defence of the D-Mark priority over international undertakings.[119]

> In spring 1973 we contravened ruling international constitutional law, the IMF agreement, in several ways. We adhered neither to the overall rules of the game, the procedural rules, nor to the material legal regulations. We freed the Bundesbank from the obligation to intervene against the dollar, solely with the motive to gain manoeuvring room within our country for a stable policy, one

that was geared to stability. In accord with the Bundesbank leadership and with the finance minister, the then Government, the then Chancellor approved this. We did not notify previously, when the Federal Republic became a member of the IMF, that we would apply *clausula rebus sic stantibus*.* We didn't even write it down. We did it when it was the only way out.

A further sign of harmony between the Bundesbank and Schmidt came in a discussion on how EMS exchange rates could be changed when inflation rates became out of line. Helmut Schlesinger, responsible for economics on the Bundesbank's Directorate, asked whether the chancellor foresaw that weaker countries might choose to leave the EMS rather than devalue[120] – accurately predicting the circumstances of the exchange rate crises in September 1992. Schmidt, for his part, showed clairvoyance when he foresaw that the dollar would rise in the next few years, as a result of the Carter administration's sudden switch to monetary rigour.[121]

Towards the end of the Bundesbank session Schmidt turned again to a favourite theme: the interaction between foreign policy and monetary policy. He criticised the Americans' previous neglect – which he said had turned 'malign' under Carter and Blumenthal – of their 'anchor role' within the Bretton Woods system.[122] And he forecast: 'The anchor of the new system [EMS] is the French and Germans together. I hope they will not say it is the Germans.' Schmidt put forward a far-reaching vision for the future of the ECU: in perhaps two or three years, a developed European currency – which he termed 'ECU-2' – could take on genuine international status.

If this comes, it will be a great opportunity for the future. This will be the sole chance of preventing the D-Mark from taking on a growing role as a reserve currency next to the dollar. The only chance to prevent the D-Mark gaining more and more weight as a world currency, with all the dangers that that brings. This is the opportunity of the ECU-2. But one should not say this out loud today. Otherwise the English will say: 'You see, the Germans are doing the whole thing out of egoism.'[123]

Schmidt had the English on his mind on 30 November because he knew that, at the Brussels meeting at the beginning of December, Britain would stay out of the Exchange Rate Mechanism of the EMS.[124] The currency system duly

---

* Treaties may become inapplicable because of changes in circumstances.

started the next year with eight of the nine Community members.[125] As Callaghan's Chancellor of the Exchequer Denis Healey confirmed, the UK decision reflected not merely the economics of pegging currency rates but, crucially, a fundamental view of Britain's place in the world.

> Europe did not come first in our international league table. America came first, economically, politically and defence-wise – it was infinitely more important than our relationship with Europe. That was the fundamental reason why Britain did not join the EMS. It was a still more important argument than the issue of the rigidities of the EMS and whether we would be locking ourselves into the wrong exchange rate.[126]

Britain's decision to stay out geared the future of the EMS much more intensely to the fluctuations of Franco-German politics than would otherwise have been the case. The UK's step, too, comprehensively sealed the issue of the dominant currency of the new system. If Britain had joined, sterling, the D-Mark and the French Franc might have jostled for influence. In contrast to Schmidt's averred hopes, the anchor role in Europe over the next decade fell comprehensively to the D-Mark – an outcome that already at the end of 1978 appeared visible to some EMS critics in Paris. Jacques Chirac, Giscard's former prime minister, struck a defiantly Gaullist tone in a strong criticism of Giscard's pretensions that the EMS was a new system: 'The ECU sounds perhaps like something from the lips of Saint Louis, but its reality strongly resembles the D-Mark and the monetary discipline accepted is more German than European.'[127]

In the setting up of the EMS, Germany indeed made few concessions to the French desire to end 'D-Mark hegemony'. Currency intervention and debt settlement rules within the EMS still required weaker countries to support their currencies rather than (as favoured by France, the UK and Italy) the stronger members to weaken theirs. Although short- and medium-term credit assistance within the EMS was expanded significantly compared with the Snake, there was no comprehensive agreement on reserve-pooling.[128]

The EMS agreement set down that a European Monetary Fund would be established after two years (in 1981), but this proviso was never enacted. As long-serving German monetary official Hans Tietmeyer said in 2007, 'The Bundesbank desire to have the system based on the anchor of the D-Mark, and to prevent a move towards "symmetry" of intervention and settlement obligations, won the day. The EMS turned out to be not much more than a legal enshrinement of the basis of the Snake.'[129] Another European monetary insider, Erik Hoffmeyer, the independent-minded president of the Danish National Bank, confirmed: 'On paper, there were concessions to France; in reality, virtually nothing changed.'[130]

Forceful Anti-Inflation Action

After the EMS breakthrough, disillusionment soon set in. The oil price rise caused by the first stirrings of the Iran–Iraq war in 1979 brought higher inflation and a threat of recession. Just as the 1973 oil price tempest wrecked the Werner Plan, the second energy shock six years later severely buffeted the EMS in its opening phase, providing a key reason why Giscard lost power in 1981, followed by Schmidt seventeen months afterwards. European monetary problems were exacerbated by an uncharacteristic weakening of the D-Mark. For years, European central bankers had been pressing the US to take forceful anti-inflation action. When it came, with a progressive increase of US interest rates in the wake of Carter's November 1978 dollar support package, a frisson of European anger followed close behind.

In response to rising US interest rates, the Bundesbank increased its discount and Lombard rates by one and two percentage points respectively in the first half of 1979 – the first German credit tightening since the breakdown of the Bretton Woods system. At the monthly meeting of Community central bank governors on 10 July several central bankers put pressure on the Bundesbank not to raise interest rates further. But just two days later, the Bundesbank increased its discount rate by one percentage point and the Lombard rate by 0.5 point to 5 per cent and 6 per cent.[131] Cecil de Strycker, governor of the Belgian National Bank, sent Emminger a strong letter of protest, claiming that the Bundesbank action would provoke interest rates 'escalation' and endanger exchange rate stability.[132]

Bundesbank President Emminger fired back a rejoinder: 'Any capital outflows from Belgium to Germany are not caused by our especially attractive interest rates, but by other reasons.'[133] The Bundesbank chief drew on his bank's near-inexhaustible reserves of self-righteousness, claiming the Bundesbank's actions were in Europe's best interests. 'We do not believe that it would help our partner countries in the longer run if monetary stability were lost in the Federal Republic as a result of a lax monetary policy, because then the whole of Western Europe would slide even faster into inflation.'

Still stronger pressures were building up in America. US inflation was heading to a post-war peak of 11 per cent. Carter appointed the cigar-chomping previous head of the New York Federal Reserve Bank Paul Volcker as chairman of the Federal Reserve in August 1979, nominating the Fed incumbent, William Miller, as Treasury Secretary. Despite the discomfort caused by the Bundesbank interest rate increases, the new American central bank chief faced further German-led calls for still tougher anti-inflationary action. One of the critical points was the American fear that the oil-producing states were considering shifting from the dollar to the IMF's composite currency, the Special Drawing Right, as the official currency for pricing oil. This would not only inflict a sharp blow to America's international financial status but could also prove highly inflationary. Anthony Solomon, who had taken Volcker's old job as under-secretary at the US Treasury for international monetary affairs, wrote in an internal memo:

> We face an extremely dangerous situation in the exchange markets ... A main reason for the pressure is [the] virtually universal view that the US and Germany are in conflict on exchange rate policy, that cooperation has broken down. The market believes that the US wants the dollar stable or rising, but that Germany wants or expects it to decline ... A huge avalanche of private money is nervous and ready to move. Pressures may get extreme ... Under current circumstances and in the current psychological atmosphere, we face not a tactical problem but a situation that could quickly degenerate into a full-blown destructive crisis.[134]

Since Carter's monetary package of November 1978, the US authorities had been intervening on the foreign exchanges to shore up the dollar. But, on both sides of the Atlantic, monetary officials knew that, in the absence of tough economic measures, dollar support intervention was not the answer. 'What is totally clear is that the present situation – with Germany ambivalent at best – is untenable,' Solomon wrote. 'We are being bled to death and will have to let go.' His warning bore fruit. On a rapid trip to Europe at the end of September 1979, Volcker received recommendations for stern austerity measures from Helmut Schmidt and Otmar Emminger during a stop-over in Hamburg.[135] According to Volcker:

> Schmidt was at his irascible worst – or best, depending upon one's point of view. He left no doubt that his patience with what he saw as American neglect and irresolution about the dollar had run out. His remarks had special force because, whatever the evident irritation with Mr Carter on other grounds, no one could really doubt his goodwill towards America and Americans over a number of years.[136]

International central bankers voiced further pleas for dollar action when, immediately after his Hamburg talks with Schmidt, Volcker attended the annual meeting of the International Monetary Fund in Belgrade. The Federal Reserve chairman had already made up his mind to organise a monetary coup.[137] Back in Washington after leaving the IMF gathering early, Volcker called a secret meeting of the Federal Open Market Committee on 6 October to decide a fundamental shift in the Federal Reserve's methods of monetary control. Henceforth, the Fed would directly target the money supply rather than interest rates. Volcker had to brush aside opposition from Treasury Secretary Miller. But during a meeting with the Federal Reserve chairman, President Carter offered Volcker support for the change in the monetary control regime. The president was apparently heedless of the pain that would ensue for the economy – and for his re-election chances in 1980. Later, it transpired that the president had been unaware of the perilous consequences. As Solomon put it, 'No President really understands these things, but the disturbing thing about Carter was that he tried to use the economic jargon as though he did.'[138] In response to the new monetary constraints, the key American inter-bank lending rate – the federal funds rate – rose sharply from around 10 per cent in summer 1979 to 14 per cent in December and 19 per cent in April 1980.

Towards the end of 1979 the build-up to the outbreak of war between Iraq and Iran and the Soviet invasion of Afghanistan added to political nervousness and fuelled a rapid rise in the gold price. With consumer prices in America still increasing rapidly, Carter – backed by Miller and Volcker – announced a further package of budget cuts, credit controls and monetary tightening in March 1980. 'The economy promptly went into a nose dive,' Volcker wrote.[139]

The drastic American tightening formed an uncomfortable backcloth for Karl Otto Pöhl's assumption of the top job in European central banking when he replaced Emminger as Bundesbank president in January 1980. The Bundesbank's chief economist Helmut Schlesinger – who had spent his working life on domestic monetary issues, with little foreign experience – became deputy president. During the coming action-packed decade, polished Pöhl and stringent Schlesinger were the key force in European central banking.

Following five separate increases in 1979 the Bundesbank raised the discount rate to a post-war high of 7.5 per cent in May 1980. As a result of the credit tightening, relations between Pöhl and Schmidt cooled sharply in 1981. In February Lahnstein, who had taken over Pöhl's old job as State Secretary in the Finance Ministry, accused Pöhl of hoisting a 'guillotine' over the government[140] – the same word used as in Adenauer's complaint to the Bank deutscher Länder twenty-four years previously. But the Bundesbank responded to persistent

D-Mark weakness and further rises in US interest rates by suspending its normal methods of lending to commercial banks, driving up money market interest rates to 30 per cent. The Bundesbank's monetary squeeze had political consequences in both France and Germany. Shortly before the French presidential elections in May 1981 that produced victory for François Mitterrand, Prime Minister Raymond Barre turned to Helmut Schmidt with a desperate plea for cuts in Bundesbank interest rates. Claiming that recent American interest rate reductions made a credit thaw possible in Europe, Barre declared:

> I believe it would be very advantageous if the interest rates could be reduced to a more moderate level. This would promote an economic recovery in Germany and, as a result, in other countries ... If the desired development in Germany were to take place quite quickly, then this would save the French economy from a further interest rate increase, which would quite clearly not be justified by the present economic position.[141]

Seizing on the chance to exert pressure on Pöhl and Schlesinger, Schmidt arranged for a copy of the Barre letter to be sent to Frankfurt. Pöhl and Schlesinger discussed the issue with the Bundesbank Directorate, then wrote to Schmidt dismissing any question of interest rate cuts. Contrary to Barre's assertion that US interest rates had fallen, the Bundesbank duo pointed out that 'the interest rate difference between dollar and D-Mark deposits has increased considerably, making the desired cut in short-term rates impossible for the time being'.[142]

In the eye of the trans-Atlantic storm, Paul Volcker succeeded in bringing down American inflation, but at the cost of domestic opprobrium for tilting the US economy into recession. One high-profile casualty was President Jimmy Carter. In the November 1980 election he lost office to Ronald Reagan, mainly because of what Carter during the campaign called Volcker's 'ill-advised' increase in interest rates.[143] Volcker kept up the anti-inflation fight, raising interest rates again in 1981,[144] precipitating widespread protests from workers hit by the economic slowdown and sparking the claim from a leading Senator, 'You're high on a hit parade for public lynching.'[145]

Helmut Schmidt, a prime instigator of the American credit squeeze, finished up as yet another victim. In his last weeks in office, Schmidt maintained an increasingly bitter yet unrelentingly unsuccessful mission to persuade the Bundesbank to relax credit. In a climactic Bundestag debate in October 1982 that sealed the fate of his government and brought Christian Democrat leader Helmut Kohl to power after a parliamentary no-confidence vote, Schmidt underlined how severely his once-harmonious relationship with the central bank had deteriorated. He called on the Bundesbank to 'contribute decisively to a fall in interest rates' to stimulate investment in the economy, adding, 'I am warning about the consequences of deflation!'[146]

The Bundesbank delayed substantive cuts in interest rates until summer 1993, when Schmidt was smarting in opposition. After having drawn in massive financial inflows in the 1970s, West Germany in the early 1980s was badly hit by a transforming tide of hot money streaming out of the D-Mark into the newly-attractive US. In the twilight of his political career, Schmidt regarded it as deeply irksome that the international capital markets should bestow such favours on Carter's successor Ronald Reagan. With trademark succinctness matched only by characteristic lack of charity, Germany's disgruntled ex-chancellor later told French visitors that both Carter and Reagan were 'zeros'.[147]

At home, too, neither Schmidt nor Giscard was enamoured with the men who took their place. The two 1970s leaders were indubitably the masters of European finance. Yet, incomprehensibly, destiny selected not them but their successors, Helmut Kohl and François Mitterrand, so insufferably ill-schooled in the affairs of money, to channel its transforming power into a greater political design. Fateful decisions to proceed with a radical reorganisation of European economics and finance lay ahead. Ambush and adventure awaited, at every stage and on every turn of the journey.

THE COMING TRIAL

The Germans are a great people deprived of certain attributes of sovereignty,
with reduced diplomatic status. Germany compensates for this weakness with
its economic power. The Deutsche Mark is to some extent its nuclear force.
French President François Mitterrand, 1988[1]

The contrasting characters of François Mitterrand and Helmut Kohl, the
longest-serving French and German leaders since the 1870s, played front-line
roles in a long-running search for European equilibrium. Mitterrand was a
man of letters and master of intrigue whose many-hued background and enig-
matic personality made him the supreme metaphor for the swirling political
currents that drove Europe towards the Euro. Kohl exuded an air of jovial
certainty tinged with rumbustious brusqueness. Though he never lost his belief
in the long-term goal of German reunification, he was taken aback when the
opportunity presented itself in 1989 – and then pushed it through with break-
neck speed. France's Socialist president and Germany's Christian Democrat
chancellor, with no economic and very little international policy experience,
took office within a space of seventeen months in 1981–82. Presiding together
over their countries for a span of a dozen years, they were responsible for all the
main decisions on monetary union.

Mitterrand was respectful of history and disdainful of capitalism. He delved
daily into the works of Balzac and Chateaubriand, and never deigned to
carry coins in his pocket. Overriding interest in economics could never be
counted among his characteristics. Yet he became – still more than Kohl – the
pivotal figure behind Economic and Monetary Union. Behind the search for

rapprochement with France's large and historically troublesome eastern neighbour lay both a deep understanding of Germany's strategic position and suspicion of how it might misuse its economic power. Mitterrand eventually became France's longest-serving head of state since Napoleon III, who as Louis-Napoleon was elected president of the Second Republic in 1848 – and later suffered the indignity of defeat in the Franco-Prussian War that led to the birth of the German Empire.

Born in 1916, the year of the Battle of Verdun in the First World War, Mitterrand grew up in a conservative Catholic family in South West France.[2] Little in Mitterrand's early life marked him down as a standard-bearer of Franco-German friendship.[3] The pillage of France by German arms – the territorial losses after the Battle of Waterloo, the war with Prussia in 1870–71, the German incursions of the First World War – marked his youthful reflections, as he later recalled: 'I was full of long-standing prejudices. I saw the Franco-German relationship as a caricature. I could not pardon the damage of three occupations within a century. It seemed to me a blasphemy that an amorphous people like the Germans could invade France and absorb it, like a swelling.'[4]

After the Second World War broke out in 1939, Mitterrand enlisted as an infantry sergeant and was wounded and captured by the Wehrmacht soon after the Fall of France. His eighteen months as a prisoner of war in Germany was an important episode establishing his later Europeanism, helping him to appreciate for the first time the diverse social classes of his own country, to distinguish between workaday Germans and their Nazi overlords, and to analyse the multiple layers of European history. Mitterrand's captors transported him to a prison camp in Thuringia in a train of cattle trucks. Pondering on the 'centuries-long duel between France and Germany' he wrote shortly afterwards of the futility of French policy towards Germany since the 1790s: 'France has exhausted itself . . . in imposing on Europe its ardour of war, in spreading its blood beyond its borders, for impossible frontiers.'[5] In later decades, Mitterrand's war years in Germany made him an object of fascination – even reverence – for many Germans. As a prisoner in Bruchsal on the Rhine in March 1941, Mitterrand became acquainted with a Catholic priest who took him to dinner with the prison governor and his family. More than four decades afterwards, Mitterrand told the story:

> The governor was wearing military uniform, the wife was wearing an official decoration and the apparel of the two daughters indicated that they were members of the Bund deutscher Mädchen [Nazi Young Women's League.] We

ate goose and drank a good French red wine. The governor asked me if I knew the occasion to which we were raising our glasses. I replied that I did not. The governor told me that German troops had just conquered Serbia.[6]

Later in the 1980s, Mitterrand moved and charmed German audiences with the tale of his encounter with an old German woman as he was being recaptured by German soldiers after he had tried to escape. She gave him a piece of bread, with the words 'I hope this will help you like the Germans.'[7] After twice escaping and being recaptured, in December 1941 Mitterrand succeeded in breaking free from German captivity and returning to France. He found his country chastened by defeat and occupation. Mitterrand took up a minor post in 1942 in the collaborationist government of Marshal Pétain, based in Vichy in central France. In a precursor of his later skill – displayed notably during negotiations on monetary union – in keeping options open and intentions obscure, Mitterrand simultaneously became a Pétainist bureaucrat and a French Resistance agent in touch with undercover operators in the British army, continually changing his name to shake off German surveillance.[8] In 1943 he received a top Pétainist decoration, the Francisque,[9] which he later termed 'excellent cover' for his Resistance activities.[10] As the German secret police, the Gestapo, stepped up its hunt for Resistance fighters, in December 1943 he undertook a clandestine journey to Algiers arranged by the British military,[11] for an awkward meeting with General Charles de Gaulle, the leader of the Free French.[12] De Gaulle asked the younger man for assistance in uniting the external and internal units of the French Resistance. Mitterrand refused. This gesture of individualism sealed the two politicians' long hostility.[13] Both politicians became, in different ways but for similar motivations, advocates of Franco-German unity.

Elected to parliament as an independent deputy in 1946, Mitterrand oscillated between centre-Left and centre-Right during the crisis-torn post-war Fourth Republic. He held eleven separate ministerial posts in successive ramshackle Socialist- and centrist-led administrations, until the Fourth Republic collapsed in ignominy. He struck up a close partnership with Pierre Mendes-France, the Socialist prime minister who – well before de Gaulle – took the first steps towards post-1945 reconciliation with Germany. During the Fifth Republic, established in 1958, Mitterrand lost two presidential elections, against de Gaulle and Giscard. In May 1981 success came at last. Mitterrand compared his third bid for the presidency with his third escape from German imprisonment forty years earlier.[14] Victory over arch-rival Giscard made Mitterrand the Fifth Republic's first Left-wing president, leading a fractious coalition of Socialists and Communists. At the age of 64 – just three years younger than de Gaulle when he founded the Fifth Republic – Mitterrand was an old man in a hurry. His main aim was to rush through domestic economic and social reforms. European policy was not an immediate preoccupation. Since the formation of the European Community and the sealing of post-war friendship between France and West Germany in the 1963 Elysée Treaty, the two countries had been the closest of European partners. Yet the relationship was not free of squalls. Many on the French Left believed that Giscard's friendship with Schmidt had pushed France too far towards economic dependence on Germany.[15]

Mitterrand was neither willing nor able to emulate Giscard's cool-headed grasp of monetary affairs, but he showed strategic foresight over Germany's future that his forerunner lacked. Nearly a decade before the fall of the Berlin Wall in November 1989, the French president – in separate conversations first with Schmidt, then, a year later, with Kohl – predicted a united German nation: the result, he said, of Soviet weakness and a consequent decline in Moscow's ability to control East Germany. These forecasts – documented by French and German government archives – suggest that Mitterrand was already starting to prepare for the ending of France's special role, kept intact by its membership of the war-time alliance, as a guarantor of Europe's political contours. Ever prescient of opportunity tinged with danger, Mitterrand readied himself for the trial.

Mitterrand's conversation on German unification with Schmidt, at the president's country home of Latche in south-west France, in October 1981,[16] was overshadowed by the economic effects of his victory five months earlier. Mitterrand enacted political and economic nostrums that had been nurtured in the long years of Socialist party opposition, but no longer matched the country's needs. Early moves included nationalising France's thirty-six top private banks[17] and five large industrial enterprises, cutting working hours and the retirement age and raising social security payments. The actions exacerbated the economic overheating and double-digit inflation bequeathed by Giscard's previous policies[18] – weakening the Franc, increasing the budget deficit and increasing the French economy's lag behind Germany. A private briefing paper from Schmidt's staff shortly before the Latche meeting warned of 'regular, perhaps serious disturbances in the German-French relationship'.[19] During the talks – which took place three days after the Franc was devalued by 8.5 per cent against the D-Mark – Schmidt gave Mitterrand a brusque message: 'You have chosen a different path. I hope you succeed. But your means and your methods are such that we cannot harmonise them.'[20]

Within his own government, too, Mitterrand's policies were contested. Jacques Delors, an industrious former Banque de France functionary from the Christian Socialist wing of the party, became finance minister in 1981 – and took an immediately pessimistic line. Delors, later a ground-breaking president of the European Commission, played a significant role in setting France on course for EMU. In Mitterrand's first administration, Delors occupied an unusually modest Number 16 position in the government hierarchy. While hardly according with Delors' view of his own abilities, his lowly status gave him the independence to speak his mind. In June 1982 Delors attended the annual Group of Seven summit of the main industrial countries, held under Mitterrand's chairmanship in the ornate setting of the Palace of Versailles. The occasion underlined the contrast between the grandeur of Mitterrand's vision and the poverty of his economic policies. A ballet performance and fireworks display formed the backcloth to a panoply of bombastically unrealistic Mitterrand announcements on world monetary reform and global technological renewal. On the foreign exchanges, the Franc was enduring another bout of weakness. At the opening of the summit Delors commented sardonically: 'To think we have all this political cinema when we have run out of reserves and will soon have to devalue.'[21] Mitterrand, for his part, was not oblivious of the pressures from rampant international capital. Shortly after the summit, he informed his ministers that France was facing 'an international war' on the financial markets.[22] Delors agreed. In November 1982 the everlugubrious finance minister told Mitterrand, 'We are threatened by a grave and humiliating crisis.'[23]

Such episodes heightened the *froideur* of Schmidt's economic policy exchanges with Mitterrand. But the chancellor's overall relationship with the French president improved as the result of Mitterrand's stance in the military and diplomatic sphere, where France had acknowledged superiority. In 1981–82, a principal source of discontent within Schmidt's Social Democratic Party was the Bonn government policy on the so-called Euro-missiles. To counter a build-up of Soviet medium-range nuclear weapons in Eastern Europe, Schmidt backed deployment of US Cruise and Pershing nuclear missiles in West Germany, a stance which most of the electorate, along with leading elements in his own party, held in deepest suspicion.

In contrast to the more cautious Euro-missiles stance taken by his predecessor Giscard, Mitterrand gave full support to the German policy on Cruise and Pershing. Mitterrand believed this was crucial to maintaining full US engagement in Europe and avoiding a 'decoupling' of US and European interests. Schmidt was anxious to harness French support to shore up his own faltering position in Bonn. He invited Mitterrand to make a landmark European speech to the West German parliament in January 1983, the twentieth anniversary of the Elysée Treaty that sealed post-war Franco-German cooperation.[24] But before the speech could be made, the German government changed. Helmut Kohl – fourteen years younger than Mitterrand – took over as chancellor in October 1982 in the wake of the decision by Schmidt's coalition partners, the Free Democrats, to switch allegiance to Kohl's Christian Democrats.

Kohl was an untried leader who – reflecting his shortcomings in English and lack of international experience and economic expertise – had long suffered from a perception of innate inferiority against Schmidt. Kohl was destined to become the longest-serving German leader since Otto von Bismarck, yet he cut a crudely homespun figure, in startling contrast to Mitterrand's acerbically intellectual aloofness. The new chancellor looked up to the elder man as a potentially significant source of foreign policy advice. Lacking any common political roots, Mitterrand and Kohl had never met before Kohl took power. Their first conversation came in Paris in early October 1982, three days after the German parliament voted Kohl chancellor following the collapse of Schmidt's coalition. Mitterrand dubbed Kohl 'the first post-war German Chancellor'. He added: 'You are young – this is just a phase in your life. But the two of us can serve our countries.'[25]

During a second meeting, in Germany a fortnight later, Mitterrand spoke of German unity in similar terms to those used with Schmidt twelve months earlier, saying it could come before the end of the century.[26] Kohl, like Schmidt, told Mitterrand that his timescale was exaggeratedly bold. He claimed that reforging a united Germany 'in a nation-state, as with Bismarck' was impossible. Kohl said overturning German and European division would take 'generations' – a cautiously-worded prophecy that he maintained until shortly before the fall of the Berlin Wall.[27]

Behind Mitterrand's words lay an expanding sense of mutual Franco-German purpose. The president recognised that, although West Germany's economic prowess was growing, the country was still beset by fundamental weakness as a result of diminished sovereignty and national partition.[28] This was a source of anxiety for the US, too. President Ronald Reagan told Mitterrand in 1982 that West Germany was 'a fragile country in a bad state'.[29] Mitterrand's inventive mind started to assemble the ingredients of a political trade-off between Germany's power in economic and monetary affairs, and France's strength in military matters and defence.[30] Germany's monetary superiority was symbolised by the status of the Bundesbank and the D-Mark.[31]

France's military acumen was underlined by its ownership of nuclear weapons and position in the Second World War alliance that maintained formal leverage over divided Germany. If unification moved on to the horizon, so Mitterrand began to realise, France could attempt to persuade Germany to share its monetary potency in exchange for security guarantees that would underpin Germany's future as a nation.[32]

Power Bargain

Important elements of a grand bargain between the different components of French and German power crystallised in Mitterrand's Elysée Treaty speech in January 1983, focused on the Euro-missiles issue. Kohl was deeply dependent on the support of the French president, having staked his chancellorship on maintaining Schmidt's unpopular nuclear rearmament stance, on the grounds of protecting West Germany's credibility as a solid member of the Nato military alliance. On his visit to Bonn, Mitterrand rose to the occasion with aplomb, producing in his Bundestag oration the most important foreign policy statement of his presidency. By intervening forcefully on German soil to support a strategy backed by the US, Mitterrand departed from de Gaulle's doctrine of non-involvement with Nato issues. In a speech resonating with historical allusion, the French president said the Germans and French 'hated war' as the result of their long history of conflict. But deterrence was the key to securing peace in Europe, which would be jeopardised unless rearmament with US Cruise and Pershing missiles went ahead.[33] He coupled his statement of nuclear *Realpolitik* with an emotional confirmation of Franco-German friendship, which he said was the key to overcoming the pain of past wars: 'transitory victories ... condemning the victor to build on blood, and the vanquished to dream of revenge'. Citing Victor Hugo's portentous statement that the two nations shared the same blood line, Mitterrand proclaimed: 'The union of France and Germany shall be the peace of the world.'

The speech marked a turning point in Franco-German relations and granted Mitterrand an abundance of political credit in Bonn that was translated into the monetary sphere, with crucial effect, over the next decade. For all his mastery of the strategic dimension of Franco-German politics, in the domain of money and finance, the French president had his back to the wall. Disquiet on international financial markets had already forced two Franc devaluations against the D-Mark within the European Monetary System. A day before Mitterrand's landmark speech in Bonn, one of his advisers informed him of a 'catastrophic deficit' in bilateral trade with West Germany and recommended a cut in German interest rates and a significant D-Mark revaluation to help even the balance.[34] In advance of the general election in Germany on 6 March – called to ratify the October 1982 coalition change – Mitterrand's mercurial and inventive foreign policy adviser Jacques Attali urged the president to confront Kohl with an ultimatum. Unless the Germans agreed a D-Mark revaluation after the election, France should follow the policy taken by Giscard a decade earlier by withdrawing from the EMS and floating the Franc.[35]

Mitterrand orchestrated a contorted set of Franco-German manoeuvres in the aftermath of the German poll that confirmed Kohl in power. The president spurred his chief advisers and ministers to weigh the consequences of floating the Franc. A struggle for supremacy among different factions culminated in a turning point in the chronicle of European money. Mitterrand opted to follow finance minister Delors' austerity policies, tighten spending controls and keep the Franc in the EMS as a *quid pro quo* for a substantial D-Mark revaluation – an agreement that set France towards the long-term goal of monetary union with Germany. In a masterpiece of political pantomime,[36] Mitterrand kept accomplices and adversaries guessing as to his true intentions; a quarter of a century afterwards, one of the key players in the drama called the outcome 'an accident'.[37] The president used the Franc's weakness as a means of gauging the abilities of his key ministers and officials to stand up to financial market pressures. Ten days after the German election, Mitterrand dispatched two successive intermediaries – Jean-Louis Bianco, Secretary General at the Elysée Palace, and Michel Camdessus, director of the Treasury – to Bonn for secret talks to check the strength of the Franco-German alliance.[38] He tested the opinions of a variety of French businesss leaders – including Jean Riboud, the legendary chairman of the US–French oil services group Schlumberger, who advised him to quit the EMS. He invited German finance minister Gerhard Stoltenberg to a clandestine audience in the Elysée Palace to try to temper the Federal Republic's hard-line economic stance.[39] To avoid publicity, Stoltenberg was smuggled in to the president through a little-used side door. The conversation was fittingly opaque: 'Mitterrand asked many questions, but left his conclusions open.'[40] Philippe Lagayette, Delors' chief of staff, recalled:

> Mitterrand was affected by the memory of the UK having had to turn to the International Monetary Fund only seven years previously. There was a rumour at the time, partly based on the views of some officials at the Elysée, that France had been ready to sell part of its gold reserves. But this was never seriously considered. Mitterrand was not a strong economic thinker but he and his

closest associates saw there was something wrong in the ideas of those who wanted France to leave the EMS. He understood that if that were to take place, it would be seen as a big defeat for his European policy. France would never recover its strong influence.[41]

The president allotted a central role in the March 1983 drama to Budget minister Laurent Fabius, a youthful Mitterrand protégé and son of a wealthy Parisian antiques dealer. The episode gave him a springboard from which he later became industry minister and then prime minister. In the manner of a schoolmaster allotting an exceptionally taxing task to his brightest and most ambitious pupil, the president asked Fabius to assess the fundamental factors underpinning the French currency.

Mitterrand asked me, in the presence of Jacques Delors, for whom this was something of a surprise, what would be my recommendations if I were Minister of Economy and Finance. I was to speak to the appropriate people and come back with my findings. I talked to people such as [Treasury director] Michel Camdessus. I realised that the difficult international financial environment and the increase in the trade deficit were constraining our efforts to carry out an expansionary policy. Camdessus told me how low the currency reserves were. After these meetings I went back to Mitterrand and told him that if we left the EMS, we wouldn't be able to carry out a more expansionary policy. Rather, the opposite was true. The need to prevent a run on the Franc would oblige us to follow a policy of even greater rigour. We would have to tighten the vice twice as much as before. I said, 'Mr President, if I were you, I would not leave the EMS.'[42]

Fabius's findings did nothing to lower the tension between Paris and Bonn. The scene shifted to Brussels where Delors, in a display of well-judged histrionics, succeeded in browbeating the Germans into a 5.5 per cent D-Mark revaluation, a move that allowed France to save face with a Franc devaluation of only 2.5 per cent. On arriving in the Belgian capital on 18 March for a weekend meeting of European finance ministers, Delors strode before the TV cameras, accusing the Germans of 'arrogance' and threatening to withdraw the Franc from the EMS. Delors acted out his part unassisted and unrehearsed, playing the role, according to Michel Rocard – agriculture minister in 1983 and a long-time Mitterrand rival – of 'a solitary man, a lonely cowboy'.[43] According to Lagayette, 'Delors was quite a good actor, he knew that he had to be tough.' Delors explained later: 'I had to be provocative.'[44]

As a gesture of gratitude for Mitterrand's Euro-missiles support, Kohl intervened by telephone at a crucial moment in the evening negotiations, overruling his finance minister Gerhard Stoltenberg on the D-Mark revaluation and thus avoiding a much larger devaluation of the Franc. As the chancellor wrote later,

> The main point was to help our French neighbours and their President in a difficult situation. During this long night I prevailed against all the doubters and instructed Stoltenberg to implement a D-Mark revaluation. He could tell his ministerial colleagues [at the European finance ministers' meeting] that the German Chancellor understood nothing about monetary policy, but he had made this decision so as to avoid harming the French currency.[45]

A few days later, and with the full support of Delors, promoted to Number 2 in his government, Mitterrand inaugurated an austerity policy designed, the president told his ministers, 'to win the economic battle'.[46] Departure from the EMS would have robbed France of crucial leverage over Germany. Mitterrand declared: 'We did not, and do not, want to isolate France from the Community.'[47] Ostensibly, Mitterrand's policy switch marked a retreat from domestically orientated economic principles, and a submission to the doctrines of France's eastern neighbour. Yet by apparently bending to the precepts of the Bonn government and the Bundesbank, Mitterrand was preparing for his most audacious gamble: an attempt to harness the monetary might of Germany for France's own ends.

The German government displayed no rancour over Delors' *prima donna* performance in Brussels. Whatever his tendency to occasional emotional outbursts, the Germans saw Delors as the best (perhaps only) French guarantor of financial stability. In discreet dealings with Mitterrand, Kohl agreed Delors should become the next leader of the European Commission. Delors recalled, 'Mitterrand allowed me to go to Brussels at my own risk to force the issue to a conclusion. There was a certain amount of political cinema in all this, but the Germans never held it against me. Otherwise Kohl would certainly not have proposed me as President of the European Commission.'[48] Kohl believed he had made the right choice, calling Delors later 'a blessing for Europe'.[49]

Incongruous Alliance

The accord over the EMS realignment and the nomination of Delors as Commission president illustrated the highly personalised and exclusive nature of Kohl–Mitterrand deal-making. The two leaders shared a taste for the lessons of history and a disregard for economics. Yet this was an incongruous alliance. As a result of their mutual inability to speak anything except their native language, they never exchanged more than a few words in a common tongue. All their communications took place through the medium of a small band of translators and interpreters, redoubtable accessories to their bevy of trusted advisers. Both Kohl and Mitterrand constructed stratagems, sealed understandings, dispensed favours and settled scores through a close-knit, tightly controlled web of networks and contacts. They could show great loyalty to political allies and subordinates. And they could be merciless in discarding accomplices whose usefulness had come to an end. Perhaps reflecting his war-time experience, Mitterrand's ruthlessness appeared to surpass Kohl's. Closeness to Mitterrand could bring remarkable benefits – and, occasionally, tragic setbacks. Two of his closest one-time confidants – Pierre Bérégovoy, finance minister for two spells in the 1980s and then prime minister in 1992–93,[50] who played a vital role on monetary union, and François de Grossouvre, an old-established Elysée Palace adviser[51] – committed suicide in the 1990s after their one-time protector cut off his support. Mindful of the fickleness of Mitterrand's *persona*, Jacques Delors went to extreme lengths to keep his distance from the president. 'When I was brought into the government as finance minister, I wanted to remain separate from Mitterrand. Otherwise I would have ended up being devoured by him.'[52]

For Kohl, the intensity of the bond with Mitterrand partly reflected their joint preoccupation with the history of Franco-German confrontation – a pathos marked by their gesture in 1984 holding hands to honour the war dead at Verdun. The chancellor was brought up in the Palatinate region in the west of Germany where he maintained a home close to the border that France and Germany had fought over for centuries. Robert Kimmitt, American ambassador to Germany in the early 1990s, forged a close relationship with Kohl – and saw how his policies intermingled security and economics. 'Europe's history of war played an important role in the reasons for the single currency,' Kimmitt said. 'I recall how Chancellor Kohl took me into his garden at the back of his house saying, with emotion in his voice, how the blood of French and German soldiers has been spilled on all the land around.'[53]

According to Hubert Védrine, a long-standing counsellor to the president, and the son of one of his war-time Resistance companions, Kohl took delight in the Frenchman's knowledge of German war-time history, including the details of army officers' failed assassination attempt on Hitler in July 1944. 'Mitterrand knew the names of the families of [coup leader Claus Schenk von] Stauffenberg and his allies.'[54]

The Mitterrand-Kohl friendship appears to have been strengthened by their similar positions as long-time underdogs against their economically well-versed predecessors Giscard and Schmidt, who held them both in barely disguised disdain. Schmidt said of Mitterrand: 'We were able to cooperate personally and also politically, [but] in economic and particularly in monetary matters, Mitterrand didn't have any great knowledge and judgment. That was a handicap for him.'[55] Giscard had similar views about his successor's devaluation-strewn initial period in office: 'I had no meetings with Mitterrand on monetary questions during this period. Mitterrand did not ask for any. He was not very interested in monetary or financial affairs. If I had seen him during that period I would have warned him to pay attention to the monetary issues.'[56]

Mitterrand's view of economics was shaped by the traditional values of the rural community and the Catholic Church, leanings that were shared with Kohl. Mitterrand – like de Gaulle – showed a prickly aversion to speculation and financial markets, and a staunch belief in the monetary sanctity of gold.[57] Michel Camdessus, director of the French Treasury during a crisis-fraught early period of the presidency, related how Mitterrand displayed his opposition to selling gold during the March 1983 currency crisis with the words: 'You and I are both from the countryside. The rule for farmers is that you don't mortgage your field.'[58] According to Fabius, 'He was always very sceptical on economic policy. "You can hear all the views of the experts," he liked to say, "but when it comes to budgets, they always end up by increasing taxes on tobacco and alcohol." He had a similarly sceptical view on currency changes. I remember him saying, "Devaluations are never small enough to avoid losing face, and never large enough to really make a difference to exports." '[59]

Kohl, for his part, could be remarkably thin-skinned about his rudimentary capacity for economics. Karl Otto Pöhl, president of the Bundesbank in the 1980s, was once quoted in the *Financial Times* as saying Kohl understood nothing of economics. The chancellor sent him a personal letter hotly denying the charge. It was unusual, in fact, for Kohl to write to Pöhl; most of the Bundesbank president's letters to Kohl on economic and monetary issues went unanswered. Looking back over a long career in European economic policy decision-making, Pöhl concluded that the most impressive politician he encountered during this period was Schmidt. 'The least impressive,' he opined, 'was Kohl.'[60] Helmut Schlesinger, Pöhl's deputy during his presidency, who headed the Bundesbank for two tumultuous years after Pöhl departed, had a much better *rapport* with Kohl, partly because he understood the chancellor's impatience with theoretical analysis. 'It was not much use writing Kohl a letter,' Schlesinger recalled. 'If you wanted to communicate with him, it was necessary to see him in person. I did this on several crucial occasions. He had time and we succeeded each time in having a meeting of minds. Maybe, in writing letters to Kohl, Pöhl made a mistake. Kohl needed to see things and persons in front of him, and grasp hold of them.'[61]

Kohl showed a similar bias towards action rather than words over German unification. His generalised commitment to the goal of national unity, at some indeterminate date in the future and as part of the 'growing together' of Europe, seemed to charm and impress Mitterrand. Some of those who encountered Kohl in the 1980s believed his views were purely sentimental; others had a more positive view. Alexandre Lamfalussy, the Belgian-Hungarian banker who became president of the forerunner of the European Central Bank, the European Monetary Institute, during the 1990s, recalled meeting Kohl at a Bilderberg international affairs council in the mid-1980s.

> I sat next to him because my name was next to Kohl's in the alphabet. I was one of few at the meeting with whom he could converse in German. He left a very strong impression on me. One speaker asked him to speak about relationship between the two Germanys. He started speaking slowly and then speeded up. He reminded listeners of the German constitution and the commitment to the unification of Germany. People round the table started to look at each other in disbelief. One said, 'Chancellor, do you expect to see unification in your lifetime?' He said: 'I don't know when, but it's going to happen. Forget about your reticence, you will have to understand that German division will not endure.' As people came out of the meeting, with some Americans among the guests, the mood was that perhaps he was joking.[62]

When the hour of unification eventually arrived, the two leaders instinctively displayed common appreciation of the need for rapprochement between money and politics. According to Michel Sapin, Mitterrand's finance minister at the beginning of the 1990s: 'Mitterrand saw the danger that reunification could upset the European balance. Kohl had the conviction that if Germany was reunified in the wrong fashion, it could reawaken old demons. So both politicians came to the conclusion that Europe needed the anchor of the single currency to avoid weakening the continent.'[63]

Construction and Renewal

The three years following the March 1983 tumult were a period of construction and renewal in Europe. Successful French efforts to reduce inflation and improve the balance of payments, and the building of a cooperative relationship between Mitterrand and Kohl, helped revive efforts towards monetary integration. An important ancillary figure in the Kohl–Mitterrand relationship was the canny Hans-Dietrich Genscher, the veteran German foreign minister, who switched with his liberal Free Democratic Party to Kohl's Christian Democrats in October 1982 and became one of the first German politicians to take up the cause of monetary union. Early in his presidency Mitterrand recognised Genscher as a kindred spirit – and as both a source of information and an instrument for influence. Genscher, like the president, possessed the ability to perceive trends well before they became publicly apparent, combining this with a capacity for subterranean political intrigue, within and outside the Bonn coalition. Mitterrand turned to Genscher particularly to place pressure on the chancellor at vital moments of strain at the time of unification.

Roland Dumas, a key ally of Genscher in Paris, became France's European minister in 1983 and foreign minister in 1984, exemplifying a fresh mood of fellow-feeling between the two countries. As Genscher explained:

> The real power in the background [on Franco-German relations] was Dumas, who was nominated Europe Minister. His father had been a member of the Resistance who was imprisoned and then killed by the Germans. Dumas told Mitterrand after he came to power in 1981 that, because of his father's death, it would be impossible for him to join the Government where he would have to deal with the Germans. Mitterrand told him that, precisely because of his family history, he would need to take the job so that he would learn to deal with present-day German realities.[64]

At the European Commission in Brussels, Jacques Delors deployed his political fire-power and technocratic energy focus to drive through the Single Market agenda for border-free harmonised European trade. In this context, Mitterrand and Kohl discussed the notion of a common European currency for the first time in autumn 1985. According to Elisabeth Guigou, a senior aide to both Delors and Mitterrand, and subsequently European minister, Kohl told Mitterrand he agreed with establishing a European currency 'as the logical conclusion of all that we are trying to construct'. However, the chancellor reminded the president that the Germans would have to give up a great deal. 'The D-Mark is our flag. It is the fundament of our post-war reconstruction. It is the essential part of our national pride; we don't have much else.'[65]

The Single Market received considerable support from Margaret Thatcher, Britain's stridently free-market Conservative prime minister, who saw it as opening up enormous corporate potential for British companies, especially in financial services.[66] Otherwise, Thatcher was immensely suspicious both of Delors' efforts to build up centralised European decision-making and of ever more frequent demonstrations of Franco-German togetherness. Thatcher's stature had grown as the result of a much-improved British economy, the British victory over Argentina in the Falklands War and the international strength of sterling – reflecting Britain's North Sea oil production, as well as a spill-over of world-wide flows into the dollar. Thatcher had at one time represented the Conservative party's pro-European tradition; in 1978 she declared that James Callaghan's decision to keep the pound out of the Exchange Rate Mechanism was a 'sad day for Europe'.[67] But during the 1980s Thatcher's European view turned almost wholly negative: 'I had witnessed a profound shift in the way European policy was conducted – and therefore in the kind of Europe that was taking shape. A Franco-German bloc with its own agenda had re-emerged to set the direction of the Community.'[68]

In Delors, Thatcher saw 'a tough, talented European federalist, whose policy justified centralism'. But Thatcher's relationship with Mitterrand was of mutual cordiality and respect – in contrast to the slowly-developing frostiness with Helmut Kohl. Mitterrand, for his part, admired and feared her precision – in particular over the long-simmering dispute on Britain's budgetary rebate from the Community, which was finally settled in 1984. He told Henry Kissinger: 'She has a strong personality, and not many long-term views. She is not used to encountering resistance. I told her that one day the opposition will be tougher than merely the Argentines or the Labour party. She is wrong in thinking that compromise is always a sign of weakness.'[69]

An important figure starting to emerge in France as an arch-proponent of a new 'strong Franc' policy was the unprepossessing Pierre Bérégovoy. As a long-time Mitterrand aide who became finance minister between 1984 and 1986, Bérégovoy held views on monetary affairs that fluctuated in close harmony with those of his mentor and protector. In March 1983 Bérégovoy had advocated French departure from the EMS but as Mitterrand moved away from this line he switched sides and endorsed Delors' policies of *rigueur*. As finance minister he presided over capital market deregulation and a strengthening of Paris as a European financial centre.

Bérégovoy's fragmented family background and experience of occupation were decisive motivations for his desire for a stable European financial environment. Bérégovoy was born in Normandy in 1925 after his father, a prominent member of the White Army, fled post-revolutionary Ukraine and settled in northern France after the Russian Civil War. Nigel Lawson, British

Chancellor of the Exchequer in the mid-1980s, who described his French opposite number as 'a short bespectacled man of working class and trade union background and simple tastes',[70] said, 'I got on well with Bérégovoy in part because he was instinctively Anglophile as a result of his experiences as a youngster with the Resistance.'[71] According to Bérégovoy's long-time adviser André Gauron,

> As a result of these experiences, Bérégovoy saw the UK as fulfilling his political vision for achieving a balance of power in Europe, and not having one country too dominant. This was in spite of the fact that he spoke no English and in his younger years never visited Britain. A constant theme for Bérégovoy was to encourage the UK to join the European Monetary System so that France would not be alone with the Germans. If you know Bérégovoy's background, you realise why one of the most emotional experiences of his entire life was when, as prime minister, he was able to greet Queen Elizabeth when she visited France in 1992.[72]

Bérégovoy re-incarnated a new form of de Gaulle's 1960s hard currency policies. However, in contrast to de Gaulle's drive to strengthen France's status in monetary conflict with Britain and the US, Bérégovoy's comparator was Germany. 'Bérégovoy believed the only way to convince Germany to treat France with respect was to have a currency as strong as theirs,' said Gauron. 'Bérégovoy was fascinated by monetary matters. When I first went to see him in 1982, he was minister for social affairs. He spent one minute talking about social security, one hour talking about the European Monetary System.' Hervé Hannoun, another senior Bérégovoy aide, said, 'Bérégovoy was one of the rare finance ministers of the Fifth Republic never to have devalued the Franc. He took the risk of linking his position as a Minister to the fate of the currency. He said that if the D-Mark were to be revalued within the EMS, then the Franc would be revalued by the same amount. Any other outcome would be a reason for his resignation.'[73]

During Bérégovoy's tenure as finance minister, the Franc's improved fortunes produced unusual tension between the Bundesbank and Banque de France. Bundesbank chief Pöhl complained to the International Monetary Fund about tight Banque de France interest rate policies that were depressing the D-Mark in the EMS and putting pressure on the Bundesbank to increase its own rates. Alan Whittome, the head of the IMF's European Department, asked Banque de France governor Michel Camdessus in March 1985 to assist the Bundesbank by mitigating its 'strong Franc' policies. Camdessus' independent-minded stance on interest rates did not endear him to either Bérégovoy or Pöhl – and the relationship between the French finance minister and the Bundesbank failed to improve. 'Bérégovoy did not like the affected condescension of the Bundesbank,' Camdessus said.[74] 'The way Pöhl projected the Bundesbank's independence was a constant irritant to him.'

German financial officials still regularly travelled to the Seine as if they were on an evangelical mission. In a reflection of the physical size of the Germans, Camdessus jocularly described two of the most prominent Germans, finance minister Gerhard Stoltenberg and his State Secretary Hans Tietmeyer, as the 'two All-Blacks: while Stoltenberg was more diplomatic, Tietmeyer was very sure of himself. He believed in the image of the French with their difficulties with inflation, unclear structures and romantic view of the world, and with their requirement for others to act as teachers to bring them to their senses.'

The D-Mark's weakness was a reflection of the sharp rise of the dollar, which reached a peak in February 1985 of DM3.47, double its depressed 1979–80 level. The Bundesbank had to interrupt its lowering of German interest rates with renewed half-point rises in the discount rate and Lombard rates in 1984–85 to counter the D-Mark's slide. After a decade in which central banks and governments had mainly stayed on the sidelines, currency market activism started to gain ground, reflecting a general desire to counter the unpredictable effects of floating exchange rates. A mood developed among the main industrialised countries towards coordinated action to brake the dollar's rise. This culminated in the September 1985 Plaza Agreement (named after the New York hotel in which it was concluded). With the aid of joint intervention on the foreign exchanges, governments and central banks succeeded in lowering the US currency from its exaggeratedly high valuation.

As part of efforts towards better management of floating rates, Britain re-examined the idea of joining the European Exchange Rate Mechanism. Thatcher had briefly considered the idea in 1980, in a gesture to Chancellor Schmidt aimed at winning support for Britain's European Community budgetary plans. In November 1985 during a top-level meeting at 10 Downing Street, Chancellor of the Exchequer Nigel Lawson, Governor of the Bank of England Robin Leigh-Pemberton, and Foreign Secretary Geoffrey Howe all told Thatcher they wanted to join. Thatcher thought differently. Famously autocratic in her dealings with ministers, the prime minister brusquely ended the discussion: 'I disagree. If you join the EMS, you will have to do so without me.'[75] Lawson recorded: 'There was an awkward silence, and then the meeting broke up.'

Thatcher's opposition to Britain joining the ERM did not prevent her from agreeing the Community treaty establishing the Single Market, the Single

European Act – which laid down the ultimate goal of Economic and Monetary Union – at a summit in Luxembourg in early December. Both the UK and Germany agreed to inscribe the EMU objective into the Single Market treaty in a compromise to encourage other countries, predominantly France, to sign up to a comprehensive liberalisation programme that would include ending restrictions on capital movements.[76] At the behest of Chancellor Kohl, Hans Tietmeyer of the German finance ministry told Thatcher during the Luxembourg talks that Britain's agreement to the treaty committed the UK neither to the goal of EMU nor to joining the Exchange Rate Mechanism.[77] Tietmeyer's brusque combination of conservative leanings, technical skills and missionary zeal – as a boy, he had harboured the ambition of becoming a priest like two of his brothers – mollified the prime minister. Yet, unknown to Thatcher, Britain maintained the momentum of European monetary manoeuvring. Her Chancellor of the Exchequer Lawson was as opposed as she was to EMU – but believed that Britain could treat membership of the ERM as a separate, technical issue, as a means of bringing down UK inflation. Refusing to be blown off course by Thatcher, Lawson arranged for three top UK monetary officials to travel to Bonn for secret talks with the government and the Bundesbank on possible British membership of the ERM. Lawson recalled, 'The Germans made it clear they would welcome sterling's membership of the ERM, which in their view would help to maintain the soundness of the system despite the weakness of its southern members (they were particularly concerned about Italy).'[78]

In the following year sterling fell from DM3.60 to DM2.85 as a result of a sharp decrease in oil prices. Heavy intervention was needed in September 1986 to slow sterling's decline – including Bundesbank action to support the pound through a swap arrangement under which it lent D-Marks to the Bank of England.[79] Lawson claimed later that, had the UK joined the Exchange Rate Mechanism in 1985, member governments would have taken orderly steps to lower sterling's value as part of the system's regular realignments. Such an experience, Lawson believed, would have prepared the UK for the harsher times ahead.

I was never in favour of EMU, I was always publicly against the single currency from the Werner plan onwards. It was a different kettle of fish compared with the ERM. I saw the ERM as a useful way for us to make use of the credibility of the Bundesbank to get inflation down. I believe that if we had joined, as I wanted to, in 1985–86, we would have had a period of five years or so when the Bundesbank's credibility was still intact before German unification, which we could have used to good advantage.[80]

Relative European currency tranquillity was shattered in 1986 by two disturbances: the arrival of a neo-Gaullist administration in Paris and an accelerating decline of the dollar. Electoral disapproval of three years of austerity policies under successive Socialist prime ministers produced victory for the French Right in the March 1986 parliamentary elections. The opportunistic and unpredictable Jacques Chirac, a veteran of numerous economic policy disputes with the Germans, recaptured the post of prime minister he had held in the mid-1970s under Valéry Giscard d'Estaing. In the eyes of more censorious German officials, Chirac went on to confirm the judgement of his schoolteachers forty years earlier: 'Works, but is often disordered ... A lively and curious mind, but more spontaneous than reflective.'[81]

François Mitterrand remained in office as president, in charge of strategic, defence and foreign policies. Fine-tuning the economy was left to his now-conservative ministers. The next two years were spent in uneasy 'cohabitation' with a prime minister who appeared intent on fully living up to his appellation as 'The Bulldozer', the sobriquet applied by Georges Pompidou, for whom the young Chirac worked in 1962. Chirac's appointee as finance minister – effectively No. 2 to the prime minister – was the prim, precisely-worded Edouard Balladur, born in Turkey of an Armenian family who emigrated to Marseille in the 1930s. Balladur demonstrated self-satisfied sleekness combined with a strong leaning towards privatisation of state-owned French businesses and formidable enthusiasm for European monetary initiatives.

The new Paris government came under immediate pressure on the foreign exchanges. Fresh flows of international funds poured into the D-Mark as the long ascent of the dollar gave way to a sharp post-Plaza decline. In a similar shift to that suffered by de Gaulle in 1968–69, the Franc fell victim to the switch in currency market sentiment. As a consequence, one of the Chirac–Balladur tandem's first acts, in April 1986, was to break with Bérégovoy's hard currency policy by requesting France's European partners to approve a substantial lowering of Franc–D-Mark parity. Banque de France governor Camdessus told Balladur the idea of a Franc devaluation was mistaken, and produced an internal document arguing that the Banque de France should move towards formal Bundesbank-style independence.[82]

Balladur imperiously brushed aside Camdessus' recommendations, and proposed an 8 to 9 per cent reduction in the Franc–D-Mark rate, which he said was forced by the Socialist government's past errors and France's 'need for additional flexibility'.[83] Other European governments believed the proposal would give France an unfair boost to competitiveness. After the usual realignment bargaining in Brussels, finance ministers agreed a 3 per cent Franc devaluation and a 3 per cent revaluation of the D-Mark and the Dutch guilder. The move was accompanied by a further relaxation of French exchange controls, underlining the Chirac government's commitment to economic liberalisation, as well as continuity with Bérégovoy's financial market reforms.

In a flurry of optimism, the Bundesbank's Karl Otto Pöhl told central bankers in Basle that the realignment would provide 'two to three years' of stability in the EMS.[84] But the realignment brought only a brief respite. Mitterrand's advisers sent him alarming news of a further rise in France's chronic trade deficit with Germany.[85] In spite of falling consumer prices in West Germany (for the first time since the country was established in 1949), the Bundesbank maintained money market interest rates well above the 3.5 per cent discount rate, in a bid to rein in fast-growing German money supply.[86] France's economic problems were exacerbated by setbacks for Chirac's public sector reforms. In January 1987 Chirac and Balladur openly criticised the Germans' 'egotistical' monetary behaviour and called for the Bundesbank to cut interest rates. Chirac declared that the currency turbulence was the Germans' fault – 'There is a crisis. But it is a crisis of the D-Mark, not the French Franc' – and ordered the Banque de France to stop supporting the Franc in the EMS.[87] In a week of turmoil, coinciding with a general election campaign in West Germany, the Bundesbank faced destabilising liquidity inflows totalling $16 billion.

After hasty consultations with Pöhl and the Bundesbank directorate in Frankfurt on 9 January, Stoltenberg telephoned Balladur to agree a 3 per cent D-Mark revaluation.[88] The details of the realignment – with the Dutch guilder once again moving in step with the D-Mark – were approved at a weekend Brussels European finance ministers meeting. Just before the German general election on 25 January, which saw Chancellor Kohl returned to power with a reduced majority, the Bundesbank cut discount and Lombard rates by 0.5 percentage points in response to a weakening economy. For Balladur this was not enough. He revived French calls for more EMS 'symmetry' to help weaker currencies, including technical measures to promote the ECU and alleviate 'intra-marginal' intervention within the system before currencies reached their allowed limits.[89]

Pöhl, bruised by France's anti-Bundesbank campaign, believed pressure on the Franc would continue. He told central bankers in Basle that there had been only insubstantial liquidity reflows out of Germany after the realignment and that 'some market participants thought the 3 per cent realignment was not convincing'.[90] The French finance minister intensified his campaign to strengthen the EMS. Balladur was buttressed by the prestige of hosting a meeting of international finance ministers in Paris in February 1987 that succeeded temporarily in halting the dollar's slide. As a sequel to the Plaza Agreement that capped the dollar's rise, the so-called Louvre agreement set down a mix of currency intervention, interest rate changes and other economic measures to keep the dollar within informal fluctuation bands against the D-Mark and the Japanese yen.[91]

Profiting from resurgent international belief that currency rates could be controlled, in June 1987 Balladur proposed a European Central Bank as the ultimate means of achieving better European monetary balance.[92] By suggesting 'the creation of a European monetary institution endowed with a degree of supranational authority', Balladur carefully side-stepped the vexed issue of whether the proposed new institution would be independent from governments.

Mutually Assured Insecurity

In the second half of the 1980s France realised it needed political as well as technical measures to restrain Germany's monetary predominance. The key lever for applying pressure emerged from a combination of Mitterrand's acumen in foreign policy and the joint interest of Chirac and Balladur in monetary manoeuvring. These ill-sorted Parisian allies concocted a strategy for harnessing France's military and security strength to achieve German economic concessions – a game of curiously interlocking interdependence.

France and Germany each played upon their built-in feelings of mutually assured insecurity in the economic and military spheres. Germany did remarkably little to mitigate French fears of German strategic fragility and even went out of its way to encourage such anxieties. This was partly a ploy to lead France more deeply into economic cooperation – including, crucially, towards liberalisation of flows of investment capital, to which both the Gaullist and Socialist parties were traditionally opposed. At the same time, Mitterrand and his conservative allies realised that providing Germany with defence and security reassurances would be an invaluable policy tool. Public opinion in both parts of divided Germany was rapidly falling under the sway of a shift in East–West relations caused by the charismatic and reforming figure of Mikhail Gorbachev, the Soviet leader who took office in 1985. As the Cold War ebbed the Germans wanted firm evidence that the military alliance of the North Atlantic Treaty Organisation – including the burden of several hundred thousands of US, British and French troops on German soil – worked in their favour. West Germany's Paris ambassador warned the Elysée

Palace in January 1987 of 'an effect of seduction' by Gorbachev to tempt Germany towards a reunited German state on the basis of 'nationalism and neutralism'[93] – hinting that the Germans might be tempted to leave NATO and adopt a position of equidistance between the American- and Soviet-led military alliances.

France reacted with due promptness. Western Europe had to be made more solid and attractive to the Germans – to prevent them drifting to the East. Mitterrand told Chirac and Balladur: 'Unless we make progress in the construction of Europe, we will not escape bargaining over Germany between East and West.'[94] Speaking to Mitterrand in March 1987, Kohl stressed how France and Germany had to improve cooperation to offset the trend towards neutralism: Germany had 'lots of people who want to go in that direction – leftist intellectuals are enthralled by neutralism, teachers are starting to talk this way'.[95] Among influential neutralist voices, Kohl suggested, was *Die Zeit*, the heavyweight Hamburg weekly newspaper, which his old adversary Helmut Schmidt had joined as publisher after stepping down as chancellor.

As a way of binding Germany into a new European framework, Mitterrand proposed extending the 1963 Elysée Treaty on Franco-German cooperation. The twenty-fifth anniversary was to be commemorated with due pomp in January 1988. Mitterrand's European specialist Elisabeth Guigou spotted a means of achieving France's long-sought aim of winning greater influence over the Bundesbank. She told Mitterrand that the 'policy of small steps' inaugurated by Jacques Delors as finance minister had run its course. There had been no progress in developing the European Monetary System, which could 'be blown away on the next monetary storm'. High-profile action was required: 'Only a joint initiative by you and Chancellor [Kohl] can prompt the Bundesbank to act.'[96] In the wake of the Guigou note, at a meeting with their French opposite numbers in Bonn, German officials suggested a Franco-German Defence Council to provide for joint decision-making, particularly on the controversial issue of French battlefield nuclear weapons which could explode on German soil.[97] Mitterrand's adviser Jacques Attali innovatively linked this suggestion to the traditional French aim of emasculating the Bundesbank. The Germans were startled by Attali's proposition:

The German officials spoke about the need for concertation with the French about their nuclear weapons capability. Then Attali said, 'So that we can have a balance, let us now talk about the German atom bomb.' The German officials were astonished. We said, 'You know we don't have the atomic bomb – what do you mean?' Attali said: 'I mean the D-Mark.' This remark showed the importance in which the French held the Bundesbank's dominance in European monetary policy.[98]

Attali's remark equating the D-Mark with atomic weapons was amplified by Mitterrand, who told his ministers that Germany used its economic power as compensation for its 'reduced diplomatic status' and lack of sovereignty.[99] Attali's *démarche* in Bonn represented the first step towards establishing the Franco-German Economic and Finance Council, in tandem with the planned Defence Council. The Bundesbank protested that the proposed body should not interfere with its cherished independence. Backed by finance minister Stoltenberg, Pöhl eventually succeeded – after several months of wrangling – in winning agreement that it should be no more than a consultative body. Pöhl, who had been put under great pressure by the Bundesbank Council to uphold the Bundesbank's autonomy, vented irritation at having to attend the Franco-German Council meetings.[100]

The Bundesbank's well-publicised opposition to the Economic Council was one of the reasons why Mitterrand increasingly criticised German economic intransigence. He told visiting West German Social Democratic leader Hans-Jochen Vogel that Germany had difficulties in giving up economic power because it was politically 'amputated'.[101] Mitterrand grumbled to Franz Vranitzky, the Austrian chancellor, that 'Germany has recovered its economic power, but refuses to share it'.[102] In talks with Spanish prime minister Felipe Gonzalez, Mitterrand called for a common currency built around the ECU as a means of correcting the German problem. 'Of course the Germans resist this. . . . The Mark is the manifestation of German power. This is a very deep issue that transcends the reflexes of bankers, and goes even beyond politics.'[103]

While Mitterrand provided high-level strategic cover for European monetary action, Balladur drew up detailed guidelines. In January 1988 he presented to European finance ministers a memorandum on EMS reform designed to build on a decade of French efforts for harmonised European money. The initiative appeared to surface at a propitious time. The Bundesbank seemed to be shifting towards greater international compliance, having cut its discount rate to a record low of 2.5 per cent in December 1987, part of a coordinated round of interest-rate reductions after a world-wide stock market slump in October.[104] The Bundesbank's action reflected pressure from Helmut Kohl, who requested a rate cut on the eve of a Council meeting because wanted to make a good impression at a European summit the next day in Copenhagen.[105] In his currency reform memorandum, Balladur did not mention Germany by name. But he enlisted traditional French arguments about the lack of 'symmetry' in the EMS to spell out the fault-lines.

> Ultimately it is the central bank whose currency is at the lower end of the permitted range which has to bear the cost. However it is not necessarily the currency at the lower end of the range which is the source of the tension. The discipline imposed by the Exchange Rate Mechanism may, for its part, have good effects when it serves to put a constraint on economic and monetary policies which are insufficiently rigorous. [But] it produces an abnormal situation when its effect is to exempt from adjustment any country whose policies are too rigorous.[106]

For Hans-Dietrich Genscher, the febrile Bonn foreign minister, the machinations in Paris provided clear evidence that the pendulum of the European *Zeitgeist* was swinging back towards monetary union. Already in spring 1987 Genscher had urged a common European money to back the Single Market.[107] The foreign minister used his informal contacts with the Bundesbank to clarify technical details on European monetary cooperation, circumventing and out-manoeuvring the finance ministry. In February 1988 Genscher's EMU drive culminated in the launch of his own personal memorandum, in which the foreign minister drew on considerable Bundesbank research work.[108] Genscher's paper stressed the importance of an independent European Central Bank pledged to price stability, but failed to emphasise the condition of economic convergence favoured by the Bundesbank and the finance ministry. Mitterrand's adviser Elisabeth Guigou told the president Genscher had shown 'great tactical skill' in putting forward his plans. She termed the main thrust of Genscher's proposals – reducing Europe's dependence on the dollar, strengthening the EMS and extending use of the European Currency unit – as 'perfectly convergent with our analyses'. However, she added that Genscher's conditions, particularly the independence of the proposed central bank, 'will be difficult to accept in France'.[109]

Finance minister Stoltenberg hit back with his own, much more cautious memorandum three weeks later which claimed that monetary union should be highly conditional on political integration.[110] In contacts with the French government, Genscher did his best to undermine the finance minister, stating that Stoltenberg had a 'difficult character'.[111] Genscher later recalled, 'Stoltenberg did not realise the importance of monetary union. Therefore it was necessary that I should go to the front line.'[112]

The deep-seated differences between his two most senior ministers confronted Kohl with a dilemma that he resolved in the most forceful way: by backing French plans for accelerated European convergence. In the May 1988 French presidential election, Mitterrand resoundingly defeated his conservative prime minister Chirac, who promptly resigned. For Mitterrand, this was a threefold triumph. He won a second seven-year term, the ultimate triumph in his twenty-year battle to cauterise wounds from previous defeats against de Gaulle and Giscard. Chirac, Mitterrand's most contested contemporary political opponent, with whom he had endured 'cohabitation' for two years, was dispatched into ignominy. And the president was free to nominate a prime minister of his own choice. He appointed long-time rival Michel Rocard, a dashing pro-European on the Socialist party's Right, demonstrating the oft-used Mitterrand stratagem of weakening competitors by giving them difficult jobs. The president called parliamentary elections in June, resulting in a handsome Socialist victory.

The doggedly faithful Bérégovoy had yearned for the prime ministership, but in Rocard's new team he was directed back to the Finance Ministry. Bérégovoy's sparring partner at the Banque de France was a seasoned official of patrician demeanour and growing independent-mindedness. Jacques de Larosière, director of the French Treasury during the 1970s, had been in Washington for eight-and-a-half years as managing director of the International Monetary Fund. De Larosière returned to Paris as Banque de France governor in January 1987 in a Balladur-orchestrated job swap with Michel Camdessus, who took over at the IMF. Bérégovoy's Treasury director was another Balladur appointee, Jean-Claude Trichet, Balladur's former chief of staff, a man who mixed technocratic industriousness and prodigious ambition with a secret love of poetry.

Bérégovoy lost no time in attempting to stamp his authority on European interest rate policy. Less than a week after taking over at the ministry, Bérégovoy proposed to de Larosière a cut in interest rates to boost French and European economic growth prospects.[113] De Larosière infuriated the finance minister by taking his time over relaxing credit. Trichet backed de Larosière's cautious line. Since both men had been appointed by Bérégovoy's Gaullist predecessor Edouard Balladur, their reticence intensified Bérégovoy's belief that the forces of conservativism were arrayed against him. However, at the end of May 1988, Bérégovoy was able to announce a 0.25 percentage point cut in French interest rates – modest proof that Socialist economic policies were working.

The German chancellor profited from the victorious French president's renewed self-confidence, as well as the momentum behind the Genscher and

Balladur initiatives, to place his *imprimatur* on the monetary union drive. The popularity of Genscher's EMU paper among German business leaders helped sway Kohl's view that monetary unity could speed up Europe's political unification – and could also yield him some much-needed backing on the domestic electoral front.[114] During weeks of diplomatic manoeuvring after the French presidential poll, Kohl pressed the Community to launch full-scale EMU preparations. A milestone was reached at a meeting with Mitterrand in early June in the idyllic setting of Evian on the shores of Lake Geneva. The French and German leaders agreed that France would support the lifting of controls on movements of investment funds throughout the Community as a key component of the Single Market programme.[115] In return Germany pledged to back plans for harmonised taxes on savings to deter fiscal fraud and other misuse. Kohl's promise was essential to counter the traditional French fear that deregulating European financial markets would automatically spur cross-border banknote smuggling and other white-collar crime.

Committee of Experts

Under Kohl's chairmanship, European leaders gathered in Hanover in northern Germany on 27 and 28 June 1988 to propel forward the monetary union project. As agreed between Kohl and Mitterrand at Evian, the summit decided to set up a committee of experts to set down a route map for EMU.[116] The group was to comprise mainly governors of the twelve Community central banks, part of a ploy by Kohl to allay domestic German fears that the EMU deliberations would pay insufficient attention to monetary stability. Both Kohl and Mitterrand realised that, in view of well-known British misgivings about monetary union, entrusting the report to a supposedly conservative group of central bankers was the sole means of winning Thatcher's support for the initiative,[117] and would also bind Community central banks – specifically, the Bundesbank – more firmly into the process than would otherwise have been the case. In addition, relatively late during the Hanover talks, Kohl proposed the crucial point that had been broached with Mitterrand at Evian: to appoint European Commission President Delors as the group's chairman. This spelled a radical departure from the Werner Plan in 1970. Then, government leaders entrusted EMU preparations to a committee led by the harmlessly ceremonial prime minister of Luxembourg, the Community's smallest state. This time they placed the design of monetary union under the stewardship of a strong-minded French politician at the height of his European powers.

Genscher was delighted at the summit outcome, predicting that a European Central Bank was 'essential' for EMU and would be set up within ten years.[118] Kohl was less forthright but said he was '90 per cent certain' that monetary union would take place by the end of the century.[119] The ever-querulous Bérégovoy refused to join in the mood of celebration. In discussions with Mitterrand, Bérégovoy voiced anxieties – which turned out later to be justified – that Kohl's earlier commitment at Evian to harmonise taxes on savings was not sufficiently strong to justify a major French concession on capital controls.[120] Additionally, there were alarming signs that the Bundesbank was about to increase interest rates again, only six months after cutting discount rate to a record low. The day after the Hanover summit, Bérégovoy wrote to German finance minister Stoltenberg that 'press reports that the Bundesbank is preparing to increase interest rates perhaps by 0.5 percentage point' were 'a source of grave concern . . . I would wish that the members of the Bundesbank Council should be precisely informed about the gravity of the consequences.'[121]

In the run-up to the Hanover deliberations, Bundesbank president Karl Otto Pöhl had maintained strong public scepticism about EMU plans.[122] Like Beregovoy, but for different reasons, he was displeased with developments. Partly he blamed Thatcher for the additional political stimulus imparted to monetary union: 'She fell for the idea of setting up the group with Delors as the chairman. She must have known it would have a political dimension.'[123] The new impetus behind EMU, combined with a renewed rise of the dollar that was stoking up concern about inflation on the Bundesbank Council, raised pressure on the Bundesbank chief to mount a counter-strike. A day after Bérégovoy wrote to Stoltenberg, the Bundesbank confirmed Parisian fears by reversing the December 1987 cut and announcing a 0.5 per cent increase in discount rate – the first increase in its leading interest rates for more than four years.

Onno Ruding, the Dutch finance minister, was aware of the Bundesbank president's state of mind. 'Pöhl was extremely unhappy with developments – he was pushed by German politicians into being cooperative.'[124] For his part, Pöhl said, 'I was worried as President of the Bundesbank about the conflict of interest that would arise in being part of proposals that effectively would lead to the abolition of the D-Mark and the monetary policy powers of the Bundesbank . . . I was not happy with the make-up of the [Delors] committee, which I believed contradicted what had been agreed with the Government.'[125] Pöhl's immediate reaction to the Hanover news was to refuse to participate in the Delors Group. He telephoned his closest central banking counterpart, Wim Duisenberg of the Nederlandsche Bank, to try to persuade him to do the same. In the end, Duisenberg and others convinced Pöhl that his presence would ensure the committee was imbued with Bundesbank-style orthodoxy – and would consequently fail to generate radical action. Kohl's predecessor Helmut Schmidt, watching impatiently from the sidelines as an increasingly crusty elder statesman, came to the same conclusion.

> The composition of that committee seems inadequate ... It does not contain enough people with global strategic understanding of what is necessary in this world. These central bankers are technicians. They will not want to dilute their power ... They are in a similar position to a Ministry of Bread or Aluminum in Moscow asked to sit on a restructuring committee aiming to cut down their area of competence.[126]

The Delors Committee deliberations – mainly carried out in Basle at the Bank for International Settlements – in fact produced a workable set of guidelines for monetary union. However, the document eventually published in April 1989 listed a series of options and recommendations rather than policy decisions. The Delors Report laid down the EMU objective as combining complete liberalisation of capital movements, full integration of financial markets, irreversible convertibility of currencies, irrevocable fixing of exchange rates. Replacement of national currencies with a single currency was seen as just one of a range of options.[127] Echoing the findings of the Werner Committee in 1970, the Report recommended a three-stage move to EMU, starting with closer economic and monetary coordination. The Delors document resembled a giant jigsaw puzzle where many important pieces were missing. There were few clues where they might be and only a vague timetable for finding them. For EMU to become reality, governmental action was required.

The document was clearest in laying down the need for a 'new monetary institution' to run EMU. This should be 'organised in a federal form, in what might be called a European System of Central Banks (ESCB). This new system would have to be given the full status of an autonomous Community institution. It ... could consist of a central institution (with its own balance sheet) and the national central banks.' The proposed European System would 'be committed to the objective of price stability ... The ESCB Council should be independent of the instructions of national governments and Community authorities.'[128] The document stated the need for 'parallel advancement in economic and monetary integration ... in order to avoid imbalances which would cause economic strains and loss of political support for developing the Community'.[129]

With parities irrevocably fixed, foreign exchange markets would cease to be a source of pressure for national policy corrections when national economic disequilibria developed and persisted ... None the less, such imbalances, if left uncorrected, would manifest themselves as regional disequilibria. Measures designed to strengthen the mobility of factors of production and the flexibility of prices would help to deal with such imbalances.[130]

There were strong differences on the vital issue of whether, in advance of monetary union, the Community should set up mechanisms for sharing currency reserves and carrying out joint currency intervention. The old ideological split between the Economists and Monetarists reasserted itself. As on similar occasions in the past, reserve-pooling was backed by the French and Belgians but opposed by the Germans and Dutch. The report stated that 'a number of Committee members advocated the creation of a European Reserve Fund (ERF) that would foreshadow the future European System of Central Banks'. This Fund would carry out 'concerted management of exchange rates' and would pool a suggested 10 per cent of Community foreign exchange reserves. However, 'other members of the Committee felt that the creation of an ERF was not opportune at this stage ... Common interventions by such a fund cannot be a substitute for economic adjustment to correct imbalances within the Community.'[131]

In the debate over the ERF Italy crucially came down on the side of the Germans and Dutch. According to Fabrizio Saccomanni, a senior Banca d'Italia official who was chairman of the Foreign Exchange Policy Committee of the ERM central banks:

At that time Jacques de Larosière was still thinking of a European Monetary Fund to provide balance of payments financing to deficit countries in order to stabilise currencies. We [the Italians] thought the idea was not addressing the real problem and would never command the support of the Bundesbank. This would endow Europe with a cumbersome new financial agency, which would duplicate the IMF and bring about a conflict of interests. The Germans agreed with us.[132]

The members of the committee had highly diverse views about the outcome. No-one believed a full-scale breakthrough had been achieved; one of the two *rapporteurs*, Italian financial expert Tommaso Padoa-Schioppa,[133] who was particularly close to Delors, told friends that little would come of the report. Jacques Delors focused on the need for more effective European economic coordination. 'Fundamentally EMU was a political issue that could only be decided by the governments. In the report, I wanted to draw attention to the need for sufficient economic coordination as a precondition for EMU.'[134] For Alexandre Lamfalussy, general manager of the Bank for International Settlements, one of the three outside experts on the Committee flanking the governors and Delors,[135] the overall political content was all-important.

> Delors wanted a politically integrated Europe. The first step was the single market, once you have a single market you have a single currency, and then the door is open to political integration. Delors displayed a stroke of political genius. He accepted the proposal of carrying out the meetings at the Bank for International Settlements, a non-Community institution based in Switzerland. He knew it was crucial to have the support of key central bankers. He knew they could work well at the BIS. It gave them a sense of importance, and a kind of protection from the outside world. Delors was extraordinarily respectful to central bankers. He didn't try to interrupt their frequently long monologues. One of the reasons for this may have been that most of the conversations were carried out in English, where he is clearly not as fluent as in French.[136]

Lamfalussy pinpointed Franco-German differences on the central issue of institution-building. 'All the French efforts were geared to building the institutions first and then allowing for convergence to happen after that. The submission by de Larosière suggested setting up the European Central Bank immediately instead of the European Monetary Institute [the EMI – the forerunner of the ECB]. The French plan was that the Central Bank should be there from the beginning of Stage Two [in 1994]. The Bundesbank strongly opposed this. The priority was to demonstrate convergence.'

Jacques de Larosière regarded the Committee as setting a path to Banque de France independence – a goal that he personally backed, but which the French government sternly resisted. 'It is a kind of miracle that this committee was set up and had the effect it did. When I was appointed as a member, the Banque de France was completely dependent on the Government. The responsibility for monetary policy was with the Finance Ministry, implementation was with the Banque de France.'[137] De Larosière, like the other governors, was appointed to the Delors Committee on a personal basis – and he used this to enlarge considerably his room for manoeuvre in Paris. A turning point came when – about half-way through the Delors Committee deliberations – de Larosière resolved to broach central banking independence directly with

Mitterrand. 'I knew that this was non-negotiable. This view was not very popular with the Ministry of Finance. So I said to myself, "I'm going to have to talk to the President." ' De Larosière saw the president for a secret half-hour meeting alone in his office on 1 December 1988.

> He said, 'What have you got to tell me?' I explained that I was participating in the Delors committee and that we were advancing towards a concept for monetary union. I said that if France wanted an agreement with the Germans, we had to accept that monetary policy would be a single policy, and that national central banks would be members of a system of central banks where all would have to be independent from governments. The European Central Bank would work only if its policies were not subject to negotiations between governments. Additionally, this was a crucial condition for our German partners. President Mitterrand did not answer specifically. It wasn't in his nature. I feared he might say: 'This is out of the question.' But he didn't. He gave a complex commentary on how the world was evolving towards regulatory systems that were no longer directly under the control of states. It was not a technical answer; it was a sociological reflection on world governance. I said to myself, 'I'm going to take that as giving me the green light.' Armed with this reassurance, I continued with my work, to the surprise of some of my colleagues on the committee, such as Karl Otto Pöhl, who thought we would be faithful to the traditional subservience of the Banque de France to the French state.

Bundesbank President Pöhl was the most senior central banker on the Delors Committee – and the most sceptical:

> The Delors Report was a confused piece of work. There were some wild ideas in it. When it was formulated, I did not believe that monetary union with a European Central Bank could come about in the foreseeable future. I thought it might come in the next hundred years. I thought it was very unlikely that the other Europeans would simply adopt the Bundesbank model. I believe that, upon the conclusion of the Delors Report, the French didn't want this either – they wanted something else. They were more keen on a system where currencies would remain separate but where the parities would be underpinned by large-scale central bank intervention.[138]

Philippe Lagayette, deputy governor of the Banque de France, and a former aide to Delors, took a more benevolent line than Pöhl:

Very few people such as [former Banque de France governor] Renaud de la Genière or [former prime minister] Raymond Barre were convinced at the end of the 1980s that establishing a single currency was in the logic of deepening the Single Market. The Delors Report was an immense step forward clarifying all these discussions and bringing the idea that no other system than a single currency, managed independently from political authorities, was viable.[139]

Robin Leigh-Pemberton, governor of the Bank of England, agreed with this view – although he realised he would not be popular with his own prime minister.

I realised that it was a perfectly practical proposition to create and distribute the single currency. I let it be known that I was in favour. I saw this as a way of re-establishing the Bank of England's independence, and introducing a more stable monetary regime in the UK. My brief from Mrs Thatcher was to follow Pöhl. I wrote a letter to Mrs Thatcher saying that, once Karl Otto Pöhl had signed, I saw no reason why I should not do the same. I would look ridiculous if I was the only governor who did not sign. I would look like Mrs Thatcher's poodle.[140]

Assembly of Grievances

The final phase of discussions on the Delors Report in early 1989 brought behind-the-scenes confrontations between the Paris Finance Ministry and the Bundesbank. President Mitterrand, his advisers and ministers laid bare the full extent of French frustrations over Germany's economic policies. There was no clear line on EMU in the capitals of Europe. National political and economic differences were overlaid by an intricate assembly of personal grievances, vexations, sensitivities and rivalries. American monetary policy, under the aegis of Alan Greenspan as Federal Reserve chairman since August 1987, remained tight throughout 1989. Bundesbank interest rate rises in 1988–89, in response to the climbing dollar,[141] forced up rates in France. Finance minister Bérégovoy had achieved partial victory in his goal to harden the Franc – yet paid a significant price through high interest rates that further depressed a sluggish economy. At a meeting of the Franco-German Economic and Finance Council in February 1989, Bérégovoy voiced anxiety that the Bundesbank was about to launch 'interest rate escalation'. Pöhl, bristling at attempts to emasculate the Bundesbank, replied that German interest rates were decided not by the president but by the eighteen-member Central Bank Council. Bérégovoy retorted, 'You must be preparing something.'[142]

A few days before the clash with Bérégovoy, prime minister Margaret Thatcher visited the West German central bank immediately in advance of a bilateral meeting with Kohl in Frankfurt. Pöhl was flattered by the attention from a figure who – for all her high-heeled stridency on the European stage – commanded both influence and fascination. Thatcher held the Bundesbank as an institution, and Pöhl personally, in the highest regard. This was the first, and almost certainly the last, British prime ministerial visit to the Bundesbank and Pöhl prefaced the lunch with a light-hearted quip. He told his guest that Kohl had telephoned him and suggested that he might like to show Thatcher the Bundesbank's coin collection – but he was sure that she would prefer to debate EMU.[143] Pöhl was right. Thatcher did most of the talking, as Pöhl recalled:

> I invited a couple of bankers as well, including Alfred Herrhausen [of the Deutsche Bank]. The lunch took place in the Bundesbank Guesthouse. The ambience was not entirely to her liking because of the 1960s style and the modern art. I started off the conversation and then she asked in her high voice: 'What do you mean by monetary union?' Then she started to give the answers herself and dominated the conversation for the rest of the meal. The lunch went on so long that Helmut Kohl was kept waiting for her at the Römer [Frankfurt City Hall]. Kohl was annoyed that this was because of the Bundesbank.[144]

Thatcher's attitude towards EMU was heavily scrutinised in Paris. Mitterrand's adviser Elisabeth Guigou warned the president about the British prime minister's tactics in a confidential memorandum: 'She has been actively preparing the ground for several weeks. She does not want Economic and Monetary Union. She has made this known through her Chancellor [of the Exchequer] M. [Nigel] Lawson. She is banking on associating the President of the Bundesbank, M. Pöhl, with her refusal – and thus dividing France and Germany.'[145]

Guigou's note recorded finance minister Bérégovoy's hostility towards an independent central bank. 'While not denying that our autonomy vis-à-vis Germany was always very weak, [he] believes that EMU would reinforce the German point of view ... A future European Central Bank, being independent of governments, would be entirely dominated by the Germans.' A month later, Mitterrand revealed his own extreme anxieties about the ECB's potential power.

I am not hostile to the Central Bank, but to certain of its modes of operation. The Bundesbank is completely beyond the control of governments. Our Central Bank [Banque de France] is independent, but it is the Government that defines the economic and monetary policy. How can we bring the Germans to accept progress on the road to monetary union? I have the impression that if they had the guarantee that monetary union would not endanger their good economic health, they would be ready to go forward. But I hesitate to make this concession. It is dangerous that the Central Bank, in the absence of a political authority, should have sovereign power. The [European] Monetary System is already a German zone. But the Federal Republic of Germany does not have authority over our economies. With the [European] Central Bank it would have it.[146]

Bérégovoy told Lagayette, deputy governor of the Banque de France, that the UK should be part of monetary union – to protect France from exposure to an overpowerful Germany. Bérégovoy told him angrily: 'I will never let you go in that direction. I don't want to do anything without the British.'[147] Reflecting opinions such as these, Pöhl believed that France would be unable to accept the proposed independence of the European Central Bank. As Fabrizio Saccomanni from the Banca d'Italia explained, 'The Germans put forward the idea of an independent, truly European central bank running an international currency. They must have thought, from a tactical point of view, that no one would accept it.'[148]

For the British prime minister, however, the Bundesbank president's softly-toned tactics showed lack of straightforwardness.[149] According to Foreign Secretary Geoffrey Howe, Thatcher 'thought that Pöhl's presence on the Delors Committee would ensure that there would be no hasty rush to monetary union. From that point of view, she thought afterwards that Pöhl let her down.'[150] Thatcher commented, 'Most damaging of all was that [his] known opposition to the Delors approach simply was not expressed.'[151]

Another facet of the European monetary tug-of-war was laid bare at a sometimes heated Anglo-Dutch meeting in April 1989. The Netherlands was the Germans' staunchest monetary supporter. It was also the European country closest to the US and Britain on defence policies. The Nederlandsche Bank closely followed German interest rate policy, and the guilder's parity had remained unchanged against the D-Mark since 1983. As finance minister Onno Ruding put it:

The Dutch gave up their monetary sovereignty many years before I became a minister. We tied ourselves to the anchor currency of Europe. If the

Bundesbank announced their changes in interest rates at 4 o'clock in the after-noon, they would telephone the Nederlandsche Bank at five minutes to four to let them know the decision. The Dutch central bank would announce the same move at five past four. That was the limit of our autonomy. For the Netherlands, this situation was a source of strength. If you imagine France in a similar situa-tion, it would have been thought a source of weakness.[152]

Mindful of the Netherlands' hard currency credentials, Geoffrey Howe prevailed upon Thatcher to invite Dutch prime minister Ruud Lubbers to Chequers in April 1989 with his finance and foreign ministers. 'A conservative, intelligent, good-looking and unfanatically tenacious, [Lubbers] was one of the few European statesmen whose company Margaret almost enjoyed.'[153] Howe wanted Lubbers to persuade her to join fully the European Monetary System, favoured by Howe and Chancellor of the Exchequer Nigel Lawson. Thatcher was at her most vituperative. 'She said that by joining the EMS Britain would lose its flexibility,' Lubbers recalled. 'I said that it was the same as putting on a seat belt when you drove in a car. It did not mean you would drive less fast, but you'd have more safety.'[154] Finance minister Ruding said of Thatcher's performance: 'She did not listen to her Ministers. She treated them very harshly. She saw the meeting as a set-up to try to get the Dutch to convince her to join EMS. She was very polite to us, but every time she used an argument that was plainly wrong in economic terms, and we said so, she switched to another argument.' Lawson labelled the dispute-ridden meeting 'ghastly and embarrassing'. After the meeting Thatcher told him 'what nonsense Ruding had talked about the ERM' and ruled out as 'particularly damaging' Lawson's suggestion of setting a date to join the ERM, declaring: 'I do not want you to raise the subject ever again. I must prevail.'[155]

In parallel with British ministerial efforts to change Thatcher's mind on the ERM, a heated dispute was building up in Paris on the independence of a future European central bank in the wake of the Delors Report. In the vanguard of the critics of the pro-independence Banque de France governor Jacques de Larosière was Jean-Claude Trichet, destined to succeed him at the French central bank and, a decade later, to take over as head of the ECB itself. One of the most testing challenges in de Larosière's long career came on 27 April 1989, in an encounter of ceremonial severity in an ornate ground floor conference room of the Louvre Palace, the headquarters of the Finance Ministry since 1871.[156] According to de Larosière, 'The Ministry received the finished report from Jacques Delors. I was summoned to a Finance Ministry conference room. M. Bérégovoy and M. Trichet sat on one side of the table, with a number of officials. I sat alone on the other side; M. Bérégovoy's manner was very cold. He said that the Ministry had been surprised and dissatisfied by the report as it had been elaborated. He gave the floor to the director of the Treasury.'[157]

In essence, the Director [Trichet] said the Delors Report went too far in proposing a degree of independence for the European central bank that went even further than the independence of the Bundesbank. He thought that I had made excessive concessions. M. Bérégovoy then said: 'What do you have to say?' I said I had heard the word 'concessions'. That indicated I had ceded points during a negotiation to reach an accord. This was not the case. 'When I insisted on the independence of the central bank, I did not regard this as a concession or a sacrifice to the detriment of France. The system would only work if the central bank at the centre, as well as its constituent parts, were independent. Anything else would be destabilising. I didn't say this because I was forced to, or because it was a German condition. I said it because I support that sentiment.' M. Bérégovoy turned to his advisers and said, 'The Governor is right.' He stressed that, instead of criticising the Delors Report, the Trésor should be working to put together a political counterweight to the European central bank. He said, 'There's going to be a super-monetary power. We need a *gouvernement économique* [economic government] to balance that.' I said to Bérégovoy, 'What you have just said is wisdom itself.'

The extraordinary tale of the theatrical confrontation between the present and future governors of the Banque de France was later passed on by word of mouth within the international central bankers' circuit. The story explains why, for years, the Bundesbank and Nederlandsche Bank were sceptical about Trichet's suitability to head the independent ECB. The French government criticism of de Larosière, however, went beyond mere showmanship. Trichet and Bérégovoy were genuinely angry, not only about the tone and content of the Delors Report's conclusions but also because of several other economic setbacks in dealing with Germany. A week before the Louvre showdown, the Bundesbank had raised its discount rate again, confirming the accuracy of the finance minister's premonition of 'interest rate escalation'.[158] An internal Elysée Palace note for Mitterrand revealed deep French worries about the sharply rising bilateral trade deficit: 'The deficit with Germany, which was FF50 billon last year (against FFr44 billion in 1987), is growing further. The persistence of this enormous deficit requires an improvement in our competitiveness.'[159] The French cabinet, meeting a day before the

Louvre session, noted with massive disapproval that the German discount rate increase coincided with a Franco-German summit meeting. 'The Bundesbank's decision to raise interest rates without warning at the same moment as the summit symbolises Germany's go-it-alone practice in the monetary sphere.'[160]

The most important source of irritation for the French government stemmed from a Bonn Cabinet reshuffle in mid-April. Chancellor Kohl displaced from the Finance portfolio the efficient but colourless Gerhard Stoltenberg, dispatching him to the Defence Ministry – a traditional graveyard post for German parliamentarians. Theo Waigel, a self-confident, wise-cracking southern politician who was leader of the Christian Social Union, Kohl's Bavarian conservative partners in the Bonn coalition, took over Stoltenberg's job. Waigel had strong ties to Bavarian bankers who deeply disliked Bonn's plans to introduce a 10 per cent withholding tax, the centre-piece of Franco-German European tax harmonisation efforts. The proposal had already sparked strong opposition from the UK and Luxembourg. Waigel insisted he would join the Cabinet only if Kohl abandoned the idea. On 27 April, the day of de Larosière's Louvre inquisition, Kohl went before the Bundestag in Bonn to announce he was scrapping the withholding tax. Suddenly, the arduous EMU compromise Kohl and Mitterrand had forged at Evian in June 1988 fell apart. According to Mitterrand's diplomatic adviser Hubert Védrine, this was a 'supplementary blow against fiscal harmonisation, confirming the profound divergence of views between France and Germany, a unique case of German desertion'.[161] Elisabeth Guigou wrote: 'Despite his personal engagement in favour of Europe, the Chancellor has been forced, for the first time since he came to power, to adopt a number of policies which will make a joint Franco-German position very difficult if not impossible.'[162]

The German U-turn reduced still further French desire to proceed with the controversial goal of making the Banque de France independent. Prime minister Michel Rocard, like Bérégovoy and Mitterrand, was no advocate of Bundesbank-style autonomy and saw no reason for haste. A close personal friend of Governor de Larosière, Rocard kept his official dealings with him to a minimum. However, to Bérégovoy's annoyance, Rocard met de Larosière shortly after publication of the Delors Report. According to Rocard's later account,

I said: 'You have issued your report, and you now want your independence?' He [de Larosière] said: 'That doesn't bother me. I have independence already: you appoint me, but you cannot sack me, except for some grave misdemeanour. You

are not permitted to give me overt instructions . . . You cannot give me something that I have already.' That impressed me. I felt liberated of the obligation to
carry out the procedure for making the Banque de France formally independent
of the Government. I left the formal step to the prime minister who took over
after the Right won the parliamentary elections in March 1993: Edouard
Balladur.[163]

Confronted by European reticence on ECB independence, the Germans
stepped up lobbying. At his first meeting of European finance ministers, on
the Spanish Costa Brava on 20 May 1989, Waigel tried to shape views in
Germany's favour when he spoke to Spanish finance minister Carlos Solchaga,
chairman of the European finance ministers.

France has always had a totally different attitude on the role of the state.
Germany made its position clear early on in the EMU process. Any weakening
of independence would be unthinkable. At the meeting on the Costa Brava,
Solchaga asked me three or four times to explain the relationship between the
central bank and the government. 'Who's the boss?' he asked. I explained the
checks and balances; it was not so bad to have the central bank responsible for
raising interest rates. When a separate institution has responsibility for monetary
policy, this can take pressure off the politicians.[164]

The finance ministers' meeting was part of the build-up to a European
summit meeting in Madrid in June – and coincided with a notable landmark
on expanding the Exchange Rate Mechanism, with the entry of the Spanish
peseta into the system in mid-June.[165] The twelve European Community
leaders – including Thatcher – agreed that the first stage of Economic and
Monetary Union should start in July 1990 with the progressive abolition of
exchange controls and completion of the Single Market. No date was set for
the inter-governmental conference required to start the three-stage move
towards irrevocably fixing exchange rates. Meeting privately at Madrid,
Mitterrand and Kohl sketched out a trade-off between the D-Mark and
Europe. Kohl told the French president: 'Abandoning the D-Mark is a great
sacrifice for the Germans. Opinion is not yet ready!' Mitterrand retorted: 'You
are moving towards German unification. You must continue to show that you
believe in Europe.'[166] But Kohl demurred on fixing a timetable. Mitterrand's
adviser Védrine was reminded of the Ancient Greek paradox: the arrow taking
Europe towards monetary union was perpetually in motion, but would never
reach its target.

Thatcher provided a distraction at Madrid by declaring Britain would put forward an alternative to the Delors Report. She failed to give advance warning to her Chancellor of the Exchequer; one senior Treasury official who heard the news on the radio while driving was so astonished that he nearly crashed into a tree.[167] Lawson's Treasury team worked out proposals for a scheme of competing currencies, under which the most stable currency would become the most oft-used – and could thus form the basis of a possible monetary union. Following Lawson's resignation in October over ever-deeper differences on policy and decision-making, the 'competing currency' proposal was formally launched in early November by his successor John Major.[168] Europe's reaction ranged from polite indifference to derision.

At the Bundesbank, Pöhl intensified the message that, if the politicians were determined to establish a European central bank, the price would be suitably high. Pöhl's relationship with Kohl was fast deteriorating. But the German central bank's hard line on independence ultimately worked in the chancellor's favour, by supporting Kohl's hard-line negotiating position on the ECB. In public statements, Pöhl cast doubt on whether the Bonn parliament would agree to transfer abroad the Bundesbank's right to set monetary policy.[169] Echoing Thatcher's thoughts, Pöhl said EMU could be accomplished without a European central bank and without a common currency; it would be sufficient to liberalise capital movements and fix exchange rates irrevocably. At the same time, to put pressure on the French and lower inflationary pressures at home, Pöhl started to voice support for a ERM realignment. He pointed out that, as a result of an absence of exchange rate changes over the previous two years, German exporters were gaining undue competitiveness.[170] The trend was underlined by booming German economic growth of close to 4 per cent, the highest for a decade. In 1989 the German economy was growing dangerously fast: the economic prelude to a political earthquake that was about to rip turbulently through the European landscape.

SHOCK WAVES

We are bringing the D-Mark into Europe ... The treaty on Economic and Monetary Union, agreed after long and intense negotiations, bears the German hallmark. Our stability policy has become the Leitmotif for the future European monetary order.

Theo Waigel, German finance minister, 1991[1]

In 1989 the Cold War ended in a blaze of hope and a crescendo of confusion, providing the spark that lit the way to a European currency. The fall of the Berlin Wall brought the sudden prospect of rapid unification of East and West Germany. The upheaval in East Germany was prompted by shifts in the East–West power balance, above all in the changed political climate between Moscow and Washington. But it also reflected the magnetic pull of the fast-growing West German economy on the East German population disillusioned by forty years of Communism. Across continental Europe, especially in Paris, Rome and Brussels, the mood was that a greater Germany must be accompanied by the age-old vision of an integrated Europe. Crucially, by bringing the D-Mark and the Bundesbank under international control, the new European monetary order would hold in check Germany's emerging muscle.

Strains over German and European unity between Kohl and Mitterrand neared breaking-point in autumn 1989. Mitterrand's mounting annoyance over Kohl's backtracking over European policies intensified when the Chancellor showed early reluctance to guarantee united Germany's border with Poland – stemming from his fears of a backlash from Right-wing voters harbouring claims on German land lost after 1945. Kohl's subsequent assurances to

Mitterrand on the single currency allayed French suspicions over Germany's increased weight. There was never a formal bargain under which Germany gave up the D-Mark in return for unification. Mitterrand, by far the most powerful and resourceful politician among Germany's neighbours, knew by autumn 1989 that German unity was unstoppable; his aim was to manage it, not to hold it up.[2] However, the fusing of the two Germanys, and the birth of the single currency, are intimately intertwined. If unification had not happened, it is highly unlikely that France would have been able to persuade Kohl to agree the EMU timetable to replace the D-Mark by the Euro.

After eighteen years on the European currency sidelines since it left the Snake in 1972, Britain re-entered the monetary mainstream when it joined the Exchange Rate Mechanism of the European Monetary System – at what turned out to be a highly unpropitious time. Although widely welcomed, the move – just days after Germany's political unification in October 1990 – helped propel Europe towards massive financial turbulence. The UK's flirtation with the politics of European money coincided with the worst British recession since the Second World War and progressively bitter wrangling between the Germans and the rest of Europe over the terms for EMU. The deep misgivings about the currency transition in German public opinion, persuasively relayed by the media and the Bundesbank, allowed Kohl to set a high price for sacrificing the D-Mark. Since the plan's unpopularity evidently gave him so little room for manoeuvre, Kohl was able to forge EMU on essentially German conditions, above all through the stipulation that the European Central Bank had to enshrine Bundesbank-style independence.

After the Maastricht summit that sealed the single currency timetable, the mood turned vitriolic. The inflationary consequences of German reunification, inflamed by the over-valuation of the East German Mark when it was replaced by the D-Mark, became increasingly evident. In a partial re-run of unrest in the 1970s, a persistent spell of dollar weakness from the late 1980s onwards sent speculative capital rushing into the D-Mark, at a time of unusual buoyancy in the West German economy and a sharp slowdown in the US in 1990–91. The dollar's frailty was exacerbated by doubts about the US economy during the 1992–93 White House transition between George Bush and Bill Clinton. As American interest rates tumbled, the Bundesbank raised the German discount rate to the highest for sixty years. Foreign exchange upheaval erupted over a period of more than a year in 1992–93, centred on the D-Mark and hitting the British, French, Italian, Spanish, Portuguese, Belgian, Danish, Irish, Greek, Norwegian, Swedish and Finnish currencies. This forced unprecedented central bank intervention totalling well over $250 billion[3] – the greatest foreign exchange crisis since the Bretton Woods system collapsed twenty years previously.[4] The turmoil caused Italy and Britain to leave the Exchange Rate Mechanism – the former, for four years, the latter, more or less permanently.

Still more significantly, the D-Mark turbulence led to drawn-out currency attrition between France and Germany in the Battle of the Franc lasting from autumn 1992 to summer 1993 – a full account of which has never hitherto been disclosed. A series of bruising incidents between the French and German monetary authorities included secret negotiations under which Mitterrand and Kohl launched strong-arm tactics to persuade the Bundesbank to underpin the Franc in September 1992. As with the 1970s Werner Plan, economic shock waves during and after German unification looked set to scupper another grand design for fixed European exchange rates. Yet destiny dictated a different outcome. Amid the clamour of currency turmoil, governments had little option but to rally anew behind the battered cause of a single European money – as the sole means of curtailing the destructive energy of world financial markets.

Radical Transformation

Events in Central Europe rumbled on during summer 1989 towards a radical transformation. East German unrest intensified as the East Berlin leadership set its face against Gorbachev-style political and economic reforms. Tens of thousands of discontented East Germans streamed out of the country via neighbouring countries such as Poland and Czechoslovakia. In September, Hungary – despite Warsaw Pact membership – opened its border to Austria, allowing free passage to the West. President Mitterrand had been ruminating over German unification longer than any other government leader (including Kohl). He started actively to prepare conditions for it, including monetary union. The problem was that the Germans, preoccupied by fast-moving events in the East, no longer appeared to be listening with the same intensity to their allies and partners in the West.

Kohl and Mitterrand were caught in a kaleidoscopic switching of positions and tactics among West Germany and the four Second World War victor powers, Britain, France, the US and the Soviet Union. In the period immediately before the fall of the Berlin Wall, the French and German leaders entered a period of mutual antagonism as Germany's own preoccupations – including the problem of unrest in East Germany – took priority. 'Kohl put on the brakes towards monetary union in the second half of 1989,' said Mitterrand's European adviser Elisabeth Guigou. 'Kohl sent business people and other representatives to Paris to explain why he was slowing down because of domestic difficulties.'[5] Mitterrand's security adviser Jacques Attali, highly suspicious of Kohl's motives and actions, believed the chancellor's unification policy changed once he realised, from late 1988 onwards, that Gorbachev could do little to stop it. 'A passionate defender of his country's interests . . . [Kohl] carried out a forced march to accomplish his great work: reunifying the two Germanys.'[6]

France and Britain had similar concerns about the speed of German transformation. They reacted in diametrically opposed ways. According to Guigou, who accompanied Mitterrand to talks with Thatcher at Chequers in early September 1989, 'Mrs Thatcher said she had spent her summer reading books about the origins of the wars of the twentieth century. She asked Mitterrand whether he feared being beaten down by reunited Germany. Mitterrand said he had no problem with unification as long as it was carried out peacefully and democratically' – a condition that, crucially, included the inviolability of the post-1945 German–Polish border.[7] Mitterrand said the answer to increasing German power lay in Economic and Monetary Union:

> Even if Germany becomes stronger once it recovers from its post-unification difficulties, I believe it is the European Union, and only the European Union, that can contain this German power. In contrast to you, I see the perturbations in the East as one more reason to realise the [European] Union. Without a common currency, we are all of us – you and we – already subordinate to the Germans' will. If they increase their interest rates, we are obliged to follow suit, and you do the same thing – even though you are not in the monetary system! So the only way of having the right to speak is to establish a European Central Bank, where one will take decisions jointly.[8]

Thatcher was not convinced: 'If we have a single currency and the Germans are unified, that will be insufferable.' Three weeks later, Thatcher took her scepticism to Moscow, attempting to persuade Gorbachev to join the UK (and France) in preventing unification. Years later, after reading various accounts of Anglo-French diplomatic manoeuvring, Kohl accused Mitterrand of playing 'a double game'. 'He like Mrs Thatcher was relying on Gorbachev not accepting a unified Germany within Nato.'[9]

Relations between Mitterrand and Kohl on EMU turned icy in October. Mitterrand told Kohl at the Elysée Palace he wanted to speed up Economic and Monetary Union.[10] However, citing his 'extremely difficult position' at home, Kohl said the time was 'not ripe' for the single currency.[11] Exuding (according to Guigou) 'cold anger', Mitterrand told Kohl the French government would launch the EMU timetable at the European summit at Strasbourg in December: 'You need to make up your mind.' The two patched up their quarrel in Bonn in early November 1989, when Kohl attempted to explain to the president his apparent hesitancy on EMU on the grounds that a political 'campaign' against monetary union was under way in Germany.[12] Never in fulsome sympathy with the Germans, despite a warm early encounter with his opposite number Theo Waigel in August 1989,[13] French finance minister Pierre Bérégovoy provided a jarring note. On 6 November Bérégovoy proclaimed to an audience of bankers in Frankfurt, with Karl Otto Pöhl sitting in the front row, his opposition to an independent central bank: 'No to technocracy. Yes to democracy! Central bankers have no right to be given superior authority!'[14]

Bérégovoy's Frankfurt protest raised eyebrows, but was of little relevance. Events in Central Europe were out of the hands of mere finance ministers. On 9 November the East German authorities announced that ordinary East Germans could travel freely across the internal Berlin border. The Berlin Wall was breached. Having lost its purpose, like much else in Central and Eastern Europe in 1989–90, the iconically ugly concrete wall simply expired. Kohl, apprised of the startling news while on an official visit to Poland, flew quickly to West Berlin, where he was jeered and whistled by a Left-wing crowd with no wish for speedy unification. Mitterrand, too, saw no reason to rejoice. He told his advisers that Soviet military commanders would prevent Gorbachev from accepting German reunification, adding, 'Without knowing it, people are playing with world war.'[15]

A day after the fall of the Wall, Pöhl was in Basle for a monthly meeting of central bankers at the Bank for International Settlements. He told them the East German economy was in basically good shape: 'The country does produce goods that can be sold in western markets. International reserves are $10 billion, external debt less than $20 billion.'[16] He said he expected unification in the economic arena, but – reflecting his own wishful thinking – added, 'Political unification is a long way off.' Events turned out differently. Rising clamour among ordinary East Germans for speedy bonding with the West led Kohl to accelerate plans for economic and political coordination with the East: a necessary prelude to unification. As the march to German unity intensified, a Medici-like chronicle of rivalry, jealousy, bluff and intrigue unfolded among European leaders. Accusations abounded of falsehoods, half-truths and double-dealing. Less than a week after the fall of the Wall, Gorbachev told Mitterrand by telephone that Kohl had informed him 'secretly' that he was trying to slow down unification. 'I cannot go further [in supporting Kohl on

German unity],' Gorbachev said. Mitterrand's acerbic counsellor Attali concluded that neither Gorbachev nor Kohl was telling the truth.[17]

At a stormy dinner for Community leaders at the Elysée Palace on 18 November, Kohl recalled the long-standing NATO commitment to a united Germany.[18] Thatcher replied archly that this assurance dated from a time when no one believed reunification was possible. When Kohl told her, 'You will not stop the German people following their destiny,' Thatcher 'stamped her foot in rage' – an outburst of truculence that, Kohl observed, appeared to find Mitterrand's approval.[19] The German chancellor incensed Mitterrand by not giving him (and other European leaders) advance notice of a ten-point plan for German unity unveiled to the Bundestag on 28 November.[20] Two days later Kohl sent his foreign minister to the Elysée Palace to face the cold blast of Mitterrand's displeasure.[21] Mitterrand told Genscher that Germany was no longer a 'motor' but a 'brake' on European integration, thus playing into Thatcher's hands.[22] Mitterrand called on Germany to agree serious negotiations on Economic and Monetary Union before the end of 1990.[23] Otherwise, Mitterrand said – with a certain melodrama – Germany risked a 'triple alliance' between France, Britain and the Soviet Union that could isolate Germany in similar fashion to the eve of the First and Second World Wars. 'We will return to the world of 1913.'[24] Under this extreme threat, Kohl backed down. He agreed that the Strasbourg summit on 8 December would approve the start of an intergovernmental conference on EMU in the second half of 1990. This was the essential deal that launched Europe on to the Maastricht monetary union path. As French prime minister Michel Rocard explained later:

> There was a balance between unification of Germany and the establishment of European monetary union. Both processes accelerated after the fall of the Berlin Wall. Kohl and Mitterrand were already engaged in both efforts. Mitterrand had to accept reunification more quickly than he thought likely, in the same way that Kohl had to accept monetary union more quickly than he had intended.[25]

Kohl's adviser Joachim Bitterlich helped prompt the change of heart, telling him that Mitterrand was giving priority to monetary union, although France's traditional reservations about giving up sovereignty made an accompanying agreement on further-going political union highly unlikely.[26] Bitterlich warned that, by accepting liberalisation of capital controls and the Bundesbank's primacy over EMU, and in view of lingering French bitterness over Germany's rejection of a European withholding tax, France believed it had already made abundant concessions to win a monetary deal.

A key component in the politicking over German unification – and the monetary measures that would accompany it – was the attitude of Mikhail Gorbachev and the Soviet leadership. On 6 December, in Kiev, the capital of the Soviet republic of Ukraine, Gorbachev told Mitterrand Kohl was issuing a 'Diktat' on unification, and said he was behaving 'like a bull in a china shop'. Gorbachev told the French president: 'Help me to prevent German unification, otherwise I will be replaced by a soldier; otherwise, you will bear the responsibility for war.'[27] Mitterrand said afterwards he was unsure what Gorbachev was really thinking. 'At Kiev, he was very severe on Kohl. When he meets the Germans, he is much more flexible. What is the reality?'[28] On 8 December European leaders gathered in Strasbourg in fraught circumstances. The meeting agreed to start preparations on the EMU inter-governmental conference in summer 1990, with a formal opening in December. Kohl said the summit was the most 'tense and unfriendly' he had ever attended.[29] Italian prime minister Giulio Andreotti warned against 'pan-Germanism'.[30] Thatcher declared: 'Twice we beat the Germans, now they are there again.' Dutch prime minister Lubbers, hitherto one of Kohl's closest allies as a fellow Christian Democrat, also voiced misgivings about German unity; reflecting Kohl's elephantine memory for slights, the episode cost him the 1995 prize of succeeding Delors as European Commission president[31] – and was one of the background reasons why Amsterdam never became a serious candidate to site the European Central Bank. During two bilateral meetings with Thatcher at Strasbourg, Mitterrand repeated his warning to Genscher that Germany could face 'encirclement' from a triple Alliance of Britain, France and Russia.[32] Thatcher took out of her handbag and brandished maps of Germany's borders before and after the Second World War.[33] Pointing to Silesia, Pomerania and East Prussia, she told Mitterrand: 'They'll take all of that, and Czechoslovakia too.'[34]

The Strasbourg summit appeared to push Germany towards EMU far more rapidly than it wanted. Germans on both sides of the Elbe were critical of abandoning the D-Mark. The West Germans regarded their currency as a badge of honour for past successes – and a talisman for future upheavals. The East Germans saw it as the most potent symbol of the western system they sought to join. In his dealings with the US administration of President George Bush – who was considerably more sympathetic to German unity than most European leaders – Kohl adroitly turned the apparent self-sacrifice of monetary union into a diplomatic instrument to show evidence of Germany's benign intentions. Days after the Strasbourg meeting, the chancellor told US Secretary of State James Baker that he was supporting EMU even though it was 'against German interests. For instance, the President of Bundesbank is against this development. But the step is politically important, for Germany needs friends.'[35]

The fragility of the tightrope Kohl was treading – and his need of friends – was underlined in January 1990 by a conversation between Thatcher and Mitterrand in Paris, when both leaders again voiced doubt and uncertainty about German developments. Mitterrand complained:

> The problem of reunification has provoked a psychological shock with the Germans. This has revived certain characteristics that one had forgotten, a certain brutality and an elimination of all other problems apart from those corresponding to their own preoccupations. I say that the Germans have the right to self-determination, but I say also that I have the right to take into account the preoccupations of the rest of Europe.[36]

In February 1990 Kohl advanced further on a collision course both with the Bundesbank and, as it turned out, with the rest of Europe. Without consultation with the Central Bank, and without considering the sizeable international implications for the D-Mark as the anchor currency of the European Monetary System, he decided at short notice to introduce the West German currency into East Germany.[37] Exporting the hallmark of the country's prosperity across the River Elbe to the eastern part of the divided nation was a blatantly political move. The aim was to induce East Germans to stay at home rather than leaving in ever more destabilising waves for the Federal Republic. The decision wrong-footed the Federal Republic's monetary helmsmen Pöhl, Schlesinger and Waigel, who shortly beforehand had dismissed the idea, respectively, as 'fantastic', 'very unrealistic' and 'hair-raising'.[38] Bonn's apparent generosity carried a sizeable price tag. The decision suspended the principles of financial probity on which West Germany had built its forty-year post-war success. The terms of the monetary conversion greatly exacerbated the East German economy's lack of competitiveness and inflated the overall German monetary supply.[39] The action increased unemployment in the East, heightened inflation in the West, and led to higher interest rates across the whole of Europe.[40] It was the moment when Germany served notice that the D-Mark, the cornerstone of Europe's currency stabilisation arrangements, would become – for several years – a force for disturbance rather than stability.

Immediate reaction in Paris to the Bonn D-Mark changeover plan was mixed. The Elysée Palace seemed determined to see it as positive news, even though it was clear that economic turbulence would ensue. Mitterrand's adviser Elisabeth Guigou told him:

The initiative has led to a rise of the D-Mark. On the financial markets interest rates have firmed abruptly: the markets anticipate higher inflation in Germany and hence a continuing rise in interest rates. It is certain that economic and monetary union [with East Germany] will be expensive for West Germany and this will lead to more growth (as a result of an increase in demand) and more inflation and, as a result, a reduction in the German trade surplus – that is to say precisely what we have been asking from the Germans for years without success.[41]

UK Treasury economists, in an internal paper that was sent to the prime minister's office, forecast that German monetary union would increase German inflation and lead to higher Bundesbank interest rates.[42] 'The safest conclusion is that a period of turbulence for the DM cannot be ruled out.' Margaret Thatcher expressed anxieties about the effect of German monetary union on currency markets. She told a cabinet meeting discussing German unification: 'Aren't we lucky not to be in [the Exchange Rate Mechanism]. What's the East German Mark going to do to the D-Mark?'[43]

Immediately after the D-Mark plan was announced, the East German population stepped up demands for parity between the East and West German currencies. The German government subsequently decided a 'headline' conversion rate of one for one for the switchover of wages and salaries implemented in July. The Bundesbank's proposal for a less generous conversion rate went largely unheeded.[44] For many East Germans parity conversion was gratifyingly unexpected. According to Helmut Schlesinger, 'I spoke to [East German Economics Minister] Christa Luft. She told me she was worried that the Bundesbank would call for 5 to 1 conversion. At the time, I had not thought of such a high rate. After unification, I found out that the rate used by East Germany for its own official internal conversion operations was 4.8 to 1.'[45]

Parallel international negotiations on German unification and EMU accelerated in 1990.[46] East Germans voted for national unity in March by giving Kohl's Christian Democrats overwhelming victory in the country's first free elections. Thatcher maintained an uncompromising line on Germany and EMU. In mid-March she told ten French industrialists at a private dinner in London that Germany would add to its existing economic strength by becoming politically dominant. 'It is not by building Europe that one can bind Germany. France and the UK need to join forces in the face of the German danger.'[47] She repeated the message to French prime minister Michel Rocard that European integration would increase Germany's dominance by '[giving] Germany Europe on a plate'.[48]

Rocard, in common with most of the rest of Europe, disagreed. The European Community had decided at the Strasbourg summit to 'bind in' a larger Germany through enhanced monetary integration. The plan was put into action. Gradually, a *quid pro quo* between Bonn and Paris started to emerge. Bundesbank president Karl Otto Pöhl, as chairman of the Committee of European Community Central Bank Governors, prepared to follow up the Delors Report by drafting a proposed statute for an independent European Central Bank.[49] Pöhl gradually saw that the French might be willing to sacrifice traditional opposition to central banking independence, in order to accomplish a higher goal.[50] In June the Community agreed to start not one but two inter-governmental conferences – on EMU and political union – to strengthen Europe's structures on the way to closer union.

During the summer Britain moved closer to a decision to climb aboard the European integration bandwagon by joining the Exchange Rate Mechanism. Ministers and officials were eager to gain some strategic hold over the newly-formed monetary contours of Europe.[51] Hans Tietmeyer, who became the Bundesbank's international director in January 1990, optimistically told Nigel Wicks, the top international official in the UK Treasury, that German monetary pressures would subside by the autumn.[52] In a belated bid for influence, in June Thatcher's Chancellor of the Exchequer, John Major, launched the Treasury's reworked proposal for a 'Hard ECU' parallel currency that could, under certain ill-defined conditions, develop into a single European money; the proposal was largely ignored.[53]

Despite Thatcher's uncompromising EMU stance, she acknowledged the Exchange Rate Mechanism had some merit. Thatcher told German foreign minister Hans-Dietrich Genscher the UK would join the ERM 'to use the D-Mark as a sort of Gold Standard which would help bear down on inflation . . . But there was no case for going further than the existing ERM for the foreseeable future. Europe needed time to adjust to the full consequences of the single market and did not need the fresh turmoil which would be caused by the attempt to move to a single currency.'[54] There was no doubt about rising momentum behind EMU. Across the Atlantic, the New York Federal Reserve Bank devoted a large part of its September board meeting to discussing the implications for New York's status as a financial centre and for the dollar.[55] Britain's ERM membership was clinched in September. The British government came to the collective view that joining the mechanism was the only way to bring down the Bank of England's base rate, stuck at 15 per cent for a year, and stoke up much-needed recovery after a sharp fall in 1990 economic growth.[56]

After the last obstacles were swept away, including agreement between Kohl and Gorbachev that a united Germany could remain in NATO, on 3 October Germany was formally reunified – amid a pronounced lack of national euphoria. Kohl warned, 'A difficult economic path lies in front of us.'[57] Karl Otto Pöhl told Federal Reserve chairman Alan Greenspan he feared 'the consequences for Germany would be severe'.[58] Just two days later, Britain announced its long-awaited decision to join the Exchange Rate Mechanism. The move was hailed as strengthening European monetary cooperation[59] – but ended up perilously close to wrecking it.

Congratulations and Contradictions

The UK entered the ERM, and cut interest rates by 1 percentage point at the same time, on a congratulatory wave of contradictory policies. The congratulations soon died away. The contradictions endured – as did prime ministerial pugnacity. Three weeks after ERM entry, and after other European governments had given the political green light to EMU (at a summit in Rome), Thatcher – less than a month before quitting as prime minister – succinctly summed up in the House of Commons whether Britain would join the single currency: 'No, No, No'.[60] She made her preoccupations clear to German ambassador Hermann von Richthofen at a Buckingham Palace state dinner.

Thatcher:	'Now that Germany has been reunified, Helmut Kohl must be very happy. He can now carry out more national policies.'
Von Richthofen:	'Chancellor Kohl will continue with European integration, including commitment to monetary union.'
Thatcher:	'What are you saying? So you want me to go to Her Majesty the Queen and explain to her that, in a few years, her picture will no longer be on our banknotes?'[61]

For all Thatcher's causticity, at the outset in 1990, the rewards from the Exchange Rate Mechanism appeared greatly to outstrip the risks. The ERM gave the UK a prominent place on the European economic policy journey. The British government failed to see it had climbed aboard a monetary vehicle that was about to veer out of control. The Treasury's Nigel Wicks said, 'We certainly underestimated the trauma of German reunification, but so did everyone else, including the Germans.'[62]

In October 1990 the temptations of membership were beguiling. Britain could harness the stature of the Bundesbank to burnish its own monetary reputation. It could attempt to stimulate the economy by bringing down interest rates. And it could profit from the perceived resilience of the ERM to prevent any inflation-generating fall in sterling. ERM realignments had become a rarity.[63] Reflecting the build-up to monetary union, European countries increasingly saw the system as a precursor to full fixing of currencies. France wanted to keep the Franc parity unchanged at all costs, part of its strategy of shackling the D-Mark. The Paris authorities ignored the Bundesbank's warnings about the need for a realignment. Britain's position was thus over-stretched. It was striving for a goal that all post-Second World War governments had sought yet failed to accomplish: improving economic growth while keeping inflation permanently under control. The chosen method was to cut interest rates, while putting a floor under the pound. Britain sought to use for its own ends the *de facto* fixing of ERM exchange rates caused by the drive to Economic and Monetary Union: an aim the government both opposed, and believed would not happen. Contrasting policies, objectives and expectations were convolutedly intermingled. Not surprisingly, developments did not turn out exactly as planned.

At the pivotal point of ERM entry, Thatcher was determined to lower borrowing costs for British companies and house-owners.[64] The Bank of England rate cut was designed to 'make the move more popular in the press and with the public', according to Kenneth Clarke, later Chancellor of the Exchequer. 'People tend to forget that Mrs Thatcher's economic thinking was not that purist. She was above all a Right-wing populist.'[65] The interest rate reduction[66] imparted a clear signal. Should sterling weaken while the economy remained in the doldrums, the UK would be unlikely to raise rates to defend the pound. Thatcher brushed aside Bank of England governor Robin Leigh-Pemberton's genteel protest.[67] 'Robin believed we should not cut interest rates on the day we announced entry into the ERM,' Major said. 'That was his view, and Margaret knew it was his view, and she knew it was my view, and that of Terry Burns [Treasury Permanent Secretary]. But that was the price for her agreement. That was the only deal on offer.'[68] The entry level for sterling – the market rate of DM2.95 – was a compromise between German and French opinions.[69] According to Major, who became prime minister in late November after Thatcher's resignation:

Every time we went to see European leaders, they would press us: 'When are you going to join the ERM?' We went in at the middle of the range proposed by the French and the Germans. The French wanted DM3, the Germans DM2.92. We went in smack at the market rate. Anything else would have been punitive for us, or would have amounted to a small devaluation. Not a single person – not Kohl, not Pöhl, not Mitterrand – asked us to go through the Monetary Committee to discuss the rate at which we joined. All the European governments wanted us in. That was the overriding consideration, not the exchange rate.[70]

The Bundesbank's Hans Tietmeyer, who attended a 6 October Brussels European Monetary Committee meeting to formalise British entry, confirmed there was dissent on the exchange rate, but no major discord.

Both Pöhl and I believed that the UK had entered at too high an exchange rate. We told the UK government that, including at the Monetary Committee. We were somewhat annoyed that there had been no prior consultation on the exchange rate . . . However, our objections were relatively mild. After their public announcement, we could hardly tell the British to stay out because the rate was too high. On the timing, we believed that this was perhaps a little too early. But this was not a significant point.[71]

Amid the helter-skelter of events, the UK had no time for thorough analysis of all the ERM membership issues. Britain gave little heed to the likelihood of future rises in European interest rates caused by unification-induced German economic imbalances. The government failed to realise that it was entering the ERM on the brink of a recession, with a headline inflation rate (although falling rapidly) three times that of Germany, during the most imbalanced period for European growth since the Second World War, and in the midst of Germany's longest period of credit tightening for seventy years.[72] In 1991 Britain's economy declined by 1.4 per cent while France's grew by only 1 per cent – but Germany forged ahead by 5 per cent – hardly a recipe for exchange rate stability. There were voices advising caution. According to career central banker Eddie George, who was deputy governor of the Bank of England in 1990 and became governor three years later,

We had tried all kinds of monetary targets, including shadowing the D-Mark. There wasn't a great deal of debate within the Bank of England, or as far as I was aware, the government on the economic issues involved. We were trying to find a monetary framework that was more robust. There was quite a lot of business backing for establishing a more stable exchange rate framework with Europe. So there was support for tying ourselves to the Bundesbank . . . I was somewhat sceptical about joining the ERM in 1990. People in the Bank and in the Treasury would have known that I was less than enthusiastic. I did however think that, in an extreme situation, we would be able to pull out. For the system to work you had to have a much more cohesive approach to a whole series of issues. I felt that there was not sufficient coherence among the different economic cultures . . . I was not at all confident that it would work. And it didn't.[73]

Underlining the flaw in Britain's timing, between the fall of the Berlin Wall in November 1989 and British ERM entry in October 1990, the Bundesbank did not once raise its discount or Lombard rates.[74] This was in spite of a series of exceptional developments that would normally have sparked tough Bundesbank action: an over-heated German economy, the introduction of the D-Mark into East Germany at an inflationary exchange rate, and a considerable fiscal boost from Kohl's reunification financing. All this marked pent-up pressure for higher German interest rates. The reason why the Bundesbank delayed resumption of its credit offensive until late 1990 was because it was embroiled in deep-seated wrangling with Kohl. The Bundesbank had voiced public misgivings over German monetary union, and was attempting a dialogue with Bonn to mitigate the consequences. Furthermore, it was trying to ensure acceptable terms for EMU. The central bank did not want to take tough measures that would further disturb the power balance with the government.[75] Pöhl explained: 'We were too much involved with German reunification. The Bundesbank didn't want to create any additional complications.'[76] Britain thus entered the ERM at what turned out to be the end of a phoney war. UK officials with European responsibilities could have foreseen at least some of this. From Germany there were few overt indications, and many mixed messages, of what was about to happen. But, Tietmeyer said, Britain should have read the signs:

> When the British entered the ERM, from an economic point of view, I do not know how they could have expected that this would offer an opportunity for a continued substantial cut in UK interest rates. It was clear that German interest rates were on a rising trend because of policies on German reunification. If the UK really wanted to cut interest rates, then they should have entered the ERM at a lower exchange rate, or they should have stayed out for some more time.[77]

Rather than ebbing, pressure for higher German interest rates increased in 1991. German inflation rose towards 5 to 6 per cent – contrasting with decelerating prices in the UK and the rest of Europe as economies slowed. The Bundesbank ended a thirteen-month cease-fire by raising its Lombard rate by 0.5 percentage points in November 1990, reigniting increases in its leading interest rates that had begun in summer 1988 and went on for four years. The scale of German challenges was underlined in May 1991 when Pöhl resigned from the Bundesbank after eleven and a half years at the helm. This was the climax of a simmering dispute with Kohl over what Pöhl considered as Kohl's reckless financing of German reunification.[78] Helmut Schmidt commented acidly,

> I expected Pöhl to tell Chancellor Kohl what was necessary, and what was impos-
> sible, with regard to his ideas for bringing the East and West German economies
> together. Pöhl did do that, but that he drew the consequences [by resigning] only
> later. This was disappointing. I expected him to say to Kohl: 'The policies that
> you are about to put into place are nonsense.' He should have resigned earlier to
> dramatise the issue.[79]

Drama erupted when Pöhl's long-standing deputy Schlesinger took over the top job. The new president was a career central banker with a trademark image for robustness and austerity. He believed monetary diplomacy required action, not words. He prevailed upon the Council to slam on the brakes. As annual German inflation edged towards 5 per cent, the Bundesbank announced a fearsome 1 percentage point increase in discount rate, and a smaller 0.25 percentage point rise in Lombard rate, in mid-August 1991, at the height of the European holiday season.[80] The step was necessary, Schlesinger confirmed later, to counter 'the wrong policies decided for the exchange rate of the East German Mark'.[81]

At the same time, US interest rates and the dollar declined as the US economy slowed sharply. German interest rates, having been 3 percentage points below US levels in summer 1989, rose within three years to 6 percentage points *above* American rates – the sharpest trans-Atlantic mone-tary turnaround in the post-war era.[82] As Britain entered an exceptionally severe economic downturn – with GDP declining in both 1991 and 1992 – the UK was caught in a three-pronged financial and political trap. First, as Thatcher and Major had planned, the UK was able to cut interest rates within the ERM. But, as Germany intensified its own monetary squeeze, the differ-ence between British and German interest rates diminished rapidly, making sterling vulnerable to speculative attrition, and preventing any further UK cuts. Second, UK inflation fell rapidly, so that – despite the fall in *nominal* interest rates – *real* (that is, inflation-adjusted) interest rates rose sharply.

Third, British exporters reliant on US sales were badly hit by a sharp rise in the pound to $2, which made American sales prohibitively expensive. For all these reasons, Britain's long-awaited economic recovery stubbornly refused to take off. The Treasury's international expert Nigel Wicks wrote later, with what might seem to be understatement, 'The reunification trauma meant that the mismatch between the requirements of German and UK policy would be especially pronounced.'[83] As ERM membership wore on, the UK exhausted the benefits of the system – and became increasingly exposed to the risks.[84]

The Countdown Starts

Europe's monetary travails increased after the Maastricht summit in the Netherlands in December 1991. Closely following the findings of the Delors Report and the work on the European Central Bank statute by European central bank governors, the treaty laid down a three-stage timetable for monetary union by 1997 or, at the latest, 1999, depending on the accomplishment of criteria for economic convergence – inflation, interest rates and budgetary and debt positions. The most significant of the Maastricht 'convergence criteria' was the stipulation that countries' general government budget deficits (counting all main areas of public expenditure and income) should not exceed 3 per cent of Gross Domestic Product (measuring a country's total economic output). Jean-Claude Trichet, director of the French Treasury, suggested the target, reflecting the 3 per cent deficit ceiling set by France in its 1983 economic restructuring.[85] The Maastricht deal was choreographed by President Mitterrand and Italian prime minister Andreotti, who then secured Kohl's blessing at the summit.

The summit agreed that EMU would automatically take place by the end of the decade for all Community countries which fulfilled the convergence criteria (apart from the UK and, later on, Denmark which secured exemptions). Knowing that the German electorate disliked EMU, France and Italy hatched the plan to ensure that not only Kohl but also his successors would be bound to the EMU goal. The Maastricht deal ensured that the Germans could introduce no further conditions for EMU, for example, on parallel establishment of 'political union'. This was an objective that both Kohl and the Bundesbank said they wanted, in order to anchor German-style stability culture throughout Europe. The goal was never precisely defined; furthermore, it was running into increased scepticism, within and outside Germany.[86]

Although setting no explicit path towards political union, the treaty established firm constraints for economic policy among EMU members, all of which were to have deep and controversial implications. It prohibited direct financing of public entities' deficits by national central banks, stipulated that neither the Community nor any EMU member was liable for the commitments of any other member (the 'no bail-out clause') and stated that members should avoid excessive government deficits, under procedures to be policed by European finance ministers.[87] The Maastricht treaty enshrined extra Community support, through the so-called Cohesion Fund, for weaker countries that would face economic constraints from the single currency. However, these measures fell a long way short of the thoroughgoing fiscal redistribution for weaker regions of individual countries that is normally available within industrialised countries' national budgets.

The Maastricht summit saw a new spirit of Bundesbank–Bonn cooperation. Finance minister Waigel phoned Schlesinger during the meeting to seek his advice on the independence of the future European Central Bank with regard to the crucial issue of the external exchange rate.[88] Once the Maastricht countdown started, no country could escape it. In view of the Germans' distaste for giving up the D-Mark,[89] Dietrich von Kyaw, Germany's craggy-faced ambassador to the European Community, termed the agreement 'a time bomb that could explode under Kohl'.[90] The chancellor, for his part, displayed ebullient self-confidence. At Maastricht he agreed a wager that the UK would become a member of EMU by 1997, the earliest date set in the treaty. 'The Government always does what the City wants ... The City will ensure that Britain joins monetary union.' He duly lost the bet, and paid out the stake – six bottles of wine – in 1997.[91]

The timetable to replace the D-Mark goaded the Bundesbank into action. If a European Central Bank was going to take its place, it would need to follow the toughest standards. Alarmed by accelerating wage claims despite a slowing of the post-unification boom, only days after Maastricht the Bundesbank struck back. It raised discount rate to 8 per cent and Lombard rate to 9.75 per cent, the highest ever in West Germany. France, which had briefly cut money market interest rate below German levels, was forced to raise rates again.[92] A detailed Elysée Palace briefing note analysed the German move in uncompromising terms, claiming that the 0.5 percentage point increase was higher than the 0.25 point rise the German central bank had indicated was likely during the Maastricht summit. 'The President of the Bundesbank and his acolytes accompanied this decision [to raise interest rates] with devastating comments ... This indicates in the most direct manner that the Bundesbank in its heart of hearts wants a D-Mark revaluation to import disinflation, even if such a revaluation has no economic justification.' Mitterrand stuck fast to the position

1 Central bank chiefs patching together 1920s monetary understandings, New York, 1927: (*from l.*) Hjalmar Schacht (Reichsbank), Benjamin Strong (US), Montagu Norman (UK), Charles Rist (France).

2 Bonn, November 1968: at an ill-fated monetary conference German Economics Minister Karl Schiller (*middle*), surrounded by his international opposite numbers, fended off pressure for a D-Mark revaluation.

3 German Chancellor Konrad Adenauer (*l.*) with President Charles de Gaulle, September 1963.

4 Bundesbank President Karl Blessing (*l.*) with Economics Ministry State Secretary Johann Schöllhorn, Brussels, 1966.

5 Retired Bundesbank President Karl Klasen (*l.*) with successor Otmar Emminger, Basle, June 1978.

6 1970s monetary negotiators: (*from l.*) Karl Schiller (German Economics Ministry), Karl Otto Pöhl (Finance Ministry and Bundesbank), Paul Volcker (US Treasury and Federal Reserve).

7 France's top international monetary team in 1967: (*from l.*) Finance Minister Michel Debré, Jean-Yves Haberer from the French Treasury, Banque de France Governor Jacques Brunet.

8 Chancellor Helmut Schmidt at the Bundesbank, 30 November 1978, accompanied by (*from l.*) Finance Minister Hans Matthöfer, Bundesbank President Otmar Emminger and monetary adviser Horst Schulmann.

9 Guadeloupe summit, January 1979: (*from l.*) Chancellor Helmut Schmidt, US President Jimmy Carter, British Prime Minister James Callaghan and French President Valéry Giscard d'Estaing.

10 Franco-German monetary discussions in Rome, May 1984: International Monetary Fund Managing Director Jacques de Larosière and Bundesbank President Karl Otto Pöhl.

11 Anglo-French understanding on Europe, 1986: French President François Mitterrand with British Prime Minister Margaret Thatcher, flanked by foreign ministers Roland Dumas (*l.*) and Geoffrey Howe (*r.*).

12 British Prime Minister Margaret Thatcher with European Commission President Jacques Delors, 1986: she was wary of Delors' plans for centralising European decision-making.

13 Franco-German meeting at the Bundesbank, 16 September 1988: (*central group from l.*) Bundesbank President Karl Otto Pöhl, French Treasury Director Jean-Claude Trichet, Finance Minister Pierre Bérégovoy (with back to camera), Banque de France Governor Jacques de Larosière.

14 Chancellor Helmut Kohl with President Helmut Schlesinger at the Bundesbank, 19 March 1992. Unlike Karl Otto Pöhl, Schlesinger placed emphasis on personal meetings with Kohl, rather than writing him letters.

15 International agreement on German unity in 1990 opens up the road to EMU: (*from l.*) Foreign Ministers Roland Dumas (France), Eduard Shevardnadze (Soviet Union), James Baker (US), Soviet General Secretary Mikhail Gorbachev, German Foreign Minister Hans-Dietrich Genscher, East German Prime Minister Lothar de Maizière, British Foreign Secretary Douglas Hurd.

16 President François Mitterrand and Chancellor Helmut Kohl in 1994.

17 Chancellor Helmut Kohl's first visit to the Bundesbank in July 1988; here he is viewing part of the central bank's gold stocks.

18 (*from l.*) Wim Duisenberg, president of the newly-established European Central Bank, Bundesbank President Hans Tietmeyer and German Finance Minister Theo Waigel celebrate the D-Mark's 50th anniversary in Frankfurt, June 1998.

19 European Central Bank Executive Board, 2006: back (*from l.*) Jürgen Stark, José Manuel González-Páramo, Lorenzo Bini Smaghi; front (*from l.*) Gertrude Tumpel-Gugerell, Jean-Claude Trichet (President), Lucas Papademos (Deputy President).

20 German Chancellor Gerhard Schröder with French President Jacques Chirac at the Franco-German summit in Nantes, November 2001.

21 ECB monetary policy conference in Frankfurt, November 2006: Jean-Claude Trichet with Federal Reserve Chairman Ben Bernanke.

22 President Nicolas Sarkozy exchanges confidences with Chancellor Angela Merkel at the ceremony for the 2008 Charlemagne Prize, Aachen, May 2008.

of his advisers that France could not countenance any change in the Franc–D-Mark parity – on the grounds that French inflation was lower than in Germany.[93]

Underlining trans-Atlantic divergence, the US cut the discount rate to 3.5 per cent, reflecting pressure for domestic reflation from embattled President Bush and his Treasury Secretary Nicolas Brady. The Bundesbank's interest rate action, meanwhile, sparked an unusual protest from the Netherlands, hitherto Germany's most robust monetary ally. Prime minister Ruud Lubbers wrote to Kohl,

> The Netherlands, too, has been alarmed by the considerable increase in Germany's leading interest rates. The Nederlandsche Bank has followed this interest rate increase, or rather, has had to follow it. There is great concern that this is strengthening recessionary tendencies … As a result of the Bundesbank's rigid monetary policies, tension within the European Monetary System is increasing (I am thinking especially of the English pound). Above all, this is seriously endangering acceptance of further economic and monetary integration.[94]

The chancellor was still piqued by the Dutchman's earlier querulousness over unification, and ignored the message. The Bundesbank found out about it only after an alarmed Nederlandsche Bank wrote to the Bundesbank to apologise.[95] Later, Lubbers explained,

> I thought Kohl could use the letter in a positive way, in trying to persuade the Bundesbank to modify the policy of higher interest rates … My cooperation with Helmut Kohl had been exemplary up to the time of unification in 1990. But cooperation with Kohl became much more difficult afterwards. He no longer wanted stronger people around him to help make the decisions. He thought he could do it himself. He changed as a person, into someone I call 'Kohl-II'. He started to believe in his own legend.[96]

The European monetary expansion process received a minor fillip when Portugal joined the Exchange Rate Mechanism in April 1992;[97] of the twelve-nation European Community, only Greece remained outside the currency scheme. In France, however, the mood was dire. The same month, Pierre Bérégovoy became prime minister,[98] fulfilling a long-held ambition, but at a time when the economy was becalmed and the Socialist party's standing was plummeting. Bérégovoy doggedly defended Mitterrand's EMU policies when he introduced the Maastricht Bill in the National Assembly, spelling out the reasons – based on emotion, psychology and wishful thinking as much as economic facts – Parliament should back the treaty,

> I belong to the generation that witnessed the Europe of blood and fire, when nationalism aroused war, when war fuelled nationalism. In a generation where we have seen reconciliation and the construction of the European Community, we have erased centuries of fratricidal strife. It is time to hold up Europe and to unfurl as our banner 'Never, never again.' Yes, I believe in Europe, because I passionately want peace.[99]

Bérégovoy attacked Gaullist EMU opponents who claimed it would bring 'obligatory monetarism and the end of autonomous economic policies'. Bérégovoy declared, 'Our monetary policy is not constrained primarily by Europe, but by an open world economy. The single currency gives us the means to cope with this constraint . . . The dollar's omnipotence has allowed the US to make others pay for its deficit. Is this not another reason for a European currency, on an equal footing with the dollar and the yen?' Bérégovoy reiterated the need for a counter-balance to the European Central Bank. 'The treaty creates a political Europe, makes possible a social Europe, [and] establishes an 'economic authority' in the Economic and Monetary Union.'

Europe's hopes of a smooth monetary transition were dealt a severe blow when, in June 1992, a wafer-thin majority of the Danish electorate rejected the Maastricht Treaty in a referendum. Adding to Europe-wide scepticism about Maastricht,[100] the Denmark vote disrupted the international ratification process – and financial markets' expectation of a smooth road to EMU.[101] Reflecting weakness in the Italian economy and long-standing foreign exchange market doubts whether Italy was competitive at its ERM exchange rate against a D-Mark that was climbing rapidly against the dollar, the foreign exchanges turned against the lira as 'the weakest link in the chain'.[102] French Treasury director Jean-Claude Trichet told the European Monetary Committee, a day after the Danish vote, that the other eleven Community states should proceed without the Danes. Denmark 'should be punished for its foolishness'.[103] This led to a clash with the head of the Bundesbank's international department Wolfgang Rieke, who described the No as 'a well-timed reminder'. Rieke commented on 'Trichet's arrogance in arguing that it is outrageous that "the people" (of an insignificant country) should be allowed to derail these grand plans'.[104]

Immediately after the Danish No, President Mitterrand called a referendum on Maastricht in France, scheduled for September. Constitutionally unnecessary, this was a high-risk gamble. Polls showed France was turning sceptical on the treaty. As John Major put it, 'It would be difficult for a novelist to come up with such a concatenation of events. The Danish No led to a French decision on a referendum. This in turn led to the possibility of the death of the Maastricht treaty, and a halt to European integration – which would have caused a bloodbath on a mega-scale on the financial markets.'[105] Nerves were on edge all across Europe – particularly in the UK, where Major faced persistent sniping over Europe from the Conservative party, including his predecessor Thatcher.[106] As the UK recession deepened, growing numbers of mainstream British economists and bankers questioned Britain's ERM policy.[107]

In the first of a series of controversies over Bundesbank policies, Bundesbank president Schlesinger apologised to the British ambassador over a press report that the Bundesbank advocated an ERM realignment.[108] Finance minister Waigel visited the Bundesbank Council in June and urged the central bank to hold firm.[109] Shortly after the Federal Reserve cut discount rate to 3 per cent, the lowest for thirty years, Major wrote to Kohl in July 1992: 'I am very concerned about the effect of any further increase in interest rates in Europe. In Britain there have been signs of recovery, but if interest rates are forced up again, that could falter. I believe the same is true in Europe.' Kohl did not reply. The Bundesbank's answer came, Major said afterwards, 'from the barrel of a gun'.[110] Two days later, the German central bank announced its tenth successive increase in discount rate, to 8.75 per cent, the highest since 1931.[111] Commenting on the German rate rise, Pierre Bérégovoy, the French prime minister, told the cabinet in Paris how, in the future, everything could change for the better: 'If a common Central Bank existed for the 12 states of the Community, then a decision such as the one the Bundesbank has just taken would not be possible.'[112]

In mid-August, the Bank of England – in an internal paper that bore the hallmarks of deputy governor Eddie George – sought to reassure the Treasury on the underlying strength of the UK's foreign exchange reserves.[113] To discuss the rising ERM tension, finance ministers and central bankers from France, Germany, Britain and Italy travelled to Paris for secret talks on 26 August. Before setting off for the Seine, Norman Lamont – a politician who distrusted European integration and had been given Major's old job as Chancellor of the Exchequer when the latter became prime minister – formally announced he wanted to remove 'any scintilla of doubt' about the UK's ERM commitment. This was followed by overt intervention from the Bank of England to shore up sterling.[114] The effect was undone when Reimut Jochimsen, a sturdily self-opinionated member of the Bundesbank Council, pointed publicly to 'potential for realignment' within the ERM – creating a fresh wave of sterling selling.[115] Just before the meeting, Kohl and Mitterrand held talks on the North Sea island of Borkum.

Kohl:	'This evening there is an important meeting of the four European finance ministers. The real problem is Britain.'
Mitterrand:	'Yes, I have received some desperate phone calls from Major.'
Kohl:	'The Franc has held up well.'
Mitterrand:	'Yes, but it has still suffered a shock.'
Kohl:	'It has managed!'
Mitterrand:	'If we have to raise interest rates, that will accelerate the recession.'[116]

The finance ministers' meeting in Paris on 26 August displayed growing helplessness in the face of the coming European currency storm. According to Bundesbank deputy president Tietmeyer (standing in for Schlesinger who was on holiday),

> The other finance ministers came with a message wanting a cut in German interest rates. I said this was out of the question, but I added that I could imagine, from a personal point of view, that Germany could be ready to have a unilateral revaluation for the D-Mark . . . However, the other finance ministers rejected this. They didn't want to discuss currency adjustments, only interest rates.[117]

France was adamant it would maintain the D-Mark link. Britain did not want to devalue alone (or with the Italians). Lamont explained, 'I was reluctant to have a unilateral devaluation of the pound because that would have exposed us to higher interest rates. If we had devalued, we would have continued in the ERM and would have paid an interest rate penalty. The French would not play on realignment, because of the approach of the Maastricht referendum.'[118] After the Paris session, Major telephoned Kohl to browbeat him on interest rates. He called Giuliano Amato, the Italian prime minister, to urge him to do the same.[119] Amato had already been growing increasingly worried about growing pressure on the lira and other weaker currencies in the ERM. Four days after the finance ministers' meeting, he flew to Paris for a secret Sunday encounter with Bérégovoy to explore whether France could join in a general ERM realignment. The French prime minister said he understood Italy's plight but could do nothing to help – because any sign of Franc weakness would reduce the chances of a Yes vote in the 20 September referendum. Amato told him it was highly unlikely that the lira could hold out for that long.[120]

Major wrote again to Kohl saying the Bundesbank had to choose 'between a cut in interest rates in Germany and an increase in rates across all Europe . . . The collapse of the dollar has pushed the D-Mark to record highs and forced up other ERM currencies too. The pound has now reached $2, an absurd level . . . The ERM has become stretched, with the pound, the French Franc and the lira all close to the bottom of their bands.' Major warned Kohl that UK interest rates might rise to 12 per cent, and that the French and Italians would have to follow suit. 'I urged him to tell the Bundesbank Council that higher interest rates risked turning the recession into a slump.'

At the end of August, Major wrote to Kohl for the third time. 'German reunification is at the heart of these problems . . . Britain strongly supported [this] but many in Britain believe they are now having to pay a high price . . . The attitude adopted by the Bundesbank . . . is difficult to understand.'[121] Finally stung into action, Kohl summoned his monetary helmsmen to the Bonn chancellery on 2 September to work out a common Bonn–Frankfurt policy – effectively healing months of disputes between the Bundesbank and the government. 'The Major letters were totally counter-productive,' Waigel explained. 'This brought the two sides together.'[122] Tietmeyer commented that Major's action in trying to influence the Bundesbank via Bonn was particularly flawed – although similar pressure applied by President Mitterrand later accomplished greater success.[123] Later, Major robustly defended his tactics:

> There was no point in discussing a detailed economic point with Helmut on the telephone . . . I was not in a position to write directly to the Bundesbank. If I had asked the Governor of the Bank of England to write to the Bundesbank, this would have had less clout. If I had dispatched a 'round robin' letter signed by Amato, Bérégovoy and myself, there would have been the danger of a leak which would have caused turmoil on the markets. The only available option for me as British prime minister was to write to Helmut. To have done nothing would not have been the right course.

The Bonn crisis meeting gave the Germans a dress rehearsal for an ill-tempered European finance ministers' gathering at the spa town of Bath in south-west England on 4 and 5 September. Italy raised its key interest rate to 15 per cent. The British government announced a 10 billion ECU international bank loan to defend sterling – a sign of British defiance, as well as misplaced confidence.

Italian prime minister Amato had been considering a similar 'jumbo loan' for Italy – but turned down the idea on the grounds that, if his country had to devalue against other European currencies, repaying the loan would be prodigiously expensive. Lamont, who was chairing the Bath meeting, repeatedly asked Schlesinger to cut rates. Increasingly impatiently, Schlesinger said 'no'.[124] 'Everyone in Europe saw a fall in German interest rates as the solution to the economic tensions,' said Leigh-Pemberton.[125] 'The Germans' position at Bath was obstinately resolute. They were egging each other on to stand fast. They knew a crisis was coming up.' Dutch finance minister Wim Kok recalled, 'Everyone dug in their heels.'[126] According to Lamont, 'I had to ask for interest rates to fall. I was aware of the Bundesbank's independence and that the move might be counter-productive, but it was our last resort. I was speaking on behalf of others too – the French, the Italians, the Irish. They all asked me as chairman to make the points I did.'[127] Lamont's successor Kenneth Clarke later criticised British tactics: 'There was a ludicrous assumption that, if things got difficult, the Germans would bail us out. However, Kohl was not interested in economics. He was always very respectful of the economic judgement of Schlesinger and Tietmeyer at the Bundesbank.'[128]

The Bath meeting was followed by fresh currency attrition. Sweden, which was not in the ERM but kept the krona pegged to European currencies, implemented drastic monetary tightening that subsequently pushed overnight lending rates to an astronomical 500 per cent. The Finnish markka was floated and fell 14 per cent against the ECU.[129] Speculative pressure mounted on the Italian currency. The Banca d'Italia's Lamberto Dini said:

> The crisis came about not because of balance of payments weakness in any particular country, but because of speculative action by the markets. After the liberalisation of capital movements in 1990–91, Italy experienced a major inflow of short term capital and the lira tended to appreciate against the D-Mark. The large Italian budget deficit was perversely seen as a source of strength, because it encouraged this inflow of capital. Operators speculated against lira by borrowing through Italian banks. During the crisis period in September 1992, we had an outflow of reserves of $40 billion to $50 billion. Everyone underestimated the strength of capital flows.

The Emminger Letter Reappears

On Friday, 11 September, a day after the Banca d'Italia publicly complained about 'excessively high' German interest rates,[130] the lira fell to its lowest permitted ERM point, triggering enormous obligatory intervention from the Bundesbank and Banca d'Italia.[131] In the light of massive inflows of liquidity threatening to disrupt the German money supply, the Bundesbank invoked the shadowy 'Emminger letter' of 1978 under which the central bank could ask the government to free it from the constraint of making unlimited support purchases of weak European currencies. The news shocked the Italians. Carlo Azeglio Ciampi, governor of the Banca d'Italia, was conferring with Amato and finance minister Piero Barucci at the prime minister's office in Rome when Ciampi was called to the telephone to be told that the Bundesbank would stop intervening on Monday. 'When he came back, he was pale, almost white,' Amato recalled.

At 9 p.m. on 11 September Kohl, Waigel and leading German officials gathered for a crisis meeting at the Bundesbank.[132] 'The message from the Government,' Tietmeyer said, 'was that they were ready for a D-Mark revaluation, while Schlesinger indicated that, in this case, a German interest rate cut would be possible. It was decided that [finance ministry State Secretary Horst] Köhler and I would travel the following day first to Paris and then to Rome.'[133] The key interlocutor in Paris was French Treasury director Jean-Claude Trichet, chairman of the Monetary Committee, in charge of European realignment procedures, while the Rome journey was necessary to win the support of the Italians that the lira would be devalued as part of the package. Schlesinger recalled, 'The order to Köhler and Tietmeyer was that they were to seek to carry out as broad realignment as possible' – involving a formal lowering of the ERM currency values of the four weakest currencies, the lira, sterling, peseta and escudo. Schlesinger told Kohl and the others at the Friday evening Bundesbank meeting: 'The stronger and wider the realignment, the more I will be able to ask for a cut in interest rates among the Central Bank Council.'

The Germans maintained afterwards that they believed, erroneously, that – after discussions with Köhler and Tietmeyer – Trichet would convene a full-scale European realignment meeting on Sunday in Brussels. The German monetary authorities – normally so outspoken in international monetary councils – were distinctly *sotto voce* in their conversations with other countries that weekend. The Paris talks with the visiting Germans were unclear and inconclusive. Only a week before the potential earthquake of the Maastricht referendum, France never had any intention to hold a full Monetary Committee meeting.[134] The Germans complied with this view – believing that the risks of a full-scale realignment outweighed the advantages. French finance minister Michel Sapin explained:

We [the government] were obsessed by the Maastricht referendum on 20 September. We were convinced that Maastricht was indispensable for the creation of the new Europe. If we created additional tensions on the foreign exchange markets, there would be a greater risk that the referendum would end in a No. At the meeting with the Germans [on 12 September], everyone was ambiguous. We were playing for a calm outcome. We French were certain in our minds that we did not want to have a full meeting of the European Monetary Committee, but we did not express this clearly. The Germans were trying to test whether there was an opportunity for a full EMS realignment, in exchange for a larger cut in German interest rates, but they also did not express themselves clearly.[135]

According to Nederlandsche Bank director André Szász, who was telephoned by Trichet over the weekend on the possibility of a Monetary Committee meeting, 'When facing political disagreements or politically sensitive issues, central bankers tend to refer to controversies indirectly rather than addressing them bluntly. This may have contributed to any misunderstanding.'[136] German finance minister Theo Waigel understood France's reasoning. 'They had kept the rate stable against Germany for many years, even at the cost of high interest rates. They were proud of this achievement. A devaluation would have been a catastrophe. Maintaining the Franc's rate had become part of the central doctrine of the French state.'[137]

The Rome talks with the two German emissaries were far more clear-cut. By invoking the Emminger letter, Germany forced Italy's hand. Tietmeyer told his Italian hosts, led by finance minister Piero Barucci, 'There's no way we can support the lira any more.'[138] Italy agreed to devalue the lira that weekend. But the agreement was reached in a telephone conference of the Monetary Committee, rather than in a full-scale meeting, and no other European currencies were involved – leaving many ERM members overvalued against the D-Mark, a legacy that was to dog the exchange rate system for months. Crucially, the Germans – who seem to have significantly over-estimated the strength of the German economy – did not communicate to the UK over the crucial weekend any suggestion that a wider realignment would have brought deeper cuts in Bundesbank interest rates.[139] Barucci recalled:

[Köhler and Tietmeyer] maintained that the German economy was booming. In order to avoid inflation they could not further reduce their interest rates. In fact the German economy in the third quarter of 1992 was starting to decline. The two officials held out the chance of a wider reduction of the discount and the

Lombard rate in the event of a multilateral realignment. That would have required UK and French approval.

John Major made clear that no wider ERM change was ever broached, since neither France nor Britain wanted it.

If we had called for such a meeting, would we have got it? If we had tried to press for a general realignment, with sterling and the French Franc moving down together, then the French would have flipped – it would have cut them off at the knees. We wouldn't have got the realignment that we needed. There would have been a huge row and no outcome. This might have led to the French voting No in the referendum on 20 September. That would have led to the wrecking of the Maastricht Treaty I helped to negotiate. And the other Europeans would have blamed the wrecking of Maastricht on perfidious Albion. No doubt Jean-Claude Trichet saw things the same way that we did. And that's why – in his capacity as chairman of the Monetary Committee – he did not call a realignment meeting.[140]

Against this background, Italian efforts to cajole Britain into a wider realignment were doomed from the start. Following a brief conversation between Lamont and Italian Treasury Minister Barucci, Amato spoke to Major on the telephone on Sunday morning, while the British prime minister was staying with the Queen at the Scottish castle of Balmoral. 'I wanted to convince him to take part in a general realignment,' Amato said. 'He said sterling would not take part in the operation. I asked him if sterling would still be stable after the Italian realignment. He said, "Yes, we feel safe".'[141]

Fabrizio Saccomanni of the Banca d'Italia said, 'It was a terrible thing that weekend. We were left isolated . . . The British attitude was "We can handle that." They said they had recently contracted large loans on the international markets. They had plenty of reserves. I told the Bank of England, "This is going to be a very difficult moment for all of us." But the Bank did not consider that this danger was real.'[142] After the Monetary Committee agreed an overall 7 per cent lira devaluation on Sunday afternoon,[143] the Bundesbank Council met on Monday morning to decide a cut in interest rates. The move, prepared by Schlesinger in telephone calls with his colleagues on Sunday, and announced prematurely by Theo Waigel in a radio interview that evening,[144] resulted in a relatively modest 0.25 point cut in the internationally-significant Lombard rate and 0.5 point cut in discount rate and money market rates – the first Bundesbank credit easing for nearly five years. Although international currency traders viewed the cut as insufficient to quell unrest, the view of the French government – and many market participants – was that Waigel, backed up by Kohl, had press-ganged the Bundesbank to soften its stance.[145] Adding to controversy in Germany over apparent Bonn pressure, German newspapers had a few days earlier carried stories mentioning President Mitterrand's view that future European central bank officials would be no more than 'technicians' carrying out government orders.[146]

Amid the build-up to the coming currency storm, Monday, 14 September saw a quixotic mission by the Treasury and Bank of England to Frankfurt and Bonn to try to persuade the Germans that the sterling exchange rate was economically viable. Treasury chief economic adviser Alan Budd was accompanied by Bank of England chief economist and future governor Mervyn King. The unsatisfactory visit to the Bundesbank and Finance Ministry added to King's general scepticism about European monetary integration. This was 'one of the great wasted journeys', according to Budd: 'My thoughts were that we had done our best to persuade them on the sustainability of the sterling exchange rate, but we weren't at all sure that we had done so.'[147]

On Tuesday, 15 September, Schlesinger received in his twelfth-floor Bundesbank office two reporters from the *Handelsblatt* and *Wall Street Journal*. Schlesinger's newspaper interview marked the turning point of the 1992 crisis. The seeds of the turmoil had been planted years previously, but the press encounter unleashed a trail of disorder: one of the largest bouts of currency intervention in history; the ERM departures of Britain and Italy; a further long-lasting intensification of British suspicions about fixing exchange rates with its European neighbours; and an over-valuation of the D-Mark that lasted several years and significantly depressed economic growth in Germany and Europe. A less principled (or stubborn) central banker than Schlesinger would have foresworn seeing journalists during severe foreign exchange unrest; Schlesinger had plenty of experience that an ill-chosen word could be costly. But Schlesinger was determined to talk to the press to correct the weekend impression, stemming from Waigel's radio broadcast, that politicians were dragooning the Bundesbank into interest rate cuts.[148]

The reporters agreed to check Schlesinger's quotes before publication. However, the *Handelsblatt* did not believe it should seek Bundesbank approval for an abbreviated version – without quotes – sent to news agencies on Tuesday evening.[149] This 'unauthorised' story said Schlesinger had wanted 'a wider-ranging realignment' the previous weekend.[150] Quickly flashed on to bank dealing screens around the world, the news was immediately interpreted as an attack on sterling. During afternoon trading in New York, steady selling of the pound turned into a rout. Among the sellers were the traders of hedge fund manager George Soros, whose flagship Quantum Fund earned a reputed $1 billion from the pound's September 1992 plight. '[Werner] Benkhoff [the *Handelsblatt* journalist] wrote his article using indirect speech. The news agencies gave prominence to a one sentence extract saying that I had wished for a larger realignment,' Schlesinger said. 'This was clearly taken out of context. I couldn't deny what I had actually said. The tape recorders recorded it. Another person might have denied this, but I could not do so.'

In London in the early evening of 15 September, as reports came in of Schlesinger's comments, the reaction was explosive. Britain's top monetary officials were meeting at the Treasury to discuss a renewed fall in sterling which – even before the Schlesinger news surfaced – had suffered a bad day. Norman Lamont agreed with Eddie George of the Bank of England that Britain should suspend membership of the ERM if overt Bank of England intervention and higher interest rates failed to stabilise the pound.

Our plan, as agreed that night [15 September – before news of Schlesinger's remarks] for the next day, was that overt intervention should begin between 8 and 8.30 a.m. If that did not succeed, we would put up rates. If that failed to hold the rate, we would have no option but to suspend our membership.[151]

Budd recalled, 'We were in a meeting in the Treasury discussing what to do, when someone came in saying that Schlesinger had given an interview stating that sterling could not survive. Norman Lamont's immediate reaction was to ask Robin Leigh-Pemberton to contact Schlesinger and ask him to withdraw the remarks. Robin left the room and then came back. Lamont asked him whether he had got hold of Schlesinger. Robin explained that we must understand that this was the president of the Bundesbank and getting him to withdraw such a statement was not all that easy. I thought, "It's all over." '

At an American embassy dinner party later that evening,[152] Lamont gave full vent to his feelings. Another guest, *Financial Times* editor Richard Lambert, recalled, 'Norman Lamont arrived late and kept popping out of the room. Lamont came up to me, somewhat agitated, and said, 'The FT is running a story that you know to be a lie, which will have awful consequences.' I got on the telephone to the office, and found out that the Schlesinger statement was the front page story.'[153] From the dinner Lamont ordered further Bank of England efforts to seek Bundesbank clarification. Leigh-Pemberton said, 'Norman Lamont rang up from his dinner to ask me to get on the phone to Schlesinger, to ask him to retract what he had said. I was quite agreeably surprised that I was able to get through to Schlesinger at his home. He said he was trying to sort it out. His attitude was rather apologetic. It was along the lines of: "I'm terribly sorry, Robin, Oh dear, I never thought of that." '[154] Major commented, 'I believe this was incompetence and clumsiness rather than malice. Had it not been for the Schlesinger statement, I think we would have survived the week. If you have the governor of the second most important central bank in the world pointing markets in a certain direction, markets will follow that lead.'[155]

Throughout the next day – Black Wednesday[156] – sterling was pressed to its ERM floor against the D-Mark. Total intervention by the Bank of England, the Bundesbank and other central banks to underpin sterling was around $30 billion.[157] At 9 a.m. Major presided over a gathering of ministers and officials in Whitehall, including Foreign Secretary Douglas Hurd, Trade and Industry Secretary Michael Heseltine and Home Secretary Kenneth Clarke, scheduled to discuss responses to France's forthcoming Maastricht referendum.[158] Instead, the meeting focused on the immediate currency crisis. The plans for a speedy ERM withdrawal were thwarted by British ministers, as Treasury permanent secretary Terry Burns recalled:

> One of the things I underestimated was how long it would take Britain actually to leave the ERM. In 1985, when the Treasury was looking at joining the ERM, [Treasury second permanent secretary] Geoff Littler drew up a paper on the circumstances under which Britain could suspend intervention obligations at a time of extreme crisis. It was always anticipated that we would make use of this in an emergency. On the morning of 16 September there was terrific pressure on sterling early on. Interest rates were raised at 11 o'clock [from 10 to 12 per cent] but the increase had almost no effect. At a subsequent meeting the chancellor, supported by the Bank of England, decided to pull out as soon as possible. In the event, other ministers had to be consulted and it took the rest of the day. It would have been less untidy if we had suspended intervention earlier and not announced the second increase in interest rates. We didn't, because the politics were extremely difficult.[159]

Major rejected immediate suspension.[160] Hurd agreed, stressing that 'the rules of the ERM [should be] followed'.[161] Hurd was guided by the political reflection that the UK decision to leave the ERM was 'probably temporary . . . It would be unwise to act in bad faith to partners whose help in the matter we had sought and might seek again.'[162] Clarke said afterwards: 'After the Bank of England put up interest rates by 2 percentage points and it didn't work, we should have left. But then Douglas Hurd put forward the opinion of the Foreign Office lawyers that we were under a treaty obligation to stay in the mechanism and carry on intervening ... This was rather pedantic. Who would enforce this point of law? Who was going to challenge us in the courts? The only person who could perhaps have claimed later that he was damaged would have been George Soros.'[163] A more forceful Treasury mandarin than soft-spoken Terry Burns would, perhaps, have overruled ministers, saving billions of dollars from British reserves. Alan Budd recalled: 'I felt as if I knew what it's like to be a German general at the end of the war, with defeat after defeat and people coming into the room with more bad news. The question is then raised: When do you surrender? In a sense it's always too late, because if you had surrendered a day earlier, fewer people would have been killed.'[164]

At 2.15 p.m. the government announced a further 3 percentage-point rise in interest rates, again with negligible effect.[165] Major telephoned Bérégovoy and Kohl to inform them of the dire circumstances and request support. 'Bérégovoy was hugely supportive, and very agitated. The focus was partly on his own referendum. He was worried that the pressure would intensify.'[166] At the cabinet meeting that day, Bérégovoy told French ministers, 'Britain is paying dearly for the policies of Mrs Thatcher.'[167] Kohl informed Major the affair was a matter for the Bundesbank: 'I am powerless to intervene.'[168] At 4 p.m. the Bank of England told other central banks sterling's ERM membership was being 'temporarily' suspended – four hours after the Treasury had intended, a delay that cost many billions of dollars from the reserves.[169] In New York trading, sterling immediately fell 3 per cent against the D-Mark – reaping spectacular rewards for traders who had sold the currency (which they had themselves borrowed) at higher levels only twenty-four hours earlier.[170]

Sterling's agony ended when the European Monetary Committee met shortly before midnight in Brussels under Trichet's chairmanship to formalise the ERM withdrawal. The Treasury's Nigel Wicks related how 'within a few hours Britain's foreign exchange reserves had been transformed from a plus of more than $20 billion into a significant negative position'.[171] Italy suspended its membership too. The Spanish peseta was devalued by 5 per cent. Lamont announced: 'We are floating and we will set monetary policy in this country to meet our objectives. It will be a British economic policy and a British monetary policy.'[172] Helmut Schlesinger delivered an acerbic postscript (in secret) six weeks later when he told France's ambassador to Bonn that Britain's ERM departure had been 'inevitable'.[173]

The Battle of the Franc

In the wake of the sterling, lira and peseta upheavals, the focus of European currency unrest switched to the French Franc. This was a state of affairs that France had faced many times in monetary hostilities with the Germans. But the complexity and bitterness of the Battle of the Franc were unique. During four separate skirmishes during an eleven-month period, the French and German monetary authorities engaged in frequently vitriolic confrontation. The Battle of the Franc ended in an uneasy truce in August 1993. Cooperative spirit between the two countries was restored – but only after deep-seated tussles that left lasting wounds. The Bundesbank – though frequently pressed into a series of seemingly inextricable corners – emerged with its fighting spirit untamed. France rescued its currency policy, which finished basically intact – but at an enormous political and economic cost. This contributed to a legacy of resentment and frustration on sporadic display in France at the end of the first decade of the twenty-first century.

There was one significant difference compared with past tension. For the first time, the upheaval on the foreign exchanges coincided with a period where France had a lower inflation rate than Germany – and felt under no obligation to devalue; this was a point on which the German government (but not always the Bundesbank) concurred. However, financial market speculators were selling Francs in unprecedented quantities, in an opportunistic quest to force France away from the 'strong Franc' policy decided by Mitterrand and Delors, and make profits by buying back the currency later on at a lower level. Great issues of national and European policy were at stake. On the one hand, France was attempting to draw level with Germanic standards of currency management as a fundamental part of its European aim of bringing the Germans into monetary union. All Left- and Right-wing administrations during Mitterrand's long presidency maintained this commitment. As John Major put it later, 'The difference between the French position and ours in 1992 was that the whole of the French establishment wanted a single currency as a means of tying down Leviathan, of binding the Bundesbank.'[174]

On the other hand, successive French governments also had a desperate need to reduce interest rates to promote recovery, lower unemployment and gain electoral popularity. There were built-in contradictions in the two aims. By raising interest rates to maintain the D-Mark parity, France deepened its economic downturn, hampered the task of meeting the Maastricht convergence conditions – and thus made accomplishing EMU more, not less, difficult.

In contrast to sterling and the lira, the German central bank believed the Franc was correctly valued in 1992–93.[175] However, the Bundesbank repeatedly criticised France's politically-induced propensity to accelerate interest rate cuts in the interests of economic growth. Each time the Banque de France went too far in reducing interest rates, it was punished by the markets and by the Bundesbank. The result was that French borrowing costs had to stay at more punitive levels, and for a longer period, than during comparable occasions in the past.

The Paris government and the Banque de France did not confront only banks and currency traders; the conflict was engaged with the Germans, too – in particular, the Bundesbank and its president Helmut Schlesinger. The policy survived but – ominously for France – at nearly every stage the Bundesbank succeeded in maintaining the upper hand. British officials for many years were jealous of what they believed was Germany's far greater political commitment to support France rather than the UK during the 1992–93 upheavals. Yet hitherto secret French and German documents reveal that the Bundesbank frequently aided the Franc only with great hesitation. Furthermore, the Germans attached conditions on French interest rates that would have been unacceptable in the UK.[176] However, the record shows that, at the very top – between Kohl and Mitterrand – the alliance was incomparably stronger than that between Major and his two Continental European partners. It was this factor, far more than fundamental understanding between the French and German monetary authorities, that tipped the balance for France to win its long struggle to maintain the D-Mark parity.

The relationship between Kohl and Mitterrand was put to an immediate test four days after Black Wednesday. On Sunday, 20 September the French Maastricht referendum resulted in a Yes vote by a tiny majority. Mitterrand was stricken by the after-effects of an operation for prostate cancer. But he showed himself on peak political form by cajoling an initially hesitant Kohl into propping up the Franc. The German government, for its part – for the second time in ten days, following wrangling over the 14 September interest rate cut – exerted forceful pressure on the Bundesbank to achieve a pro-European outcome.

When the foreign exchange markets opened on Monday, 21 September, the narrow pro-Maastricht referendum victory led to severe Franc selling. The currency markets believed that French political opposition to Maastricht was unlikely to die down – and question marks would remain on the 'strong Franc'. Speculators borrowed massive quantities of Francs from French banks and then sold them against D-Marks, leading to heavy Franc intervention purchases by the Banque de France to defend the currency. As French finance minister Michel Sapin explained, 'The referendum result created a difficult situation for the French authorities. If it had been a No, then that would have been the end of the treaty, so the result would have been clear-cut. If it had been a significant Yes, that would have calmed down the markets. The French authorities were uncertain how to react.'[177]

European finance ministers and central bankers were in Washington for the International Monetary Fund annual meeting. Complex interactions ensued, including a myriad of trans-Atlantic telephone calls. On Monday, 21 September, finance minister Sapin, Treasury director Trichet and Banque de France governor de Larosière, held inconclusive talks with the German delegation to the IMF, led by finance minister Waigel and Bundesbank president Schlesinger, to try to resolve the extreme tension on the foreign exchanges. The Germans rejected a major Franc support plan, with Schlesinger adamant that the Bundesbank would not cut interest rates. On 22 September speculative attacks against the Franc intensified. As a sign of solidarity, the Bundesbank offered to intervene by openly purchasing Francs in the markets for the account of the Banque de France – but the gesture did not go far enough for the French, who wished the Bundesbank to make an open-ended commitment to purchase Francs against D-Marks on its own account. Mitterrand's advisers told him in Paris, 'The meetings at Washington have produced nothing. Messrs. Waigel and Schlesinger do not wish to speak of a cut in their interest rates . . . M. Sapin has had his requests rejected . . . We are at a crossroads. Will the European Monetary System and, with it, Economic and Monetary Union survive unbridled speculation?'[178] Trichet, director of the French Treasury, told Ciampi, the governor of the Banca d'Italia, at a private Washington breakfast meeting that the Franc would probably have to devalue.

Fulfilling a long-scheduled plan to meet after the Maastricht referendum, Mitterrand and Kohl conferred at the Elysée Palace on 22 September. French prime minister Bérégovoy wrote to Kohl the previous day requesting fresh German support. Mitterrand said at the beginning of the meeting that France might have to leave the European Monetary System 'unless other ways can be found to keep it alive'.[179] Mitterrand said 'billions [of dollars] of drugs money' were attacking the Franc and blamed the Bundesbank for talking down other currencies following the cut in German interest rates the previous week. Showing characteristic insouciance on monetary issues, Kohl initially claimed to be unaware of the gravity of the crisis.

Mitterrand: 'The speculation has been unleashed. It will be enough if we hold out for three days, and then it will have failed. I am aware of the independence of the Bundesbank, but what does it want? To remain the last one standing on a field of ruins? Because it will be a field of ruins.'

Kohl: 'I'm surprised by your dramatic tone. People told me yesterday that everything was calming down. I read Bérégovoy's letter in the aeroplane. I don't understand.'

Mitterrand re-affirmed that France would not devalue the Franc. Kohl used a break in his talks in Paris to telephone Horst Köhler, Number 2 in the German Finance Ministry, in Washington to receive an update on the currency position. Kohl returned to the meeting with Mitterrand. According to the Elysée Palace transcript, Kohl declared that whatever action was to be taken would have to remain secret.

Kohl: 'They have told me that the situation is not that serious and the Bundesbank is prepared to help. It will announce that it will not raise rates, is considering a rate cut and will extend a further $5 billion credit line to defend the Franc.'

Mitterrand: 'Only implacable political will can stop the speculation. We have to show that.'

Kohl: 'I cannot say that the parity will be maintained. I cannot go over the head of the Bundesbank. That's not my business. That is the Bundesbank's business. This should not appear like political manipulation. I had a terrible discussion with the Bundesbank last week. That has become known. I cannot start that again. I will try, all the same, to see if we can obtain a rapid declaration from the Governors. But I don't wish anyone to know about this. If I am asked, on coming out of here, I will say that we have discussed the situation in Europe after the referendum. As to monetary affairs, I will say that the discussions have taken place in Washington.'

Kohl broke off from the meeting for a second time, telephoning Hans Tietmeyer in Washington. On returning, the chancellor was more business-like:

Kohl: 'I had Tietmeyer on the line. He shows no sign of nerves. I told him I would like a declaration from the Governors within the next hour on maintaining the parity between the Franc and the D-Mark. That is also his view. In addition, they will make available DM19 billion to support the Franc and the Bundesbank will lower money market rates below 9 per cent. But it is not up to the politicians to say that.'

Mitterrand: 'Let us try to go forward on this basis. The most important message is that the Governors say that the parity must be maintained. I am not so much in favour of the independence of central banks, but the advantage is, for them at least, that when they speak, they are believed. We have two great advantages. The first is my own unwavering will that we shall maintain the Franc–D-Mark parity. The second is the will of Germany and France, to be expressed in the communiqué of the Governors.'

Kohl's crucial phone call with Tietmeyer catalysed the German and French delegations in Washington into a flurry of action to restart the stalled talks. In a series of telephone exchanges with the leaders of the German monetary establishment in Washington, the chancellor left none of his interlocutors in any doubt about the force of his will.[180] Just forty-five minutes after the Mitterrand–Kohl meeting finished in Paris, a tumultuous Franco-German monetary gathering got under way in Washington – starting at 12.15 Washington time and lasting around four-and-a-half hours.[181]

Treasury director Jean-Claude Trichet faced what appeared a highly unequal contest in the German delegation's offices at the Sheraton Hotel. Sapin and de Larosière had left central Washington to return to France.[182] Trichet sat down accompanied solely by Banque de France official Francis Cappanera.[183] On the other side were Waigel and Köhler from the German finance ministry and Schlesinger, Tietmeyer and Rieke (head of the international department) from the Bundesbank. Gert Haller from the finance ministry, and Otmar Issing, the Bundesbank's Directorate member for economics, joined the discussion.[184] Tensions ran high. Waigel, who sympathised with Trichet, angrily asked Schlesinger to stop Rieke taking souvenir photos of the French Treasury director squirming under unequal odds. After two highly pressurised days in Washington coping with the Franc's travails, Trichet's showdown at the Sheraton was the supreme test of his nerves. He surmounted the trial. With martial pride – 'I felt I was "on the front" ' – Trichet wrote an extraordinary handwritten letter to Mitterrand fifteen months later recalling the episode, enclosing his own twelve-page note of the meeting.[185]

In his letter to Mitterrand, Trichet said that on 21 September Kohl had given the German monetary delegation in Washington an 'instruction' – a step that would have formally contradicted the Bundesbank Law. Trichet's message to Mitterrand underlined striking – and long-lasting – differences in perceptions about central banking independence between Germany and France. Schlesinger and Tietmeyer, for their part, subsequently rejected Trichet's interpretation as a misunderstanding of the Bonn–Frankfurt dialogue, and affirmed that Kohl – despite deploying forceful arguments – left the final decision to the Bundesbank. The affair had a wry sequel: in 2008, ensconced as the highly independent president of the European Central Bank, Trichet publicly recalled the marathon Washington encounter, describing it as 'particularly tense, and particularly successful' at a ceremony in Berlin in which he received one of Germany's highest honours, the Grand Cross, from the hands of Horst Köhler – by then, Germany's federal president.[186]

During the 1992 gathering, according to Trichet's own *aide-memoire*, and the accounts of others who were there, passions rose to great heights. Schlesinger – who did most of the talking on the German side – argued that France had either to raise interest rates or devalue. The Bundesbank president initially refused to sign a declaration that the Franc's parity was inviolable. According to Trichet's own account, the exchange went as follows:

Schlesinger: 'I will not sign any joint declaration by the French and German central banks on maintaining the parity. Don't count on me for that. I am only the president of the Bundesbank, nothing more. I do not wish to face the ridicule of being contradicted by the facts twelve hours, twenty-four hours or forty-eight hours later. That is not the attitude of a responsible central bank! If you are in the situation of the French Franc, you devalue. France has done nothing to defend the Franc! Nothing serious! It has not even made use of our offer to buy Francs in Frankfurt for your account . . .!'

Trichet: 'The German finance minister will understand that I am stupefied and indignant. The remarks that we have just heard do not correspond to the orientations of the heads of state and government of the two countries. This language is the language of break-down . . .'

Waigel: *(visibly moved, makes conciliatory gestures)*

Trichet: *(turning to Schlesinger)*: 'The alliance of France and Germany has been the pivot of the European system since the reconciliation. Your speech and your tone indicate the system is going to burst apart.'

Trichet gave a long exposition of why a Franc devaluation was unjustified and what France had done to support its currency, including $15 billion in intervention before the referendum and $10 billion afterwards, as well as a rise in interest rates. He said the Banque de France would be willing to accept that the Bundesbank intervened for France's account in Frankfurt, on condition that the markets were not told that this was the case.

There followed a meeting break in which Kohl – in a Parisian restaurant after the talks with Mitterrand – telephoned Waigel and Schlesinger in Washington. Trichet gave a telephoned report to the French finance ministry and prime minister's office. During the pause, Trichet, by his own account, took the future German president Horst Köhler aside, and imparted a message 'of rare violence' regarding Germany's European priorities.

> I told him with brutality that the Bundesbank (and Germany) were making a mistake if they thought they could treat us in the same way that England and Italy had been treated quantitatively and qualitatively. We were not comparable, neither economically nor politically nor strategically.

After the phone calls with Kohl, the German side showed more conciliation; Köhler said the Germans would accept a common declaration.[187] Schlesinger said he would sign it only if the two other Directorate members at the meeting, Tietmeyer and Issing, agreed. The Bundesbank agreed to raise total credits to the Banque de France to DM39 billion – DM4 billion more than granted to the Bank of England during the Black Wednesday turmoil. Again (as in the case of Italy on 11 September) citing the principles of the 1978 Emminger letter, Schlesinger declared that support by the Bundesbank could not be unlimited, in view of the danger to Germany of a liquidity build-up from massive intervention. The Bundesbank president insisted that if automatic intervention to support the Franc on its ERM floor exceeded DM10 billion, Germany would convene the European Monetary Committee as a prelude to a Franc devaluation.[188]

Schlesinger won Waigel's agreement for his tactics by cannily telling him that the Bonn government's budget would face extra pressure if unlimited intervention continued.[189] On this crucial issue of possible German intervention suspension, the meeting ended without agreement. In an argument that France was to use again during further stages of the Battle of the Franc, Trichet insisted that, if the Bundesbank was to limit its automatic Franc support, the D-Mark would have to leave the ERM.

After all-night preparations in Paris, the French and German central banks and finance ministries published a joint communiqué early on 23 September, declaring the sanctity of the D-Mark–Franc parity.[190] Accompanied by large-scale central bank intervention funded by the Bundesbank (totalling $32 billion in the week to 23 September[191]), increases in money market interest rates in France and cuts in Germany, the communiqué succeeded temporarily in quelling anti-Franc speculation. 'Germany had its own interest in signing this statement', Sapin said. 'Schlesinger must have realised that, because of unification pressures, Germany was starting to lose its position as the 'top pupil' in the European class. He saw the economic situation getting worse. Preventing a large Franc devaluation against the D-Mark was important to help not just the French but also the German economy.'[192] Mitterrand's economics adviser Guillaume Hannezo told the president that France's hard line had paid off: 'M. Schlesinger gave in only when the French delegation broke off the negotiations and when it was clear that we would not devalue but would require the Germans to respect or repudiate its EMS obligations.'[193] Hannezo reiterated Paris's surprise over the discovery of the Emminger letter limiting the Bundesbank's intervention obligations. 'This is singular: a treaty from state to state can be repudiated by an independent public organ.'

The Paris–Washington struggle represented only the opening salvo in the Battle of the Franc. The UK government watched the Franc's rescue closely. When John Major visited Mitterrand in Paris at the end of September to discuss the Maastricht process, the two leaders swapped criticism of the Bundesbank.

Major: 'The monetary business has been the root of all evil. The recent actions of the Bundesbank have created enormous difficulties between Britain and Germany. I have found it very difficult to quieten things down. We believe in London that the Bundesbank gave all the information necessary [to the foreign exchange markets] to damage sterling . . . You have also had to make great efforts to support the Franc.'

Mitterrand: 'We have intervened after the difficulties of the pound, and we have kept an eye on the markets.'

Major: 'The shock was caused by Schlesinger's remarks after the Bundesbank lowered its interest rates. We could no longer save the pound. The Bundesbank refused to lower its rates any more. We increased ours by 2 per cent and then by 5 per cent, without effect. We had no choice but to leave the system. That led to the most serious government crisis for 25 years . . .'

Mitterrand: 'I am not surprised . . . We have had to face up to a financial crisis which has been sudden, powerful and unjust . . . Without doubt there was a certain brutality in the attitude of the Bundesbank and its president.'[194]

Major mentioned to Mitterrand an incompetent attempt by Bonn's London embassy to correct British press stories about alleged Bundesbank misdeeds. The embassy leaked to the *Financial Times* part of a Schlesinger letter to

Lamont explaining the Bundesbank's role. 'That letter was personal and confidential,' Major said. 'This afternoon the embassy has given a version of the letter to the press. It has led to a real explosion – politically it's a catastrophe for the Conservative Party.'[195] In view of British sensitivities about Germany's apparently more generous treatment for France than for the UK, French officials agreed to keep secret the nature of Kohl's conversation with Mitterrand on 22 September. According to an internal Elysée Palace note, 'We have been instructed to say nothing to the press, so as not to put Kohl in difficulty, and not to give credibility to the idea that a political authority could give instructions to central banks.'[196]

A new round of monetary tension flared up in November with devaluations of the peseta and escudo, necessitating steady Banque de France intervention to prevent the Franc from falling to its ERM floor. In a meeting with Italian prime minister Giuliano Amato, Mitterrand set down his philosophical vision why the solution was monetary union.

Mitterrand: 'If there wasn't this interplay among European currencies, speculation wouldn't exist. The Franc nearly succumbed. It is intolerable. There is no reason why the policy of a state should be at the mercy of volatile capital which does not represent any real wealth, or creation of real goods. It is an intolerable immorality.'

Amato: 'I agree with you.'

Mitterrand: 'It has to stop.'

Amato: 'That does not just depend on us. We need to go further down the road of integration.'

Mitterrand: 'One day the only important currencies will be the Ecu, the dollar and the yen.'

Amato: 'Two centuries ago, the Socialists believed they could abolish money. In any case the single currency would be very useful.'[197]

On the eve of an end-year Edinburgh summit meeting in December 1992, Europe-wide ratification of the Maastricht Treaty seemed to have run into political setbacks nearly everywhere. This spilled over into renewed pressure on the Franc. Finance minister Sapin asked Mitterrand to send 'a very firm letter' to Kohl reminding him of German 'responsibilities' in the EMS.[198] Mitterrand told Kohl, 'We have suffered two monetary squalls as a result of Schlesinger's declarations. We nearly came to disaster . . . If we didn't have the support of your political will, I ask myself how we would have been able to resist.'[199] A week later Jean-Claude Trichet forecast new tussles:

The situation is extremely dangerous. The Anglo-Saxon markets, in London and New York, are playing for the destruction of the European Monetary System. It's the same with the British media. The European recession, which is becoming more and more visible, is creating supplementary element[s] of uncertainty and trouble. German interest rates have not fallen since September, which strengthens the market's conviction of the vulnerability of the exchange rate mechanism. We continue to be under very great pressure. We need to envisage all eventualities, including that we will be in an acute crisis ... We must be ready to take all possible joint action ... We should be ready to lower German interest rates because the survival of the system itself is at stake; and also to announce a rapid acceleration of European monetary construction built on the D-Mark and the Franc ... France will not limit its interventions to defend the parity. Each of us will have to live up to our responsibilities. We will not quit the system. Germany will have to choose.[200]

Prime minister Bérégovoy intensified pressure on the Germans with a strong letter to Helmut Kohl pointing out that French real (inflation-adjusted) interest rates were at an unprecedented level and asking the Bundesbank to ease credit. He continued, 'A slowdown in economic activity in Europe has deep repercussions on employment, both in France and in Germany ... I must alert you once more to the consequences.'[201]

But the Bundesbank delayed further cuts in its leading interest rates until February 1993.[202] Further currency unrest hit another weaker currency in the ERM, the Irish pound, which was devalued in February, amid a further upsurge in attacks on the Franc.[203] Heavy defeat for Bérégovoy's Socialist government in the March parliamentary elections – resulting in a new spell of 'cohabitation' between Mitterrand and the Gaullists – lifted confidence in the French economy. Mitterrand's new prime minister was former finance minister Edouard Balladur. Like Bérégovoy before him, Balladur hardened his previously lukewarm support for monetary union[204] and – benefiting from close links to de Larosière and Trichet (his former chief of staff while finance minister) – started the process of making the Banque de France independent.[205]

The French government remained haunted by fears of fresh unrest. Balladur told Mitterrand that he would support an unchanged D-Mark–Franc parity 'even if it cannot be excluded that in three or six months, as the result of developments in Germany, I will experience failure'.[206] France faced a 'cruel dilemma', one of Mitterrand's advisers told him in April. Either the Balladur government could run 'a very restrictive budgetary policy' which would secure EMU and stop the 'vertiginous' rise in public debt, but would reduce growth and raise unemployment. Or the government could give clear priority to growth rather than lowering budget deficits, and face diminishing prospects for EMU and a 'severe attack' on the Franc.[207] The Elysée Palace was aware of German doubts on the Maastricht timetable. 'The Germans are hiding their scepticism less and less. Tietmeyer is speaking of 2002 [for realising EMU].'

The EMS was rocked by further devaluations of the peseta and escudo in May – the fifth realignment in eight months. However, the Banque de France cut interest rates by 3.5 percentage points in the first ten weeks after the arrival of the Balladur government. For a time, from mid-June onwards, short-term French interest rates fell below German levels.[208] A cautionary note from the Elysée Palace warned, 'The Franc is not totally protected from speculative attacks.'[209] Unfortunately for France, in an unguarded radio interview on 24 June, Balladur's new finance minister Edmond Alphandéry suggested that Germany should discuss interest rate cuts at the next Franco-German Economic Council in Paris in early July.[210] The ever-watchful Schlesinger immediately interpreted the statement as an attack on the Bundesbank's independence. Waigel promptly rang Alphandéry to cancel the scheduled meeting. Gloomy French figures on sluggish growth and rising unemployment compounded the markets' view that, in spite of its low inflation rate, France would have to devalue. At the same time, German economic data showed a slight economic improvement, leading financial operators to believe that cuts in German interest rates were coming to an end. This was the prelude to the final round of the Battle of the Franc – which would ultimately suck in most countries in Europe.

According to a lengthy, detailed contemporaneous memorandum from the Bundesbank's Hans Tietmeyer, the new Franc crisis was sparked by the 'increasing doubts of the markets that France could use interest rate policy as an effective defensive weapon [against a declining Franc]'.[211] An ominous signal came when the Bundesbank cut its discount and Lombard rates on 1 July. As if in revenge for the flurry of disagreements that preceded the interest rate move, the D-Mark did not weaken, but firmed against the Franc. Banque de France intervention to support the Franc rose steadily. 'Speculation from the Anglo-Saxon markets' (as an Elysée Palace note put it[212]) rose to new heights on 22 July when the Banque de France purchased DM22 billion worth of Francs to stop the currency falling to near its ERM floor. Balladur asked Jacques Delors, the European Commission president, to phone Kohl to seek a resolution. A secret Franco-German meeting in Munich on the night of 22 July, which started at 10.30 p.m. and lasted until 4 a.m., failed to calm the storm. The French side[213] asked for renewed Bundesbank 'swap' credits of DM15 billion to support the Franc. In exchange for agreement on DM10 billion, the Germans required the Banque de France to lift its own Lombard rate from 7.75 per cent to 10 per cent – an unprecedented degree of conditionality for a 'swap' agreement. The Bundesbank agreed to discuss a 0.25 per cent Lombard rate cut at the next Council meeting. The foreign exchanges were initially calm the next day until Bundesbank Council member Reimut Jochimsen, the bane of Britain during the September 1992 crisis, ruled out Bundesbank interest rate cuts during a lunchtime TV interview – sparking DM4.5 billion in Banque de France foreign exchange intervention to shore up the Franc.[214]

Franco-German currency antagonism reached a peak after the Bundesbank – despite a larger-than-promised 0.5 percentage point cut in Lombard rate – kept its discount rate unchanged on 29 July. Currency markets carried out further heavy Franc sales, triggering large-scale Banque de France intervention. Kohl and Balladur agreed the French and German monetary authorities would meet again in Paris the next day, 30 July. 'The amounts [of intervention] are even larger [than September 1992],' said an Elysée Palace note on 30 July. 'Every European country points to the Bundesbank for unleashing this crisis.'[215] Balladur wrote to Kohl protesting that the Bundesbank's Lombard rate cut was 'insufficient', proclaiming that the latest crisis had cost France $27 billion in intervention and calling on Germany to 'face up to [its] responsibilities'.[216] Balladur suggested unlimited Bundesbank intervention, an 'immediate and adequate' cut in interest rates and direct purchases of Francs for the Bundesbank's own reserves. The move – reminiscent of Edward Heath's plea for unlimited German support in 1973 – would have effectively merged the French and German money supplies and created premature monetary union on inflationary French terms.

Simultaneously Balladur enraged the Germans by sending a faxed letter to other European governments obliquely suggesting that the D-Mark should quit the ERM to lower tensions for the other currencies.[217] If the D-Mark were to leave, in line with a goal repeatedly put forward by senior French officials over the previous nine months, this would give France the long-sought prize of the EMS 'anchor role'. This was an objective that France was eager to attain, and the Germans were totally determined to frustrate.

On Friday 30 July, Waigel, Schlesinger, Tietmeyer and the new Finance Ministry State Secretary Gert Haller arrived – irritated and late – at the Paris Finance Ministry at 10.30 a.m.,[218] amid heavy international Franc selling. The Banque de France was supporting the Franc with purchases of $100 million a minute at one stage, selling D-Marks borrowed from the Bundesbank. The German visitors' arrival was delayed because the French authorities sent slow-moving mini-buses, not fast cars, to meet them at the military airport south-west of Paris.[219] Waigel commented ironically: 'We meandered through Paris in the early morning and of course arrived too late at the Finance Ministry. I told Alphandéry I had enjoyed watching the mists rise in the grey dawn of Paris and also appreciated visiting the many Parisian bridges that we repeatedly crossed.'

Tietmeyer said the meeting was unprecedented in his twenty-five years of international monetary discussions.[220] Waigel told Alphandéry that the suggestions in the Balladur letter to Kohl were 'unacceptable'. Schlesinger commented: 'The French received us very coldly. We felt that it was like standing in the Hall of Mirrors of Versailles, ready to sign the German capitulation [after the First World War]. It was made clear that either we had to carry out unlimited intervention in favour of the Franc, or that Germany had to leave the EMS.'

At 10.45 a.m. Jacques de Larosière declared that the French authorities were letting the Franc fall to its ERM floor – triggering unlimited automatic support intervention, under EMS rules, by the central banks of both the stronger and weaker currencies. Waigel said: 'The French were running out of money. The Bundesbank had intervened to an unbelievable extent. Alphandéry said we should carry on. He could not see that the reserves were running out. We wanted to make a joint Franco-German request to change the D-Mark–Franc parity [at the European Monetary Committee]. But Alphandéry wanted us to make the request by ourselves. He wanted to put the blame on us.'[221] As the meeting was about to end, Schlesinger cold-bloodedly pointed out the enormous sums that the French had borrowed to defend the Franc. He reminded the French that, as a result of currency intervention action, the Banque de France owed the Bundesbank DM34 billion – and that repayment was due shortly.[222]

Waigel, Schlesinger, Tietmeyer and Haller flew to Austria on the afternoon of 30 July to see Kohl in his holiday residence. The chancellor backed the Bundesbank's uncompromising line, and Waigel's stated desire to free the Bundesbank from obligatory intervention on Monday morning.[223] The scene shifted to Brussels where the Monetary Committee (convened unilaterally by Germany) met on Saturday 31 July, followed by a session with finance ministers and central bank governors on Sunday. After many hours of vexatious disagreement, the crisis was resolved at around 2 a.m. on Monday, 2 August – just before currency trading re-opened in the Far East – through a drastic widening of the ERM's fluctuation bands.[224] This was a proposal that the Germans had first put to the French on 22 July, but had been initially rejected. De Larosière recalled:

The initial French proposal was to ask the Germans to leave the EMS, on the grounds that it was German policy that was creating strains in the system. One of the first to speak on this idea were the Dutch, who immediately indicated that they would follow the D-Mark. So did the Belgians. I then telephoned M. Balladur to say that the idea would not work. I realised that the system would only survive with a very large widening of bands.

De Larosière said Balladur's initial proposal of a 6 per cent fluctuation band would be insufficient to deter speculators: 'It would be like putting a big piece of raw meat in front of lions. It would be swallowed in two to three days.'[225] Britain's pro-European Chancellor of the Exchequer Kenneth Clarke, who had replaced Lamont in June, attended the Brussels meeting. Just as the meeting appeared to be breaking up without agreement, Clarke intervened forcibly late at night to promote the growing consensus on wider bands.[226]

Balladur and de Larosière agreed by telephone to press for an exceptional widening of 15 per cent each side of central rates and – after a telephone conversation in which Balladur told Kohl that France would leave the system unless margins were increased to this level – Balladur gave instructions to Alphandéry to proceed accordingly. Allowing currencies to fluctuate by an exceptional wide margin effectively suspended the Exchange Rate Mechanism – but the emergency measure avoided formal devaluations and prevented speculators from making profits. The French prime minister was pleased with his handiwork. 'The next morning Mitterrand phoned me and said: "You've made quite an effort, you put forward 6 per cent, but you have ended up with 15 per cent." So we fought the speculators and we won.'[227]

At the weekly cabinet meeting two days afterwards, Mitterrand acknowledged that the optimal solution would have been to persuade the Germans to leave the ERM. He blamed the unrest squarely on Germany. 'The difficulties stem from Germany's problems in managing its reunification and trying to make the other Europeans pay for it, in the same way as the US has done with its deficit. We are still in a crisis, rather than at the end of it.'[228] The July–August flare-up marked the final skirmish in a series of bitter tests for Franco-German relations, at a pivotal period for shaping post-Cold War Europe. The final struggle brought the break-up of the old European monetary order, and a new campaign – accompanied by fresh strife – for a more durable construct.

EUROPE'S DESTINY

The overall political situation in Europe made monetary union both necessary and desirable. If the political will was there, it would have been wrong – and impossible – for the Bundesbank to oppose it. We had good fortune since we could construct the European Central Bank on the Bundesbank model.
Helmut Schlesinger, former Bundesbank president, 2007[1]

The after-shocks of Maastricht brought a variety of strains and fissures, just when the Europeans should have been celebrating the rebirth of a unified Europe, the arrival of the single market and the blueprint for the single currency. A triumphant wave of western liberal capitalism had crashed on to the beachhead of central and Eastern Europe in 1989–90, tearing away the hold of communism. Yet only three years later the western part of the continent was caught up in the turbulent backwash of its own previous success. This was largely the result of a serious recession in 1993 – on some counts, the worst since the 1930s depression – a delayed legacy of the exchange rate crises of the previous two years. In the East, fragmentation took hold, illustrated by a series of bloody conflicts in former Yugoslavia, the disintegration of the Soviet Union and, less cataclysmically, the break-up of Czechoslovakia. Western Europe's answer, to proceed with tighter integration through monetary union rather than to proceed with a drastic widening of the Community, looked to many observers like the wrong choice for shaping Europe's destiny. Rather than spurring an outward-looking spirit of expansive dynamism, Maastricht gripped Europe in a mood of often contradictory resentments and fears.

One reason for the polarisation was that – as a consequence of the previous monetary turmoil – Western Europe was effectively split across a north–south divide of 'hard' and 'soft' currency blocs. In the first camp were Germany and the other stronger currency countries – Belgium, the Netherlands, Luxembourg and Austria (which joined the Community, along with Sweden and Finland, in 1995) – that had not suffered devaluations in 1992–93. The weaker southern countries included Portugal, Italy, Greece and Spain, later referred to sardonically by foreign exchange traders as the 'Club Med' (and, even less flatteringly, as the PIGS). They all had higher inflation rates than the German-led group, came under recurring foreign exchange attack from rumours of devaluation – and were therefore eager to lock exchange rates against the D-Mark and gain protection from rampant flows of global capital. The schism represented an ideological as well as an economic divide – bearing some resemblances to the split between the Economist and Monetarist approaches to the Werner Plan in the 1970s, with the former group placing priority on economic convergence as prerequisites for monetary union, the latter giving precedence to harmonising monetary regulation of exchange rates.

France, despite Herculean efforts over ten years to maintain German-style economic discipline, straddled an uncomfortable position between the two blocs – and consequently faced the worst of all worlds. To maintain foreign exchange markets' often-faltering belief in the sustainability of the 'hard Franc', France was forced to hold interest rates significantly higher than German levels, despite recording a lower inflation rate than Germany's – circumstances that would normally have produced the reward of lower borrowing costs. France thus endured a vicious circle of slow growth, high budget deficits and rising government debt, generating long-lasting political and social burdens. Tension between the two European blocs ebbed only when, later in the 1990s, a broad-based European recovery gained pace, driven by a much-overdue rally in the dollar and weakening of the D-Mark that mitigated speculative capital inflows into Germany and allowed lower interest rates throughout the continent. The dollar rally during President Bill Clinton's second four-year term effectively rescued the EMU project – a somewhat ironic twist, considering that one of the fundamental aims of EMU was to lessen European exposure to US monetary vicissitudes.

On the discord-studded final journey to the single currency, one of the few issues on which the Europeans could agree was the name for it. The neutral-sounding 'Euro' was chosen in December 1995 as a compromise between other options with more nationalistic connotations. 'Crown' or 'krone' (too central European), 'ecu' (too French), 'gulden' (too German or Dutch) or the prefix 'Euro' in front of existing currency names (too reminiscent of national money) were all rejected. Much dissent surrounded the selection procedure for EMU members, based on the statistical 'convergence criteria' set at Maastricht. Supporters of fiscal and monetary orthodoxy in Germany included Bundesbank president Hans Tietmeyer, the flag-bearer of the Economist view of monetary union, who replaced Schlesinger in 1993. Tietmeyer and his supporters leaned strongly towards a smaller and more homogeneous EMU excluding Italy, which they believed would be a more durable and stable construct than a larger selection of countries.

At the same time as many Germans were plagued by fear of contagion from their neighbours' perceived monetary instability, the weaker bloc of European countries worried that they faced isolation and disruption through exclusion from monetary union. Such concerns ran alongside an opposing anxiety among the stronger currency bloc that exporters from weaker states such as Italy, if they were not permitted to join EMU, would benefit unfairly from permanently devalued currencies. Both the Snake and the European Monetary System had assembled at their core a small number of economically compatible states: if EMU did little more than group these countries into a single currency, then where would be the political and economic advance? As Dietrich von Kyaw, Germany's long-time ambassador to the European Community, put it,

> There were two views regarding the Bundesbank and the future of European currencies. One school of thought held that we should defend our stability culture and uphold the strength of the Bundesbank at all costs. The other strand of opinion was that Germany's export interests depended not merely on a func-tioning internal market but also on the avoidance of currency devaluations in it.[2]

Tension between the stronger and weaker countries was heightened by suspected 'creative accounting' and statistical manipulation by Italy, Greece and other countries to fulfil the Maastricht conditions. Even Germany, in a dramatic reversal of its traditional orthodoxy, at one stage appeared guilty of doctoring accounting procedures in order to meet the EMU conditions – inflaming worries that the new currency, when it was eventually formed, would be inevitably weak.

Swirling controversies over the shaping of Europe were exacerbated by the departures of leaders who had earlier established the momentum behind the monetary plan. In France, President Mitterrand bowed out after two seven-year terms and was replaced by his long-time Gaullist adversary Jacques

Chirac, who immediately injected a strident national tone into French policies. Chirac compounded Europe's problems by rashly calling parliamentary
elections ahead of schedule in 1997, resulting in a Left-wing victory, and – for
the third time in just over a decade – a further volatile period of 'cohabitation'
between a French president and prime minister of different political hues. In
Germany, Helmut Kohl was voted out of office after sixteen years and replaced
by Social Democratic leader Gerhard Schröder, just a few weeks before the
Euro was introduced. While Kohl, with weighty pathos, called the Euro and
European unification 'a matter of war and peace',[3] the new chancellor took a
much more prosaic line, describing the planned new currency as a 'premature
sickly child' that would be weaker than the traditionally strong D-Mark,
would increase German unemployment and would also raise Germany's
economic dominance in Europe.[4] All three predictions were the opposite of
what Kohl had forecast – and all came true.

Radical Shift in Performance

After the 1993 shake-up in the European Monetary System, Europe's four
most important economies underwent a radical shift in economic performance. Germany suffered a substantial revaluation of the D-Mark – the opposite of what was warranted by its flagging economy and relatively high
inflation – sparking a substantial downturn. France, having resolutely nailed
its colours to the D-Mark mast, was similarly damaged by exaggeratedly high
interest rates. Italy, despite benefiting from a falling lira after it left the
Exchange Rate Mechanism, was not able to cut interest rates as fast as the UK.
Italy was caught up in the general downturn, and – like Germany and France
– suffered an economic contraction in 1993, the first time since the Second
World War that these three economies had simultaneously recorded negative
growth. Of the European Big Four, Britain provided the only bright spot,
using post-ERM freedom of manoeuvre to engineer a sharply lower pound
that sparked an unexpectedly robust low-inflation recovery, putting considerable competitive pressure on other countries that remained in the ERM.

The UK brought down interest rates to below German levels by 1993, a
triumph for new methods of monetary control and greater monetary
autonomy for the Bank of England. The result was one of the most radical
transformations in European economic fortunes of any period since the
Second World War. Britain's annual average growth rate in 1988–92 had been
only 1 per cent; in the five years thereafter it rose to 3 per cent. Growth in
Germany, France and Italy declined precipitously from 4, 2.7 and 2.1 per cent

respectively in 1988–92 to around 1.3 per cent in all three countries in 1993–97.[5] Consumer price inflation over the two five year periods fell in all four countries, but the decrease was most significant – and most welcome – in the UK.

Black Wednesday shattered the political credibility of the Major government, paving the way for defeat by Labour in the 1997 election,[6] but produced a far more benign economic outcome than almost anyone had forecast – thanks to the effect of ERM membership in markedly lowering inflation expectations of UK consumers and employers. Just days before Black Wednesday, Major had predicted that any realignment of sterling within the ERM would bring 'rising import prices, rising wages, rising inflation and a long-term deterioration in Britain's competitiveness.'[7] In fact, as he said in 2007, 'If you take out the political cost of leaving, and concentrate on the economics, even though the whole process was quite painful, ERM membership accomplished what no policy prescription had done for fifty years. It brought inflation down and kept it down. Every other policy option tried by Britain had failed to do that.'[8] According to the Treasury's Alan Budd, the coercive element of the ERM served its purpose: 'It worked because interest rates were held at a high level (though they were cut from their peak) for a further two years after we joined the ERM ... The great benefit of ERM membership was that it gave us no choice in the matter.'[9]

Britain's post-Black Wednesday repositioning was helped by Germany's mishandling of the episode. Sterling's ejection from the ERM was the result of interlinked policy errors for which the UK, Germany and the rest of Europe all bore responsibility. Yet the Bundesbank's clumsy communications that led to the September 1992 crisis deflected international attention from UK policy flaws and highlighted those of the Germans. Britain had in fact toyed with the idea of suspending ERM membership on several occasions before Black Wednesday.[10] Schlesinger's *Handelsblatt* interview afforded Britain an exit route, even though it was an uncomfortable and undignified one. By giving Britain little option but to leave the ERM, the Bundesbank enabled Britain to escape in the role of the victim – and to uphold the view on financial markets that it was intent on a resolutely anti-inflation policy.[11]

A further British benefit centred on bargaining with Germany over the political make-up of Europe. After the September storm, Chancellor Kohl believed he owed Major a favour. Sarah Hogg, head of Major's Downing Street policy unit (later chairman of British private equity investment company 3i), said, 'Kohl had led the British prime minister to believe that there would be more support for sterling than there actually turned out to be. I believe

Kohl had a guilty conscience about this afterwards. This was one reason why he helped Britain on a number of occasions during the post-Maastricht process.'[12]

Britain's enormously improved performance was of immeasurable significance to the rest of Europe, because it provided an alternative model to policies elsewhere. The British example of a successfully floating currency increased the pressures on the rest of Europe to move to a single currency within the Maastricht time-frame – or risk a return to generalised floating that could break up the Common Market. Britain's economic revival bolstered the British government's spirits. In an over-confident statement a year after Black Wednesday, John Major echoed Margaret Thatcher's traditional disdain for the Europeans' currency plans:

> Last autumn, when the pound left the ERM, I warned of the fault lines throughout the system ... These fault lines lie across Europe; the ERM as a whole has foundered ... I hope my fellow heads of government will resist the temptation to recite the mantra of full economic and monetary union as if nothing had changed. If they do recite it, it will have all the quaintness of a rain dance and about all the same potency.[13]

In Germany, high interest rates and the price-damping impact of the strong D-Mark accomplished the Bundesbank's aim of squeezing out inflation from the unified nation – yet this looked like a Pyrrhic victory. The sharp increase in the D-Mark's real (inflation-adjusted) exchange rate was the most significant since the collapse of the Bretton Woods system twenty years earlier – and it produced a similar outcome, a sharp economic downturn.[14] Because of the economic dependence on Germany of the rest of Europe, the German slowdown fed through immediately into reduced growth among its partners. Falling tax receipts and higher outlays for unemployment forced up budget deficits, reducing the ability of these countries to meet the Maastricht fiscal criteria and impairing the German government's task of convincing a reluctant German public of the merits of monetary union.

Scepticism about the Maastricht treaty was particularly deep-rooted within the Bundesbank. Ernst Welteke, who joined the central bank's Council in 1995 (and in 1999 succeeded Tietmeyer as Bundesbank president[15]), became aware of this early on. 'Before I joined the Council, I took part in a monetary workshop in 1993 with one of the Bundesbank Directorate members. He made such a negative speech about EMU that I said to myself, "If this is so complicated, then perhaps we shouldn't bother." '[16]

Germany's politicians skilfully orchestrated the Bundesbank's doubts to put maximum pressure on would-be EMU participants to fulfil German-inspired stability conditions. Bundesbank president Tietmeyer, solid of build and solemn of countenance, led the hard-liners' chorus. He liked to compare himself with an oak tree from his native Westphalia, and habitually stressed the ethical dimension to the Bundesbank's policies. Underlining the differences between the UK's relatively settled history and Germany's past upheavals, Tietmeyer once said, 'You have the House of Lords, the Queen and your established traditions – we have the Bundesbank.' The Bundesbank's legendary independence, although never as absolute as often portrayed, gave Chancellor Kohl and other leading German politicians an important advantage in the fight for a German-style EMU. On all the key issues regarding the setting up of the European Central Bank – its independence, location, internal structure, monetary instruments and leadership – German views prevailed.

In Paris, the Franc's survival at the end of the Battle of the Franc provoked no Gallic outpouring of triumph. Instead, the French government expressed regret at the pain of the exercise, combined with fear of a possible collapse of the single market if more countries joined Britain and Italy in floating. Prime minister Edouard Balladur gave priority to maintaining high interest rates and shoring up the Franc. He pointedly shunned the opportunity for lower interest rates offered by the drastic widening of fluctuation bands in August 1993. After the disastrous experiment earlier in the summer to reduce Paris interest rates below Germany's, the Banque de France and French Treasury were taking no chances. French short- and long-term interest rates remained consistently above German levels. Balladur insisted to finance minister Theo Waigel that France would stick to monetary orthodoxy, in a clandestine bilateral meeting in early August 1993 – a gesture of conciliation after the Franco-German storms over the previous month. 'I said from now on French and German policies on interest rates had to move in step. I had the impression that Waigel was very satisfied with the outcome. Afterwards Kohl telephoned me to thank me for my gesture.'[17]

Under government orders, the big French banks kept base rates at 10 per cent for several months in late 1993 in spite of inflation of just over 2 per cent. The Franc rose against the D-Mark for its over-sold levels, and currency traders bought back the Francs they had earlier sold – making losses on the transactions rather than their expected speculative profits. 'The Franc was very competitive [because of low French inflation],' recalled governor Jacques de Larosière.[18] The Banque de France was able to buy back dollars and D-Marks more cheaply than it had earlier sold them, in operations to restock its exhausted foreign exchange reserves. Faster than expected, the central bank repaid its large intervention credits raised from the Bundesbank and the European Monetary Cooperation Fund.[19] The Banque de France made a profit on the 1993 intervention operations, in stark contrast to the UK's large losses over the Black Wednesday turmoil.

However, maintaining the hard Franc policy with exceptionally high interest rates brought an explosion of public sector debt as tax revenues fell and social security outlays rose. French government debt in 1992 was 40 per cent of Gross Domestic Product, below the ratio in Germany and the UK,[20] but it rose rapidly thereafter[21] as France accumulated an additional €500 billion worth of debt during the 1990s. The politician responsible for much of the build-up was Nicolas Sarkozy, budget minister between 1993 and 1995 under prime minister Balladur. The huge debt increase, by significantly raising debt service costs, significantly narrowed successive governments' room for manoeuvre on economic policy. One episode that led to long-running antagonism was violent disagreement at the end of 1994 between the future President Sarkozy and Jean-Claude Trichet, governor of the Banque de France, over the government's budgetary targets.[22]

The scars left by such experiences became visible only later; shortly before winning the presidency in May 2007, Sarkozy summed up the results of France's 1990s 'hard franc' stance in extremely negative tones: 'With its exorbitant interest rates and over-valued exchange rate, the monetary policy of the 1990s penalised investment, lowered the competitiveness of French products and French labour, led to an explosion in unemployment and provoked recession.' He added that if France had left the Exchange Rate Mechanism in the early 1990s, as the UK did, and allowed the Franc to float and interest rates to fall, it would have been a great deal better off.[23]

Sarkozy's criticism of the *franc fort* policy was no surprise. The currency battles caused by German reunification left deep disillusionment about the shortcomings of European currency cooperation. As Michel Sapin, Mitterrand's last Socialist finance minister, put it, 'German unification was an exogenous shock – an event that hit the system from outside. European governments could have made an effort to resolve the situation together. In fact they didn't. The affair had some of the elements of a Greek tragedy.'[24] Mitterrand's adviser Elisabeth Guigou, who later became Europe minister in the post-1997 Socialist government, commented, 'It was already apparent at the beginning of the 1990s that each government would carry out its own policy on its own terms and by itself. When Germany decided to introduce the D-Mark in East Germany at a rate of 1 to 1 instead of 1 to 2, this led to an increase in German interest rates. Neither France nor Germany took account of each other's situations. This set a pattern which has lasted.'[25]

Looking back at the lessons of the 1990s, Christian Noyer, Alphandéry's chief of staff at the Finance Ministry during the tumult, who later became director of the Treasury and then governor of the Banque de France, said Europe missed an opportunity after German unification to let the D-Mark find its own level through floating. Probably this would have allowed the D-Mark to rise in 1990–92 – and then to have fallen later after the foreign exchange markets realised the extent of Germany's post-unification problems. 'If all three of the larger EU countries – France, UK, Germany – had said after German unification that the D-Mark should float, on a temporary basis, since this was the centre of the problem, then this idea might have worked. But the three countries didn't think of this. They were fragmented. And so the idea only came up [in 1993] when it was too late.'[26] Noyer said the Battle of the Franc hardened French determination to press on with EMU – to ensure that past sacrifices had not been in vain.

> If we had been wise and had run a strong currency in previous decades, leading to low inflation and strong competitiveness, we would have been in a different position. But that didn't happen. At the beginning of the 1990s, France held the viewpoint: 'We have wanted monetary union with Germany for so long. Let us not jeopardise it by floating.' If France had followed the path of floating, we would have devalued by perhaps around 20 per cent at the same time as Italy and Britain. By not doing that, France saved EMU.

French anxieties about other countries following the British and Italian devaluation route increased when the Portuguese escudo and Spanish peseta came under new attack, despite the wider ERM margins. In reaction to relatively high inflation and only sluggish growth in both countries, they were devalued in early 1995, for the third and fourth time respectively since September 1992. Yves-Thibault de Silguy, France's European Commissioner for monetary affairs, commented frostily after the devaluations, 'If the single currency does not arrive, the very existence of the single market would be threatened.'[27]

The flurry of competitive devaluations made even the hard men on the Bundesbank Council more attentive to a single currency's potential merits. Otmar Issing, who became the Directorate member for economics in 1990, and later took the same job at the European Central Bank, was a well-known hawk on EMU at the time of the Maastricht summit. In the first few years after

1992–93, Issing voiced doubts on whether Europe could move to monetary union without parallel moves to political union.[28] However, later on, the currency upheavals focused attention on the need to protect German exports – and made him and others see the advantages of EMU.

> I would not previously have forecast that the European currency would start during the 1990s. The decisive moment came with the currency crises of 1992–93. The status quo was not tenable. We faced a 30 per cent devaluation of the lira. Some companies in southern Germany competing with Italy went bankrupt. There was a danger of controls on movement of goods. I and others came to the conclusion that the Common Market would not survive another crisis of this dimension.[29]

Helmut Schlesinger, too, changed his tone. During his presidency, he displayed great stringency on monetary union. After he retired from the Bundesbank in 1993, he suddenly showed benevolence, a transition that surprised former colleagues. Schlesinger wrote an article for *The Economist* in 1996 which generally welcomed EMU and said it was likely to take place in 1999 with six to ten participants.[30] Schlesinger's successor Hans Tietmeyer complained that Schlesinger was contradicting official policy that economic convergence took precedence over the Maastricht timetable. Schlesinger later even went so far as to change his earlier view that political union in Europe was necessary to achieve monetary union.[31] Schlesinger's new stance partly reflected a realisation – born mainly of down-to-earth patriotism – that Chancellor Kohl deserved support for his Euro policies. But Schlesinger had also become frustrated by the near-impossibility of making timely realignments in a system of fixed but adjustable rates:

> The exchange rate crises of 1992 and 1993 gave rise to a great deal of emotion and were highly politicised. One example was the way that English newspapers wrote about the Bundesbank and portrayed Hitler standing in front of the Bundesbank building. It was extremely difficult, if not impossible, to bring about realignments that would have been sensible for economic reasons. The problem of the EMS was that it was no longer a risk, but an encouragement, for speculators. I realised there was no option but to proceed directly to monetary union for the countries that were ready for it.[32]

The most striking convert of all was Jean-Claude Trichet, the former director of the French Treasury, who took over from Jacques de Larosière as governor of the Banque de France in September 1993.[33] Trichet arrived just in time for the formal independence of the central bank under the legislative process inaugurated by Prime Minister Balladur.[34] Four years previously, in the aftermath of the Delors Report, he had virulently opposed just such a step. Trichet adapted smoothly to the new rules – and gave every sign that he had always been their most trenchant advocate.[35]

Meanwhile, with unemployment of close to five million, Germany's growing economic problems impeded the Germans' task of fulfilling their own economic convergence conditions. In the rest of Europe, too, the recession in 1993 took its toll. The automatic effect of the downturn in lowering tax revenues and increasing social security payments drove up European government budget deficits to nearly 6 per cent of Gross Domestic Product – double the 3 per cent Maastricht target that was seen as a key instrument for lowering inflationary pressure and securing the stability of the single currency. The chief fiscal culprits in 1993 were Greece with a budget deficit of 12 per cent of GDP, Italy (10 per cent), Spain, Belgium and Portugal (7 per cent), and France (6 per cent). The Netherlands (4 per cent) and Germany (3 per cent) were more or less in line with the target. There was also good news from Ireland, which restricted budget deficits to less than 3 per cent of GDP (and later even recording surpluses) – part of a decade-long transformation that would send economic growth rates soaring to 8 to 10 per cent annually in the latter 1990s, earning it the sobriquet as Europe's 'Celtic tiger'.

In the light of strong fiscal miscreancy elsewhere, both Germany's conservative-led government and the Social Democratic Party opposition redoubled their assurances that potential members would face the most stringent appraisal for meeting the convergence criteria. Finance minister Theo Waigel's Bavarian Christian Social Union, partner with Kohl's Christian Democrats in the Bonn coalition, led a particular outcry over a potential weakening of German stability. This gave Waigel, as a supporter of monetary union, a highly delicate diplomatic role in winning public acceptance.

The significance of the Maastricht criteria was far less economic than political. Fulfilling the targets was a symbol of governmental commitment to the disciplines of the new system. Germany set down an additional marker by steering through a key decision in October 1993 on the location of the European Monetary Institute (EMI), the forerunner of the European Central Bank. The EMI was due to take up its functions when Stage 2 of EMU began in January 1994. In line with its long-held views backing the Monetarist rather than Economist approach to monetary union, France had wanted the new body to embrace central bank-like powers – giving it the ability to intervene, using Europe's pooled (mainly German) monetary reserves, to hold exchange rates steady and protect Europe from disruptive capital flows. Additionally France was reluctant to base the EMI in Frankfurt fearing that the new body would come under undue influence from the Bundesbank and German-style monetary doctrines. Germany and the Netherlands, on the other hand, wanted to ensure that the EMI avoided conflicts with national central banks' continued operational activities, and ensured that the EMI concentrated on necessary but low-profile statistical and economic work such as harmonising different countries' collection of monetary data.

Furthermore, Kohl brushed aside the candidature of other cities such as London, Edinburgh or Amsterdam. In contradiction to the French, the chancellor wished to symbolise continuity with the Bundesbank. As Edouard Balladur, French prime minister, recalled:

> I did not wish to place the European Central Bank in Frankfurt, but I'm afraid I failed. As prime minister I said to Kohl, 'We are ready to put it in Bonn, because the ministries will go to Berlin, you will have room in Bonn.' I said the same to Mitterrand, but in a private conversation with Kohl [in autumn 1993], he made the concession of establishing the ECB in Frankfurt, without discussing it with me before. Afterwards I said to Mitterrand, 'Why did you do that without consulting me?' He said. 'You must accept it. That was necessary to get the Germans to accept the end of the D-Mark, to allay their anxieties.' But I persisted in believing it was a mistake. If today the European Central Bank was in Bonn, that would be different.[36]

Following the decision to place the European Monetary Institute in Frankfurt, the man chosen to head the new body was Alexandre Lamfalussy, general manager of the Basle-based Bank for International Settlements. Sharp of mind and wry of manner, Lamfalussy was the most polished of monetary technocrats, commanding English, French and German with cut-glass precision. He left his native Hungary for Belgium in 1949 to escape Communism – a similar experience to arch-ERM speculator George Soros (who fled Hungary for the UK in 1947). Lamfalussy honed his international skills at Nuffield College, Oxford in the 1950s. As a long-time BIS official, he was a working central banker, but did not have the power to raise or lower interest rates – an apt compromise to lead a hybrid central bank-in-waiting. With the aplomb of long experience, Lamfalussy bridged the inevitable monetary and political divisions at the heart of EMU.

The ambiguities of the Maastricht process partly reflected its curious mix of elements of certainty and doubt. Politicians like Kohl and Waigel put forward, with varying levels of plausibility, two essentially contradictory propositions. On the one hand, the Maastricht Treaty committed Europe 'irreversibly' to monetary union. On the other, it soon became clear that the final fixing of exchange rates would not go ahead in 1997, the first EMU completion date fixed at Maastricht, because hardly any countries met the convergence targets – numerical criteria for debt, deficits, interest rates and inflation – deemed (particularly by the Germans) as crucial conditions for EMU stability. Assuming introduction of the single currency in 1999, question marks had to remain up to the last moment about the final choice of participating countries – or even whether EMU would be postponed. This was an unsatisfactorily rancorous procedure, but there was no way round it. The Bundesbank and the German Finance Ministry, in particular, backed by their traditional allies the Dutch, argued that any other approach would relax the necessary political pressure of the selection criteria – and would automatically lower confidence in the planned currency on the financial markets and among European electorates.

Lamfalussy took over the secretariat of the Committee of European Central Bank Governors and started in Frankfurt with a skeleton staff of twelve. The first meeting of the EMI board, made up of central bank governors from all fifteen European Union members, took place in the rebuilt medieval surroundings of the Frankfurt City Hall. But the early home of the EMI was in Basle, since Lamfalussy and his team worked from the BIS headquarters to lay the groundwork for permanent premises.[37] This led to the EMI agreeing to take over, floor by floor, the thirty-six-storey former head office of the German trade union-owned Bank für Gemeinwirtschaft (BfG) in the Kaiserstrasse in the city centre. The BfG building, constructed in 1977, was soon dubbed the Eurotower. The principal tenant, Commerzbank, progressively made over sufficient space to allow the EMI to start at end-October 1994 with 150 people and to build up later to 300 to 400. (When the Euro started in 1999, the ECB had 600 staff. It grew to 1,400 employees in 2008.)

During the EMI's start-up period, an intriguing divergence of views came to the fore over the future Central Bank's financial market activities. Banque de France governor Jean-Claude Trichet opposed the Lamfalussy and Tietmeyer line that the EMI should be equipped with a central operations and dealing room for money market and foreign exchange dealing. Trichet believed that too strong an operational role for the ECB would, over time, unduly promote Frankfurt as a financial centre. Trichet pleaded, in contrast, for national central banks to carry out the ECB's market operations in even more of a decentralised fashion than was planned. The aim was to protect the international financial market importance of Paris. However, Lamfalussy and Tietmeyer prevailed, and the EMI was equipped with a central dealing room. This became the hub of the European Central Bank's centrally-coordinated money market operations. It gained particular importance during massive injections of banking liquidity into the financial markets in 2007–08 to offset the effects of the US sub-prime credit crisis.

Lamfalussy's job involved political as well as technical challenges. Part of his challenge was to help 'sell' EMU to the reluctant Germans – a task where he was given full support from Chancellor Kohl.

> I went to see Kohl four times during my three-and-a-half years in Frankfurt. German people who knew me and who were in favour of EMU used me to press home the positive case with him. I said: 'I don't know how you will get the German people to give up the D-Mark,' He said: 'It will happen. The Germans accept strong leadership.' Kohl made clear he was ready to give up the D-Mark and that unless there was monetary union, Europe would be in danger. His view was that 'Europe needs a balancing force.' I said it was difficult. He said, 'I know it is difficult, but you must go ahead with it.'[38]

As the European Monetary Institute took up its duties, debate resounded around Europe on which countries would join the prospective currency bloc and how it would be run. Since the Werner Plan in 1970–71, Germany had always called for some form of political union to accompany monetary union, as a means of implementing economic coordination in areas such as budgetary and wage policies. It became increasingly clear during the 1990s, however, that Europe would not implement anything like 'political union' – not least because no one could agree on what it entailed. The purest German objective foresaw a common political system as a guarantor of strict monetary policies. The French version was quite different: to set up a political body to coordinate economic and monetary policies and essentially supervise the European Central Bank. Despite these basic differences, a broad range of German politicians – ranging from ex-Chancellor Helmut Schmidt to functionaries in Kohl's ruling Christian Democratic Union – spoke out in favour of a 'fast track' route to EMU built around a core Franco-German group that would espouse the basic principles of stable money.[39] German finance minister Waigel cast perennial doubt on whether Italy, in view of its large budget deficit and past propensity to inflation and devaluation, would be selected as a founder member of EMU. This sparked sporadic criticism around Europe about alleged German monetary nationalism but, equally, fears among German and French industrialists that they could face ruinous competition from cheap Italian imports if Italy stayed out and the lira fell.[40]

A new president in Paris heralded fresh bouts of nationally-minded sparring. Neo-Gaullist leader Jacques Chirac won the May 1995 presidential election against Socialist opponent Lionel Jospin. Chirac's two spells as prime minister in 1974–76 and 1986–88 had been marked by Franco-German monetary turbulence. The new president's appeal to the diverse forces of French Republicanism, especially to Gaullists who opposed diluting political sovereignty, partly reflected long-lasting hostility to German monetary principles that he had already displayed during the 1970s.

During his election campaign, Chirac cast doubt on the Maastricht timetable by advocating policies to stimulate the French economy at the expense of the EMU convergence criteria. He clashed frequently with Trichet over the Banque de France's anti-inflationary monetary policies.[41] Once ensconced as president, Chirac appeared to be plotting openly to remove the central bank governor from his post. In a prelude to a contorted juridical investigation into large public subsidies for the costly restructuring of the state-owned bank Crédit Lyonnais, Chirac publicly blamed the Treasury and Banque de France in 1996 for having failed to exercise adequate supervision.[42] This was widely seen as an attempt to destabilise Trichet by focusing on his previous Treasury banking supervision responsibilities. However, Trichet remained in his post, displaying the same tenacity and devotion to anti-inflation orthodoxy that he was later to show as president of the European Central Bank. Beyond this, in the function that he had gradually assumed as guardian of the 'strong Franc', Trichet had made himself indispensable: he (and Chirac) knew that replacing him with a less independent and more politically pliable governor would have led to the Franc sharply falling on the currency markets – and ended the Gallic dream of tying down Germany through monetary union.

Chirac exhibited a similar mix of aggression and frustration with regard to Germany. In place of Mitterrand's subtle *Realpolitik*, Chirac put on show his impatience and irritation with German policies on EMU – causing frequent ructions with Kohl and, less often, his successor Schröder. Chirac's problems were partly of his own making – a foretaste, in some ways, of difficulties that were to dog his successor Nicholas Sarkozy a decade later – and led to a spiral of worsening difficulties. Constant presidential sniping at the Banque de France's efforts to maintain German-style policies were counter-productive, as they lowered confidence on the financial markets and forced the central bank to maintain interest rates 2 percentage points higher than in Germany (and 5 points above France's inflation rate) in order to persuade foreign investors to hold Francs and prevent the currency falling on the foreign exchanges.

High borrowing costs held back consumption and investment and depressed French growth – and this – reflecting the automatic impact on government receipts and spending – kept France's budget deficit at the unhealthily high figure of 5 per cent of GDP in 1995. This in turn led Germany to step up lobbying for reinforcing the Maastricht treaty with rules on member countries' debts and borrowing after monetary union. This precipitated further disputes with France, Italy and other southern countries such as Spain and Portugal about whether Germany was trying to dictate unduly strict policies to the rest of Europe. Otmar Issing, the Bundesbank Directorate member responsible for economics, said, 'It is decisive that the [European] Union has a financial constitution that durably rules out fiscal misbehaviour either at the level of the Community or by member states.'[43]

In autumn 1995 Waigel launched German proposals for a 'Stability Pact'.[44] The plan was to levy fines on countries whose budget deficits exceeded the Maastricht reference level 3 per cent of GDP.[45] Coinciding with the Stability Pact initiative, and following well-publicised German scepticism about Italy's chances of meeting the Maastricht criteria, the Rome government launched proposals for postponing EMU. Prime minister Lamberto Dini suggested delaying the fixing of currency rates for two or three years beyond the planned 1999.[46] Some of Germany's European partners interpreted German insistence on stringent application of the convergence criteria as a sign that Bonn was trying to torpedo the entire single currency project.[47] None the less, the EMU project seemed to be inching towards the point of no return. Stephen Wall, John Major's European adviser, was sent to Brussels as Britain's permanent representative to the European Union. Almost immediately, he noticed the momentum towards the single currency.

When I look back at the issues surrounding EMU over many years, I am struck by the way that we have tended to look at everything through the prism of our own politics . . . One example was the prevalent feeling in the UK, when I arrived in Brussels in 1995, that EMU would not go ahead. When I got to Brussels, I could see that everyone was gearing up for EMU. There was no doubt that it would happen. The British wish that it shouldn't happen was father to the thought that it would not happen.[48]

At a summit meeting in Madrid in December 1995, European leaders reaffirmed January 1999 as the starting date, agreed the outlines of the Stability Pact – and reached an accord on baptising the currency the 'Euro' rather than the French-proposed 'Ecu'. Waigel confirmed Germany's overriding interest in sealing monetary union: 'No other country has such an interest in free competition, free export markets and a large internal market.'[49]

Conflict and controversy dogged European decision-making until the final selection of EMU members in May 1998. Reports that EMU would be postponed, some fed by the Bundesbank and German politicians, circulated ceaselessly in political rumour mills and on the foreign exchanges, but became progressively less credible. As growth slowly picked up throughout the Community, friction over the monetary selection process gradually eased. The dollar's rise from mid-1995 onwards, after it had descended to a record low below DM1.40, helped Europe's transition – by cheapening exports and opening up a route to moderate economic expansion. Governments stepped on the fiscal brakes to ensure that budget deficits in the all-important 'reference year' of 1997 were in line with the target of 3 per cent of GDP.

The fiscal tightening, often through 'one-off' measures that were later reversed, turned out to have a positive effect. Profiting from a benign international environment – a pick-up in the US economy, a stronger dollar and low inflation of around 2 per cent – Europe recorded a fortunate near-doubling of growth in 1997.[50] The Bundesbank engineered a helpful fall in borrowing costs, bringing down its discount rate and Lombard rate from the 1992 highs to 2.5 per cent and 4.5 per cent respectively by 1996. These were levels that remained in place until the final fixing of currencies in 1998 – and prefigured the 'corridor' for interest rates when the European Central Bank took over during the first decade of EMU. Still more significantly, interest rates throughout Europe started to converge on German levels, as the financial markets became increasingly confident that EMU would start on time with a relatively large group. Yves-Thibault de Silguy, France's hyper-active European Commissioner for monetary affairs, summed up the mood of aspiration when he stated in autumn 1996 that the single currency would be 'quickly understood in New York and London, sooner than in Paris or Frankfurt, as the tangible sign of re-emerging European power'.[51]

Lower interest rates significantly reduced the cost of servicing debts for some of the hard-pressed southern countries, which had a direct effect in reducing budget deficits. This was of enormous assistance to traditionally high-interest countries like Italy and Spain as they sought to achieve the 3 per cent deficit target. A key figure on the European EMU path was veteran Banca d'Italia governor Carlo Azeglio Ciampi. Against the background of ever-changing Italian prime ministers, rampant political corruption, and high budget deficits and government debt, Ciampi had won an unusual amount of trust from the Italian electorate and from foreign governments. As a key component of Italy's untiring efforts to join monetary union, Ciampi became prime minister at the helm of a technocratic administration in 1993, the first non-parliamentarian to head an Italian government in the twentieth century. He later joined the Left-of-centre governments of Romano Prodi and Massimo D'Alema as Treasury Minister.

Prime minister Prodi accomplished the key task of pushing through pensions reforms in 1997 that secured crucial agreement on the 1998 budget needed as a condition for EMU membership. According to the Bundesbank's former president Helmut Schlesinger, the campaign against Italian membership by some members of the German central bank Council never had much chance of success. Excluding Italy was arithmetically valid, but politically impossible: Italy's public debt was 120 per cent of GDP, double the Maastricht target of 60 per cent. But Belgium had a still higher debt level – 130 per cent – and the Belgians were certain of membership because of their link in an existing monetary union with high-stability Luxembourg, which could not possibly be kept out. Schlesinger added,

> As for the 3 per cent deficit criterion, this was always going to be realisable for Italy because of lower debt service costs as a result of Italian interest rates falling towards German levels in the two years before EMU. I remember Ciampi explaining this to me by scribbling down some numbers on the back of a serviette in Rome.[52]

Ciampi's successor as governor of the Banca d'Italia, Antonio Fazio, fought a rearguard action against his own country's membership – the sole European central bank governor to do so. His stance echoed the views of former Banca d'Italia governor Paolo Baffi, who had opposed Italy's joining the European Monetary System in 1979 on the grounds that, under the constraints of an unchanged exchange rate, Italian industry would quickly become uncompetitive against lower-cost European rivals such as Germany. According to prime minister Romano Prodi,

> To say that Fazio was doubtful about the Euro is an understatement. He was strongly against it. He did what he could do to stop it. His scepticism went beyond Baffi's. Fazio of course knew the decision to join was political; it was not

the central bank's decision. But Ciampi and I still had to do a great deal of work to contain him.[53]

Fazio's views were not shared by others at the Italian Central Bank. 'We believed that monetary union would be the mechanism by which we would regain some sovereignty at the European level. We would sit on the board of the ECB, and we would have a say in shaping the monetary strategy of Europe,' explained long-time foreign exchange chief Fabrizio Saccomanni. 'Although it is painful to admit for a central bank governor, Fazio felt we had to devalue from time to time to regain competitiveness and to support economic activity.' Fazio gave little hint of his adversarial views on monetary union during his interventions at regular European Monetary Institute meetings in Frankfurt. However, Fazio's stance led to strong discord with Tommaso Padoa-Schioppa, the veteran Banca d'Italia foreign specialist and celebrated EMU supporter who eventually joined the European Central Bank's six-member board in 1998.

Italy showed its pro-EMU colours by rejoining the Exchange Rate Mechanism in November 1996.[54] Greater likelihood that Italy and other traditionally high-inflation countries would join monetary union countered worries among exporters in Germany and France that Italian companies would gain future market share with a perpetually devaluing currency. But – as Italian experts such as Fazio were aware – Italy faced the risk of higher unemployment and other painful side-effects if it failed to match up to the competitive conditions of a perpetually fixed currency. Echoing the orthodox views of the Economist group of German monetary practitioners that had been put forward for thirty years, Bundesbank president Tietmeyer was tireless in insisting on the deep-seated issues at stake:

Monetary union means a restriction on national sovereignty, on national manoeuvring room and the ability to go it alone. Participants lose the instrument of exchange rate adjustments. That strengthens pressures towards internal flexibility. In a monetary union, countries have to tackle and solve their economic problems and challenges in a similar way and with similar speed. If the countries decide fundamentally different answers, then great problems will arise. Countries which implement the right solutions soon become more competitive against those which react wrongly or late.[55]

To be weighed against such dangers were the risks that EMU would not go ahead on time. Finance minister Waigel spelled out the problems: 'If monetary union were to fail, that would bring a further strong revaluation of the D-Mark with catastrophic effects on employment and growth.'[56] The political impact, too, of a setback for Europe's integration efforts could be dire. Arch-EMU advocate Valéry Giscard d'Estaing pointed to the German threat. 'If monetary union does not go ahead, that will be a very dangerous situation for France ... That would be the end of a long period of Franco-German organisation of Europe, and the transition to a preponderant influence by Germany.'[57]

The European growth outlook started to improve towards the end of 1996, but the objective of EMU – though gradually coming into reach – still seemed to require enormous sacrifices. Politicians and electorates appeared to perceive the negative effects as outweighing the potential benefits. Franco-German divergences were again on show. Giscard made a surprising call for a Franc devaluation against the D-Mark as a condition for entry into monetary union. 'Since 1990 all French governments have stuck to the Franc–D-Mark parity. This has not been a policy of the 'stable Franc' but has bound our money to a foreign currency that would drive the Franc higher.'[58]

Shortly before a bilateral summit at Nuremberg in December, Chirac's prime minister Alain Juppé re-emphasised Franco-German historical and cultural differences about EMU decision-making and the role of the central bank. 'We do not want a technocratic, automatic system that will be exclusively under the control of the European Central Bank.'[59] Chirac and Juppé wanted monetary power to be balanced by political power. They used the summit to plead for a political EMU Advisory Council with the ability to influence ECB decisions. But Waigel and his State Secretary in the Finance Ministry Jürgen Stark beat back the French proposal with such force that Chirac complained to Kohl about Stark's behaviour.[60]

There were more tantrums between Kohl and Chirac at the mid-December European summit in Dublin. After more than a year of heated debate, the European Union at last approved the Stability Pact. But after a furious personal disagreement between Kohl and Chirac (according to observers at the scene they almost came to fisticuffs), the French president succeeded in toning down German proposals for large automatic fines on miscreant countries. The Dublin meeting saw vitriolic discord between Theo Waigel and the French finance minister Jean Arthuis. The thirty-year-long German campaign for an anti-inflation 'stability policy' in the hands of a non-elected central bank collided with France's traditional support for political power over central bankers – and its refusal to give up national sovereignty to a European body that would have the last word on France's budget. On French insistence, the EU Council declared that growth as well as price stability would be an explicit goal of future EMU monetary policy. The arrangement for policing budgetary policy was renamed 'Stability and Growth Pact'.

Greater political control over the Pact weakened its disciplinary effect, but proved a boon for France and Germany – since they both failed to meet budgetary targets in coming years. The Dublin summit agreed that Wim Duisenberg, the president of the Nederlandsche Bank, should take over from Lamfalussy as head of the European Monetary Institute.[61] But in another sign of Franco-German divergence, Chirac rejected Kohl's view that Duisenberg – seen as too strong a supporter of German policies – would automatically become the head of the ECB later on.

The softening of the Stability Pact accompanied a range of other political steps casting doubt on the rigour of the monetary union process. Manifold examples of statistical manipulation of the entry criteria weakened public confidence – especially in Germany – in the stability of the new currency, and were greeted with derision by Anglo-Saxon commentators hostile to EMU. Italy announced a special 'Europe tax' for the 1997 budget to allow its Maastricht targets to be met. With considerable justification, the European Commission questioned the short-term budgetary palliatives agreed by a number of countries to meet the Maastricht criteria, arguing that these countered the sought-after 'sustainability' of European convergence. Germany attacked French proposals to use pension fund transfers from the French telecommunications company France Telecom to reduce its budget deficit. Gerhard Schröder, the charismatic Social Democrat prime minister of the northern German state of Lower Saxony, bidding to dispossess Kohl in the forthcoming general elections, adopted Euro-scepticism for his polling campaign. He was dismissive about the Kohl government's ability to meet the self-set convergence criteria, and called for EMU to be delayed: 'Germany won't meet the criteria without creative accounting.'[62]

Europe's efforts to forge common policies on EMU became still more convoluted during a summer of uncertainty in 1997. In the UK general election in May, the Labour Party took power for the first time since 1979. The new government under prime minister Tony Blair pledged a constructive line on European integration. Not least because of the memories of Black Wednesday, the Blair government was deeply divided on the Euro issue, and decided not to join the Euro on the 1 January 1999 starting date. But, to maintain influence over European policies, the UK held out the prospect of EMU membership in coming years. One of Labour's first moves was to make the Bank of England operationally independent from the Treasury. This was part of the plan by

Blair's Chancellor of the Exchequer Gordon Brown for improving running of the economy – but it also fulfilled a formal condition for Britain to join the Euro. The plan was kept secret during the election campaign. When asked why he had not revealed it before, Brown replied gruffly, 'No one asked me.'[63]

In Paris, Jacques Chirac was under pressure from political in-fighting and poor economic performance, with unemployment at a post-war high of more than 3 million in spite of tentative economic recovery. To try to win a mandate for more robust economic reform, he dissolved the National Assembly and called general elections nine months ahead of schedule. This was a spectacular gamble, and he lost it in grandiose style. Chirac's incaution allowed a Socialist government under Lionel Jospin to take over from prime minister Alain Juppé and launch an awkward five-year period of Left-wing 'cohabition' with a Right-wing president. Rather than underpinning France's commitment to the Euro, the election outcome undermined it. Jospin's scepticism on the austerity measures needed to fulfil the Euro entry criteria compounded Chirac's own fundamental doubts on the issue. In addition, Jospin launched legislation for a 35-hour week – imitating a similar move for German metalworkers, but without compensating steps to boost productivity – that weighed down significantly on French competitiveness in coming years. On the key issues of national sovereignty and anti-inflation policy, the Chirac–Jospin combination set the scene for repeated conflict with Germany on the rules for running EMU.

The shake-up in British and French politics coincided with a setback for financial probity in Germany. In May 1997 finance minister Waigel – after discussing the idea in private with Tietmeyer – unexpectedly suggested revaluing the Bundesbank's gold reserves to help bridge a budgetary shortfall and allow Germany to meet the 3 per cent budgetary target for 1998.[64] The central bank publicly rejected the idea as setting a poor example of statistical manipulation that could be imitated by other countries. The episode laid Germany open to allegations of hypocrisy and damaged both Tietmeyer's and Waigel's public standing. With greater foresight the Bundesbank president could have prevented the issue from becoming publicly controversial. Waigel recalled: 'If I had known before how virulent the Bundesbank reaction would be, I would have reconsidered the action . . . I let the Bundesbank enjoy its moment of glory. In fact they had shot their bolt and on the question of the Euro they were not able to deploy their influence again in any similar way.'[65]

In July 1997 Wim Duisenberg took over leadership of the European Monetary Institute from Lamfalussy, as planned, but only after considerable discussion over the terms. Nout Wellink, the long-time member of the Nederlandsche Bank's governing board, who took over as president when

Duisenberg moved to the EMI, said, 'Duisenberg had substantial doubts about whether 1999 would be realised as a starting date. He didn't want to go to Frankfurt and remain as EMI president if EMU did not go ahead on time.'[66]

In the end Duisenberg agreed to relinquish his post in Amsterdam and move to Frankfurt, reassured from most European countries that he would later become head of the European Central Bank. France, however, opposed an automatic succession, and the new Socialist finance minister Dominique Strauss-Kahn publicly suggested a French candidate for the ECB.[67] Furthermore, Strauss-Kahn strengthened the Socialist government's activist credentials by casting doubt on the German-backed Stability Pact. He urged a new 'balance' between policies to beat inflation and measures to help Europe's eighteen million unemployed. France's finance minister made clear that France was likely to miss the chief Maastricht condition of a budget deficit of 3 per cent of GDP – but then announced tax increases to try to meet the target. Discussion flared up again on whether EMU could be postponed, or could even go ahead without France. But the debate was quelled by a combined coalition of European politicians, aided by some influential outside supporters. Karl Otto Pöhl, the former Bundesbank president, said that – even though neither Germany nor France would meet the criteria precisely – 'the train towards monetary union has started and can only be halted at the risk of running off the track.'[68] Jean-Claude Trichet, governor of the Banque de France, declared 'unthinkable' that France would not get its budget deficit under control and meet the January 1999 starting date.[69] According to Duisenberg's successor Wellink, fatalism was in the air:

> Expectations about EMU starting on time in 1999 were at first dampened, then we [at the Nederlandsche Bank] gradually realised there was no escape ... I remember a discussion with Duisenberg when he said. 'We will get EMU from 1 January 1999 and whatever happens Italy will be part of it.' Italy was a founding member of the European Community. These people knew enough how to construct the figures [on Italy's economic performance] to satisfy the convergence criteria.

As 1997 drew on, Bundesbank president Hans Tietmeyer briefly rekindled speculation of a postponement by declaring that 'the heavens would not fall in' if EMU were delayed.[70] But such rumours became steadily more sporadic. In Britain, the Labour government added to confusion about its future European plans by dropping hints – and then dashing them – that it might want to join EMU shortly after the 1999 launch.[71] Bank of England governor

Eddie George said he was unconvinced that EMU discipline would help single currency participants to improve labour market flexibility and reduce unemployment.[72] Blair's Chancellor of the Exchequer, Gordon Brown, was also hostile to the idea, telling Parliament the UK would become a member only if the Euro was a success and if the UK and European economies converged.[73]

Amid the politicking, European central banks took decisive action to harmonise interest rates ahead of formal fixing of exchange rates. The Bundesbank raised its key money market intervention rate in coordination with five other European central banks to produce a single market interest rate of 3.3 per cent in the core countries of the prospective EMU area.[74]

Jospin and Strauss-Kahn launched a further instalment of the long-running initiative for an 'economic government' for Europe as a political counter-weight to the ECB.[75] In October 1997 Germany bowed to French insistence on establishing a formal political authority to balance the ECB. Waigel and Strauss-Kahn agreed that the so-called 'Euro-Group' of finance ministers from Euro members should meet regularly with the European Central Bank president to discuss how to run the European economy. A crucial issue was exchange rate policy. The Maastricht Treaty divided responsibility for the external value of the Euro between the ECB and European governments. The French intended the Euro-Group to gain responsibility not just for overall exchange rate strategy, but also for short-run currency movements. For example, the finance ministers would make decisions not simply on whether a target rate should be set for the Euro against the dollar or yen, but also for interest rate changes needed to influence rates in the short term. Dominique Strauss-Kahn rammed home the political necessity of reinforcing governmental supervision of the ECB. 'In the absence of a visible and legitimate political body, the ECB might soon be regarded by the public as the only institution responsible for macroeconomic policy.'[76]

The minor German concession over the Euro-Group failed to damp simmering French resentment about Germany's *de facto* control of monetary union. Disagreement came to a head in November 1997. The issue was the presidency of the European Central Bank. The Governing Council of the EMI – made up of central bank governors of the European Union members – unanimously proposed Institute president Duisenberg as head of the ECB, to be founded the following summer. The final decision was however in the hands of governments. France was determined to make its voice heard by proposing its own candidate. Duisenberg was the representative of a country which had traditionally backed orthodox German policies. President Chirac and his prime minister Jospin caused an uproar by declaring in early November they were backing Banque de France governor Jean-Claude Trichet for the post. Chirac was forced to play down his earlier furious criticism of Trichet's stringent monetary polices.[77] Trichet earned the ire of his colleagues on the EMI Council. The governor had been summoned to Paris in October to be told of the French government's plans for him – and had accepted without reservation. Tietmeyer, a strong Duisenberg supporter, believed that Trichet had played a double-game by allowing his name to go forward as the French candidate – even though, as a member of the EMI Council, he had voted for Duisenberg.[78]

Mounting evidence that, in spite of Franco-German tensions, Europe was serious about starting monetary union set off a wave of reaction in the US. In a parallel with the establishment of the European Monetary System twenty years earlier, critical views were clearly in the ascendancy. William McDonough, president of the New York Federal Reserve Bank, was cautious about any immediate challenge to the international role of the dollar. 'While some decline in the reserve role of the dollar is certainly plausible, I believe the risk of a dramatic shift in official dollar reserves both in and outside Europe has been exaggerated. It will take time before the objectives and operating procedures of the European Central Bank become clearly understood.'[79]

Other leading Americans took a less benevolent line. The prevalent view of Alan Greenspan, the Federal Reserve chairman, during the run-up to EMU – was that 'I didn't think it was going to happen'.[80] His reasoning was clear: 'I was extremely sceptical whether a central bank with the same power as the celebrated German Bundesbank could impose itself on the whole continent. Besides, I had my doubts if such an institution was necessary, since Europe already had a *de facto* central bank, in the shape of the Bundesbank.'[81] Nobel prize-winner Milton Friedman called into question the Euro area's suitability for monetary union on account of limitations on internal movements of goods, labour and capital and exposure to external shocks, that could affect some countries more than others. 'The Euro has been motivated by politics, not economics ... Monetary unity imposed under unfavourable conditions will prove a barrier to political unity.'[82] Most critical of all was Martin Feldstein, economics professor at Harvard, who argued, 'The adverse economic effects of a single currency on unemployment and inflation would outweigh any gains from facilitating trade and capital flows ... The independence of the ECB and the goals of monetary policy will become a source of serious conflict among member countries ... A French expectation of equality [with Germany] and a German expectation of hegemony are not consistent.'[83]

Resistance continued in the monetary heartland of Germany. Four German professors – including former Bundesbank Central Council member Wilhelm Nölling – launched a lawsuit against EMU at the Constitutional Court.[84] No less than 155 German university professors signed a letter calling for an 'orderly postponement' of EMU on the grounds that economic conditions were unsustainable.[85] Only 30 per cent of German voters said they favoured exchanging the D-Mark for the Euro.[86] Ralf Dahrendorf, the German-born economist and politician who had joined the British House of Lords, wrote:

> Pretty soon the people of Europe will realise that the great promises with which their leaders have sold them the project will not come true. Growth will be dependent on the same old internal and external factors, and Asia will be more important for them than EMU. Unemployment may even rise if EMU encourages companies to fall prey to the epidemic of merger-mania.[87]

A series of official reports on the convergence of European economies at the end of March concluded that eleven countries – including Italy – were ready to join.[88] Helmut Kohl remained optimistic, telling a Bundestag committee that Frankfurt would become a 'very big financial centre' as the result of the advent of the Euro.[89] Switzerland would be in the Euro within ten years, Kohl said, and Britain would be a member in a few years, too. 'The City [London] is on a trip [to the Euro] and where the City goes, Downing Street goes too.'

As the date neared for turning the European Monetary Institute into the European Central Bank on 1 June, all countries except France backed EMI president Duisenberg for the top job. France suggested that the formal eight year-term for the ECB presidency should be split between the Dutchman and Trichet. Germany and the Netherlands turned down a formal decision to limit Duisenberg's term of office, declaring this would be inconsistent with the ECB's independence. However, the Germans accepted that Duisenberg might want voluntarily, for reasons of age, to step down around half-way through his mandate.[90] The tussle coincided with separate politicking in Germany over the Bonn government's choice for the six-person ECB Executive Board. In a structure that consciously mirrored the Bundesbank's, the board together with member countries' central bank governors would make up the ECB's Governing Council that would be the supreme arbiter of European interest rates. Bonn's first choice for the post was Jürgen Stark, State Secretary at the Finance Ministry, who had previously worked for Kohl in the Chancellery.[91] However, Stark's nomination would have relayed to other countries that the German government was giving a top post to its own man. The Germans feared this would compromise ECB independence – and would encourage Chirac's campaign for Trichet. As a result, finance minister Theo Waigel decided to appoint Otmar Issing, the hawkish Bundesbank Directorate member for economics. Chancellor Kohl regarded the Issing proposal with distaste, on the grounds that the Bundesbank man 'had never said a good word' about the Euro.[92] However Kohl's aides convinced him that Issing's well-known scepticism would stiffen confidence by convincing public opinion that the Euro would be in sound Bundesbank hands.

The Issing nomination formed part of the preparations for the European summit in Brussels on 2 May that was designed to launch the single currency. Britain's prime minister Tony Blair was in the chair, reflecting Britain's rotating six-month presidency of the European Union. Believing that the Netherlands, France and Germany would resolve in advance the ECB leadership imbroglio, the UK failed to prepare adequately for the summit tussling. Wim Kok, the Dutch prime minister, was – like Jacques Chirac – in no mood to compromise. The French insisted that Duisenberg be confirmed as ECB chief, with a specific leaving date in July 2002, half-way through the year when Euro notes and coins were to be introduced. The arguments oscillated back and forth for nearly twelve hours.[93] The bickering among the French, Dutch, German and British leaders bordered on the comical:

Chirac: 'Who is this man who says we must waste all this time talking about a few weeks longer he stays in the job?'

Kok: 'You say, "Who is this man?" He is not someone who just turned up off the street, you know.'

Chirac: (*snorting*) 'Boeuf!'

Kohl: 'I don't like the tone of this conversation. I'm assured this is a man of quality and honour. It is important we discuss this honourably.'

Chirac: 'We learned about Duisenberg through the press. I will not be treated like that. We have already accepted the Bank would be in Frankfurt.'

Blair: 'This is not very productive.'

Chirac: 'Nor dignified.' (*To Blair*) 'You are a very clear and precise person. This is not a clear and precise process.'[94]

After Chirac threatened to veto Duisenberg's candidature, and the Germans declared they were ready to wreck the summit by departing early, France followed the pattern of earlier EMU negotiations and backed down on the main points. In a decision announced after midnight on 3 May, Duisenberg was given the job for the official term. He declared on a 'voluntary' basis that he would not serve the full eight years. He would remain in the job at least until the introduction of notes and coins. The horse-trading added to public doubts in Germany whether the European Central Bank would really be free from political interference. Chirac declared: 'We are in a system of European nations where each one defends its interests'.[95] Kok said the decision was a 'victory for the Netherlands'.[96] Duisenberg called the Brussels proceedings 'slightly absurd' and drew applause from the European Parliament when he said he might stay on for the full eight-year term after all.[97]

The European Monetary Institute was transformed into the European Central Bank on 1 June 1998. Christian Noyer from the French Treasury was appointed deputy president.[98] The independence of the Central Bank was even more strongly anchored than the Bundesbank's. The ECB's statutes laid down that it was illegal for either the Central Bank or any of the national central banks making up the Euro system to 'seek or take instructions from Community institutions or bodies, from any Government of a member state or from any other body'.[99]

In power-sharing with governments over exchange rates, European finance ministers had formal responsibility for the relationship between the Euro and international currencies. Yet it was clear that day-to-day influence on currency movements would be wielded by the ECB. The central bank's overriding objective to maintain price stability was more precisely defined than with the Bundesbank. The ECB's Governing Council defined 'price stability' in October 1998 as maintaining consumer price inflation for the Euro area 'below 2 per cent over the medium term' – a target that in May 2003 was adjusted to 'below but close to 2 per cent' to guard against the risk that the ECB might try to aim for an unduly deflationary policy. This was very close to the Bundesbank practice of building into its monetary control methods 'unavoidable price rises' of 2 per cent.

The ECB selected monetary instruments and monetary control techniques that were closely aligned with Bundesbank practices. The Bundesbank's discount and Lombard rates set a corridor between higher and lower interest rate levels. Similarly, the ECB decided to run its money market intervention operations between bands (normally 2 percentage points apart) defined by its 'marginal lending rate' and 'deposit facility'. Rather than operating an overt money supply target, as was the case with the Bundesbank, the ECB opted for a so-called 'two-pillar' approach using both monetary and economic analysis for its methods of monetary control. As the guardian of the Bundesbank's monetary traditions, ECB board member Issing was particular eager to maintain the importance of the 'monetary pillar' in the bank's analysis of financial developments. Another landmark decision during the run-up to Euro intro-duction in 1999 was opening the future Euro international banking payments system – known as Target – to the UK, even though Britain was outside mone-tary union.[100] This was a vital step that allowed the City of London, from outside the Euro area, to play a leading role on the Euro financial markets once the European currency was established.

Final Euro preparations got under way amid an international economic environment that was turbulent, but on the whole favourable. Currency crises broke out in 1997 and 1998 affecting the emerging economies of South-east Asia and Russia. The unrest strengthened the mood that Europe needed to forge a strong bulwark to the monetary uncertainties in the rest of the world. Inflation across the European Union was only 1.5 per cent in 1998, helped by a steady fall in the oil price to an average for the year of just under $12 a barrel – the lowest dollar oil price since 1974.

On the political scene, a generational change of European leaders took place. Kohl was voted out of office in Germany's September elections. Gerhard Schröder took the helm, with an unsentimental stance on the single currency; he declared it would be weak and would help German companies to boost exports throughout Europe and lay off staff by using improved restructuring and rationalisation investment opportunities in other countries. Among the original line-up of European leaders who had started the EMU journey at Maastricht, only one – Luxembourg prime minister Jean-Claude Juncker – was still in office. In the weeks before the permanent fixing of exchange rates and the birth of the Euro, it became clear that Germany would grant its European partners a striking favour by starting off the new currency at a rela-tively high conversion rate for the D-Mark. This was one of the long-range effects of the currency's excessive rise after Black Wednesday – giving other Euro area countries an initial competitive boost.

Europe showed greatly varying views about the advent of EMU. ECB pres-ident Wim Duisenberg praised Europe's ability to withstand the international currency unrest that had befallen emerging markets in 1997–98. 'On former occasions, there were always flows into the dollar and D-Mark, sometimes tearing apart the European exchange rate system. This time there has been nothing of the sort.'[101] In France, prime minister Lionel Jospin, like many other French politicians, was sceptical about handing over economic control to an unelected central bank. But he declared that 'European economic coor-dination' would carry the day, thanks to the 'political fundament' of the Euro-Group of finance ministers –[102] a forecast that grossly overstated its importance. A lone voice of pessimism was sounded by Antonio Fazio, governor of the Banca d'Italia, who outlined the risks for Italy of permanently fixed exchange rates. The sharp reduction in Italy's budget deficit, allowing it to qualify for EMU, had been due mainly to lower interest rates on Italian government debt: 'The country is enjoying a virtuous circle.'[103] Fazio warned that the future health of Italy and other countries that, in the past, had relied on devaluations to gain competitiveness would depend on ability to make necessary adjustments in economic structures. 'Otherwise,' he said, 'the circle will turn vicious' – a warning that, for the whole of Europe, provided an apt overture to the forthcoming monetary transition.

COPING WITH IMBALANCE

Independence of the Central Bank is a means to an end, to win Germany's approval for monetary union, but it is not the end of the story. We will not be able to escape a situation taking place where the Government will have to give orders to the Central Bank. This could take place in a war, or as a result of an American financial collapse. If the American financial tsunami explodes – $12,000 billion external debt and $2 billion in new borrowings every day – then European governments and the European Central Bank will have to act in concert.

Michel Rocard, former French prime minister, 2007[1]

The single currency brought a radical change of monetary authority across many nations with proud heritages. Under the banner of the Euro gathered the ancient cities that had spawned dynasties, civilisations and empires: Lisbon and Antwerp, Genoa and Paris, Vienna and Amsterdam, Athens and Rome. Some of the currencies that were extinguished, such as the French Franc, the Spanish peseta, the Portuguese escudo, the Dutch guilder, or the Greek drachma, were genuinely antique. Others like the D-Mark, Italian lira, Austrian schilling and the Belgian Franc were relatively modern inventions. All contained the seeds and the spirit of centuries of European experience. The coins for Cortez' men looking out on to Darien; the money of Mozart for his music and Molière for his manuscripts; of Tiberius for his treasure and Krupp for his cannon: all this was fused and remoulded into a new currency for a new age.

When the dawn of the EMU era broke on 1 January 1999, there was a supreme mismatch between politics and money. The Euro marched in; but no regime was overthrown, no monarch tumbled, and no new potentate bestrode the throne. The European Central Bank, acting independently from governments, took over monetary control and inaugurated a 'one-size-fits-all' interest rate policy among the Euro members. They became the only sizeable nations in the world without their own currency, pooling sovereignty in the hope and expectation that each would derive more benefit than it had given away.

The Central Bank's objective was of utmost simplicity: to maintain price stability, taking priority over a secondary aim 'to support the general economic policies in the Community'.[2] The instrument of change, the Euro, was initially brought in merely as a financial unit of account, and then, in 2002, as real money, as national notes and coins were withdrawn from circulation and replaced by the new legal tender. This was a bloodless, noiseless, bureaucratic revolution. But it was a revolution, all the same: an unprecedented, self-willed abrogation of state prerogative.

The additional power channelled to the Central Bank in Frankfurt was manifested in diverse ways. The monetary writ of the ECB extended across a slowly expanding area, with Greece joining the eleven founding states in 2001, Slovenia in 2007, Malta and Cyprus in 2008 and Slovakia in 2009. The status and clout of the new monetary institution grew, too, in line with the increased volumes of Euros held by international investors and transacted on the capital markets. The ECB became, by common consent, the second most important central bank after the Federal Reserve in Washington, responsible for the world's top internationally-traded and reserve currency after the dollar – and even took over the dollar's leading role in some dealing and investment categories.

In the first ten years of the Euro, however, the ECB remained beset by an awkward series of imbalances. Differences came to the fore over the division of economic policy responsibilities with EMU governments, some of which remained jealous of the power they had given away. A gap yawned between the significant monetary might that the ECB was perceived to have amassed, and its actual ability – rather slender, it might appear – to improve the lives of the ordinary Europeans who had been enjoined to give it their trust.

The volume of international payments disequilibria overhanging world financial markets began to increase inexorably – rising current account deficits in the US, UK, Spain, France and Italy on the one hand, and large surpluses in China, Russia and Middle East oil exporters on the other. And there was a progressively growing divergence between the financial fire-power at the ECB's disposal and the far greater monetary ammunition assembled by private and public sector institutions on the world investment scene. These ranged from hedge funds and private equity firms to the shadowy para-state

Sovereign Wealth Funds running the surplus capital of wealthy developing economies from the Middle East and Asia.[3] All these institutions were surrounded by potent mythology – and frequently attracted blame from politicians and electorates for the manifest malfunctioning of the world financial system.

Homely Bluntness

The man chosen to preside over the European Central Bank in its formidable set of initial challenges, the laconic, tousle-haired Wim Duisenberg from the Nederlandsche Bank, brought to his duties homely bluntness combined with notorious stubbornness. His down-to-earth phraseology resonated with the echoes of his rural homeland of Friesland in northern Netherlands: the Dutchman's description of the German central bank's traditional resilience to political pressure – 'The Bundesbank is like whipped cream. The harder you beat it, the stiffer it gets' – came to apply to the European Central Bank under his leadership, too. Unfortunately, his penchant for plain speaking turned into a reputation for simply speaking too much.[4] Even before he took his post in June 1998, Duisenberg had been politically weakened by previous bruising encounters with the French government over the terms and length of his mandate. He frequently described his arch adversary, President Jacques Chirac, with ill-disguised contempt as 'that man' – hostility that was certainly mutual.

Duisenberg's early statements on financial market communication were well-meaning. Expounding his desire to follow the lead of the famously Delphic chairman of the Federal Reserve, Duisenberg declared, 'I have to watch my words with the same intensity as Alan Greenspan.'[5] However, in the problematic first three years of the Euro, when the currency existed only as a financial instrument and not as a freely-circulating physical currency, Duisenberg did not always proceed with appropriate care, committing numerous public relations gaffes, particularly over the exchange rate, that made him (not wholly justifiably) a byword for waywardness.

Duisenberg's overall record was much more positive than his somewhat bumbling public persona might indicate. He spearheaded a crucial period of build-up of the ECB's functions, welding together staff from across Europe and inaugurating a collegiate spirit among the policy-making Governing Council – made up of the ECB's six-person Executive Board and the governors of the national central banks from the Euro area – meeting twice a month on Thursdays on the thirty-sixth floor of the Frankfurt Eurotower.[6] 'I had my hesitations about the number of people around the table at the Governing

Council and whether this would impede effective decision-making', admits Nout Wellink, Duisenberg's successor as Nederlandsche Bank president – and one of the only four who, in 2008, had been a member of the Council since it was set up. 'But this was not a problem. Much of this is due to Wim Duisenberg and the way that he started in 1998–99.'[7]

A substantial part of the early difficulties of the ECB and its president stemmed from the acceleration of an eight-year run of dollar strength that started in 1995, straddling the presidencies of Bill Clinton and George W. Bush. In a similar pattern to the dollar's firmness two decades earlier, between 1979 and 1985, under Presidents Carter and Reagan, the US currency's gains at first helped European economies – by making Europe's exports cheaper – and then put them under pressure, because higher interest rates were needed to counter currency depreciation. Starting with an exchange rate of $1.18 when the Euro was introduced in January 1999, the Euro declined by 30 per cent to a low of $0.84 against a rampant dollar during its first three years. The US currency profited both from relatively high Federal Reserve interest rates and from buoyant American growth at around 4 per cent a year.

The ECB was forced to raise its benchmark interest rates seven times from late 1999 onwards to protect the currency and offset fears (especially in Germany) of imported inflation. The ECB intervened with the New York Federal Reserve Bank in September 2000 to try to brake the currency's decline – one of the only two occasions in the ECB's first decade that it intervened on the foreign exchanges.[8] The action was ineffective, partly because of what was regarded as only lukewarm support for the Euro from Clinton's Treasury Secretary Lawrence Summers. The Euro tumbled further the following month when, in a celebrated blunder, Duisenberg ruled out fresh support intervention connected to an outbreak of tension in the Middle East. The statement, in an interview with the London *Times*, broke the central bankers' cardinal rule of not discussing foreign exchange intervention tactics in public, and confirmed Duisenberg's accident-prone reputation.[9]

Even as the US economy slowed in 2001 after the election victory of George W. Bush, and US interest rates started to decline, the Euro lost ground further. This reflected the foreign exchange markets' view that the ECB's caution about cutting interest rates – based on worries about the expansion of the European money supply – was holding back expansion in the core economies of Europe, Germany, France and Italy, mired in a period of sluggish growth. The problems in the Big Three Euro economies – making up 70 per cent of EMU GDP – overshadowed positive news elsewhere, above all in countries like Spain, Ireland and Greece, which were all able to make use of the Bundesbank legacy of low interest rates to expand economic dynamism in the early years of monetary union. Negative views on the European economy were reinforced by evidence of policy divergences between Chancellor Schröder and President Chirac, who had conspicuously failed to rekindle the alliance between their predecessors Kohl and Mitterrand.

Referring to disagreements between Chirac and Schröder on agricultural reforms and on voting weights at the European parliament, Pierre Muscovici, the French minister for Europe, said the two countries were taking positions on the basis of 'national interest that are not identical . . . Undoubtedly, this has weakened the EU.'[10] The ECB somewhat reluctantly started to cut borrowing costs in 2001 to bolster growth, joining in a round of coordinated interest rate reductions with the Federal Reserve after the September 2001 terrorist attacks on the US, a move that sent a further flurry of international funds into the US as a 'safe haven' from world political turmoil.

The Euro's initial weakness under Duisenberg's stewardship sparked an outpouring of *schadenfreude* from Anglo-Saxon detractors.[11] Public confidence in the currency across the Euro area plummeted – especially in ultra-sensitive Germany.[12] But there were some beneficial offsetting factors. Reflecting low international commodity prices, the Euro's weakness did not lead to any resurgence in European inflation, which was restricted to less than 2 per cent during its first five years – an important triumph for Duisenberg. Additionally, potentially the most taxing episode of the ECB president's tenure – the physical introduction of Euro notes and coins in January 2002 across a vast area stretching from Finland to the Canary Islands – proceeded far more smoothly than almost anyone had predicted, a tribute to the organisational skills of the ECB and the national central banks.

The changeover – marked, in perhaps the most overt display of Euro enthusiasm, by Italians hurling their old lire into the Trevi fountain in Rome – was a continent-wide logistical operation involving transfer of 8 billion new banknotes and 38 billion coins to banks, retail stores, and vending machines, and the withdrawal of 6 billion national banknotes and 29 billion coins.[13] The ECB coordinated the printing of a total reserve stock of 15 billion banknotes worth €633 billion, and 52 billion coins worth €16 billion. The notes, if laid end to end, would reach the moon and back about two-and-a-half times. By 3 January 2002, 96 per cent of all automated teller machines in the Euro area were dispensing Euro banknotes; one week after the introduction more than half of all cash transactions were being conducted in Euros, and the cash changeover was completed within two months, when national banknotes and coins ceased to be legal tender by the end of February.

The changeover produced none of the disastrous setbacks that many (frequently, but not solely, Anglo-Saxon) commentators had predicted, but it was accompanied by widespread public discontent throughout the Euro area about price mark-ups by shops and restaurants. This dissatisfaction – although difficult to substantiate in statistical data on Euro area inflation – had a large-scale political impact.[14] Jean-Claude Juncker, Luxembourg's prime minister and finance minister, who plays an important role in Euro policy coordination as president of the Euro-Group of EMU finance ministers, said:

> Those businesses that took advantage of the Euro introduction to implement unwarranted and unjustified price increases did enormous long-term damage to the single currency project. Ever since the 'Teuro' episode,* the suspicion that something not quite right is happening to prices has not gone away, even though in many members, inflation is actually lower than before the introduction of the Euro.[15]

Romano Prodi, president of the European Commission during the Euro's preparatory years, and twice Italian prime minister, also pointed to the Euro's problems of public acceptance: 'The Italians are not blaming the Euro for the slow growth [in Italy]. They blame the Euro for specific inflationary effects, for increased prices in restaurants and for other services. This happened because the changeover was not managed well.'[16]

Soon after the successful Euro changeover, in February 2002, Duisenberg finally declaimed his retirement with the words, 'Enough is enough.'[17] However, he did not leave the ECB until more than eighteen months later, in view of the time needed to clear his designated successor, France's Jean-Claude Trichet, from allegations of misdemeanour after a long-running investigation – initiated by Chirac – into Trichet's role in the ill-starred affairs of state-owned bank Crédit Lyonnais. When he finally stepped down, Duisenberg took issue with his critics: 'If you read the Anglo-Saxon press, then we paid too much attention to monetary growth. It seems that money shouldn't matter for monetary policy. If you read the German press, the story was different. Some said we communicated too little. Others said we communicated too much. When you are flanked on both sides, then you must be somewhere in the middle of the park.'[18] Like his successor Trichet, Duisenberg recognised that the ECB was fighting a near-continuous battle against largely sceptical public opinion:

---

* A play on the German word *teuer* meaning expensive.

It was not so long ago that most people doubted that the single currency would ever see the light of day. Then, when they saw that it would, they speculated that only a few countries would be able to join. But they underestimated the resolve of European governments to be part of this great step forward in Europe's history.

Trichet benefited from a fortunate coincidence. Almost as soon as he took over, the dollar started to weaken, driven down on the foreign exchanges against the Euro and other leading currencies by the view that a major dollar decline was needed to correct the burgeoning current account deficit in the American balance of payments. The change in the Euro's fortunes, which was accompanied by a slow recovery in the overall European economy, helped imbue Trichet with a Bundesbank-style aura of monetary firmness, strengthening his credentials for warding off political attacks on the ECB's independence. In contrast to Duisenberg, who frequently found himself under external pressure, Trichet appeared – at least initially – in masterly control of the agenda. This was an invaluable settling-in period. The ECB Council was able to keep interest rates unchanged for Trichet's first two years in the job, reflecting an absence of inflation pressures in a generally weak European economy.

Europe's sluggish expansion was caused above all by a long bout of economic doldrums and high unemployment in Germany, where the economy showed virtually no growth between 2002 and 2004, causing rising budget deficits and prompting Chancellor Schröder's government to abandon any attempt at adhering to the fiscal rules of the Stability and Growth Pact. Economists throughout Europe warned that, at a time of slow growth, implementing rigid rules for public sector borrowing would risk turning downturn into depression. A more flexible stance was backed, too, by Romano Prodi, president of the European Commission and one of the architects of Italy's Euro membership. He called the Pact 'stupid' and urged 'intelligence' in interpreting its fiscal limits.[19] In November 2003 France and Germany joined forces to suspend the sanctions mechanism of the Pact – sparking resistance from many smaller states which claimed that EMU's largest members should set a good example.[20]

After that, the tide turned again. Guided in particular by a gradual improvement in the German economy from 2005 onwards, Trichet masterminded a gradual increase in ECB interest rates from December 2005 to June 2007, in eight separate quarter-percentage 'point moves starting from the low point of 2 per cent bequeathed by Duisenberg. In contrast to his predecessor, Trichet could justify the interest rate increases to public opinion and to the foreign exchange markets not as a reaction to a weakening Euro – which after 2003 gained ground almost uninterruptedly against the dollar – but as a pragmatic response to the welcome pick-up in Euro area economic activity.

Trichet's stature was improved, too, by his gruelling preparation for the job. This included his handling as director of the French Treasury of the 1992–93 Battle of the Franc, as well as his ten-year tenure as governor of the Banque de France. In contrast to Duisenberg's career in the Netherlands, where the Dutch central bank's adherence to the Bundesbank's policies seldom caused controversy, Trichet had been engaged in a near-continuous struggle with French politicians over stewardship of the French economy. This was a useful hardening exercise for the ECB skirmishes ahead, and also taught him valuable skills in commanding public opinion.

An intense personality with near-inexhaustible reserves of charm, stamina and cunning, Trichet was much better placed than Duisenberg – who tragically died in a swimming-pool accident in the South of France less than two years after his departure – to stamp his hallmark on the ECB. Throughout his career, Trichet had scrupulously fine-tuned his principles to match the most propitious long-term political currents; since 1993, realising that this was the essential factor for EMU, he had been a fully-fledged supporter of central banking independence. He showed himself a much more adroit, though frequently less entertaining, spokesman for the ECB than Duisenberg. Trichet showed much more cautious monetary choreography, using highly guarded language in his own commentaries to signal the ECB's policy stance, and bringing in tough new guidance for other Council members to ensure they spoke with one voice.

Trichet's presidency, combined with the climbing Euro, undoubtedly bolstered the European Central Bank's international position. A master of political dramaturgy, Trichet learnt early on the art of appealing to disparate audiences with equal verve and credibility, deploying a mixture of steel and seduction, and relishing the chameleon-like nature of his task: 'In Germany, they think of me as a Frenchman, in France, as a German.' At his first meetings of German bankers in Frankfurt or Berlin, his audiences marvelled at the spectacle of a French functionary in charge of the ECB. Speaking an appropriate smattering of German – but mostly a flow of melodiously-accented English, far more enchantingly than any Bundesbanker – he succeeded in adopting, with matchless self-conviction, the German central bank's discarded mantle.

With slightly condescending flattery and a touch of the well-appointed courtier, Trichet greets interlocutors with unfailing respect. He kisses ladies' hands with old-fashioned gallantry – whether they be Chancellor Angela

Merkel or the wives of Frankfurt-based foreign journalists – and flamboyantly addresses former British Chancellors of the Exchequer as 'Monsieur le Chancelier'. With his literary leanings, Trichet combines the jargon of a monetary technocrat with the imaginative diction of a philosopher-poet. He does not 'think about' monetary issues but 'meditates' on them,[21] he speaks of 'a good poem [as] a gold coin that doesn't lose its value',[22] and he relishes the ECB's perpetual voyage into uncharted waters: 'We know that we are making history, because we never know what will happen next.'[23] In the Netherlands in 2004 Trichet dwelled on Europe's 'enriching diversity' in the arts as well as monetary affairs, peppering his address not with economic statistics but with quotes (in the original language) from van Gogh, Shakespeare, Goethe and Chateaubriand.[24]

Trichet won praise even from those who profess doubts about EMU and the policies behind it. John Major, the British prime minister who endured Black Wednesday, said in 2007:

> EMU had a very difficult birth. It was established at the wrong time, for the wrong reasons and in the wrong circumstances. But it's been very deftly handled by the European Central Bank. I've a high regard for Trichet – he's a very able man. The ECB now has developed a reputation for monetary management.[25]

Richard Lambert, director general of the UK employers' association, the Confederation of British Industry, generally a sceptic about France's long-time stance of shackling the Franc to the D-Mark, said, 'I am full of admiration for the ECB. They have brilliantly managed the formidable task of creating a single monetary policy in Europe. Trichet is a clever, wily man who can also be very amusing.'[26] In similar vein, a senior American monetary official qualifies Trichet as 'a very smart, clever man, grandiose in his statements. He has a lot of confidence in the ability of his words to shape attitudes and expectations. But I wonder whether he's quite as clever as he thinks he is?' A man of Trichet's image-consciousness was not displeased to be the world's best-known central banker after Ben Bernanke, chairman of the Federal Reserve – nor to be considerably senior in central banking experience.[27] Taking into account his continuous period of central bank leadership since 1993, Trichet became, by 2008, by a span of four years, the Governing Council's most experienced member, ranking as the longest-serving top-flight European central banker since the 1960s.

Sitting in his thirty-fifth floor office in the Frankfurt Eurotower, Trichet playfully emphasises the collegiate nature of his ECB team, in a bid to offset the widely-held impression that, in reality, there is only one person at the Central Bank who counts: himself. 'If you think back to a forecast you might have made in 1999: "Could you imagine sitting here with the president who is French and chief economist who is German, together with all our colleagues in the Executive Board – Greek, Austrian, Spanish, Italian – and all our colleagues in the Governing Council, in charge of the Central Bank of the Euro area as a whole, and not of any particular economy?" '28

Trichet's deputy as ECB vice president since 2002 has been Lucas Papademos, the scholarly and self-effacing former governor of the Bank of Greece. Apart from Trichet and Papademos, the longest-serving Board member is Gertrude Tumpel-Gugerell, the former deputy president of the Bank of Austria, who joined in 2003 and has responsibility for the 'plumbing' of European finance, in the form of banking payments systems, including the inter-bank Target scheme. The other members are José-Manuel González-Páramo from the Banco de España, who looks after money market and foreign exchange operations; Lorenzo Bini Smaghi, from the Banca d'Italia and Italian Finance Ministry, who is in charge of international affairs; and Jürgen Stark, formerly at the Bundesbank and the Bonn Finance Ministry, who took over Issing's economic responsibilities in 2006. Three of the six-strong Board, Trichet, Bini Smaghi and Stark, previously worked at national finance ministries – giving the Board more robustness in national and international monetary diplomacy than was the case under Duisenberg.29

All the Board members have responsibility for policies that extend well beyond the Euro area. Tumpell-Gugerell and her team, for instance, work on payments systems with non-EMU states such as Poland, Hungary, Romania and the Czech Republic, and share experience with other countries including the Gulf states, Egypt, China and the Balkans. Among González-Páramo's duties in the ECB's money market operations is management of the Bank's €41 billion ($60 billion) in gold and foreign exchange reserves, pooled from part of the individual holdings of national central banks.30 Ironically, in view of the political controversy generated by the issue of European reserve pooling in previous decades, the ECB's currency reserves are tiny compared with world-wide official reserves of $7,000 billion and the hitherto fast-growing separate holdings (totalling around $3,000 billion) of Sovereign Wealth Funds set up by emerging economies. The Chinese central bank – the People's Bank of China, which could lay claim to outstripping the importance of the ECB and even rival the Federal Reserve in coming years, depending on whether the Chinese currency, the renminbi, is made convertible – holds $1,800 billion in official international reserves. This is thirty times greater than the ECB's reserve assets, and underlines how, even if the ECB wished to take an activist stance in steering the external value of the Euro, it would be unable to do so because of a lack of currency ammunition to influence exchange rates.

The explosion of reserves in the first decade of the twenty-first century was heavily linked to a sharp rise in balance of payments disequilibria and a corresponding increase in international liquidity – factors which helped trigger the sub-prime mortgage crisis in August 2007.[31] The best measure to record the imbalances is the current account balance of payments – recording all foreign trade in goods and services as well as transfers, investment income and other 'invisible' earnings. The sum of individual current account surpluses and deficits in thirteen countries with the largest individual contributions to international liquidity – China, France, Germany, Italy, Japan, Kuwait, Russia, Saudi Arabia, Spain, Switzerland, United Arab Emirates, UK and US – more than quadrupled between 1998 and 2007 to $2,300 billion.[32]

The US current account deficit tripled over this period, from $213 billion to $738 billion (although the peak was reached in 2006, as exports rose thereafter, under the impact of the weaker dollar). The relative ease with which international funds flowed into the US to finance the burgeoning balance of payments deficit underlined how, under floating exchange rates, capital flows progressively swamped purely trade-induced currency movements. During the thirty years between 1950 and 1980, the US current account fluctuated between surpluses and deficits of no more than 1 per cent of GDP, whereas already by 2005 the shortfall was six times as large. Deficits also rose sharply in the UK, Spain, France and Italy (the latter two countries had run surpluses before the advent of EMU). On the other hand, surpluses expanded fast in the developing countries and in parts of the industrialised world (from $31 billion to $360 billion between 1998 and 2007 in China, from a deficit of $16 billion to a surplus of $255 billion in Germany, from $119 billion to $212 billion in Japan, from zero to $77 billion in Russia, and from a deficit of $13 billion to a surplus of $101 billion in Saudi Arabia.)

A large excess of savings through the build-up in surpluses, along with the emergence of the US as the world's largest borrower, contributed to the trend for US banks to create ever more risky borrowing mechanisms. In the period up to 2007, the US sucked in more than $5 billion a day from the rest of the world to finance both its enormous current account deficit and the still larger volumes of international capital outflows.[33] Between 2000 and 2006 international issuance of credit instruments rose twelve-fold, from $250 billion to $3,000 billion, according to bankers' estimates – activity that appeared to accelerate after 2004 as investors sought higher returns after a long period of relatively low interest rates.[34] Most notorious was a range of debt vehicles developed in the US to re-package higher-risk loans to less trustworthy mortgage borrowers into a series of innocuous-looking debt instruments all benefiting from relatively high credit ratings that turned out in many cases to be almost entirely fictional.

Trichet and other central bankers were aware of the growing risks. In January 2007 he criticised lack of transparency in some innovative areas of financial markets and warned that there could soon be some 'repricing of credit risk'.[35] He said in May 2007 'perhaps all the risks are not fully appreciated ... Episodes in the global economy where you have "capital chasing investment" are not necessarily sustainable in the very long run.'[36] A dilemma lay behind Trichet's words: central bankers, while anxious about rising banking risk, welcomed a significant degree of financial innovation to help harness excess savings towards financing world-wide disparities in economic performance, not least within the Euro area itself. Too many Cassandra-like predictions of a bursting of the credit bubble could have accelerated the outcome with dire consequences, and the central bankers did not want to stand accused of killing geese laying golden eggs.

When the crisis eventually erupted in August 2007 with the sudden revelations of the risky and illiquid nature of many sub-prime mortgage instruments, Trichet gained for himself and the ECB, more or less overnight, and in the most difficult circumstances, an enviable reputation for practical central banking skills. The enormous – and (as it turned out) long-lasting – shock to the banking system was completely unexpected. What Trichet called 'that tsunami that came across the Atlantic' gained unprecedented virulence when it reached Europe on 9 August, causing the European financial markets to seize up, and prompting the ECB to take a highly activist stance by unilaterally pumping in €95 billion in overnight liquidity to ease the balance sheets of hard-pressed banks. Such exercises were repeated in the coming months. The European Central Bank showed considerably more effectiveness than the Federal Reserve and the Bank of England in reacting to the crisis. In particular, it scotched previous criticisms that the complexities of Governing Council decision-making made it incapable of making decisions quickly. One reason for the ECB's effectiveness was that it was able to use a wider variety of collateral from European banks' balance sheets to back the emergency lending – a legacy of the pragmatic merging of collateral rules from the member countries' central banks when the ECB was set up. Another important factor was exhaustive planning and meticulous coordination – the same qualities that the bank had shown with the Euro changeover in 2002. As Alexandre Lamfalussy, president of the ECB's forerunner, the European Monetary Institute, commented:

> Right from the massive liquidity creation during the early days of August 2007, the ECB passed the crisis management test with flying colours. The ECB's precautionary planning paid off. It carried out two stress-testing exercises a couple of years before the crisis. These showed that, despite the organisational complexity of the Eurosystem, it was possible to establish, in the event of crisis, a first-class communication system, a mechanism for decision-making and an effective division of labour among the national central banks and the ECB.[37]

The aftermath of the credit crunch raised doubts about the ECB's future policy course. On the one hand, coupled with the effects of the doubling in oil prices in 2007–08, the financial market dislocation led to a sharp slowdown in Euro area growth – especially in the peripheral countries of the Euro area that had relied most on low interest rates and booming property markets to fuel expansion. On the other, higher energy prices, combined with simultaneous increases in prices of food and other commodities – owing to a mixture of speculation and increased demand from developing countries – sent inflation to well above the ECB's 2 per cent target.

Faced with these contradictory pressures, and responding to its principal mandate of safeguarding price stability, the ECB opted to keep its benchmark interest rate unchanged at 4 per cent after the events of 9 August, in contrast to the 3.25 percentage-point drop in leading US interest rates – from 5.25 per cent to 2 per cent – in the nine months after August 2007. The switchover in US and European interest rates (although less extreme) bore some resemblance to the transformation in trans-Atlantic interest rate policy in the early 1990s. It added to the weakness of the dollar, which tumbled to a low of $1.60 to the Euro in July 2008, roughly half its value in summer 2001 – causing a further squeeze for hard-pressed European exporters.

The questions over the ECB's interest rate policies sharpened a long-standing debate over the policy credibility of one of its main instruments for measuring inflationary pressure. The more hawkish faction of the ECB's Council regarded excessive growth in European money supply as a harbinger of forthcoming inflation, whereas others were included to tone down the indicator's importance. This led to divisions on the ECB Board on whether the ECB should modify its 'two pillar' policy – involving monitoring money supply as well as general economic analysis – to a 'one pillar' stance, in line with the move away from monetary targeting by the Federal Reserve and other central banks.

The emergence of an ECB policy dilemma coincided with the advent of President Nicolas Sarkozy, who swept in to the Elysée Palace in May 2007 at the end of Chirac's undistinguished second six-year term, with a tantalisingly mixed programme ranging from liberal reforms and pro-American defence policies to a protectionist 'France-first' stance on trade and investment. Sarkozy – febrile, egotistical and thin-skinned – tended to regard France as a victim, not a beneficiary, of EMU. He displayed considerable public resentment about France's failure to establish a *'gouvernement économique'* to provide a political counterweight to the ECB – maintaining arguments earlier put by Mitterrand and Chirac, but with greater impatience. Expressing France's frustration with the political balance sheet of the Euro's first decade, a senior financial official in the Sarkozy government said: 'There is a gap between what we have created – a major currency with a lot of energy – and what we have accomplished. We were expecting a tool of monetary diplomacy. A great deal of effort has gone into this, but all the power is in Frankfurt.'

Silvio Berlusconi, the media mogul-cum-politician re-elected as Italy's prime minister in 2008, joined Sarkozy as a second leader with strong leanings towards enacting some form of political control over the European Central Bank. Once in power, however, Berlusconi toned down his anti-ECB election campaign rhetoric to concentrate on re-invigorating the country that faces the most intractable economic problems of any EMU member.

The depressed French mood on EMU stood in stark contrast to the highly positive assessment from leading politicians in Germany. According to Peer Steinbrück, the tough-minded Social Democrat finance minister in the German Grand Coalition with the Christian Democrats, that ruled between 2005 and 2009:

My feeling about the Euro's success is close to euphoric. It is one of the greatest success stories in the history of the European Community. It has produced lower inflation and has provided a welcome disciplinary force. It has been good for consumers because transfer costs have fallen – even though more needs to be done to cut costs in cross-border banking payments. And it is good for companies because they no longer have to cope with exchange rate fluctuations. The advantages outweigh the disadvantages. In the past – even with the Bundesbank's formal independence – there was a good spirit of cooperation between the German finance minister and the president of the Bundesbank. Of course I do not have this relationship with the President of the European Central Bank. I do not telephone him in the way that I might have done with the President of the Bundesbank. By entering the Euro, Germany gave up national monetary control. But we received very important advantages in return, through the fixing of European currencies and the promotion of stability culture throughout the Euro area.[38]

An important aim of better coordination between the ECB and European governments, according to Sarkozy, would be to bring down the rise in the Euro, similar to efforts enacted by the US, China and Japan.[39] Over the past forty years, France had frequently been massively hostile to American monetary decision-making. However, in 2007–08 Sarkozy and other French politicians found themselves praising the US central bank by comparison with the ECB, in particular the Federal Reserve Board's statute giving equal weight to the goals of stable prices and maximum employment.[40] Summing up views of many politicians from both Right and Left, former Socialist prime minister Laurent Fabius called for a 'more pragmatic and less dogmatic' ECB policy to bring down the Euro.[41]

> The Fed is perfectly independent, but there is concertation with the US government ... Independence means that you speak to each other, that you listen, not that you say: 'I don't want to know, I don't care.' During my time in the French government, I have seen these remarkable people at the European Central Bank. That left a negative impression, because I saw in their views, perhaps to strengthen their power, that they were concerned only with inflation. Growth and employment didn't really concern them.

The French calls for greater European policy coordination, for all their apparent conviction, were somewhat inconsistent; in the first decade of EMU France itself failed to set a lead in this area, for example, on reducing budget deficits, liberalising trade or deregulating working hours – yet such harmonisation represented precisely the goal that an 'economic government' would promote. An ancillary reason for French frustration at the workings of EMU was Germany's large increase in competitiveness since 1999, which gave a fillip to German exports and hence to German economic growth at the expense of countries such as France and Italy. This phenomenon started to become noticeable only from 2005 onwards after Germany recovered from a difficult transitional period of economic weakness and high unemployment under Chancellor Gerhard Schröder.

According to former prime minister Edouard Balladur, the elder statesman of the French Right and a confidant of Sarkozy, the international environment benefited Germany more than France in the 2000s. 'Germany's mechanical and engineering industries have an excellent reputation. Countries like China and India need such capital goods and naturally they buy them from Germany.'[42] Jean Peyrelevade, former chief of staff to French prime minister Pierre Mauroy, and an *eminence grise* on the French financial scene since the 1980s, said diverging performances emphasised a basic Franco-German divide:

> The German population realises that having a healthy structure for industrial production is important for growth and purchasing power. But supporting the productive capacity of the economy is not popular in France. German enterprises' margins are 20 per cent higher than in France. The policies that Sarkozy is following reflect the continued belief that the key to economic growth is by bolstering purchasing power through income distribution and reduced personal taxation. Sarkozy believes sincerely in his policies, but he is making a tragic error.[43]

Former German Chancellor Gerhard Schröder, previously a sceptic on the Euro, said in 2007, 'Those who were in favour of EMU were right and I was wrong.'[44] Although confessing some sympathy for Sarkozy's position on the ECB, Schröder believes the French president started a campaign that he could not win. 'The French would like greater coordination of economic polices than the Germans would normally want. Up to a point I understand the French position. A fixation on fighting inflation is not a good thing, and creates problems for politicians. But if you try to fight the German stability culture, you are bound to lose. It's better not to start that game.' Schröder urged the French to face reality:

> If France's political aim was to create the Euro as part of a plan to weaken Germany so as to reduce our supposed economic dominance, then the result has been exactly the opposite. The rise in German competitiveness means that Germany is stronger, not weaker. In a way, that is obvious and inevitable because we are the strongest economy in Europe. We have less inflation – and the others can no longer devalue.

Fraught Decision-Making

The activist French stance on managing the ECB, as well as the trials of the international credit crunch, brought fresh challenges for the ECB's decision-making procedures and communications. The institution has to tread a fine line between the openness and accountability of a public institution, and traditional central banking secrecy – and it needs to respect the independence from governments inherited from the Bundesbank and enshrined in its statute by international treaty. One weighty voice criticising the ECB's communication policy is that of former European Commission president Jacques Delors, who said it was 'a negative factor in the sense that it has added to Euro pessimism. The ECB president puts too much emphasis on inflation rather than on the total parameters affecting the economy.'[45]

The ECB's decisions are primarily negotiated and announced in English, the international language of business and finance. Yet, at a national level, the monetary stance within the sixteen states of EMU is expounded and executed in local languages – requiring an arduous linguistic balancing act.

The Bundesbank Council, meeting on Thursdays at fortnightly intervals (like the ECB), debated and negotiated in German, among Germans; the ECB Governing Council comes to its conclusions at gatherings of sixteen different nationalities, mainly speaking English.[46] In 2009 there were two native English speakers on the Council: Patrick Honohan, governor of the Central Bank of Ireland; and Michael Bonello, governor of the Central Bank of Malta.[47] Further Anglo-Saxon credentials stem from the Bundesbank's Axel Weber – whose wife is English and who has considerable international academic experience – and Mario Draghi, governor of the Banca d'Italia, who (like Federal Reserve chairman Bernanke) is a graduate of Massachusetts Institute of Technology (MIT) and also worked at New York investment bank Goldman Sachs.[48] Among other American-influenced Council members, Papademos was at MIT and Columbia University, and worked as an economist at the Federal Reserve Bank of Boston. Athanasios Orphanides, governor of the Central Bank of Cyprus, at 46 the youngest member of the Governing Council, is another MIT graduate, who worked for seventeen years at the Federal Reserve Board.[49]

Trichet brought far greater decisiveness to the Council than Duisenberg, who confined himself largely to summing up and presenting the conclusions afterwards. Trichet steers meetings with a rigour lacking under his predecessor. During Duisenberg's stewardship of the Council, Trichet coined the phrase, 'We are a team, the chairman is the coach' – a slogan that, under his own firm leadership, fell into disuse. European government representatives can attend the Governing Council gatherings, although they have no voting rights.[50] Euro-Group president Juncker and Joaquín Almunia, the Spanish European Commissioner for monetary affairs, are frequent participants.[51] Trichet, accompanied by Papademos, normally attends the monthly informal meetings of the ministerial Euro-Group hosted by Juncker.

The Bundesbank Council published minutes of its meetings only after thirty years; the secrecy surrounding its proceedings played a part in fostering its own sometimes exaggerated mythology. The Bundesbank Council's prowess as a management group was, according to Ernst Welteke, president between 1999 and 2004, less impressive than its anti-inflation policy credibility. 'Particularly the professors among the members carried out very interesting high-level discussions, but it was noticeable how they failed to solve practical questions.'[52] The ECB's disclosure rules follow the Bundesbank's thirty-year pattern, in significant contrast with the practices of the Federal Reserve Board and Bank of England, which publish minutes of their interest rate-setting sessions three and two weeks respectively after the meetings take place.

The ECB's multinational, multilingual set-up creates considerable potential for confusion on financial markets through unclear references or misleading translations, and provides a strong reason for control and circumspection.[53] The ECB's growing membership – up from eleven to sixteen countries since it started – adds further to communication and governance challenges. Germany and France still make up more than 50 per cent of the Euro area's economic weight, but – since the Governing Council operates on the principle of 'one member, one vote' – their share of voting rights has fallen.[54] The issue of disclosure is made acutely sensitive by the EMU area's lack of political unity. As part of their independent birthright, the ECB's Board and Council are supposed to represent the Euro area as a whole, rather than their own countries. In practice, the national links are enduring.[55]

The ECB believes that publishing details of Council meetings, in line with British or US practice, could place pressure on national central bank governors, and undermine the ECB's independence.[56] 'Such a measure would draw attention to individual positions,' according to Trichet. 'What counts is the position of the collegial decision maker, the Governing Council.'[57] The Bundesbank's Axel Weber, who has emerged (especially in his public statements) as one of the most hawkish ECB Council members, called publishing minutes 'old fashioned' and said this had negative effects by moving markets weeks after the event.[58]

The European Parliament, which meets Trichet five times a year in a regular dialogue, acknowledged the ECB's difficulties in publishing minutes – but called upon the Governing Council to take other measures to improve transparency,[59] including improving the information flow at press conferences that Trichet, like Duisenberg previously, holds immediately after Council meetings to explain policy decisions, starting with a formal statement approved by the Council.[60] The ECB claims that publishing a statement and allowing the press to ask questions is more informative than publishing minutes. The press conferences have occasionally revealed inconsistencies between the formal statement and Trichet's own comments, producing confusion as well as clarity. Yet the sessions with the media are also prone to a ritualistic quality that can impede revealing interchanges with the ECB's multinational squad of press followers. Incongruously, British and American journalists (despite hailing from countries that are not in EMU) habitually ask the most questions.[61]

During both the Duisenberg and Trichet presidencies, the Governing Council made monetary policy decisions either by unanimity or by a broad consensus, rather than by taking votes. The ECB's statutes formally lay down a route to decision-making by voting[62] – the method used by the US Federal Open Market Committee and the Bank of England, as well as (previously) by the Bundesbank. Yet both the larger and the smaller EMU members appear discomfited by the potential tensions inherent in the one member, one vote system. Enlargement of EMU has increased the theoretical possibility that the largest states could be outvoted by economic minnows. Malta, Cyprus, Slovenia and Slovakia, the four latest adherents, have a combined population of eleven million, compared with eighty-two million for Germany. Economically, Germany outweighs Malta by 500 times – but the president of the Bundesbank has the same vote as the Maltese governor. Over time, it seems inevitable that the ECB will move towards decision-making by voting – which could draw attention to the striking disparity of forces on the Governing Council.

Nout Wellink of the Nederlandsche Bank plays down the likelihood of speedy changes, but adds, 'The reason why there have been no votes up to now [on monetary policy at the ECB] has been partly to create a feeling of consensus and collegiality during the early years. There is now less reason to be sensitive on that issue.' John Hurley, the Irish governor, said: 'It might be expected that the ECB Governing Council would move more in the direction of voting over time.'[63] According to the most experienced observer of the ECB's proceedings, Luxembourg prime minister Juncker, 'I believe that the ECB Governing Council will publish minutes of its fortnightly meetings in the next two to three years as part of improved democratic accountability, and that they will also put monetary policy decisions such as changes in interest rates to the vote. This is more difficult for the ECB than for national central banks. Central bank governors do not want to be seen to be taking action against the perceived interests of their countries.'

The ECB's voting and communications are closely tied up with its independence, defended by Trichet with great vehemence, and – in the face of sporadic sniping from Sarkozy – strongly backed by Schröder's successor, Christian Democrat Chancellor Angela Merkel. 'For the Germans, the independence of the European Central Bank is the be all and end all,' she said. 'You won't get the Germans to change that.'[64] Germany's orthodoxy on the ECB was reinforced by her Social Democrat finance minister Steinbrück, who – following the change in German government in 2005 – proved far more adept than his predecessor Hans Eichel in bringing down the German budget deficits in conformity with the Stability and Growth Pact – a contrast with persistently higher budgetary shortfalls in Paris.[65] Steinbrück's budgetary achievements gave him greater authority in opposing French views on the ECB: 'There is no possibility that France can succeed in reducing the European Central Bank's independence. ... These criticisms by Nicolas Sarkozy of the ECB have no effect. I do not know why he rattles at the cage like this – it is completely idiotic.'

The German finance minister's policy-making vigour also has given him more clout in the monthly meetings of the Euro-Group, which Sarkozy campaigned to upgrade into a body that could put pressure on the ECB – an aim fiercely opposed by the Germans. The Euro-Group meetings provide 'a place for informal exchanges and understandings built on common sense', according to Steinbrück. 'A lot of mutual trust has been built up among the members. If we want to settle things, we reach for the telephone and speak to each other. The Euro-Group is certainly becoming more important. But I don't see it developing like a Russian doll, as the inner layer of power within the Community.' Juncker, too, showed broadly contentment with the status quo:

> I believe the Euro-Group can do its job without creating a large counterweight to the ECB. I do not want a bureaucracy that simply produces papers. I have a small team in Luxembourg and I rely heavily on the economic staff of the European Commission for help in preparing meetings ... The debate about monetary policy and the mandate of the ECB is a waste of time. France has not been able to push through its way of thinking here. President Sarkozy has no support among the finance ministers for the suggestion of tighter political controls on the ECB, even though some heads of government might agree with it. Any such policy line by President Sarkozy would always falter because of the very firm German position.

The most revealing indication of German power over the finance ministers came when – in a unique visit by a head of state – Sarkozy invited himself in

July 2007 to a monthly Euro-Group gathering in Brussels, just before the credit crisis exploded.[66] Steinbrück roundly criticised Sarkozy's statement that France would put its budget cuts on hold until 2012, prompting the French president to tell him he was bringing about 'the end of Franco-German friendship'.[67] Steinbrück commented later,

Sarkozy knows the way these meetings are conducted, because he used to be a finance minister. But he came to the meeting with a certain personal view about his position as the French president. He did not expect to be contradicted. It fell to me to make a statement correcting what he had to say. I was speaking, too, on behalf of other finance ministers at the meeting, and they all supported me. I said to my colleagues on leaving the meeting that I had perhaps made an enemy for life. They answered that I had also made a lot of friends.

Trichet's conservative central banking policies, and his strong alliance with the Berlin government over ECB independence and the power of the Euro-Group, put him on a collision course with politicians of all colours in France – circumstances that seem to have increased his obduracy.[68] This is a trait that finds favour with the hard money men in Frankfurt. One German central banker speaks approvingly of Trichet as 'our convert'; another comments that, for Germany, it is incomparably better to have a French ECB president carrying out a Bundesbank-style policy in Frankfurt than a German president carrying out a Banque de France-type policy in Paris – a possible outcome if the ECB had been located in France rather than in Germany.

Expressing general disappointment in Paris about the imbalance in government–central banking power, one of Mitterrand's closest advisers, former Europe minister Elisabeth Guigou, said, 'The economic part of Maastricht has been atrophied. One cannot give complete economic power to a European Central Bank.'[69] According to former prime minister Edouard Balladur, who keeps closely in touch with his former chief of staff Trichet, 'It is not up to the ECB to set economic policy . . . I say to Trichet during his regular visits to see me: "You are not Mr Euro. You are implementing a monetary policy where one of the fundamental issues, the desired level of the Euro against other currencies, is chosen by Euro member governments. That is what happens in all countries as part of the relationship between governments and central banks." '

Such strictures seem to have had little effect on Trichet. According to Nout Wellink of the Nederlandsche Bank, 'He is more independent than in the past. His reaction has been stronger, he is more angry than in the past [about

attacks on the ECB]. Perhaps he has gone through a new intellectual process.'
According to Jean-Claude Juncker:

> Jean-Claude Trichet is a restless defender of independence. He speaks of the need
> for an independent central bank in an almost erotic manner. He has to be more
> radical in his language because he is French. I remind him, somewhat teasingly,
> from time to time that – as a former director of the French Treasury – he was not
> always a believer in an independent ECB.

Former Chancellor Helmut Schmidt delivered a characteristically bitter-sweet
judgement on Trichet's prowess:

> The European Central Bank is the most independent in the world. There is no
> counter-balance that is anchored in a framework. The main counter-balance
> comes from public opinion and also the opinion of the financial institutions. For
> the time being, this is not a problem. How long this situation will last, I do not
> know. It cannot last for ever. We should trust Monsieur Trichet. He is better than
> anyone else. The danger of the present system is that we might get someone who
> is not as good as him.[70]

Trichet had plenty of opportunity for practising his autonomous line.
Immediately after the sub-prime mortgage crisis broke out, Sarkozy attacked
the Bank in September 2007 for pumping liquidity into the financial markets
but refusing to lower interest rates to help businesses, claiming 'They're
making life easier for speculators yet harder for businessmen.'[71] In July 2008
President Sarkozy assailed the ECB's decision to restart interest rate rises –
after a break of more than a year, with an increase from 4 per cent to 4.25 per
cent – as 'at best pointless, at worst, totally counter-productive' and declared
he would continue promoting 'debate' about what he called the bank's
misguided monetary policy.[72] A close adviser to Sarkozy called the independence of the ECB an 'historic error', and said the Central Bank should take
steps, coordinated with other countries, to bring down the Euro from a level
that he claimed was 30 to 40 per cent over-valued against the dollar.

Weakness in the Heartland

The policy discord at the heart of EMU in its first ten years would have been
far less virulent if the three largest members, Germany, France and Italy, had
shown greater dynamism. Economic weakness in these three states, continuing

their history of relatively slow growth in the immediate pre-Euro period, held back overall EMU performance. Lower-income southern countries such as Spain and Greece, and other smaller, peripheral states like Ireland and Finland, used additional economic leeway from the Euro to increase growth, helping to close the prosperity gap with the wealthy EMU core. But in many cases this was achieved at the expense of much higher public- and (especially for Spain) private-sector debt. Servicing this debt may turn out to be more onerous than expected – shown ominously in 2008 by the progressively higher interest rates exacted on government bonds issued by higher debt countries such as Greece and Italy.[73]

The dissonance extended well beyond the Franco-German differences over the status of the European Central Bank. It was exacerbated by the widespread perception that Germany – for all its remaining economic problems – gained more than other countries from EMU membership, and was less hard hit by the Euro's sharp rise against the dollar in 2007–08. France and Italy, accounting for nearly 40 per cent of EMU output, failed to use a relatively benign starting position to enact economic reforms required to compensate for past mistakes and improve potential. The greatest initial benefit for the weaker Euro members (particularly Italy, Spain, Ireland and Greece) was the reduction in EMU interest rates. The substantial reductions in governments' borrowing costs brought immediate (although not necessarily sustainable) reductions in budget deficits and, to a smaller extent, indebtedness; however, most countries failed to build on these achievements.

After a difficult first five years, Germany emerged as the best-managed of the larger EMU economies; overall, though, during the first decade its growth lagged well behind France. Average annual growth in Germany, France and Italy was 1.5 per cent, 2.1 per cent and 1.3 per cent respectively in the first ten years (very similar to the 1993–98 period of pre-EMU transition, when the growth rates were 1.4 per cent, 1.7 per cent and 1.3 per cent respectively). These states increased output at less than half the pace of the faster-growing members Spain (3.6 per cent), Ireland (6 per cent) and Greece (4 per cent) – countries which (with the exception of Greece) also showed above-average growth in 1993–98.[74] The pace of German expansion accelerated in 2004–08 until the credit crisis took hold, whereas for France it remained constant.

In the Euro area as a whole, economic growth in 1999–2008 increased to an annual 2.1 per cent compared with 1.9 per cent in 1993–98 when Europe was navigating the wearisome preparations for the single currency. The overall world economy expanded by 4 per cent annually in the Euro's first decade, against 3 per cent previously. The Euro area's 'growth gap' compared with other, mainly much poorer, countries has increased. The Euro area in its first decade recorded a general fall in unemployment, greater flows of cross-border trade and investment,[75] and a slightly smaller dispersal of economic growth compared with the previous decade. In nearly all these fields, Euro states' performance was, however, broadly similar to that of non-EMU European countries in 1999–2008.

The German economy's main problem during EMU's first decade was the weakness of domestic demand – a direct result of the fall in workers' incomes that was part of a rebalancing of the German economy after unification, and which helped spur a shift of productive resources towards exports. During the transition period at the start of EMU, the traditional consensus-based German corporate system, hinging on close cooperation between management and workforces, enabled considerable restructuring and streamlining across German industry. A combination of the fixing of exchange rates and Germany's success in holding down costs led to unprecedented increases in German price competitiveness against the other members of the single currency area. Germany's greater success in reducing its budget deficit made it more capable than France and Italy of coping with the ECB's continued monetary restrictiveness in 2007–08 to meet the renewed inflation threat that surfaced after the oil price rise.

According to the Organisation for Economic Cooperation and Development, Germany improved its overall competitiveness against all countries by more than 10 per cent between 1998 and 2007, based on labour costs per unit of output in industry.[76] At the same time, Italy's competitiveness position worsened by an astonishing 34 per cent. Germany's focus on high-value capital goods, often in niche sectors where small to medium-sized family-run businesses rank as world leaders, gave the country a powerful edge in trade with fast-growing emerging economies in Asia, Latin America and the Middle East.

German competitiveness based on price *within* EMU was thus complemented by competitiveness based on quality *outside* EMU. This combination led to sizeable increases in the German trade surplus both inside and outside Europe. In spite of a 40 per cent rise in the Euro against the dollar since 2003, Germany in 2007 maintained its status ahead of China as the world's number one exporter, with an export tally only slightly less than the combined total of the other three main economies in Europe, France, the UK and Italy.[77] German exports to EMU members grew 10 per cent a year between 1999 and 2006, well above growth in exports to the Euro area of 7 per cent for Italy, and 6 per cent for the UK and France. But German exports to the non-EMU world rose even faster, by 12 per cent a year, against 7 per cent for France, 10 per cent for Italy and 9 per cent for the UK.[78] The overall result was that Germany's trade surplus with the rest of the world tripled in the Euro's first decade.[79] Germany's trade surplus with France grew threefold, too, over this period. This was a sensitive matter for any Paris government: in 1982 President Mitterrand's advisers told him the bilateral deficit with Germany was 'catastrophic'; by 2007–08 it was more than four times larger.[80]

The competitiveness imbalance was exemplified by significant changes in EMU members' current account balance of payments – a build-up of deficits in Spain, France, Italy and Greece, and large surpluses in Germany and the Netherlands.[81] One of the reasons for overall deterioration in Euro members' competitiveness was very poor productivity growth, particularly Italy, Portugal and Spain.[82] Since the birth of the Euro, a sizeable proportion of domestic consumption in Europe has been switched to purchasing goods from abroad, particularly from Germany – generating, over time, significant (and possibly even permanent) transfers of income and wealth.

Allied to the build-up in balance of payments disequilibria was an inexorable increase in public debt due to higher budget deficits, concentrated on the Euro's three largest members. The extra borrowing reduced governments' flexibility to respond to adverse economic conditions, and heaped additional burdens on future generations for financing pension entitlements for the rising numbers of older people. Since the fall of the Berlin Wall in 1989, overall government debt in Germany, France and Italy increased by a total €3,000 billion – €17,000 per head in Italy, €14,000 in France and €13,000 in Germany.[83]

These figures represent a severe indictment of economic policy-making, particularly in Paris and Rome. Germany could blame the debt increase, at least in part, on the exertions of absorbing former Communist East Germany, a country with only slightly fewer people than the Netherlands and with entrenched economic and social problems. France and Italy, which were unable to use a period of relative economic calm to curb public spending and enhance tax revenues, did not have a similar justification. In Germany, additional debt helped finance economic revival; in France and Italy, it exposed prolonged economic errors – a poor starting point from which to tackle the exceptional challenges of the 2008–9 slowdown.

France's record was particularly disappointing. In their custodianship of public finances, the legacy of Presidents François Mitterrand and Jacques Chirac – rulers for twenty-six successive years – was even worse than that of successive Italian leaders. Over that time, France made significant strides in modernising its leading corporations, its energy industry and its transport infrastructure, but these positive developments were overshadowed by the general profligacy of public finance. As short a time ago as 1980, France's public debt was one of the lowest in Europe – only 20 per cent of GDP, compared with 31 per cent for West Germany, 57 per cent in Italy and 41 per cent for Britain. In 2007 the debt total rose to 64 per cent of GDP, against 63 per cent in reunited Germany, 104 per cent in Italy and 43 per cent in the UK. Since 1989 overall French government debt almost doubled as a proportion of GDP. This was a far greater increase than for Germany, where the debt-to-GDP ratio rose by 50 per cent.[84] Measured by its ability to keep government accounts in good order, France weathered Germany's first unification in 1871 after the Franco-Prussian War more effectively than it did the second one at the end of the Cold War in 1990. Crucially, the poor debt records in France and Italy greatly hampered these countries' ability to cope with the difficult period following the exacerbated autumn 2008 credit crisis.

In the arena of banking and finance, the Euro economies showed highly varied developments, and were affected in different ways towards the end of EMU's first decade by the US sub-prime mortgage upset. An important part of the credo behind the Euro is that integrated banking and financial markets should play a significant role in smoothing out imbalances in economic performance among member states. According to this theory, the relatively small amount of fiscal redistribution throughout the Euro area via the European Union budget (which makes up a mere 1 per cent of EU GDP) should not hinder the financing of economic adjustment, as long as private sector financial institutions can take up the strain in ironing out economic discrepancies.[85] Unfortunately, however, Euro area banking and financial organisations have registered only scant success in improving Europe-wide services for private customers and smaller businesses. The legacy of the credit crunch is that financial organisations throughout the Euro area are likely to show further caution in cross-border activities – a handicap for EMU's cohesiveness and resilience.

The main area where the Euro has driven greater banking efficiency and productivity has been in wholesale banking – producing visible benefits for large investment institutions and bigger companies, rather than for ordinary citizens.[86] In addition, there has been far less cross-border European banking consolidation than earlier predicted – partly because of differences in management culture and practices across the Euro members. The main Euro area banks to have been directly hurt by the problems surrounding US debt instruments were German institutions – a reflection of Germany's large current account surplus that made German banks the most important exporters of capital among EMU members.[87] Leading institutions in Spain, Italy and France were much less affected by the upheaval – one of the reasons why the top commercial banks in the Euro area in 2008 were Spain's Banco Santander, Italy's Unicredit and France's BNP Paribas. These three banks were all considerably larger in equity market capitalisation than the leading bank in Germany, Deutsche Bank – which in 1990, by contrast, had been by far the best-capitalised bank in Europe.[88]

German banks in general slid precipitously down the European league table, reflecting a lack of consolidation in Germany's own banking market, and showing that Germany's prowess in manufacturing was not matched by similar acumen in financial services.[89] In general, the barriers to cross-border banking have been greater than the incentives, as Michel Pébereau, chairman of BNP Paribas, pointed out:

> Today, the European market exists in practice for corporate and investment banking but there is no European market in retail banking. Europe is still split into twenty-seven national markets, due to the remaining barriers of consumer protection laws and taxation of savings, which remain nationally determined and differ widely. Therefore, banks are unable to offer the same products in all member states . . . The extension of retail banking networks into neighbouring countries is prohibitively costly, preventing a single product being offered in all member states, even a simple product such as a consumer loan. The creation of a single market in retail banking would increase competition between banks, promote innovation, reduce products' prices for consumers, strengthen the European banking industry and increase economic growth. But there is strong national resistance to harmonisation of rules.[90]

Rolf Breuer, chief executive of Deutsche Bank in the late 1990s, explained with disarming frankness that his bank's failure to build a cross-border European banking presence was partly because of exaggerated perceptions of German banks' strength. 'Every bank to whom we ever talked automatically saw themselves as the number 2 – even if we really wanted a merger of equals. The more we said that the other bank wouldn't be the number 2, the less they believed us . . . In Italy, we had a really striking position; we were the biggest non-Italian bank. We were also the biggest non-Spanish bank in Spain. We had high quality businesses in both countries and didn't feel under pressure to grow. We were somewhat complacent. We didn't take sufficient note of the consolidation taking place around us. The world was changing and we didn't notice.'[91]

Italy's Unicredit, with its 2005 takeover of Germany's second biggest bank, Munich-based HypoVereinsbank, set the most striking example of cross-border

Euro banking expansion – a feat that, according to Unicredit Chief Executive Alessandro Profumo, was largely due to the Euro and the progress of European integration.

> German unification led to weakness in the whole German economy which was compounded by mistakes in fiscal policy, and thus produced weakness in the banking system . . . All this depressed the valuation of German banks, and was a major reason for our purchase of HVB . . . We were lucky, because we invested in HVB [in June 2005] two months before the economy started to get better. Now everyone says we bought HVB cheaply.[92]

Profumo underlines cross-border adaptation as a prime condition for financial services success. 'We have the advantage of being Italian. We are used to dealing with the different cultures of people from different areas, and this is an advantage in dealing with the Germans. Italians have a high degree of flexibility. The Germans were quite depressed at the time of the HVB takeover. They went from being somewhat arrogant about the performance of their economy to a bit too down-hearted after unification.'

Sharpening Crisis

In the first twelve months of the credit crisis after August 2007, EMU area banks did not need to raise additional capital from sovereign wealth funds and other foreign investors in the same way as non-EMU institutions such as Citicorp, Merrill Lynch and Morgan Stanley in the US, Barclays in the UK and UBS in Switzerland. Nor were there any spectacular collapses in investment banking equivalent to the fall of Wall Street bank Bear Stearns, bailed out by JP Morgan and the Federal Reserve in March 2008, and – even more dramatically – the bankruptcy of Lehman Brothers and the takeover of Merrill Lynch by Bank of America in September 2008. However, shortly after the Lehman and Merrill Lynch shocks, the tide of financial market convulsions washed through into Europe with full force. The Belgian-Dutch bank Fortis, the Franco-Belgian financial group Dexia and Germany's second-biggest mortgage lender Hypo Real Estate all had to be saved from collapse with spectacular private- and public-sector financial rescue packages. Ireland took unilateral measures against financial panic by moving to guarantee all bank deposits – a move quickly followed by Greece and Germany.

At the beginning of October 2008, the credit crisis underwent a further turn for the worse – a moment of fear and panic on world financial markets, but also an opportunity for President Nicolas Sarkozy to show his mettle on the governance of the Euro bloc. Profiting from his position as the six-monthly chairman of the European Council, Sarkozy relished the chance to show leadership. Only three months after he had fiercely criticised the European Central bank's summer-time interest rate increase, Sarkozy received a remarkable vindication of his views. In the face of widespread concern about a looming recession in industrialised countries, the ECB was forced to cut interest rates in October by 0.5 percentage points, in concert with the Federal Reserve and the Bank of England – the first ECB credit easing since Trichet took over the ECB reins in 2003. Sarkozy hosted crisis meetings of European leaders on two consecutive Sundays, on 5 and 12 October, pointedly inviting UK prime minister Gordon Brown (despite Britain's non-membership of the Euro) as well as the ECB's Trichet. Sarkozy proclaimed: 'This [crisis] needs concrete measures and unity – and this is what we have today'[93] – launching a make-or-break effort to bring greater coordination to the Euro club.

Shortly afterwards, European and North American governments announced separate moves to prop up their banking systems with total pledged funding of between $3,000 and $4,000 billion to ward off the most serious financial threat to the world economy since the 1930s Depression. One result of the Sarkozy-hosted meetings was an effective suspension of the EMU area's Stability and Growth Pact as a means of offsetting recessionary risks – opening the way to a further expansion of Europe's debt and deficit levels. At the same time, the Euro extended a decline against the dollar from its over-done July 2008 high of $1.60, bringing relief to hard-pressed European exporters. As fears of an economic slump gained hold and inflationary risks subsided, the ECB executed a notable U-turn, with further interest rate cuts of 1.25 percentage points in November and December.

Well before the financial market turmoil, there had been warnings, in the key field of banking supervision, about the need for more coordinated international action to ward off economic crises. Alexandre Lamfalussy, a central banker with one of the widest experiences of cross-border regulatory challenges, called in May 2007 for the ECB greatly to enlarge its supervisory powers as a means of preventing shocks to the financial system. Lamfalussy proposed that the European Union use provisions in the Maastricht Treaty to confer upon the ECB supervisory responsibilities for thirty to forty major European banks with strong cross-border activities. Describing the ECB's structure as 'a weakness', Lamfalussy said:

> From the macro-prudential side, you have to find out what's going on inside the banks. My view is that you should have the ECB involved in supervision. The

ECB must be really close not just to the heads of large commercial banks but also to operating people at all levels. Since it is operating in the money markets and oversees the operation of the payments and settlement systems, it can capture signs of emerging trouble. But this information may come too late to be helpful. It is bank supervisors who possess privileged information on what is happening in the banking world and at present the ECB has no operational role here.[94]

As a result of recommendations from people like Lamfalussy, as well as the after-effects of the 2008 turmoil, a more centralised regime for European bank supervision seems inevitable in coming years.[95] An extension of the European Central Bank's financial watchdog duties, in coordination with national supervisory agencies, would increase still further its involvement with politics – broadening the already wide range of tasks that the ECB undertakes. For central bankers enthusiastic about empire-building, the suggestion may be warmly received, but it also sends a warning signal. If the Frankfurt institution is to take over still more responsibility for policing a highly imbalanced world economy, not only the Euro's successes but also its shortcomings will be laid at the European Central Bank's door – including those for which it is not responsible.

THE RECKONING

The tenth anniversary of the introduction of the Euro is characterised by deep crisis. Even after the events of the past few weeks, we are in a better position with the Euro than without it. The European Commission's argument that we need to do more work on the single currency is now more evident. EMU is not finished. It is unfinished business. It needs to be further developed.

Joaquín Almunia, European Commissioner for Economic and Monetary Affairs, 2008[1]

The reorganisation of Europe's money has neither healed nor destroyed the continent. The consequences of the single currency have matched neither the greatest hopes of its supporters, nor the gravest fears of its detractors. The stabilisation of currencies and the reduction of European interest rates to German levels brought some powerful benefits. But behind the apparent stability of monetary union linger a number of disadvantages caused by additional sources of rigidity built into the European economic system – handicaps that seemed particularly likely to cause problems at times of crisis.

In the first eight years of the Euro's first decade, the European Central Bank's task was eased by relatively benign external economic circumstances, in the form of generally high world growth and low inflation. Low commodity prices and a flood of cheap imports from China and other developing countries exerted downward pressure on international prices. But EMU members had also to cope with a tumultuous cavalcade of world events. The terrorist attacks on the US in 2001 and the wars in Afghanistan and Iraq brought great trials for managing currencies. They were accompanied by huge American balance of payments deficits, roughly three times larger than had been regarded as 'unsustainable' in the past.[2] The perturbations were exacerbated by the rising power of emerging economies and, towards the end of the period, the triple shock of the world-wide credit squeeze, a sharp rise in oil prices and the American economic slowdown. All these developments formed an ominous prelude to the dramatic worsening of the worldwide credit market upheaval in autumn 2008 – a period of turmoil that is subjecting monetary union to its toughest-ever test.

EMU may have indeed helped Europe withstand the pressures better than it would otherwise have done. Yet any illusions that, through the creation of the Euro, the continent could somehow insulate itself from vicissitudes beyond its borders were comprehensively dismantled. All these developments, and the searching questions they brought for Europe's new monetary order, were interlinked. Without the mobility of world capital and the activities of emerging economies' central banks and sovereign wealth funds, the US would not have been able to finance its burgeoning deficits. Without the excess of world savings driven by enormous payments imbalances, the sub-prime mortgage crisis, with its unexpected tribulations for economic policy-makers and financial market regulators, would not have erupted in the way that it did. Without apparently plentiful debt finance for funding imbalances, buoyant consumption in countries with big current account deficits like the US, Britain, France and Spain would not have supported international economic growth. Without the increase in energy use from the expansion of both developed and developing economies, the 2007–08 oil price rise, and the significant dislocations it caused, would not have been unleashed with the same ferocity. Without the drive towards 'lighter' regulatory regimes in the US and Britain, partly as a means of bolstering their financial markets, the now-apparent abuses in banks' lending and liquidity policies would not have been so extravagant. And without the inter-locking nature of world banking markets, the ravages that started with American home loans would not have spread like wildfire and engulfed the world's financial sector in autumn 2008.

Holding inflation to an average figure slightly above its target of 'below, but close to 2 per cent' in the first ten years, the ECB accomplished its primary goal of price stability. But, as is shown by the similar performance of compa-rable European countries outside the Euro, such as Britain, Sweden, Norway or Switzerland, low inflation resulted more from the forces of globalisation than from any special ECB acumen.[3] A 2 per cent inflation rate is a solid achievement. But it is by no means spectacular compared with the five years before the introduction of the Euro (where EMU countries recorded average consumer price inflation of 2.2 per cent) and the three decades before the break-up of the fixed exchange rate Bretton Woods system, when prices in the main industrialised countries rose at an average of 2.6 per cent a year – the prelude to the two inflationary decades between 1970 and 1990 of average price rises of 7 per cent (with much greater variability between countries).[4]

After the 2007–08 US sub-prime mortgage crisis and the oil price shock, the EMU inflation rate rose to 4 per cent and growth slowed sharply. The Euro and the political structures behind it suddenly faced a much more exacting environment. Ten years is a short period in the life of a new currency. The Euro withstood some important early challenges, yet further trials lie on the horizon. The years to come will be a time of reckoning.

Superficial Comforts

The single currency is plainly no panacea for economic ills; the danger is that some member governments have appeared to view it as one. Beguiled by the superficial comforts of a system of low interest rates and substantial external currency protection, many EMU members avoided making inevitably unpopular decisions on budgets, social policies and wages needed to ensure they could fully meet the new disciplines, not just over a shorter period but in the long term. Economic reforms throughout the Euro area slowed compared with the period before the introduction of the single currency when governments were straining to meet the Maastricht convergence criteria.[5] Yet the outcome was not greatly different from the past. In contrast to claims by both advocates and critics of the single currency, no firm evidence has emerged that the Euro and its 'one-size-fits-all' interest rate have brought sustainable shifts in economic behaviour, either positive or negative. This applies both to EMU members, and to other European states that are not in the single currency but have significant links to it through trade and investment.

In the first ten years, the Euro area's record for job creation and for economic growth per head was slightly better than that of the largest and richest economy in the world, the US.[6] However, a comparison solely with America, at a time when the US was building up massive debt and heading towards a severe economic slowdown, hardly provides an appropriate yardstick for an overall assessment.[7] When the Euro area is analysed by comparison with important non-EMU European economies, the conclusion is that EMU states – despite important improvements[8] – still have a lot of work to do. Looking at Europe as a whole, the Organisation for Economic Cooperation and Development concluded in autumn 2007:

> There are signs that economic reforms are paying off. While the EU average on many indicators is still mediocre, there are member states that are among the best performers in the OECD – be it Finland for its school systems, the UK and several northern European countries for their labour markets, the Eastern Europeans, Spain and Ireland for their dynamism and France and Germany for their world-beating companies. The chance is for Europe's laggards to learn from its best performers.[9]

The interlinked economic processes within EMU are similar in some ways to the workings of the nineteenth-century Gold Standard and the late twentieth-century Exchange Rate Mechanism, in which weaker member states gained initial advantages, but were forced over time to adapt to economic conditions set by stronger countries. There are two major differences: one, on the whole, benevolent; the other, less so. First, within EMU, the strongest country – Germany – bequeathed to the others lower interest rates stemming from the Bundesbank's forty-year success story. Second, monetary union, by definition, involved the constraint of permanently fixed exchange rates; by simultaneously enacting the ultimate step of a single currency, as a means of making EMU irreversible, the members of the Euro were locked still closer together. There is a risk that some member states may find themselves trapped with an exchange rate and interest rates that are out of line with overall economic requirements – and without an exit route of the sort available in the past, through departure from the Gold Standard, or devaluation within (or withdrawal from) the ERM.

The 'one-size-fits-all' monetary policy provides policy-makers with instruments that can be used with great benefit. But they need to be handled with care. If the tools are misused, or pass into the wrong hands, they can lead to self-harm, if not fatality. In the first decade, the Euro's members exploited the system's benefits, but – particularly at the beginning of the period – failed to forge an overall strategy to avoid later pitfalls.[10] It is still not too late for corrective action but, if existing economic patterns are extrapolated into the future, some countries are likely to come under pressure either to leave EMU, or to put their ties to the rest of the grouping onto a radically new footing.

Political and economic fault-lines within the Euro area hamper its capacity to manage the new post-2007 combination of risks. The divisions within Europe, and on the wider international scene, appear in some ways to mark a re-run of the 1970s. As in the final decade of the Bretton Woods system, the international economy in 2007–08 came to the end of a sustained period of non-inflationary growth. Mired in the conflict in Iraq, the US was in the throes of an unpopular and costly overseas war, with some parallels to the military engagement in Vietnam between 1965 and 1975. As in the late 1960s and early 1970s, the dollar came under pressure from American balance of payments weakness and revived forecasts of a diminished role as the world's premier reserve currency.

The policies in 2007–08 of the world's two premier central banks seemed to reflect historical as well as contemporary circumstances. The European Central Bank, with its behaviour rooted in the anti-inflation traditions of the Bundesbank, took a different interest rate course compared with the Federal Reserve. The US central bank's dual mandate of pursuing both price stability and high employment is stereotypically based on folk memories of the Great Depression, and also reflects its close ties – some would say, over-friendly – with Wall Street, and its corresponding desire to shore up unstable banks. In contrast, the single-minded anti-inflation priority of the Bundesbank and – by extension – the ECB has its genesis in the desire to avoid the monetary destruction that took place in Germany after the First and Second World Wars.

There were further reminders of history in the disharmony between France and Germany over monetary policy, exchange rates and central banking control, reminiscent of numerous past disputes. The convergence in Franco-German economic behaviour that marked France's 1980s and 1990s adhesion to the 'strong Franc' at times appeared fragile.

France, in common with other countries, certainly learned lessons from the turbulent monetary history since the 1960s. Additionally, the general support for central banking independence – rather than being a purely German speciality – has spread far beyond the Bundesbank over the past thirty years, including to the developing world. In the twenty-first century, France's inflation rate and general economic performance are far closer to Germany's, and – unlike in the 1970s – the French and the Germans are bound together by EMU. This brings stability, but also strains reminiscent of earlier discord. Former Bundesbank president Karl Otto Pöhl underlined the parallels: 'We are witnessing a return to the same type of conflicts as in the 1970s and 1980s, in terms of the disagreement between the stability policies followed in Germany and those pursued by other countries.'[11]

France's greatest hope for additional dynamism rests on the ambitious, far-sighted and overdue economic reforms brought in by Nicolas Sarkozy in 2008, centring on deregulation of the retail industry, establishment of an independent competition authority and efforts to liberalise labour markets, for example by helping companies side-step the statutory thirty-five-hour week. If these succeed, France could accomplish the task, close to the heart of every Paris government since the 1960s, of closing the economic gap with Germany. But it will be an uphill struggle – and surmounting it will be made more difficult by the drawn-out effects of the 2007–08 credit convulsions.

Economics Denationalised

A primary accomplishment of EMU was to achieve the denationalisation of money, as a means of improving the management of European economies. Yet the Euro has also facilitated a denationalisation of economics, helping propel Europe and its people further towards a pan-European financial and corporate system of globalised trade and investment. EMU has become a fertile, dynamic and creative market-place for internationally-operating companies, many of them from outside the Euro area. Borrowing and lending is incomparably more straightforward in a single European currency. Trans-national accounting and financial procedures are simpler. Banks and financial organisations, including the ubiquitous, mainly Anglo-Saxon private equity firms, hunt down business across a borderless continent. Corporations can map out their strategies and bring their products to customers across a single market that is global, not just European.

These are major factors encouraging economic expansion. Yet Europe's citizens are not universally happy about the experience. The results are widely believed to have brought downward pressure on living standards and an unequal sharing of rewards across society. The Euro is blamed for negative occurrences such as higher inflation, even when the problem is exaggerated, or the true causes have nothing to do with monetary union.[12] The Euro seems to have increased public antagonism towards US-style free-market capitalism[13] – an aversion that is particularly prevalent in France.[14] Even in Germany, the most open of the larger EMU economies, popular misgivings about the negative effects of the Euro and globalisation, fuelled by well-publicised transactions of sovereign wealth funds, resulted in protective action by the Berlin government in summer 2008 to guard against foreign takeovers of German companies.[15]

Governments' shortcomings in winning popular support for overriding European policies were exemplified by the rejection of the European Union's constitutional reform treaties in referendums in the Netherlands and France in 2005 and, in Ireland, in the 2008 voting on the refashioned Lisbon Treaty.

The referendum setbacks were not wayward expressions of independence that might have been expected from nations such as Britain and Denmark that had never fully conformed to typically 'European' behaviour. France and the Netherlands were two of the European Community's founding members, and Ireland achieved enormous economic success after it joined in 1973. European integration has always been designed to support the well-being and advancement of ordinary people – not just the business establishment. Yet the 'No' votes underlined the gulf between the immensity of the new forces that had been unleashed, and their relative remoteness from political supervision. The Irish government's unilateral decision in September 2008 to guarantee all bank deposits in reaction to the credit market turbulence was partly an effort to protect hyper-nervous Irish citizens from international financial contortions. But the move also helped trigger a chain reaction of nationally-minded measures throughout Europe that spurred an escalating crisis with 1930s-style overtones.

The gap between governments and governed was nothing new – but it seems to have gained intensity. France's 'No' to the constitutional treaty emphasised the Euro-scepticism already on show in the country's 1992 Maastricht referendum. Luxembourg prime minister Jean-Claude Juncker explained why the Euro, and the structures behind it, have not been universally popular:

> Businesses are profit maximisers, politicians are vote maximisers. The Euro makes it easier for astute businessmen to generate higher profits. But for the politician, the Euro can render vote-maximising more difficult, as a smooth and frictionless participation in the monetary union sometimes entails that difficult decisions have to be taken or that unpopular reforms have to be initiated. Before the introduction of the Euro, this could be 'sold' more easily to the public than at the end of the process, since there was a reward – namely participation in the Euro. Nowadays, the reward is less palpable.[16]

The stabilisation of European exchange rates and the smoothing out of the European economic cycle over the past ten years have plainly not been sufficient to buttress popular support for the new pan-European structures. One of the most experienced ECB Council members, Nout Wellink of the Nederlandsche Bank, pointed out:

> Despite the undeniable integration of financial markets, there are tendencies in times of crisis for a form of renationalisation of the money markets. EMU protects us against these risks, even though it doesn't remove them

altogether. When you look at the effects of the terrorist attacks of 11 September 2001 as well as the sub-prime mortgage crisis, you see the need for EMU. On the other hand, it's not a totally convincing argument for public opinion to say we need EMU to protect us against the crises we would have had if it were not there.[17]

Lorenzo Bini Smaghi, the Italian member of the ECB Executive Board – whose extrovert presence and lively turn of phrase mark his ambitions beyond the end of his eight-year term in 2013 – points to the gap in perceptions within and outside Europe:

> Wherever I go abroad – the US, Latin America, Asia – the Euro is held in great respect and great esteem. It is an obvious success story. In Europe, if you look at the economic statistics – unemployment, inflation, interest rates – hardly anything has worsened over the past ten years, on the contrary. Yet very few people from European electorates seem to have a good thing to say about the Euro. People feel the Euro is responsible for bringing lots of problems. This tells you quite a lot about the way we Europeans look at things.[18]

Popular misgivings about the Euro cast a shadow over the currency area's cohesion. Europe has an impressive monetary sub-structure for an edifice of political rule-making that has manifestly not yet been built – and probably never will be. Power over money has been centralised through the 'one-size-fits-all' interest rate. Yet the trappings and symbols of nationhood – governments, prime ministers, armies, police forces, parliaments, tax agencies, law courts, football teams, even (despite cross-border mergers) leading banks, TV stations and newspaper groups – continue, more or less unchanged, as thoroughly national institutions. The centralisation of European money, far from spurring a generalised move to supranational decision-making, has in some respects had an opposite effect. In spite of EU efforts at greater harmonisation, governments' behaviour shows divergence in areas ranging from budgetary policies to support for industry. Under pressure from public opinion, governments wish to retain maximum hold over areas of decision-making where they maintain vestiges of control.

The greatest consequence of these circumstances centres on the chimera of political union. Regarded by successive French and German governments (for different reasons) as a prerequisite for a successful currency, political union has failed to become reality – and is unlikely to do so. The much-discussed Stability Pact (with the word 'Growth' added later) was initiated by the

German government in 1995 for a dual purpose. It was a device to assure German voters that irresponsible fiscal policies from southern countries would not derail the single currency; and it also marked a potential first step towards political union. Subsequent developments provided the sole, rather ironic, example of forceful Franco-German convergence during the Euro's first decade, when Chancellor Schröder and President Chirac toned down the Pact to avoid sanctions for errant budgetary behaviour. Even though Schröder's successor Angela Merkel introduced a more disciplined approach, the legacy was long-lasting. Centralised control of borrowing necessary to guarantee the longer-term stability of the Euro was plainly anathema to governments and electorates. Any residual hopes of political union were resoundingly dashed – a message that subsequently echoed around the European Union during the credit crisis.

The electoral unpopularity of post-Euro business structures affects, too, the flexibility of Europe-wide markets in products, capital and labour. As all the experts connected with the EMU project have made clear from the beginning, a necessary precept for the 'one-size-fits-all' policy to work satisfactorily is that mechanisms for smooth-running economic adjustments should be in place within member countries and across national borders.[19] In the first ten years of the Euro, despite unquestionable advances in some areas, member countries made insufficient progress in putting this condition in place, reflecting in many cases electorates' unwillingness to change settled habits.[20] The system thus remained exposed to the risk of internal disequilibrium, with high unemployment and slow growth in some countries, accompanied by a higher rate of economic expansion in other member states that adapt better to single currency conditions.

Economic Adjustment

The principal adjustment processes taking place across EMU stem from a fundamental, if paradoxical, tenet of EMU: one size manifestly does *not* fit all. Disharmonised interest rate arrangements are designed to act as a means of adjustment for Euro members, in a similar way that flows of gold regulated economic behaviour in the nineteenth century. The ECB establishes a single basic interest rate based on average conditions throughout a relatively hetero-geneous currency area. This will result in perfect interest rate conditions only in the unlikely case of completely smooth economic performance across the entire currency bloc. In the normal course of events, there will be inevitable disparities between the interest rate set for all EMU countries, and that which would be established, in the absence of the Euro, to meet their purely domestic requirements.

Countries expanding more slowly than average, with a lower inflation rate, are constrained by a higher rate of interest than would normally be required. These punitive circumstances create incentives for increases in efficiency and productivity that eventually push down costs for manufacturing and service businesses, improving competitiveness and working through over time – though not without the negative side-effect of higher unemployment – into higher growth. As Bundesbank president Axel Weber explains, this was the mechanism that contributed to Germany's slowdown in the first five years of EMU, and to its ensuing recovery. 'The low inflation rate combined with the irrevocable fixing of intra-European exchange rates gave [Germany] a competitive advantage over higher-inflation countries. The important point is that the competitive advantage is maintained for a lengthy period of time, far outweighing the negative effect of the disadvantage of slightly higher real interest rates.'[21]

The corollary is that countries that are expanding faster than the Euro average, with a higher inflation rate, will have *lower* interest rates than would otherwise be the case. This will tend to increase their inflation, reduce their competitiveness, increase imports, worsen their balance of payments positions, and – eventually – reduce growth rates towards more sustainable levels around the Euro average. Spain and Ireland found themselves in this more expansive group of EMU members for the most of EMU's first decade, profiting from low interest rates in real (inflation-adjusted) terms. But they were either unable or unwilling to use fiscal policy to counter effects of economic overheating – and were suddenly precipitated into the category of slower-growing countries after the 2007 credit crunch.

Miguel Fernández Ordóñez, Governor of the Banco de España, said the large initial fall in Spanish interest rates, together with other structural changes in the economy, promoted the 'prolonged expansionary phase of the Spanish economy, the strong reduction in the unemployment rate (in spite of the increase in the labour force) and a rise in per capita income towards the Euro area average'.[22] Notwithstanding the post-2007 slowdown, Fernández Ordóñez believes the Spanish economy is sufficiently flexible to recover a high growth path once economic adjustment is concluded.

The lower the barriers to cross-border trade, financial, investment and labour flows, the smoother will be the adaptation to different economic performances in different countries. However, the steps that are needed to make the Euro work more effectively will themselves often prompt public discontent.[23] This is a task for politicians rather than central bankers, as José-Manuel González-Páramo, the ECB's Executive Board's Spanish member, points out:

> Some EMU member governments seem not to have learned how to manage macroeconomic policies in the new situation with economic and monetary union. Some of them behave as though they were still managing the economy within their own monetary and economic frameworks ... In cases where competitiveness has become clearly out of line with other better-performing countries, these governments don't seem to have realised that adjustments can no longer be made through changes in currencies. They can only be made through changes in costs.[24]

The Importance of London

One vitally important field where financial market adjustments take place, with significant impact on the Euro area, is located outside EMU – London, the centre of the European capital market. The complex co-existence between Britain and the Euro area was thrown into sharp relief by the consequences of the credit crisis. Efforts to find more cohesive regulatory solutions for Europan banks will necessarily influence competition between the three main European financial centres of London, Frankfurt and Paris. These cities' relative financial prowess is a highly sensitive political issue. The UK will be loath to agree any European measures with the potential to harm London's premier standing – a position that has so far proven remarkably resilient.

'I never thought that London would be seriously challenged by Frankfurt,' admits Wilfried Guth, the former head of the Deutsche Bank, Germany's largest bank. 'The strength and solidity of the financial markets in London and the deeply embedded relationships are all powerful factors, particularly in investment banking. It was always, and still is, difficult to imagine that this could diminish. There is a certain magic in the strength of London.'[25]

The City of London's relative prosperity despite Britain's non-membership – and despite the banking downturn after the sub-prime mortgage crisis – is one of the most important single factors keeping the UK outside the single currency. Much has happened to dash the expectation of Robin Cook, Britain's foreign secretary in the early years of Tony Blair's government, that UK membership of the Euro was 'inevitable'.[26] The City's relative success compared with rival centres such as Frankfurt, Paris and Amsterdam has been just one part of the story. The difficult-to-meet 'five tests', hastily assembled by the Labour government in 1997 as conditions for membership of the Euro, provided an economic justification for the UK's fundamental lack of political readiness to join. EMU's initial poor economic performance entrenched a British perception of Euro malaise that will be difficult to dislodge – whatever travails the UK faces in the aftermath of the credit crunch.

Richard Lambert, head of the Confederation of British Industry, pointed out how UK industry's interest in joining has cooled since the Euro started. 'In my discussions with [CBI] members the Euro never comes up, because the political reality of us joining in the foreseeable future is so unlikely. There is a certain degree of hostility. The further you go in the direction of smaller businesses, the more you hear that Brussels is full of hopeless bureaucrats making our lives a misery.'[27]

Earlier UK predictions that EMU would simply break up under its own contradictions have been replaced by a form of resigned cynicism, expressed by Nigel Lawson, Margaret Thatcher's second Chancellor of the Exchequer: 'EMU is a remarkable achievement. However, the Russians' feat of putting a man into space was also a remarkable achievement. Even if it doesn't all end in tears – and so much political will has been invested in it that the politicians will move heaven and earth to make it a success – whether it will achieve any great benefit is, like the achievement of putting Yuri Gagarin into space, a question that we cannot at the moment answer.'[28]

Since Britain left the Exchange Rate Mechanism, the eyes of British business have turned to a wider world. 'The British economy has moved on since 1992 to become a fully international economy,' says Sarah Hogg, chairman of British private equity group 3i and former adviser to prime minister John Major. 'We have a large European private equity business, but our fastest growing countries are India and China. For all the importance of Europe to Britain's economy, in some ways it looks like yesterday's story. When I speak to business people abroad, they don't ask me "Why don't you join EMU?" They say, "How is your business in India going?" '[29]

Within the Euro area, there is a palpable sense that the UK is drifting ever further away. According to German finance minister Peer Steinbrück:

I don't believe the UK will be in EMU in ten years. Britain's self-awareness, its identity and its self-definition are not really those of a country that believes it is part of Europe. You see this in its leanings to the US, in its permanent search for alternatives outside Europe. If you look at the City, it is not in its interest that the UK joins EMU. Membership would mean that the City would lose its special status and so Britain would suffer financially and economically.

According to Klaus-Peter Müller, president of the German Banking Association and chairman of the Supervisory Board of Commerzbank, which emerged in summer 2008 as the number two German bank through the takeover of Dresdner Bank, 'No one could doubt that London is the centre of the European financial world . . . I have given up trying to convince the British to join economic and monetary union. But there is high cultural affinity between the Germans and the British. The door to EMU is open, and the British can walk through it if they want to. But the other Europeans can also build and develop EMU without the British, and we are proud of that.'[30]

Former German chancellor Helmut Schmidt believes the gap is widening:

> I have now learned that the British don't really want to be members of the European Union. They are completely happy with the Common Market. They don't want any more than that. That goes for the widow of the dock worker in Liverpool, and it goes for the widow of the textile worker in Leeds. Europe for them is very far away, rather nebulous, dangerous, suspicious. The British are drunk on their status as the financial centre of Europe and perhaps the world. Britain's real economy doesn't play much of a role, only finance matters.

The general sympathies with UK thinking of a fundamentally pro-Anglo-Saxon member of the ECB Governing Council, Nout Wellink, have been sorely tested.

> In the Governing Council we almost never discuss the UK. We more often discuss China, the US, Japan. The Euro area is now a major currency bloc. There is a certain resistance in the system to having cooperation with the UK. The view is: 'You do not belong to our group. If you're not a member, do not seek to become involved.' In the beginning, I was in favour of the UK being a member of EMU. I thought we should need the support of the Anglo-Saxon world, for instance to offset the Germans' tendencies towards bureaucracy. However, I have now changed my mind, I do not think that UK membership is necessary.

For all such signs of a widening gulf, an ill-articulated belief remains that EMU will remain incomplete while the UK remains aloof. Yves-Thibault de Silguy, France's European Commissioner for monetary affairs in the 1990s, uses an apocryphal story to illustrate lingering regret that the UK is not part of the club:

The cultural differences between the French and the Germans are colossal. In the business community, the French find it less difficult to get on with the British than with the Germans. When a new French prime minister is elected, of course his first instinct is to travel to see his opposite number in Berlin. You get picked up at the airport by a big black Mercedes, travel to the stark-looking Chancellery, are met in a businesslike way, carry out a matter-of-fact, slightly stilted conversation and sit down to a somewhat awkward dinner with a meal served cold. You return to Paris a little bit dispirited. The British prime minister reads about this the next morning, gets on the telephone and asks the new French prime minister if he'd like to come to dinner at 10 Downing Street. There is good conversation and a charming atmosphere; the prime minister takes you by the arm and guides you from room to room as if you were in someone's home. A sumptuous dinner follows with fine French wines. The French prime minister returns to Paris and says to his ministers: 'We are spending far too much time with the Germans. We need to do more with the British.' You then go the following week to Brussels, a row erupts where the French and the Germans are forced to make common cause with each other against the British. My conclusion: You may enjoy dining with the British, but you have to work together with the Germans.[31]

The Spirit of the D-Mark

The Euro was designed to shackle Germany. In fact, after a difficult period of adaptation, monetary union appears to have helped revive its economic prowess. Germany's still sluggish domestic demand and its exposure to the broad streams of the world economy make it vulnerable when currents turn adverse – as happened towards the end of 2008. But the Germans exude considerably greater self-confidence than at the start of EMU. This is not simply a matter of revived economic output and exports. As a result of below-average German growth for much of the past twenty years, the French economy in 2007–08 was exactly the same size in relation to Germany – equivalent to 73 per cent of German GDP – as it had been before unification, when Germany had twenty million fewer people.[32] Germany's greater clout reflects its success in winning battles for influence. France and Germany fought long struggles during the post-war era to construct a European framework in line with their predilections: the French wanted European institutions to protect high-growth policies from external monetary disruption; Germany wanted Bundesbank-style principles to protect Europe from inflation. The final word has not been spoken. The extraordinary upheaval in the European and world economy at the end of 2008 could yet unleash a change in the balance of power between the European Central Bank and European governments. However, it appears as if German precepts, for the moment at least, have won the upper hand. A Bundesbank-style system that worked well in Germany for most of the post-Second World War era has been spread to the rest of Europe – with consequences that appear to have benefited the Germans more than others. The result – predicted by some arch EMU-sceptics such as Margaret Thatcher, as well as seasoned Bundesbanker Wilhelm Nölling[33] – contrasts with the semi-ideological purpose of EMU exemplified by politicians like Michel Rocard, who acknowledges: 'I was one of the few Frenchmen who said that if we wanted to create a new European architecture including monetary union – a strong structure that the US would listen to, and not neglect amid the cacophony of a crowd of irrelevant dwarfs – then we would need the Germans to sacrifice the one unique, prized element in their post-war cultural framework: their currency.'[34]

Another leading French politician who, like Rocard, made no secret of his distaste for the initial consequences of monetary union is Dominique Strauss-Kahn, France's Socialist finance minister in the late 1990s during the final preparations for the single currency, who became managing director of the International Monetary Fund in 2007. In October 2008, during one of the most dramatic days of the financial crisis, Strauss-Kahn proclaimed the need for change in the Euro:

I know of no country that has a currency but with no finance minister in charge of that currency. We have a very strong central bank, but in front of that no real person in charge of the economy. I remember having a discussion with [then German finance minister] Theo Waigel: he was very much opposed to the Euro-Group as a starting point for the *gouvernement économique*. I told Theo, 'You meet [then Bundesbank president] Hans Tietmeyer for breakfast once or twice a month. You don't just talk about bacon and eggs, you talk about economic policy.' Independence of the central bank is not at stake if you talk about interest rates and so on. There was a step forward with the Euro-Group under [Luxembourg prime minister] Jean-Claude Juncker. This was useful – but it is not enough in a crisis like this. It is very difficult to make decisions without a centralised power.[35]

As Strauss-Kahn's palpable frustration indicates, the D-Mark may have been sacrificed, but its spirit appears still to be alive. With greater or less willingness, and in varying degrees, other countries regard Germany as the benchmark for their own policies and performance – and as a catalyst for Europe-wide change. According to former Bundesbank president Karl Otto Pöhl, 'German industry is by far the strongest in Europe. France has maintained its position in some areas, but does not have Germany's sustainable strength. The other European countries have no choice but to adapt to the German pattern and embark on a course of cost cutting. This will take several years and will be very difficult politically and economically.'

Edmond Alphandéry, former French finance minister, points to the reversal of French and German positions: 'Up to 1999 France made tremendous efforts in improving wage policies and competitiveness. Germany suffered during that time as a result of financing unification not through increasing taxes, but through debt, creating difficulties for the rest of Europe. Through excessive wage hikes the Germans lost competitiveness. When Europe started monetary union, France thought it was entering a more comfortable world where the crisis was over, and we relaxed our efforts on competitiveness. So, ten years later, France has lost competitiveness, just as the Germans did fifteen years ago.'[36]

For former French prime minister Laurent Fabius, the Germans have built-in advantages:

> The Germans do not suffer as much from the expensive Euro because they have industrial specialisations and products in areas like engineering that are less sensitive to price. And if you look at the areas where they have taken market share, it has often been to the detriment of France, Italy and Spain. We need to find a policy that is good not for just one country, but for the whole of Europe. The Germans must see that ill-coordinated economic policy risks costing them employment. In the long term, they have a considerable demographic problem. It would be an error for the Germans to think that the EMU system can continue to function without serious changes.[37]

Former Italian prime minister Romano Prodi, by contrast, is a believer in German strength. 'I was one of the few people continually telling Kohl and Schröder that German industry was stronger than any other in Europe. This is the engine for Europe. Germany is by far Italy's biggest export market. It is a good thing for Europe if they are stronger. I am absolutely not afraid of German economic domination of Europe. Exports are driving Germany, but that produces German growth that is positive for our exports.'[38]

Alessandro Profumo, chief executive of Italy's largest bank, Unicredit, believes German influence is positive for Italy:

Italy has now digested the single currency shock. The Italian position is starting to become more like Germany's. The Italian corporate sector has done some catching up. The strong currency has weeded out the weaker companies. Italian exports have lost ground to competitors in terms of sheer quantity but have improved qualitatively by rising up the value scale in areas like shoes and textiles – the machine tools sector has been performing fantastically . . . I support an independent central bank. It prevents you from having illusions about the real economy. Some people might say they don't like the ECB being similar to the Bundesbank. I think that this is a good thing.[39]

Former German chancellor Gerhard Schröder backs up this message: 'Now that Germany has gone through a difficult time, lowered its costs and has recovered competitiveness, the other countries have to do the same. There is no way that Germany is going to produce significantly more inflation to help out the others.' Hans Eichel, Schröder's finance minister, does not hide the danger of future strains. 'German companies have been better overall at coping with globalisation than French or Italian firms. Now other European countries must make the same efforts. I would have nothing against a partner country in EMU making a decision to leave the system. It would force them to recognise the extent of the benefits they would give up. This could be a salutary shock.'[40] According to Bundesbank president Axel Weber:

Within the European Union, there may be a move to Germany specialising in industrial activity, leaving other countries to be strong in services. Countries have the ability of altering the economic conditions that will attract certain industries by making changes to their economic structures, improving productivity, encouraging research and innovation and so on. Germany has embarked on this path, and this provides a model for others to follow. There is really no alternative to the path that Germany has taken. Hopefully politics will keep Germany on this path.

Experienced British politicians believe Germany will forge ahead of the rest. Denis Healey, Labour's Chancellor of the Exchequer in the 1970s, said, 'France has always been guided by the desire to counter what it saw as Germany's post-war economic dominance. But France's chances of winning full control of

Germany's monetary and economic policies in the long run are zero. The Germans will run the show in Europe. They are the best performers economically. German reunification has been a staggering success. It has taken fifteen years, longer than many expected – but that's not a long time in history.'[41] According to former British prime minister John Major:

> The Germans will get east Germany right. It will take a lot of time, a lot of money, but they will do it . . . When you have east Germany as a powerhouse in twenty years, this does make Germany look different than the rest of the Euro area. This could bring strains similar to those in the ERM in the early 1990s. There may be some turbulence affecting the European currency, but the real strains are likely to be more in the real economy of individual countries, in a currency zone that is driven increasingly by German economic strength.[42]

A Threatening Combination

Under the pre-1999 Exchange Rate Mechanism, realignments generally took place whenever member countries' different inflation rates caused production costs to become significantly out of line with each other. This was the crucial step required to prevent large payments imbalances that would spark destabilising capital flows from weaker to stronger countries. With the advent of EMU, currency crises have been banished to the history books. Individual countries' payments surpluses and deficits within EMU are automatically financed at a constant exchange rate through the balancing mechanism of Euro capital flows. Countries with misaligned economic structures have more time to take policy action, by adjusting production costs in line with those prevailing among their competitors.

In 2008 a large number of factors exerted an impact on European economies: shortcomings in EMU reforms to make markets more flexible, a world-wide economic slowdown, a high (although later declining) Euro–dollar exchange rate, a roller-coaster oil price, and near-breakdown of the world's financial markets, necessitating massive banking bail-outs by governments in Europe and America. All this added up to a deeply threatening combination. The danger for the Euro's next decade is that necessary structural changes in uncompetitive industries will be forced by rising unemployment. Companies and factories in weaker Euro members will lose market share, facing losses, lay-offs and closures. Job losses and weaker tax receipts – unless offset by other factors – will raise budget deficits and threaten individual countries with a debilitating spiral of decline – exacerbated by demographic changes that will see a drastic increase in elderly populations.[43] In the more taxing times ahead, higher-debt countries may face pressures to renege on EMU membership, relinquish the painful discipline of 'one-size-fits-all' monetary policy and return to their pre-Euro currencies. Such a departure might appear beneficial, but it would also bring terrible retribution, says Bundesbank ex-president Karl Otto Pöhl – who, with some regret, singles out Italy as a possible exit candidate.

I believe it was a mistake to let Italy in. I thought it was a good idea at the time, because [Banca d'Italia governor and Treasury Minister Carlo Azeglio] Ciampi was my friend and because I believed he was right in thinking that it would exert a useful discipline on Italy. Yet now I am not so sure. Italy has not made good use of the benevolent starting conditions of EMU, in particular the significant fall in interest rates which has led to a large reduction in Italy's debt service costs. Before too long, the widening in the competitiveness gap with other countries will put Italy in a critical position. On the other hand, it is not realistic to think that Italy would leave EMU. The longer it stays in, the higher the price a country like Italy would have to pay if it were ever to depart.

European Central Bank Executive Board member Lorenzo Bini Smaghi reflects that an EMU exit would confront world capital markets with a repeat of two notable past crises. It would amount to a combination of the forced restructuring of Russian debt in 1998 and Argentina's default on foreign payments in 2002.

It cannot be totally excluded that a country goes through a recession and gets into difficulties, and comes into a situation where it might consider leaving the Euro area and returning to the former domestic currency. But a currency break-up has never happened in a fully integrated system such as EMU. It is not comparable even with cases in the past such as the breakdown of the Soviet Union after 1991. What would happen to the country's debt? Would it be in Euro or – in the case of Italy – in new lire? That would amount to a default vis-à-vis debt holders in a lot of other European countries, so such an occurrence would be less like Russia in 1998, and more like Argentina in 2002. Such a state of affairs would not be merely a currency crisis but a full-scale political crisis. It would lead to capital controls, and probably suspension from European Union.

Christian Noyer, governor of the Banque de France, spells out the immense implications:

> The price to pay would be huge. The assumption is that leaving EMU would mean a depreciation of the currency against the Euro. This would inevitably lead to large debt service problems. Most of the country's public debt would be in Euros, so debt service costs measured in the new domestic currency would rise by the amount of the depreciation. If the country decided unilaterally to re-denominate its debt into the new national currency, this would keep the value of the debt service unchanged for the debtor, but would lower it for the creditors – a move that would ruin the country's credibility. In both cases, market interest rates would rise sharply, seriously penalising the economy.[44]

The ultimate master of monetary *Realpolitik*, former Chancellor Helmut Schmidt, speaking in 2007 (several months before an election that saw Silvio Berlusconi return as Italian prime minister), summed up how Italy might be tempted to take such a step – and why it would ultimately be ruinous:

> The only country which might do this and might have a political leader ridiculous enough to do that would be Italy. The fact would be disastrous for Italy because the financial centres of London and New York would play football with the new Italian lira. The exchange rate of that new currency would be destroyed in less than a year. This is the great strength of the Euro, that nobody can leave it without damaging his own country and his own economy in a severe way. Let Signor Prodi be replaced by Signor Berlusconi, and Berlusconi tells the world: 'We are going to leave the Euro, we are going to revive the lira.' Once the first utterance to that effect is being televised, from that moment the lira goes into decline – even though it still does not exist.'[45]

German finance minister Peer Steinbrück bluntly sums up the general assessment: 'The Euro is irreversible. If any member was to withdraw, it would lead to disaster for that country's economy – so they would never do it.' An intriguing question for the future is whether the first step to quit EMU could come not from one of the weaker members, but from a stronger country such as Germany perturbed about the lack of 'stability culture' elsewhere in EMU and worried about the potential danger of being outvoted in the ECB.[46] Such a step would require a somewhat unlikely 'nightmare scenario' of a substantial and long-lasting economic downturn outside Germany coupled with continued prosperity within Germany – but it cannot be ruled out altogether, especially if Germany turns out to recover more quickly from world economic strains than other Euro members.

Patterns for the Future

In the next ten years, sporadic threats to the well-being of EMU will bring a kaleidoscope of reactions from Euro policy-makers – assertiveness and defensiveness, popularism and passivity. Nicolas Sarkozy's criticism of the ECB and its policies are more likely to be made behind the scenes rather than in public, in reaction to stiff opposition to his anti-ECB attacks from the German government and other Euro finance ministers. Sarkozy realises that formally changing the Central Bank's independence-guaranteeing statute is practically impossible, but – as the Bundesbank's rich history has shown – there are other ways for politicians to bring pressure to bear on independent central banks, without contradicting the formal prohibition on politicians giving 'instructions'.

The ECB's stream of interest-rate cuts and liquidity-boosting measures since the September 2008 Lehman Brothers collapse have won Sarkozy's favour, but the true test of the ECB's mettle will come when it decides to tighten credit and withdraw money-market liquidity as the European economy returns to more normal conditions. Sarkozy can be expected to use occasional private meetings with ECB president Jean-Claude Trichet to put his views in forceful terms. Trichet's long experience of withstanding sniping from Paris, and his solid support from the German political and economics establishment, will stand him in good stead. The hawkish faction on the Governing Council, with prominent roles played by the two German members, Jürgen Stark and Axel Weber, is likely to back a firm interest-rate policy to the hilt. Sarkozy can be expected to seek allies elsewhere in Europe in his campaign for a more 'pragmatic' ECB policy to promote European recovery after the credit crisis.

However, Sarkozy's efforts to remodel the ECB's standing and influence appear unlikely to succeed. The swing to the right in Germany's 2009 parliamentary elections has strengthened the position of Chancellor Angela Merkel and led to a new centre-right Berlin government linking the Christian Democrats and Free Democrats – more demonstrably in favour of traditional sound-money policies than the previous Grand Coalition. Alongside a general increase in Germany's influence as it moves out of recession well ahead of other weaker European countries, the formation of the new government is expected to stamp Germany's imprint on EMU even more strongly than in the past – a timely reminder of Willy Brandt's injunction to his economics minister in 1970. In spite of occasional pressure from the European Parliament, the forces calling on the ECB to give more information on its decision-making are likely to abate. It would be reasonable for the ECB to start to release minutes of its proceedings – in anonymous form to protect Central Bank governors from possibly unfavourable publicity in their home countries – but this flies in the face of the Bundesbank's long-term practice, and is unlikely to happen.[47] The ECB already faces an extension of its powers as the result of a move into the field of overall supervision of Europe's largest banks, and the complexities engendered by this change are likely to put other reforms on hold.

In this climate, proposals such as the ministerial Euro-Group taking over from the ECB responsibility for defining 'price stability' and thus setting the EMU inflation target are unlikely to find favour. In addition, there is likely to be a defeat for French-inspired monetary 'pragmatism' with regard to the ECB's 'monetary pillar' in its interest-rate-setting analysis. Rather than being downgraded, as had at one time appeared likely, the analytical focus on monetary and credit statistics is likely to be preserved or even enhanced in reaction to the setbacks for international central banks' inflation-targeting efforts in the run-up to the credit crisis. The post-crisis consensus is that the ECB, Bank of England and Federal Reserve failed to do enough to stop credit and asset bubbles developing in the years before 2007. Once the worst of the recession is over, central bankers' instincts will be to revert to tried-and-tested methods of monetary control to prevent a reappearance of such disturbances. The ECB will take on an even greater resemblance to the institution from which it was spawned – the German Bundesbank. This development will not win plaudits from Paris. Nicolas Sarkozy still has the opportunity to show assertiveness over the ECB Governing Council before his presidential term ends in 2012 – but he is fast running out of options.

Sarkozy failed to make use of one potential opening when in October 2009 he renewed the six-year mandate of Banque de France governor Christian Noyer – a long-time Trichet protégé – and passed up the opportunity to replace him with a candidate with views closer to his own.[48] The French president may be hoping that Noyer's support for a less dogmatic interest-rate policy and a more formal ECB dialogue with European governments could help advance France's perennial campaign for a 'gouvernement économique' – but that may turn out to be a pipe dream.

Sarkozy will play a crucial role in deciding the successor to Trichet, whose eight-year non-renewable term ends in 2011. In his efforts to find a candidate who is 'pragmatic' (that is, less hard-line) on inflation, and more in tune with his desire for a stronger state role in economic management, Sarkozy can be expected to show strong displeasure with German efforts to appoint Bundesbank president Axel Weber to the top job. Sarkozy will probably deploy considerably more intelligent tactics than President Chirac displayed during the nomination battle over the first ECB president, Wim Duisenberg, in 1997–98. The main front-runner to succeed Trichet has been Banca d'Italia governor Mario Draghi, whose nomination could be brought about through ECB board member Lorenzo Bini Smaghi taking over the governorship in 2011. (By the same token, Weber could accede to the number-one position by changing jobs on the ECB board with Jürgen Stark, who would then take over as head of the Bundesbank.) Both France and Italy argue that Germany has implicitly given up the right to choose a German national to head the ECB, as the result of the 1993 decision to site the central bank in Frankfurt. However, an increasing assertive German government is likely to state the case for Weber's nomination on the grounds of his acknowledged monetary competence and relative youth (he will be fifty-four in autumn 2011, against Draghi's sixty-four) – as well as the paucity of top international jobs allocated to Germans.

In the key area of budgetary policy, the economic slowdown has blown off course the German government's previous policy of balancing the budget by 2011. None the less, the Germans are likely to be more successful in budgetary consolidation than other Euro countries. A constitutional amendment introduced in 2009 forcing Germany to balance its budget from 2015 onwards sets an exacting standard for the rest of EMU. International investors are likely to demand higher yields on the bonds issued by the more indebted countries, led by Italy and Greece, with debt-to-GDP ratios of 114 per cent and 103 per cent respectively – well above the Maastricht reference level of 60 per cent. (As a result of additional public borrowing to withstand the financial crisis, debt ratios in Germany and France, too, rose strongly towards 80 per cent in 2009.) Heavily indebted governments will have little choice but to accept higher yields on their bond issues as a condition for staying in EMU; if any such countries were to leave the Euro as a way of winning back export competitiveness, they would face a very much bigger interest-rate premium.

During the coming phase of adjustment, the Euro's smaller members are likely to be more successful than the larger ones in improving competitiveness through boosting productivity, lowering wage costs and lengthening working hours. Because of the shortcomings of labour market reforms to allow smoother transition, in some countries the adaptation will come via the brute force of higher unemployment.

Italy poses an intriguing set of questions for other EMU states. On his third attempt as prime minister, Silvio Berlusconi cannot afford further failure as he struggles to rectify the dire state of Italy's finances and make the country fit to remain a permanent EMU member. In an attempt to avoid further unsettling the capital markets, Berlusconi and his ministers are unlikely to repeat the anti-Euro diatribes that were occasional features of his earlier administration between 2001 and 2006.

Among the other main problem countries, Spain and Ireland – which suffered most from boom-and-bust conditions prompted by the 'one-size-fits-all' policy – will recover only gradually from the 2008 slowdown. Yet Italy is the weakest link. Despite the resilience of many Italian companies, Italy's slow growth and internal adjustment problems (particularly in the south) will raise speculation of a EMU break-up. If government bond borrowing costs rise already within the Euro area for countries hit by such fears, the relative costs of departure would effectively be less onerous than otherwise. In practice, the ruinous consequences of leaving EMU are such that the political and economic environment would have to be unbearably negative for governments to quit. However, politicians may consider other steps to alleviate pressures, such as import controls, tax incentives for exports and other protectionist measures. Traditionally hard currency countries such as Germany and the Netherlands may face pressure from the weaker states to modify their stability-orientated policies in areas like budgets – and maybe even to modify the 'no-bail-out' clause in the Maastricht Treaty that rules out reciprocal state guarantees on debt. It is unlikely, however, that Germany and its followers will accede to such pressure.

The new entrants to the Euro area in the next decade will be concentrated on smaller states, where the economic and political advantages of member-ship appear more clear-cut. However, even the speedy addition of Estonia, Lithuania and Latvia – whose currencies are pegged to the Euro within a new version of the Exchange Rate Mechanism – is uncertain, reflecting these states' fears of loss of economic flexibility. Denmark – badly affected by the credit crisis – may adhere if it is persuaded that EMU is a 'safe haven' – and if it can overcome its equal and opposite fear that membership will cause assimilation by Germany. Sweden, Hungary, the Czech Republic, Poland and even the UK face a similar flurry of challenges in balancing their priorities.

The UK, however, will take a 'safety-first' line on EMU. Whatever the outcome of the election that must take place by 2010, and despite occasionally-heard views that the Euro area could represent a 'safe haven' from economic storms, the UK is highly unlikely to make any decision to join in the next parliament. In practice, the UK will probably stay out at least until 2025, marking continuity with the policies that Gordon Brown has followed in the Labour government, both as Chancellor of the Exchequer and as prime minister. With memories of Black Wednesday still strong, the ability to let the pound take the strain on the foreign exchanges represents a source of flexibility that few British policy-makers would wish to renounce. The only position from which a future British government would be likely to seek to join the Euro would be one of great weakness; in these circumstances the other EMU members would hardly welcome the UK with open arms.

On world capital markets, the Euro will gradually increase further its share of world foreign exchange reserves from an indicated 27 per cent in 2008 compared with 63 per cent for the dollar.[49] (The remaining proportions are held by currencies such as sterling, the yen and the Swiss Franc.) America's innate size and stability will ward off any threat that the Euro can take over the dollar's preponderant role in the next twenty to thirty years.[50] The lessons of the past should anyway teach European politicians to guard against hubris. Unduly large Euro holdings by foreign central banks could expose Euro members to instability, especially as EMU's internal fissures are likely to become more apparent. Over the next ten years, the Federal Reserve, the ECB and the People's Bank of China will work out a more coordinated system for regulating the renminbi's exchange rate. Other emerging country central banks, as well as the Bank of England, Swiss National Bank and Bank of Japan will be part of that system. Political inertia, the inconvertibility of the Chinese currency – and the still relatively small size of the Chinese economy – will hold down the People's Bank of China's international profile, but visits to Beijing from representatives of the ECB and the Euro-Group will become more frequent.

Surmounting the Tests

The international turbulence faced by EMU members at the beginning of its second decade in some ways represented sheer misfortune. The sub-prime mortgage crisis did not originate in Europe. The European Central Bank, under both Duisenberg's and Trichet's leadership, has lived up to its international responsibilities at least as adeptly as the Federal Reserve. The ECB did not invent the rules of the single currency, and cannot be blamed for political squabbling between France and Germany. Yet these quarrels are likely to continue. For France, which has staked so much on the Euro and is still disappointed with the outcome, the sharp slowdown in European growth in and after 2008 represents yet another setback. On the other hand, if the more rigorous climate intensifies pressures on the Euro's weaker members to adapt more quickly to the need for improved financial discipline, the new circumstances could be salutary.

Some realities are clear, though painful. EMU has contributed to strengthening, not weakening, Germany, but has also made Europe's largest economy more vulnerable to unfavourable alliances of other countries, especially if they feel threatened by a perception of new German power, or irritated by the Berlin government's reluctance to take more active economic stimulus measures to counter the recession. The corrective economic action that EMU members most urgently require is the most difficult to enact. The countries that have done best to diversify their trade and investment outside Europe are likely to fare best within it. The repercussions on Europe of the international credit upheaval may in some ways prove longer-lasting and more pernicious than those on America. Without better economic coordination, much of what the Euro area has built up could be lost. The cathartic shock of a severe EMU crisis, centred perhaps on Italy, could clarify the obligations required to guarantee weaker states' continued membership. History is written by the victors, not the vanquished. EMU's unfinished history so far contains neither. In coming years there will be both. The lesson of the first decade is there is no certainty that the single currency will survive the next one unscathed. Yet if the Euro overcomes its trials and becomes a durable success, that accomplishment, measured by all that has gone before, will truly be the richest of triumphs.

NOTES

Introduction: The Story of the Euro

1. Duisenberg speech, Charlemagne Prize ceremony, Aachen, 9 May 2002.
2. IMF data base, April 2008. In 2008 the world's top economies ranked by nominal Gross Domestic Product measured in dollars were: the US, Japan, China, Germany, UK, France, Italy, Russia, Spain, Brazil, Canada, India.
3. Britain, Denmark and Ireland joined the European Community in 1973, Greece in 1981, Spain and Portugal in 1986. Austria, Finland and Sweden joined the European Union in 1995, Cyprus, the Czech Republic, Estonia, Hungary, Latvia, Lithuania, Malta, Poland, Slovakia and Slovenia in 2004, Bulgaria and Romania in 2007. After EMU started in 1999, Greece joined in 2001, Slovenia in 2007, Malta and Cyprus in 2008, and Slovakia in 2009.
4. According to ECB and US Treasury figures, Euro notes and coins in circulation overtook those in dollars in October 2006 – $759 billion for the dollar against just over $800 billion for the Euro. *Financial Times*, 27 December 2006. The subsequent rise in the Euro against the dollar further widened the difference, so that in summer 2008 dollar volumes were around $780 billion against $940 billion for the Euro. The gap then narrowed markedly as the Euro fell towards the end of 2008.
5. There is a vast literature on the need for flexibility of product, capital and labour markets to allow appropriate economic adjustment mechanisms to make a single currency area function satisfactorily, starting with Robert Mundell, 'A Theory of Optimum Currency Areas', *American Economic Review* 51: 657–65, 1961. The theory lays down a further condition in the existence of fiscal redistribution to allow tax income to flow from regions of high economic activity to weaker areas hit by falling output and rising unemployment. See also Barry Eichengreen, 'Lessons of the Euro for the Rest of the World', Vienna, 4 December 2002.
6. OECD Economic Outlook No. 83, June 2008. The US budget was in surplus to the tune of 0.4 per cent of GDP in 1998, the year before the Euro came into being, while the current account deficit – recording trade in goods and services, transfers and investment income – was 2.5 per cent of GDP.
7. Gianni Toniolo, *Central Bank Cooperation at the Bank for International Settlements, 1930–73*, 2005, p. 327. The EPU came into being in July 1950, settling import and export balances among eighteen European countries, and enabling net surpluses to be used for trade outside Europe even though European currencies at the time were not convertible.

8. The Treaty of Rome referred to a common monetary policy in Articles 103 to 108. However, neither the Council of Ministers nor the European Commission had any binding powers in monetary coordination.

9. The literature on the 'Impossible Trinity' is wide-ranging. See, for instance, Bank of Greece Governor Nicholas C. Garganas' speech, 'Exchange-Rate Regimes on the Road to EMU: Lessons from Greece's Experience', Budapest, 28 March 2003.

10. *Survey on European Union*, OECD, p. 20, September 2007. Western European GDP per capita reached a peak of just over 80 per cent of US levels in 1980 (against only 46 per cent in 1946 and 67 per cent in 1957) before falling back to only 75 per cent in the first decade of the twenty-first century. Figures are based on purchasing power parity GDP figures for Austria, Belgium, Denmark, Finland, France, Germany, Italy, Netherlands, Norway, Sweden, Switzerland, UK.

11. European Commission, *EMU@10: Successes and challenges after ten years of Economic and Monetary Union*, May 2008, p.6. Goldman Sachs, *The Euro at Ten: Performance and Challenges for the Next Decade*, June 2008.

12. For a review of the tendency of the public and politicians to blame the ECB for Europe's poor growth performance, as well as other more negative effects of the Euro, see Charles Wyplosz, 'European Monetary Union: The Dark Side of a Major Success', *Economic Policy* 46, pp. 207–61, 2006.

13. *Financial Times*, 29 January 2007.

14. Eurobarometer opinion poll No. 69, June 2008. This showed that 43 per cent of Europeans saw globalisation as a threat to employment and national companies against 39 per cent saying it was an opportunity thanks to opening up of markets. 18 per cent of respondents said 'don't know.'

15. In Denmark, the proportions regarding globalisation as a threat rather than an opportunity were 17 per cent against 78 per cent; in Sweden, 29 per cent against 64 per cent; in the Netherlands 27 per cent against 63 per cent. In Britain and Germany the responses were in the middle-ground of the EU range: 47 per cent against 37 per cent, and 50 per cent against 41 per cent. In Ireland, Italy, Greece and France the percentages seeing globalisation as a threat rather than an opportunity were 40 to 34, 41 to 34, 67 to 32 and 66 to 25 respectively.

16. Germany made up 26 per cent of the twelve-member European Community's economy in 1980, against 23 per cent in 2008, according to IMF statistics. Britain's share rose from 17 per cent to 18 per cent over this period, Spain's from 7 per cent to 10 per cent, Ireland's from 0.7 per cent to 2 per cent, while France's share fell from 22 per cent to 18 per cent and Italy's remained the same at 14 per cent.

17. For a summary of the balance of political and economic factors impinging on the journey to EMU, see Carsten Hefeker '*Die Europäische Währungsintegration nach dem Zweiten Weltkrieg: Politik, Ideologie oder Interessen?*', Hamburg Institute of International Economics, 2006.

18. Padoa-Schioppa interview with author, Rome, 24 July 2007.

19. European Commission, *op. cit.*, pp. 4 and 35. Intra-EMU trade flows accounted for one-third of Euro area GDP in 2007–08, up from one-quarter ten years earlier, with half of the increase attributable to elimination of exchange rate volatility. 'The Euro has increased trade between Euro area countries in a range of 5 to 15 per cent so far and there may be more to come.'

Chapter 1: Blood and Gold

1. Victor Hugo, *Actes et paroles*, 'Pendant l'Exil', 24 February 1855.

2. BArch-P, 25.01/6428. Plans for 'Bank for European Settlements', Note from Reich Economics Ministry, 3 July 1940. See also Walther Funk, *Wirtschaftliche Neuordnung Europas*, 1940. European currencies would be stabilised in relation to the Reichsmark. Berlin would gradually replace London as the world's financial centre.

3. There are a few cases where successful monetary unions have persisted for many years, despite the lack of political union. One example is the monetary union between Switzerland and Liechtenstein (both using the Swiss Franc with the Swiss National Bank running monetary policy). Another was the long-standing currency union between Belgium and Luxembourg. Both link-ups concern small and highly homogeneous states. See Xavier de Vanssay, 'Monetary Unions in Historical and Comparative Perspective', 1999.

4. Helfferich joined the board of Deutsche Bank in 1908 and served as State Secretary in the Reich Treasury from 1915 to 1916, when he became State Secretary in the Interior Ministry and Vice Chancellor.

5. Karl Helfferich, *Das Geld*, 1903/23, pp. 31–32. The English translation *Money* was published in 1927.

6. The *livre* – the derivation of the modern pound – was a unit of both money and weight worth 20 *sous* (from the Latin *solidus*). It was primarily an accounting device, and never actually minted.

7. The Grately Law Code of Athelstan (924–939) lays down that every borough was entitled to operate a mint with one 'moneyer', and larger towns were accorded two or more 'moneyers'.

8. Philip Cottrell, Gérassimos Notaras and Gabriel Tortella Cottrell (eds), *From the Athenian Tetradrachm to the Euro – Studies in European Monetary Integration*, 2007, Cecilie Morrison, 'Money for an Empire – Achievements and Limitations of Byzantium's Currency from Constantine the Great to the Fall of Constantinople'.

9. Podiebrad's plan was turned down by Louis XI, King of France, and by Pope Pius II, and nothing further was done about it. Denis de Rougemont, 'The History of the Ideal for a United Europe', *The Meaning of Europe*, 1965.

10. Letter from Napoleon to the King of Naples, 6 May, 1807. 'Brother, when you issue coins I would like you to adopt the same valuations as in French money. In this way there will be monetary uniformity all over Europe, which will be a great advantage for trade.' Glyn Davies, *A History of Money from Ancient Times to the Present Day*, 2002.

11. John Driffill and Massimo Beber (eds), *A Currency for Europe*, 1991, James Foreman-Park, 'The Gold Standard as a European Monetary Lesson'.

12. Hugo speech on the opening of Peace conference, Paris, 21 August 1849.

13. Churchill speech, Zurich, 19 September 1946. 'France and Germany must take the lead together. Great Britain, the British Commonwealth of Nations, mighty America – and, I trust, Soviet Russia, for then indeed all would be well – must be the friends and sponsors of the new Europe.'

14. See for instance, German Chancellor Helmut Kohl speech, Vienna, 18 May 1993. He declared he would no longer use the term 'United States of Europe' because it could be 'misunderstood'.

15. Rueff article, *Synthèses de Bruxelles*, 1950.

16. John Maynard Keynes, *A Treatise on Money*, 1930.

17. Andrew Crockett, *International Money*, 1977, p. 7.

18. BNL Quarterly Review, No. 184, March 1993, Sylvester Ejefinger and Eric Schaling, 'Central Bank Independence in Twelve Industrial Countries'.

19. Michael D. Bordo, 'The Classical Gold Standard – Some Lessons for Today.' *Federal Reserve Bank of St. Louis Review* 63, No. 5, May 1981, pp. 2–17. 'The Bank of England generally abided by the rules during 1870 to 1914. A balance-of-payments deficit and a decline in the gold reserves normally led to the Bank raising its discount rate, lowering domestic investment, spending and prices and attracting short-term funds from abroad. Most other countries on the Gold Standard – notably France and Belgium – did not, however, follow the rules of the game. They never allowed interest rates to rise enough to decrease the domestic price level.'

20. Helfferich, *op. cit.*, p.141. Esquirou de Parieu was Vice President (later President) of the French Chamber of Deputies.

21. Bamberger speech to Reichstag, Helfferich, *op. cit.*, p. 148. See also Deutsche Bundesbank, *Währungen im Übergang – Die Einführung der Mark 1871–1876 in aktueller Perspektive*, 2001.

22. The proximate cause for war was disagreement over a Hohernzollern incumbent on the throne of Spain, an option that France opposed.

23. H.O. Meisner, *Denkwürdigkeiten . . . Waldersee I*, 1922, p. 162; Fritz Stern, *Gold and Iron*, 1977, p. 153.

24. Jules Favre, *Gouvernement de la défense nationale du 29. janvier au 22. juillet 1871* (Paris, 1875), III, p. 96, in Stern, *op. cit.*, p. 153.

25. Allinson, *War Diary of the Emperor*, 1926/71, p. 325. Stern, *op. cit.*, p. 154.

26. The peace agreement was signed on 26 February, only hours before expiry of the armistice. Paris was still under siege when the Commune was declared on 18 March.

27. *The Economist*, 4 March 1871.

28. Deutsche Bundesbank, *History of the German Central Banking System*, 2006.

29. The name 'Mark' was chosen as a neutral appellation for the new currency that would not raise resentment in either the taler or gulden areas. Deutsche Bundesbank, *Währungen im Übergang*, 2001, p. 12. See Dieter Lindenlaub, 'The Confidence in a New Currency: The Introduction of the Mark in Germany 1871–76', in Philip Cottrell, Even Lange and Ulf Olsson (eds), *Centres and Peripheries in Banking*, 2007.

30. BFA, *Evénements 1870–71, Vol. VIII, La Libération du territoire et la rôle de la Banque de France*. The main component of the reparations was FFr2.5 billion worth of talers. The other currencies used were Frankfurt florins, 'Banco' Marks and Reichsmarks, Dutch florins, Belgian Francs and British pounds, as well as German and French bank notes.

31. Léon Bizouarne, *La Haute Banque: Son Rôle dans la Libération du Territoire Français en 1871–72 & 1873*, Paris, 1892. The Banque de France's role was described in heroic terms. 'Thus was manifested not only the financial genius of the High Bank but also its inexhaustible reserves and the profound science of the economic life of nations.'

32. BFA, *Evénements 1870–71, Vol. VIII, La Libération du territoire et la rôle de la Banque de France*. Report by Budget Commission of the National Assembly by Deputy Leon Say, 1875.

33. Hugo, '*Pour la guerre dans le présent et pour la paix dans l'avenir*' ('For war in the present and for peace in the future'), Bordeaux, 1 March 1871.

34. Germany's population grew from 41 million in 1871 to 68 million in 1913. Around the turn of the century the proportion of younger people in Germany was, with the exception of Russia, the highest in Europe.

35. Deutsche Bundesbank, *Währung und Wirtschaft in Deutschland 1876–1975*, Knut Borchardt, 'Währung und Wirtschaft', p.28

36. Stern, *op. cit.*, p. 180.

37. Stern, *op. cit.*, p. 180. Bleichröder letters to Bismarck, 11 and 19 December 1874.

38. Borchardt, *op. cit.*, p. 29.

39. Georg Kalbe, 'Die Bank von Frankreich und die Deutsche Reichbank – Ein Vergleich'. Inaugural Dissertation, Friedrich-Wilhelms-Universität, Berlin, 1902. The Banque de France relied on its gold stocks as a buffer against interest rate changes. Between 1898 and 1913 the Banque de France altered its discount rate 14 times, against 79 times in Britain and 62 times in Germany. See Barry Eichengreen, *Golden Fetters: The Gold Standard and the Great Depression, 1919–1939*, 1992.

40. Georg Schwalenberg, 'Die Bank von Frankreich und die Deutsche Reichbank – Ein Vergleich'. Inaugural Dissertation, Vereinigte Friedrichs-Universität Halle-Wittenberg, 1903, pp. 99–112.

41. Alex Snyckers, *La Reichsbank et la Banque de France*, 1908. 'The discount rate of the Banque de France is permanently well below the rates of the Reichsbank . . . The happy situation of the French market is juxtaposed against one that is less favourable in Germany.'

42. Helfferich, *op. cit.* pp. 208–13. The suspension of convertibility of banknotes took place in Germany and France by direct legislative action, whereas in Britain it was accomplished by more practical means and 'moral suasion'.

43. *L'Information*, 11 September 1914. Moving the gold reserves required 132 10-tonne lorries or six or seven large trains.

44. BFA, 106999534/1. Banque de France Extraordinary General Council meeting, 1 September 1914. 'The Governor does not hide the fact that the departure of the Government of the Banque elicits in this house a profound emotion.'

45. Helfferich speech to Reichstag, Berlin, 20 August 1915. Five months earlier he spelled out the policy of relying on war loans and Treasury bills rather than taxation to supply war finance: 'We maintain the hope of being able to present our adversaries at the conclusion of peace with the bill for the war forced upon us.' Speech to Reichstag, 10 March 1915.

46. The debt total was fixed on 1 May 1921 after 23 meetings of the Reparations Commission.

47. BFA, 1064198804/83. Havenstein letter to Montagu Norman, Berlin, 25 November 1921. A copy of the letter was sent by Norman to Georges Robineau, Governor of the Banque de France.

48. BFA, 1064198804/83. Norman letter to Havenstein, London, 3 December 1921. By giving precise technical reasons for the refusal of the loan request, Norman intended his wording to be helpful to German efforts to call a moratorium and change the basis of reparations payments. See Gerald D. Feldman, *The Great Disorder: Politics, Economics and Society in the German Inflation, 1914–1924*, 1993, and BEA, OV34/71 with further Havenstein–Norman correspondence in December 1921.

49. Poincaré, *Documents Diplomatiques, Réponse du Gouvernement Français à la lettre du Gouvernement Britannique du 11 août 1923 sur les Réparations*, Paris, 20 August 1923.

50. BArch-K, R.43/1/632. Reichsbank directorate letter to Reich finance minister, 23 August 1923.

51. Law of the Autonomy of the Reichsbank, 26 May 1922. This was a condition of agreement by the Allied victors on a partial moratorium on the Versailles Treaty payments.

52. John Maynard Keynes, *The Economic Consequences of the Peace*, 1919.

53. The title of a book in 1939 by Norbert Mühlen.

54. Schacht was appointed Currency Commissioner in November 1923 by the government of Gustav Stresemann, with the job of overseeing the over-burdened and ageing Reichsbank President, Haverstein, whom the government was trying to dislodge. Haverstein died of a heart attack on 20 November.

55. In February 1929, in a final effort to resolve Germany's reparations under the Versailles Treaty, Schacht joined a commission set up under the US businessman Owen Young to reschedule the country's obligations. Schacht reluctantly signed the Young Plan in June 1929 which reduced the reparations total but maintained payments for 50 years into the future. The Bank for International Settlements, owned by leading international central banks, was set up in Basle on Schacht's instigation to handle Germany's reparation payments.

56. Toniolo, *op. cit.*, pp. 146–9.

57. BFA, 1064198804/83. Schacht letter to Moret, 30 September 1933. Moret letter to French finance minister, 30 September 1933; Moret letter to Schacht, Paris, 5 October 1933. Moret told the French government that, although the planned modification of the Reichsbank's independence was formally incompatible with international regulations covering Germany's debt payments, he did not intend to oppose the matter.

58. Harold James, *The End of Globalization: Lessons from The Great Depression*, 2001, pp. 191–2. The influential Emmanuel Monick, financial attaché at the French embassy in London, a post-war Governor of the Banque de France, told prime minister Blum that exchange control would represent a 'German path' that would bring France close to the German war economy. Devaluation, in a deal agreed with

the US and Britain, would, on the other hand, give the allied democracies the means for political collaboration against dictatorship.

59. 'Two hundred families are the masters of the French economy, and in effect of French politics', said prime minister Edouard Daladier in 1934. Daladier became Defence Minister in the Popular Front government. See also Leon Trotsky, *Où va la France?*, 1936: 'Each one of the 200 families is incomparably more powerful than the Blum government.'

60. BFA, 'Aperçu historique', Conseil Général, June 1947. Legal changes in July 1936 reduced the General Assembly's power to choose members of the bank's 20-strong Council, most of whom were henceforth chosen by the state. The position of the governor and the two deputy governors remained unchanged. The Council's composition was changed from a preponderance of bankers and industrialists.

61. The presence of foreign credit representatives on the Reichsbank's general council – a relic of the Versailles Treaty – was ended in 1930. But the Reichsbank still required foreign central bank approval up to 1937 for important changes such as modifying banknote rules.

62. BArch-P, RB 25.01/7035. Schacht, *Zeitschrift der Akademie für Deutsches Recht*, 1 March 1937.

63. BFA, PF/Fournier. Around 300 tonnes of gold were moved abroad for use as potential guarantees for supply contracts. The rest was moved to 51 branches close to the Mediterranean or Atlantic, for ease of shipment in case of war.

64. BArch-K, R43 II/234. Reichsbank memorandum, 7 January 1939.

65. *La Lumière*, 27 January 1939. 'Après Schacht l'aventure: La course au désastre'.

66. The Banque de France succeeded in sending more than 1,000 tonnes abroad on a variety of naval vessels embarked from Toulon in the south, Verdon in the south-west and Brest in Brittany. The cruiser *Émile-Berlin* returned for a second voyage from Brest and took out 254 tonnes on 11 June.

67. BFA, 1065199801/46. Conversation at Banque de France building between de Bletterie and German officer, 15 June 1940, around 20.15 (German time).

68. BFA, PF/Fournier. Following the incineration, only negligible stocks of banknotes, out of a total note issue of FFr 220 billion, remained in the central bank.

69. BFA, 1065199801/46. 'Compte rendu de l'enlèvement des drapeaux', Paris, 16 June 1940.

70. The British government's offer, which first surfaced on 15 June and was agreed by the War Cabinet on 16 June, was a political ploy, not a statement of realistic policy.

71. The southern zone came under full German occupation after Allied forces landed in French North Africa in November 1942.

72. BFA, 10620200101/65. 'Le Commissariat allemand près de la Banque de France'. The Commissariat officially took up its duties on 25 June 1940. Schaefer was installed in his functions by the German military administration on 29 June 1940.

73. SHA/Schaefer. Schaefer became President of the Bank of Danzig in 1933. When the Danzig central bank was wound up after the German invasion of Poland, Schaefer was made a member of the Reichskreditkasse in Lodz in September 1939. His appointment to the Banque de France came in June 1940.

74. BFA, 10620200101/65. 'Le Commissariat allemande près de la Banque de France Juin 1940–Août 1944', 2 September 1945.

75. BFA, 2210198101/12; BFA, 2210198101/2; BFA, 2210198101/11. Correspondence in September 1943 and February 1944, standardisation of French banking accounts. Correspondence, industrial and supply questions, banknote issue, 1941–44. Correspondence, February 1942 regarding Bank for International Settlements share certificates. Correspondence, industrial and supply questions, banknote issue, 1941–44.

76. BFA, 1065199801/45. Account of meeting with Schaefer and German officials with French bankers at Palais-Bourbon, Paris, 1 July 1940.

77. The rate was set at 20 Francs to the Reichsmark, against a rate based on purchasing power parities of 17 to 1. A full account of German policies on French war indemnities was written after the war by Heinrich Hartlieb, a Reichsbank official who was part of the Franco-German Armistice Commission and later (1947–53) became Deputy President of the Bavarian Land Central Bank and (1954–65) a Directorate member of the Bank deutscher Länder and the Bundesbank. DBA, Hartlieb/'Tätigkeitsbericht'. Hartlieb concluded: 'France made a significant contribution to the German conduct of war, without a severe deterioration of its economy, finances or currency . . . In the course of the occupation, France was in no way exposed to the same economic burdens as the nations of Europe involved in the fighting, and especially Germany.'

78. BFA, 1065199801/46. 'Note on questions of monetary order posed by the occupation,' Paris, 10 July 1940.

79. BFA, 1060200101/65. Letter from President of French Economic Affairs delegation to Minister Plenipotentiary Hemmen, president of German Armistice Delegation for the Economy, 18 March 1941.

80. The Germans sought, too, the bullion holdings of Poland and Belgium, which had been transferred to France for safe-keeping in November 1939, 'Nazi Gold, Information from the British Archives', Foreign and Commonwealth Office, September 1996. Toniolo, *op. cit.*, pp.249–51. The Pétain government acquiesced in the transfer of Belgian gold to the Nazis, but most of the French gold was kept abroad for the duration of the war. BFA/de Boisanger. Note by Breart de Boisanger after Liberation of France. 'Exposé de ma gestion depuis juin 1940'. Governor Bréat de Boisanger claimed that he resisted the German order to restitute Belgian gold in Dakar to occupied Belgium, but he was overridden by prime minister Pierre Laval. Note by Breart de Boisanger after Liberation of France. See Gérard Cornu, *L'or monétaire au vingtième siècle, En marge de l'histoire de la Banque de France : Aventures de l'or monétaire.*

81. BFA/de Boisanger. De Boisanger note after Liberation of France.

82. Filippo Occhino, Kim Oosterlinck and Eugene N. White, Rutgers University, 'How much can a victor force the vanquished to pay?', 2006. According to post-war estimates, French indemnities to Germany from occupation payments and looting amounted to nearly double the reparations bill under the Treaty of Versailles, and nearly six times French payments to Germany after the 1870–71 war.

83. BFA, 1060200101/65. Meeting, Banque de France, Paris, 19 January 1943.

84. BFA, 1060200101/65. Meeting, Banque de France, Paris, 17 June 1944.

85. Fournier stepped down as governor in September 1940 to become president of the French Railways and was replaced by Yves Bréat de Boisanger.

86. Schaefer was in Germany at the time of the Liberation. He was held in a military prison in Germany, in the French occupation zone of Baden-Baden.

87. BFA, 1060200101/65. Henry de Bletterie, deputy governor of Banque de France, letter to Commander Mitzakis, France post-war Commissioner at the Reichsbank, 9 May 1946. Schaefer was accused of aiding illegal money exports through his position as deputy president of the Aero-Bank (Bank deutscher Luftfahrt), set up in 1939 to further the operations of the Luftwaffe, and through Banque Charles in Monaco. Schaefer claimed his functions at the Aero-Bank and at Banque Charles had been 'completely secondary'. In a letter to de Bletterie on 16 April 1945, Mitzakis wrote, 'The former Commissioner has been relatively correct in the exercise of his functions and his control has not been unduly arduous. . . . Schaefer has been imprisoned not because of his former functions as Commissioner but in view of his position as Deputy President of Aero-Bank.' De Bletterie wrote to Mitzakis: 'Dr Schaefer's behaviour during his functions as Commissioner at the Banque de France should not motivate, from my point of view, the prolongation of his imprisonment.'

88. Schaefer was finance minister in 1953–54 and 1958–61. In 1957–58 he combined this with the post of deputy prime minister of Schleswig-Holstein.

89. Couve and other French war-time officials took part in negotiations with Hartlieb from the Reichsbank at the Franco-German Armistice Commission. (See note 77 above.)

90. Couve was director of External Finances in the Vichy regime in 1940.

91. Wilfrid Baumgartner was head of Credit National during the Second World War, before he was deported to Germany in 1943. He became governor of the Banque de France between 1949 and 1960 and was finance minister under de Gaulle. Jacques Brunet became director of the French Treasury in 1940 and was Baumgartner's successor as governor between 1960 and 1969.

92. Morgenthau, Bretton Woods, July 1944, *Proceedings of Bretton Woods*, p. 81.

Chapter 2: At the Epicentre

1. Alistair Horne, *Macmillan 1957–1986*, 1989, p. 256. Macmillan diary, 9 June 1960.

2. BEA, OV34/10. 'Note on visit to the Ruhr, 19 May–8 June 1945'.

3. BEA, OV34/10. MacDonald visit to Germany in July 1947, 'General Impressions' to Sir Otto Niemeier and others, 9 July 1947.

4. DBA, B330/8375. Letter from Col. (retd.) William G. Brey, former director, OMGUS Foreign Exchange Depository, to Klasen, 17 May 1973.

5. The Federal Reserve and the Treasury contributed to pressure on sterling that was a major factor behind the British decision to halt the Suez military adventure. Harold Macmillan, *Riding the Storm*, 1971, p. 164. 'Northwest of Suez: The 1956 crisis and the IMF', James M. Boughton, IMF Staff Papers, Vol. 48, No. 3, 2001.

6. The payments imbalances were not primarily a reflection of the US current account, which was in balance or small surplus for most of the 1960s – and where large deficits started to appear only as late as 1977. The real problem stemmed from the outflow of military dollars to support the armed forces in Vietnam, coupled with increased domestic social spending, which led to a sharp rise in the US budget deficit.

7. Deutsche Bundesbank, *Fifty Years of the Deutsche Mark*, 1999, 'Monetary Stability: Threat and Proven Response', Manfred J. Neumann, p. 276. The military law setting up the Bank deutscher Länder in 1948 stated, 'The Bank is not subject to instructions from any political body or public office, with the exception of the courts.'

8. Communiqué, US and British military governors, 14 February 1948.

9. DBA, BDL2/4. As early as June 1948, the Bank deutscher Länder rejected an Allied wish to maintain the discount rate at 8 per cent, compared with the Reichsbank's wartime discount rate of 3.5 per cent. The rate was set at 5 per cent before being reduced in two stages to 4 per cent in summer 1949. See Dieter Lindenlaub, Deutsche Bundesbank, 'Bemerkungen zum Einfluß der Alliierten Bankkommission auf die westdeutsche Geldpolitik 1948–1951,' Frankfurt, 27 November 1992.

10. Christoph Buchheim, 'The establishment of the Bank deutscher Länder and the West German Currency Reform', in Deutsche Bundesbank, *Fifty Years of the Deutsche Mark*, 'German influence on the details of the plan for currency reform was slight, in contrast to the subsequent – and in view of its success, quite understandable – tendency to paint it larger than it actually was.'

11. The Allies overruled a vote by the Bonn government for a 25 per cent devaluation. This decision appeared guided by the wish of the French government to avoid a devaluation that would give the West Germans undue competitiveness.

12. The ECB's dual decision-making structure, combining a central Executive Board (the German appellation is *Direktorium* – the name of the old Bundesbank Directorate) and a decentralised group of central bank governors (together, making up the Governing Council), directly reflected the Bundesbank's structure. The Bank deutscher Länder's inheritance is seen in the shareholder structure of the ECB, owned by the European Union's national central banks, in the same way that the BdL was owned by the Land central banks of Germany's regional states. (The Bundesbank, by contrast, came under the ownership of the Federal government in 1957). Dieter Lindenlaub pointed out

this nuance. See Jürgen Stark, speech on '60 Jahre Währungsreform', Bad Homburg, 20 June 2008. See Chapter 7, p. 208.

13. Otmar Emminger, *D-Mark, Dollar, Währungskrisen*, 1986. p. 463.

14. Comment by Alec Cairncross, in report on German visit, 9 November 1950, Ludwig Erhard Stiftung, 1986, p. 208. Vocke supported the British government's unsuccessful last-ditch attempts in September 1931 to stay on the Gold Standard. BEA, OV34/3.

15. DBA, CF/Vocke. BDL/BBK–2/4. Vocke letter to Adenauer, Frankfurt, 31 October 1949.

16. The BdL wanted tighter money to counter world-wide inflationary pressures caused by the Korean War as well as German import liberalisation. At a meeting of the BdL Council on 26 October 1950, Adenauer protested against the bank's plan to raise interest rates. The Council voted – after the Chancellor had left – to raise the discount rate to 6 per cent from 4 per cent.

17. DBA, CF/Vocke. Vocke letter to Schäffer, Frankfurt, 7 March 1950. Vocke wrote: 'The main theme running through your new rules is mistrust. As you say, your primary concern is that the Central Bank can topple the Government.'

18. Toniolo, *op. cit.*, p. 318. Donald MacDonald, 'Interest rates on our dollar deposits', 24 October 1955, BISA 1/19. The BIS suggested that the West German central bank place $100 million on deposit with the BIS for two years.

19. BFA, 1489200205/1. 'Note du Secrétariat Comité des chefs de délégation, Conférence intergouvernemental pour le Marché Commun et l'Euroatom', 17 February 1957. The West Germans proposed a clause banning 'measures susceptible of compromising monetary stability.'

20. *Die Kabinettsprotokolle der Bundesregierung*, Volume 9, 1998. Cabinet meeting, Bonn, 14 March 1956.

21. DBA, CF/Vocke. Vocke letter to Adenauer, Frankfurt, 20 April 1956.

22. Adenauer speech, Federation of German Industry, Cologne, 23 May 1956. Deutsche Bundesbank, *Fifty Years of the Deutsche Mark*, Manfred J. Neumann, p. 291.

23. Volker Hentschel, 'Die Enstehung des Bundebankgesetzes 1949–57, Politische Kontroversen und Konflikte', *Bankhistorisches Archiv*, December 1988.

24. See Dieter Lindenlaub, 'Karl Blessing im Spiegel der Politik', Frankfurt, 2007.

25. Blessing was put in charge in March 1938 of the Reichsbank's takeover of the Austrian National Bank after the *Anschluss*. In 1941 Blessing became a member of the three-man management board of Kontinentale Öl, the German state-controlled oil company.

26. DBA, B330/242. Adenauer letter to Blessing, Bonn, 12 November 1958. The Chancellor proposed that the Bundesbank's economic reports should point out 'the danger of a still greater widening of the gap between wages and productivity'. DBA, B330/242. Blessing letter to Adenauer, Frankfurt, 24 November 1958. Blessing replied that the bank would gladly take up the proposal. The exchange led to the 'Blessing Memorandum'. See DBA B330/242. Blessing letter to Adenauer, Frankfurt, 14 November 1958.

27. Between 1950 and 1959, Germany registered average annual growth in Gross Domestic Product (GDP) of 7 per cent, compared with 1.7 per cent in the US, 3.9 per cent in France, 2.1 per cent in Britain and 5.1 per cent in Italy. Inflation averaged 1.1 per cent in Germany, against 2.1 per cent in the US, 6.2 per cent in France, 4.3 per cent in Britain and 2.7 per cent in Italy.

28. Excess German foreign exchange as a result of the foreign trade surplus was converted into gold at the Bundesbank under the Bretton Woods arrangements. By 1960 West Germany's official stocks were 2,640 tonnes, against 2,490 tonnes for Britain and 1,460 tonnes in France – the world's second largest holdings after the US (15,820 tonnes). World Gold Council statistics, 2008.

29. DBA, CF/Emminger. Emminger letter to Vocke, Frankfurt, 12 November 1956.

30. DBA, B330/242. Blessing letter to Adenauer, Frankfurt, 6 August 1959. The letter held out the prospect of a rise in the Bundesbank discount rate and recommended

reduced short-term Bundesbank financing to the government and cuts in public sector construction.

31. DBA, B330/242. Blessing letter to Adenauer, Frankfurt, 4 March 1960. DBA, B330/242. The Blessing letter was a reply to an Adenauer telegram to Blessing, Bonn, 3 March 1960.

32. DBA, Emminger/ CF. See also Emminger, *op. cit.*, pp. 104–8.

33. Deutsche Bundesbank Annual Report, 1960, p. 5. See also Emminger, *op. cit.*, p.110. The Bundesbank described the US credit easing as a 'tragic coincidence'.

34. Deutsche Bundesbank, *Fifty Years of the Deutsche Mark*, Carl-Ludwig Holtfrerich, 'Monetary Policy under Fixed Exchange Rates (1948–70)', p. 372. While Blessing and Adenauer clung to the old dogma of defending the D-Mark parity, Erhard recognised that 'politicians and the public at large considered domestic price stability to be more important than retaining D-Mark parities'.

35. DBA, B330/242. Adenauer letter to Blessing, Bonn, 28 February 1961. Blessing letter to Adenauer, Frankfurt, 1 March 1961.

36. Hermann Josef Abs, Speaker of the Management Board of Deutsche Bank, and Fritz Berg, president of the Federation of German Industry, opposed revaluation.

37. DBA, B330/175. Bundesbank Council meeting, Frankfurt, 25 February 1961.

38. DBA, B330/175. Bundesbank Council meeting, Frankfurt, 3 March 1961.

39. Blessing press conference, Bonn, 5 March 1961.

40. ECBA. Marjolin statement, Committee of European Central Bank Governors, Basle, 12 October 1964.

41. André Szász, *The Road to European Monetary Union*, 1999, p. 8. Marjolin article, January 1965.

42. Hans Tietmeyer, *Herausforderung Euro*, 2005, p. 47.

43. Francisco Torres, 'The Long Road to EMU: The Economic and Political Reasoning behind Maastricht', Working Papers in Economics, University of Aveiro, 2007.

44. Toniolo, *op. cit.*, p. 439. Article by Nouk Wellinck in Nederlandsche Bank Quarterly Bulletin, 2003, pp. 27–8.

45. ECBA. Committee of EEC Central Bank Governors, Basle, 6 July 1964. The meeting was attended by Marjolin.

46. Blessing remarks, NDR radio, 27 January 1963.

47. BEA, G1/188. Blessing letter to Cromer, 10 October 1962. 'It is intended to keep things in the hands of the Central Bank Governors of the Six.'

48. ECBA. Holtrop, Blessing statements, Committee of EEC Central Bank Governors, Basle, 12 October 1964.

49. DBA, B330/245. Blessing letter to Erhard, Frankfurt, 23 October 1964.

50. Charles Coombs, *The Arena of International Finance*, 1976, p. 175.

51. Milton Gilbert, *Quest for World Monetary Order*, 1980, p. 135.

52. Hugo Young, *This Blessed Plot*, 1998, p. 118. Macmillan message to Foreign Secretary Selwyn Lloyd, December 1959. Expanding European economic cooperation 'may have the effect of excluding us both from European markets and from consultation on European policy.'

53. Céline Paillette, 'Stratégie monétaire française, candidatures britanniques à la CEE et SMI 1961–1967', 16 April 2002. See CAEF, B17749. Note anonyme 'Marché commun, Angleterre, Etats-Unis', April 1962. 'Les problèmes de coopération monétaire posés par l'adhésion éventuelle de la Grande-Bretagne au Marché commun', 20 July 1962.

54. John Newhouse, *De Gaulle and the Anglo-Saxons*, 1970, p. 211.

55. BISA, 2.1 – *Federal Bank of New York – Policy*, Vol. 4, 'Continental Dollar Market', October 1960. The Eurodollar market arose partly because banks from Soviet-dominated Eastern Europe preferred to leave dollar balances in London or Paris rather than depositing them in the US.

56. DBA. Johannes Tüngeler, 'Die D-Mark im internationalen Währungsgefüge' (unpublished manuscript), pp. 91–2.

57. Toniolo, *op. cit.*, p. 356. The French announcement turned what had previously been a discreet policy of purchasing gold into a 'publicised policy creed'.

58. De Gaulle press conference, Paris, 4 February 1965.

59. James, *International Monetary Cooperation since Bretton Woods*, 1966, p. 169.

60. Giscard speech, Paris, 11 February 1965.

61. The phase 'exorbitant privilege' appears in de Gaulle's memoirs, *Mémoires de l'Espoir, L'Effort 1962–1971*, 1971, p. 202, but is nowhere to be found in the General's speeches. Giscard used the phrase in an article in *Le Figaro*.

62. Raymond Aron, *In Defence of Decadent Europe*, 1979, p. 190. See also Alan J. Dillingham, 'The Evolution of France's European monetary diplomacy', European Community Studies Association, Charleston, South Carolina, May 1995.

63. Giscard article on 'La politique monétaire internationale de la France', *Politiques Economiques*, March 16 1965, pp. 1–7.

64. James, *op. cit.*, p. 170.

65. The exception to West Germany's gold supremacy in Europe came in 1965–67 when it briefly relinquished the No. 2 position to France.

66. West Germany made direct troop payments to the western Allies up to the ending of the formal occupation statute in 1955. Afterwards Germany defrayed the costs of foreign troops with compensation payments for buying Allied goods.

67. DBA, B330/242. Vocke letter to Erhard (with copy to Blessing), Frankfurt, 22 February 1965. Vocke proposed that Bonn should support de Gaulle on gold, but Blessing told Erhard that Vocke had misrepresented de Gaulle's suggestions. DBA, B330/242. Blessing letter to Erhard, Bonn, 22 February 1965.

68. DBA, B330/246. Blessing letter to Schiller, Frankfurt, 12 December 1966. The Bundesbank warned that Kiesinger's government could lose 'respect and authority' if it pushed too hard for an immediate interest rate reduction. Schiller attended the Council meeting on 15 December when interest rates were left unchanged. He wrote to Blessing on 23 December pointing out that the economy gave 'rise for concern' and calling on the Bundesbank to take steps to support 'our economic recovery'. The Council's next meeting, on 5 January 1967, decided to cut discount rate and Lombard rate. A further three reductions took place in the next four months.

69. Leo Brawand, *Wohin steuert die deutsche Wirtschaft?* 1970, p. 56.

70. IMFA, CF S1813.7. Blessing letter to William McChesney Martin, 30 March 1967. James, *op. cit.*, p. 192. The Blessing letter was coupled with a pledge to buy $500 million in medium-term US government securities. Kiesinger letter to Blessing, 30 March 1967.

71. ECBA. Ansiaux statement, Committee of European Central Bank Governors, Basle, 8 May 1967.

72. Information from Helmut Schlesinger.

73. Toniolo, *op. cit.*, p. 414.

74. Blessing's backing for American gold policies earned him approval from US monetary officials: 'What a blessing we have a blessing.'

75. AAPD, Document No. 358, p. 1407. Conversation between Kiesinger and Spanish Foreign Minister Castiella on a journey to El Escorial, 30 November 1968. Kiesinger reported that de Gaulle had described France as 'abimé' ('damaged' or 'spoiled').

76. James Callaghan, *Time and Chance*, 1987, p.172.

77. BEA, OV44/14. 'Sterling balances', Bank of England note, 20 February 1969. The balances were partly a relic of sterling's nineteenth-century dominant share in world trade. They also reflected Britain's success in persuading the British Empire to maintain sterling reserves during the Second World War. Toniolo, *op. cit.*, p. 389.

78. Callaghan, *Time and Chance*, p. 159. Conscious that the 1931 departure from the gold standard and the 1949 devaluation had occurred under Labour governments, the incoming Wilson administration decided against devaluation for both political and economic reasons.

79. UKNA, Treasury papers, T 318/93. 'Secret note – the international credits', December 1964 – UK balance of payments: short-term assistance to sterling under the Basel arrangements, 1962–65. The $3 billion was made up of $1 billion from the Americans, $1.55 billion from eight European central banks and the BIS, with the rest from the Bank of Canada, Bank of Japan and US Export-Import Bank.

80. Gilbert, *op. cit.*, p. 68. 'The real surprise was that the devaluation was fended off for three years. . . . By quite fantastic manoeuvring, the Government found the means to finance and disguise the basic deficit and the flight from sterling.'

81. Callaghan, *op. cit.*, p. 176. Early in 1965, Kuwait, which hitherto had held all its reserve in sterling, announced that it had decided to replace 50 per cent of its holdings with dollars. In January 1965 French finance minister Giscard telephoned Callaghan informing him that France was about to offer a large amount of dollars to the US to acquire gold.

82. BEA, OV44/14. Telegram from British Embassy Paris to Foreign Office, 21 September 1965. 'The Economic Correspondent of the ORTF told my labour attaché that the guidelines of the French National Broadcasting System include instructions to bear in mind, in commenting on sterling, the opinion of Ministry of Finance experts that the pound will eventually be devalued. This briefing is evidently available to the Gaullist newspaper.'

83. BEA, OV44/125. 'Note for the record' by Leslie O'Brien, London, 1 September 1965.

84. Toniolo, *op. cit.*, p. 399. O'Brien told central bank governors in Basle on 12 November 1967 that the pound would have to devalue unless a large medium- to long-term support package could be agreed, since the Bank of England was already overburdened with short-term debt. Since the governors could not pledge this, the only other alternative appeared a $3 billion IMF standby commitment.

85. Coombs, *op. cit.*, p.149. 'The cost of keeping the sterling market open on that final day of the $2.80 parity was appalling.'

86. Emminger speech, German Industry Federation, Frankfurt, 28 November 1967.

87. Callaghan, *op. cit.*, p. 223.

88. Peter Hennessy, *The Prime Minister*, 2000, p. 317. Jenkins' conversation with Jon Davis and Peter Hennessy, 5 May 1999.

89. Most of the loss was borne by the US and UK – 5,400 tonnes (36 per cent of gold reserves) and 870 tonnes (43 per cent of reserves) respectively. France and West Germany increased their reserves during the Gold Pool, by 2,770 and 800 tonnes respectively. See also H. Zimmermann, *Money and Security, Troops, Monetary Policy and West Germany's Relations with the United States and Britain, 1971*, 2002.

90. Coombs, *op. cit.*, p. 165.

91. US presidential aircraft were used for transporting some of the central bankers to and from Washington. DBA. Johannes Tungeler, 'Die D-Mark im internationalen Währungsgefüge,' (unpublished manuscript), p. 71.

92. Toniolo, *op. cit.*, p. 424. The facility, provided by twelve central banks through the BIS, was made up of foreign currency swaps on which the Bank of England could draw to offset reserve losses deriving from the conversion of sterling balances.

93. Volcker interview with author, New York, 28 August 2007. See also Volcker and Gyohten, *Changing Fortunes: The World's Money and the Threat to American Leadership*, 1992, p. 69.

94. ECBA. Committee of EEC Central Bank Governors, Basle, 10 September 1968. Blessing declared his recent remarks had been 'misinterpreted' and blaming a flurry of speculation on a D-Mark revaluation on 'an English press campaign'.

95. Schiller declared in September 1968 that revaluation would be 'an absurdity' since it would damage German export competitiveness.

96. Emminger, *op. cit.*, pp. 141–2. BEA, OV44/130. 'The Bonn Conference of November 1968', HM Treasury, p. 1. The Basle meeting mooted a 15 per cent adjustment between the D-Mark and the Franc.

97. AAPD 1969, Document 13, p. 53 footnote 9. Couve letter to Kiesinger, Paris, 9 November 1968. Couve warned that, if foreign exchange unrest continued, the Paris government would be forced into 'extreme measures' which would have 'grave consequences especially for its immediate partners'. German ambassador in Paris Braun letter to Brandt, 14 January 1969. The German government claimed the letter reached Kiesinger only shortly before the 20–22 November monetary conference. AAA, B52–532. Meeting between Ortoli and Johann Schöllhorn, State Secretary in West German Economics Ministry, Paris, 14 November 1968. Schöllhorn reported: 'Ortoli described the situation as exceptionally dramatic . . . The pressure from the French government for an immediate and massive revaluation of the D-Mark was emphasised with all possible harshness.' AAPD 1968, Document 383, p. 1493. Meeting between Kiesinger, Schiller, Strauss, Fowler, Bonn, 18 November 1968. Fowler gave Kiesinger a message from President Johnson commenting on reports that France was about to devalue the Franc because Germany was unwilling to revalue the D-Mark. The US asked Kiesinger to make immediate contact with de Gaulle to avoid unilateral action by France that could seriously undermine Bretton Woods. AAPD 1968, Document 385, p. 1498. German ambassador Herbert Blankenhorn message to Brandt, 20 November 1968. Wilson received Blankenhorn in the early hours of the morning in the Cabinet Room of 10 Downing Street, accompanied by Foreign Secretary Michael Stewart and Chancellor of the Exchequer Roy Jenkins. Wilson termed the German refusal to revalue (announced in the evening of 19 November) and the imposition of border taxes as 'irresponsible' and 'far from being adequate'. Britain would make a 'fundamental reappraisal' of its contribution to Nato, including troop stationing in Germany, unless a solution was found that included a revaluation of the D-Mark and a devaluation of the Franc. Wilson threatened to float the pound unless a currency realignment took place. BEA, OV44/130. 'The Bonn Conference of November 1968', HM Treasury, p. 4. Jenkins had written to Schiller on 19 November backing up the American call for Germany to revalue. Just before receiving Blankenhorn, Wilson sent a message to President Johnson. 'If there is to be any satisfactory outcome in our opinion it is vital for all of us to concentrate on getting the Germans to do much more than they have so far indicated. The only satisfactory solution is a revaluation of the DM.' (Annex A to Report on Bonn Conference.) Immediately after seeing Blankenhorn, Wilson sent a second message to Johnson on 20 November. 'We spoke to him [Blankenhorn] in the sternest language about the inadequacy of the measures announced tonight by the German Government and expressed our strongly held view that the right answer would be a substantial revaluation of the DM.'
98. AAPD 1968, Document 385, p. 1498, footnote 4.
99. BEA, OV44/130. 'The Bonn Conference of November 1968', HM Treasury.
100. Coombs, op. cit., p. 182.
101. Communiqué, Group of Ten meeting, Bonn, 22 November 1968.
102. Coombs, op. cit., p.183
103. DBA, B330 / DRS 142. Message to Government, Bundesbank Council, Frankfurt, 21 November 1968.
104. AAPD 1968, Document 386, p. 1500. Note on 'Die währungspolitischen Vorgänge in außenpolitischer Sicht' by ministerial director Harkort, 21 November 1968. The Bonn government was moving towards acceptance of a D-Mark revaluation, which it believed could help win concessions from the Allies in other fields.
105. Cabinet meeting, Paris, 23 November 1968.
106. Debré, Mémoires: Gouverner autrement 1962–70, 1993, p. 325.
107. DBA, B330/DRS 142. Bundesbank Council meeting, Frankfurt, 5 December 1968.
108. ECBA. Committee of EEC Central Bank Governors, Basle, 9 December 1968.
109. AAPD 1969, Document 13, p. 53. Talks between German ambassador von Braun and de Gaulle on 1 January 1969, Paris, von Braun letter to Brandt, Paris, 14 January 1969.

110. AAPD 1969, Document 99, pp. 377–8. De Gaulle conversation with Kiesinger, Paris, 13 March 1969.
111. AAA, B52/587. Karl Schiller, 'Antrag auf Verbesserung der Währungsparität der Deutschen Mark um 6.25 prozent', West German Economics Ministry, 9 May 1969.
112. Deutsche Bundesbank, *Fifty Years of the Deutsche Mark*, Holtferich, *op. cit.*, p. 388. Statement by Conrad Ahlers, government spokesman, 9 May 1969, following a Cabinet meeting in which Blessing took part. This came a day after the Bundesbank Council came out unanimously in favour of revaluation.
113. NYFA, CF/Foreign Exchange 260. 'The French Devaluation: A First Assessment' by Foreign Exchange Research Division of Federal Reserve Bank of New York, 11 August 1969. 'It is paradoxical, but possibly true, that a franc devaluation, which would serve to reduce the extent of the mark revaluation that many believe necessary, might, at the same time, increase the pressures for undertaking that revaluation in the near future.'
114. DBA, B330/244. The election came just after a sharp increase in Bundesbank interest rates and an equally sharp exchange of letters between Blessing and finance minister Strauss. Blessing warned Strauss on 2 September that inflationary pressures made a 'moderate' discount rate increase likely at the next meeting of the Bundesbank Council on 11 September. The letter ended: 'I would be grateful, dear Minister, if . . . you will not contradict the possible credit policy decisions that I have indicated above.' Strauss countered that a discount increase was unnecessary. The Bundesbank went ahead with a 1 percentage point increase in discount rate and 1.5 percentage point rise in Lombard rate on 11 September. Strauss wrote on 18 September that he was 'extraordinarily surprised'. On 22 September – just six days before the 28 September election – Blessing replied to Strauss that the tightening was justified by an economic boom 'that we have not seen since the [1948] currency reform', sparking off the danger of a price–wage spiral.
115. Kiesinger interview, *Der Spiegel*, 3 November 1969.
116. Debré, *op. cit.*, p. 326.
117. NYFA, CF/Foreign Exchange, 260. 'The New Mark Parity: An Appraisal', Internal Research Memorandum from Foreign Research Division for Alfred Hayes, President of the New York Federal Reserve Bank, 27 October 1969, 'Unless the appropriate measures are taken, the French run the real risk of losing not only the potential gains stemming from the German revaluation, but also of seeing their devaluation gains wiped out by offsetting price increases.'
118. Young, *op. cit.*, p. 234.
119. Pompidou statement, The Hague, 1 December 1969.
120. The communiqué on 2 December 1969 said, 'A plan in stages should be drawn up by the Council during 1970 with a view to creation of Economic and Monetary Union.'
121. Willy Brandt, *Erinnerungen*, 1989, p. 453. Statement, The Hague, 1 December 1969.
122. NRA. Arthur Burns in conversation with Henry Kissinger.
123. Volcker and Gyohten, *op. cit.*, p.81.
124. John S. Odell, *US Monetary Policy, Markets, Power and Ideas as Sources of Change*. 1982, p. 263.
125. Coombs, *op. cit.*, p. 204.
126. Brandt speech on 'Peace policy in our time', Oslo, 11 December 1971, a day after he received the Nobel Peace Prize.
127. Henry Kissinger, *The White House Years*, 1979, pp. 410, 528–9.
128. Edward Heath, *Travels*, 1977, quoted in Young, *op. cit.*, p. 217.
129. Heath statement to European negotiating teams in Brussels, 29 January 1963.
130. Brandt speech to Bundestag, Bonn, 3 December 1969. 'Our pensioners and our savers would view an inflationary policy as confiscation.'
131. Tietmeyer, *op. cit.*, p. 45.
132. ECBA. Committee of EEC Central Bank Governors, Basle, 9 March 1970. Zijlstra of the Nederlandsche Bank agreed with Klasen. DBA, B330/5876/2. Bundesbank Council in Frankfurt, 18 March 1970. The Franco-Belgian plan was put forward by

Bernhard Clappier, deputy governor of the Banque de France and Hubert Ansiaux, governor of the National Bank of Belgium and president of the Committee of EEC Central Bank Governors.

133. DBA, B330/9941. Schöllhorn letter to Klasen, 3 April 1970.
134. DBA, B330/9941. 'Diskussionsbeitrag zum Thema Wirtshaftsunion als Grundlage der Währungsunion', Bonn, 1 April 1970.
135. DBA, N2/155. 'Aufzeichnung: Wirtschafts- und Währungsunion', 13 April 1970, p.15.
136. ECBA. Klasen statement, Committee of EEC Central Bank Governors, Basle, 29 May 1970.
137. DBA, B330/9941. Letter to Brandt from Belgian prime minister Gaston Eyskens, 15 May 1970. Eyskens suggested the Franco-Belgian proposal for a European Currency Equalisation Fund should take effect in the first stage of EMU to 'stimulate greater convergence of economic policies' and 'affirm the monetary independence of the European Economic Community with respect to the US dollar'.
138. ECBA. Klasen and Clappier statements, Committee of EEC Central Bank Governors, Basle, 12 & 13 September 1970.
139. ECBA. Committee of EEC Central Bank Governors, Basle, 8 November 1970. Baffi said continued autonomy of national labour markets would prevent harmonisation of incomes and thus make monetary union impossible.
140. ECBA. Meeting of Committee of EEC Central Bank Governors, Basle, 8 November 1970.
141. BEA, 5A180/2. Paper from A. Dicks-Mireaux, on an earlier draft of the Werner Report, 22 July 1970.
142. BEA, 5A180/2. 'European Economic and Monetary Integration: The Werner Report in Perspective', from T.G. Underwood (Economic Analysis and Research), 2 November 1970.
143. BEA, 5A180/2. Paper on Werner report, October 1970. The Bank paper added, 'It would be very difficult, if not impossible, for a member, by its own policies, to correct a "balance of payments" deficit which might emerge between it and the rest of the Community . . . Deficit regions could easily become depressed areas.'
144. Brandt, op. cit., p. 456. Brandt blamed the 'retarding influence' of the Bundesbank and Bonn ministries for preventing him from developing the plan for EMU, including the pooling of Germany's reserves.
145. DBA, N2/156. Brandt letter to Schiller, Bonn, 21 October 1970.
146. Schiller speech to Bundestag, Bonn, 6 November 1970. DBA, B330/DRS142. Schiller statement, Bundesbank Council, Frankfurt, 17 November 1970.
147. Erik Hoffmeyer, Decision-making for European Economic and Monetary Union, Group of Thirty, Occasional Paper 62, Washington, 2000.
148. UKNA, FCO 59/559. Talks between Barber and Giscard, London, 24 November 1970.
149. UKNA, FCO 59/559. Talks between Sir Geoffrey Rippon, Chancellor of the Duchy of Lancaster, and Giscard, London, 24 November 1970.
150. Report on European summit, 23 November 1970.
151. DBA, N2/153. Emminger letter to Schöllhorn, Frankfurt, 23 December 1970.
152. Coombs, op. cit., pp. 206–7.
153. The Bundesbank cut the discount rate from a high point of 7.5 per cent in summer 1970 to 5 per cent in March 1971.
154. AAPD, 1971, Document 27, p. 118. Pompidou remarks, talks with Brandt in Paris, 25 January 1971.
155. AAPD, 1971, Document 27, p. 115. Brandt talks with Pompidou, Paris, 25 January 1971.
156. Pompidou leaned heavily in Germany's direction by backing a stronger role for the Banque de France – a significant concession in a country where the central bank had been habitually part of the governmental apparatus. The Banque de France was brought under government control in 1936 and nationalised in 1945.

157. AAPD, 1971, Document 27, p. 118. Brandt remarks, talks with Pompidou in Paris, 25 January 1971. 'I must ask you to consider the difference in the positions of the Bundesbank and the Banque de France.'

158. DBA, N2/154. Letter from Schöllhorn to Emminger, 4 February 1971.

159. DBA, N2/154. 'Report on results of German–French consultations', Paris, 25–26 January 1971. 'We must maintain the freedom to return to the point where we started.'

160. Debré, *Le Monde*, 26 February 1971.

161. Toniolo, *op. cit.*, p. 448.

162. Emminger, *op. cit.*, pp. 177–82. In May 1971 the German economics minister tried to persuade the Bundesbank Council of the merits of joint EEC floating. A majority led by Klasen opposed the idea, arguing instead for capital controls to deflect hot money. This proposal was contested by a pro-floating Bundesbank faction led by Emminger. Bonn rejected the Bundesbank's recommendation, and opted instead for temporary unilateral D-Mark floating until a new parity could be agreed.

163. AAA, B52-IIIA1. Report from German Embassy, TV remarks by Giscard, Paris, 11 May 1971.

164. NYFA, CF/Foreign Exchange 260. Note from Charles Coombs for Alfred Hayes, 'The Outlook for the Dollar', 22 March 1971.

165. James, *op. cit.*, p. 217.

166. 'Action Now to Strengthen the Dollar', US Congress Joint Economic Committee, Sub-Committee on International Exchange and Payments, chaired by Henry Reuss.

167. DBA, B330/9941. Klasen letter to finance minister Axel Möller, 31 March 1971. This contained a background note 'not for passing on to US authorities'. The gold was originally sold to the US at the end of 1969 when German required large quantities of dollars to help finance a significant outflow of speculative funds after the D-Mark revaluation of October 1969. The German initiative to unwind the gold sale – which fell outside the self-imposed restriction of the 'Blessing letter' of March 1967 – was backed by the Belgian, Dutch, French and Swiss central banks to help persuade the US to switch to anti-inflationary policies.

168. NYFA, CF/Foreign Exchange 260. Hayes letter to Burns, New York, 11 August 1971. 'Minister Schiller proceeded to exploit the resultant massive build-up of the dollar reserves of the Bundesbank by virtually predicting an upward float of the Mark and thereby inviting speculators everywhere to validate his prediction.'

169. Volcker and Gyohten, *op. cit.*, p. 77. Coombs, while taking part in emergency meetings in Washington, received a call from the Federal Reserve Bank's trading desk in New York saying that the British were requesting gold conversion for about $3 billion of dollar holdings. Later it transpired that the UK request had been for some combination of 'cover' to guarantee the value of the dollar holdings, but not necessarily for gold.

170. James, *op. cit.*, p. 219.

171. Kissinger, *White House Years*, p. 954. Neither the International Monetary Fund nor Kissinger was informed in advance about the ending of dollar–gold convertibility.

172. James, *op. cit.*, p. 219.

173. NRC, Department of the Treasury, Files of Under Secretary Volcker 1969–1974: FRC 56 79 15, France. Meeting in Paris, 17 August 1971. According to Giscard, 'This is how the US has financed its deficit during the last 10 years. It will have to find a new way of doing this now.' France 'didn't like to let the market fix exchange rates. The German experience was an example of how bad this could be. The mark had floated much higher than the Germans had expected.'

174. USNA, Nixon Presidential Materials, NSC Files, Name Files, Box 810, Arthur Burns. Burns letter to Nixon, 16 November 1971.

175. USNA, RG 59, Central Files 1970–73, FN 10. Telegram from US Embassy in Germany to Department of State, 'Limdis; Greenback', Bonn, 17 November, 1971, 1450Z,

reporting on conversation between Finance Attaché and Otmar Emminger. 'While Germany was willing to see a 10 per cent appreciation of DM vis-à-vis the dollar, it could not continue to accept such an appreciation vis-à-vis other currencies, and particularly vis-à-vis the Franc . . . Schiller would not be in a position to resist pressure for help from these two important industries . . . Emminger warned that one should not over-estimate the strength of Minister Schiller [who] simply was not in a position to continue the float. He had to return quickly to a fixed rate or the Cabinet would disavow him. Emminger almost visibly shuddered at the thought of what might happen in the economic policy field if Schiller, with his constant liberal and outward (beyond the EEC) looking influence, should be forced from office.'

176. USNA, RG 59, S/S Files: Lot 73 D 153, Morning Summaries, 15 November 1971. 'Key French officials have begun to warn us that, if we do not soon indicate clearly what our terms for a settlement are, opinion will turn decisively against us. There have been disturbing signs recently . . . Behind these immediate concerns lies the deeper fear that if the crisis is not ended soon nations will be increasingly inclined to take defensive measures, with the resulting contraction of world trade leading to a world recession.'

177. UKNA. Heath complained that the American action 'destroyed the then existing pattern of exchange rates, erected new barriers to trade between the US and the rest of the world, and undermined the foundation of the system of international trade and payments established in 1946'.

178. Meeting of Nixon and Pompidou, Azores, 13–14 December 1971.

179. The D-Mark was revalued by 13.6 per cent against the dollar, against the yen by 16.9 per cent, and against the French franc and sterling by 8.6 per cent. To deflect speculative pressure, Bretton Woods fluctuation bands were widened from 1 per cent to 2.25 per cent from the central currency rate, an overall 4.5 per cent.

180. James, *op. cit.*, p. 238.

181. USNA, Nixon Presidential Materials, NSC Files, Agency Files, Box 290, Treasury, Volume III, Letter from Pompidou to Nixon, Paris, 4 February 1972.

182. AAPD 1972, Document 29, pp. 127–138. Meeting between Brandt and Pompidou, Paris, 10 February 1972. Pompidou declared, 'A monetary union will not be possible without an economic union.' UKNA, PREM 15/917. Germany signalled to Britain that the French were backing economic discipline and promised Heath full involvement in Franco-German plans. Brandt letter to Heath, Bonn, 13 February 1972.

183. As a result of the widening of bilateral exchange rate bands for Bretton Woods currencies, Community currencies could fluctuate against each other by up to 9 per cent. Both France and Germany wanted to correct this position, not least because changes in internal Common Market currency relationships played havoc with European agricultural payments.

184. The UK, Ireland and Denmark joined the Snake on 1 May 1972, while Norway became an associate member on 23 May. The Basle agreement establishing the Snake took effect on 24 April.

185. Deutsche Bundesbank, *Fifty Years of the Deutsche Mark*, Jürgen von Hagen, 'A New Approach to Monetary Policy', p. 413. The half point-discount rate increases came in October, November, December 1972 and January 1973.

186. Edward Heath, *The Course of My Life*, 1998, p. 410. 'On Wednesday 21 June I met Tony Barber and officials from the Treasury and Bank of England. We discussed a proposal from Barber to increase the bank rate from 5 to 6 per cent . . . The following day we did increase the bank rate to 6 per cent, but this provided only a short-lived respite. Tony Barber returned that day at 4.15 pm for another meeting, again accompanied by officials. We were by now running down our foreign currency reserves at an alarming rate and he and his advisers saw no alternative to abandoning the existing parity.'

187. USNA. Heath message to President Nixon, 26 June 1972. An embarrassed Heath blamed the setback on lack of international monetary reform.

188. The Bundesbank recommended tough regulations obliging foreigners to seek approval for the acquisition of fixed interest D-Mark securities. This followed similar measures by the Swiss authorities.

189. Transcript, White House conversation between Nixon and Haldeman, 23 June 1972.

190. Treasury Secretary George Shultz, who took over from Connally in June, told Nixon that America's inaction in defending Smithsonian made 'a poor launching pad for a constructive trans-Atlantic dialogue on longer-term reform.' Arthur Burns, the Federal Reserve chairman, showed some emollience on European issues – but his was a lone voice.

191. AAPD 1973, Document 196, p. 884. Talks between Brandt and Pompidou, Bonn, 3 July 1972.

192. UKNA, PREM 15/917. Letter from Brandt to Heath, Bonn, 7 July 1972. 'The Federal Government, as you know, has shown understanding for your decision to forestall, through the measures taken by your government, the British monetary reserves being exhausted by speculation. I hope [a return to the Snake] can be achieved soon enough to avoid additional problems for the enlarged Community.'

193. AAA. British ambassador to Bonn Nicholas Henderson conversation with Brandt, Bonn, 15 August. 1972. '[Finance minister] Helmut Schmidt will probably tell the French that if we cannot agree on parallelism, then the path to monetary union will be longer.'

194. BEA, 7A134 10. O'Brien conversation with Sir Alan Neale, 16 August 1972. 'Neale thought it was not inconceivable that, if sufficiently frustrated, Pompidou might . . . say that we were evidently unready to play a full role as member of the Community.'

195. AAPD 1973, Document 15, p. 73, footnote 40. On 14 December 1972 Chancellor of the Exchequer Anthony Barber informed the European Commission and other European finance ministers that the UK would not re-enter the Snake on 1 January. As of 9 January, the German government calculated that sterling's *de facto* devaluation since the departure from the Snake in June 1972 amounted to 9 per cent.

196. UKNA, PREM 15/1492. Brandt letter to Heath, following Franco-German consultations, 26 January 1973. Letter from Michael Alexander to Tom Bridges on the result of Franco-German meeting. 30 January 1971. 'Both agreed on the importance of meeting the calendar laid down by the summit, particularly over economic and monetary union. They agreed that this depended largely on the United Kingdom and that the position of sterling was a major problem.'

197. Emminger, *op. cit.*, p.234. See also Deutsche Bundesbank, *Fifty Years of the Deutsche Mark*, Jürgen von Hagen, *op. cit.*, p. 413. This was a spectacular *volte-face* from the Bundesbank's backing the previous summer for administrative controls against speculative inflows – a policy that had manifestly not worked.

198. The decision to devalue was announced late on 12 February 1973 following a bout of speculation in which foreign central banks absorbed more than $8 billion.

199. NYFA, CF/Foreign Exchange 260. 'The Defense of the Dollar, January 23 – February 9 1973, as seen from the Trading Desk', by Scott E. Pardee. Charles Coombs at the New York Fed complained about the 'futility' of not being informed about US Treasury negotiations. This led to the Fed selling large volumes of borrowed D-Marks just before the dollar devaluation, causing a subsequent loss.

200. Emminger, *op. cit.*, pp. 236–7.

201. AAPD 1973, Document 75, p. 355.

202. Nicholas Henderson, *Mandarin*, 1994, p. 54.

203. UKNA, PREM 1576. FCO telegram 292 on meetings between Brandt and Heath, Bonn, 1 March 1973. Heath departed from his prepared script. Nicholas Henderson, Britain's ambassador to Bonn, noted: 'The impact of this impromptu appeal to vision was considerable, and he sat down to loud applause.' Henderson, *op. cit.*, p. 56.

204. Henderson, *op. cit.*, p. 58. Nicholas Henderson said of Pöhl's performance: 'He seemed a dashing fellow, not at all over-awed by the occasion or by the absence of his

Minister. On the contrary, he seemed to be enjoying himself, to be very relaxed and to have distinctive ideas of his own.'

205. AAA, ZA/105.688, Meeting of European Monetary Committee, 14 February 1973. The meeting called for an acceleration for the move to EMU.

206. UKNA, PREM 1576. Pöhl accepted the need to protect the sterling balances. He stressed that, if a new parity was fixed for sterling, there could be a considerable movement out of the pound into the Deutsche Mark – as much as $5 to $6 billion.

207. UKNA, PREM 1576. Conversation between Heath, Brandt and their officials, Schloss Gymnich, 1 March 1973 at 10.55 pm. Mitchell added that a European Treasury would be needed as well as a central bank. See also AAPD 1973, Documents 69 and 70, pp. 335–45. The German records report Pöhl as saying that if each member remained within the Snake, Europe would be very close to a common currency.

208. Pöhl: 'Central banks look at their reserves as misers looked at their treasure. This is a decision for the German government, not for the Bundesbank.'

209. UKNA, PREM 15/1576. 'Secret – Common Float' by Derek Mitchell, 1 March 1973.

210. UKNA, PREM 15/1576. Record of a meeting between Heath and Brandt, Federal Chancellery, Bonn, 11 am, 2 March 1973.

211. UKNA, PREM 15/1576. Record of a meeting between Heath and Brandt, Federal Chancellery, Bonn, 4 pm, 2 March 1973.

212. Recalling Schmidt's offer in Paris three weeks previously, Pöhl said the German finance minister 'had clearly contemplated large amounts of credit on easy terms'. Pöhl said he believed such facilities could encapsulate 'a nil interest rate and repayment over several years – seven or even 10 years'. Pohl confirmed, with Brandt's agreement, that the offer 'still held good'.

213. DBPO, Series III, Vol. IV, Document. 37. PREM 15/1459. Cabinet Currency Crisis – Note of a Meeting held at Chequers on 3 March 1973 at 4 pm. A British Cabinet meeting at Chequers on 3 March agreed that Britain would seek membership of a joint Community float only if the right conditions could be negotiated. Heath told his Ministers that this 'would not be easy'.

214. DBPO, Series III, Vol. IV, Document 43. Douglas-Home papers. Tel 195. Message from Heath to Brandt, 6 March 1973. 'A necessary condition of success would be the availability within the Community of financial support of the most far-reaching kind. This would be tantamount to a very substantial degree of reserve pooling, and, therefore, some at least of the support should be interest-free.' In putting forward extreme proposals for European monetary support, Heath may have been responding to a warning from Nixon that Britain should not enter too deeply into European integration. DBPO, Series III, Vol. IV, Document 43. Douglas-Home papers. Washington tel 851. Message from Nixon to Heath, 3 March 1973. Brandt received a similar letter. AAPD 1974, Document 84, p. 399, footnote 4.

215. DBPO, Series III, Vol. IV, Document 45. Douglas-Home papers. Tel 331. Brandt message to Heath, 8 March 1973.

216. DBPO, Series III, Vol. IV, Document 47. Douglas-Home papers. Tel 338. Brandt message to Heath, 11 March 1973. AAPD 1973, Document 75, p. 355. Brandt letter to Heath.

217. DBPO, Series III, Vol. IV, Document 48. PREM 15/1459. UKREP Brussels Tel 1320. 11 March 1973. Giscard told the meeting, 'The important question is to maintain the Snake.' Barber said, 'Only the knowledge that support was unlimited and free from damaging obligations would be effective in putting an end to speculation.'

218. As a contribution to stabilising Snake exchange rates, Germany agreed to revalue the D-Mark by 3 per cent. The communiqué at the end of the finance ministers' meeting said: 'The British, Irish and Italian members of the Council stated that their governments intended to associate themselves as soon as possible with the decision that had been taken to maintain the Community exchange margins.' DBPO, Series III, Vol. IV, Document 50. UKNA, PREM 15/1459. Heath message to Barber, 12 March 1973. 'I do

not think the Treasury and the Bank of England are sufficiently aware of these wider implications. I quite understand that they do not wish to see a repetition of the events of 1964 to 1967. But we did not join the Community in order to behave like Little Englanders.'

219. BEA, 6A103/4. Note from Derek Mitchell to Leslie O'Brien, 16 April 1973. Paper for Prime Minister and Chancellor Barber: 'Rejoining the EEC Snake Support Facilities'. 'A figure of 10 billion [European] units of account was mentioned by the Italians . . . This is nothing like enough. The UK lost $2.5 billion in 5 working days last June. The Germans in January and February 1973 took in $6 billion in 3 weeks. Total support for the dollar on 1 March 73 was $3.5 billion of which Germany's share was $2.5 billion.'

220. AAPD 1973, Document 93, pp. 446–51. Conversation between Brandt and European Commission President Ortoli, Bonn, 29 March 1973. Brandt asked Ortoli whether the EMU plan would enter Stage Two in 1974. Ortoli said it was possible, but foresaw 'very great difficulties'.

221. DBPO Series III, Volume IV, Document 53. UKREP Brussels tel 1513. PREM 15/1460. Talks between European Commissioner Sir Christopher Soames and Pompidou, Paris, 19 March 1973. Pompidou said that when Britain left the Snake in June 1972 he had been led to believe this was a temporary measure and the British would be back with a fixed parity by January. He had been surprised by Anthony Barber's demands (during the March 1973 monetary negotiations) as a price for returning to the Snake.

222. Deutsche Bundesbank, *Fifty Years of the Deutsche Mark*, Jürgen von Hagen, *op. cit.*, pp. 414–19. The Bundesbank Council's first move towards direct money stock control was broached in January 1973, before the switch to floating rates.

223. The Bundesbank raised discount and Lombard rates to 6 per cent and 8 per cent in May, and then by a further 1 percentage point in June. Rates remained at that level until October 1974.

224. DBA, B330/9942. Klasen letter to Brandt, 7 May 1973. 'As a result of our successful stability efforts, or because of unfavourable internal American developments, the dollar could become weaker again. This would not disturb us, as long as France or other members of the joint float did not wish for the bloc to intervene again in support of the dollar.'

225. The Bundesbank's recommendations were partly based on a report it drew up in November 1972.

226. The D-Mark revaluation was followed by a revaluation of the guilder.

227. BEA, 7A/13411. Note for the Bank of England governors of a conversation with Derek Mitchell, HM Treasury, 15 June 1973. Against the advice of his senior officials, Heath had been toying with the idea of bringing sterling back into the Snake, partly to increase Britain's bargaining power in questions like European regional aid. 'Mitchell said that for some reason, as yet unknown, the PM was now showing an interest in the possibility of an early return of sterling to the Snake, and this was the background to the question he had asked me earlier this morning on how much intervention might be necessary to put sterling back into the Snake. I pointed out how impossible it was to give an answer, but said that one might say there would have to involve discretion to spend at least several hundred million dollars.'

228. UKNA, PREM 15/1520. Heath letter to Brandt, 31 July 1973. 'There is no doubt that a decisive factor [for heavy pressure on sterling] was the attraction of funds away from London by the strong pull of exceptionally high interest rates [in Germany.] As a result, our own minimum lending rate . . . went up a further 2 percentage points at the end of last week . . . This is the highest ever figure for us, and is full of crisis overtones . . . As the effects spread through the economy – for example to mortgage rates, which are a particularly sensitive area – we may run into increasing difficulties.' See also Emminger, *op. cit.*, p. 274. Additionally, as late as September, Heath was still fretting about a possible return to the Snake, asking his officials to badger the Germans about earlier rejected proposals on unlimited credits for the pound. 'Pöhl and I met

for 1½ hours this afternoon. I asked Pöhl how he saw the possibilities of reviving the March idea of unlimited and unconditional support. Pöhl's unequivocal reply, from which he refused to be shifted, was that there were no prospects of progress in this direction . . .' UKNA, PREM 15/1564. Mitchell telegram, Nairobi, 23 September 1973.

229. DBA, B330/9942. Klasen letter to Brandt, Frankfurt, 3 October 1973. 'Premature entry could sooner or later lead to currency movements that would not only would undermine our German credit policy but also lead to a break-up of the Snake.' Klasen drew attention to UK inflation of more than 9 per cent, and foreigners' sterling balances totalling £6.3 billion.

230. UKNA, PREM 15/1564. Conversation, Chequers, after dinner, 6 October 1973. Pöhl said he saw little risk of a further decline in the dollar; an appreciation was more likely. One reason for Pöhl's pessimism on the Snake may have been to ward off any residual UK enthusiasm about rejoining it. Earlier, he had put forward a possible date for rejoining on 1 January 1974. Telegram from Mitchell for Armstrong, on meeting with Pöhl, Nairobi, 23 September 1973. Mitchell reported Pöhl as having said 'Schmidt has gone off unlimited and unconditional support for sterling within the Snake (having originally proposed it).' The meeting note added: 'Emphasis on the Snake seems likely and the PM may well be asked to consider some such idea as Pöhl's that we should accept a binding commitment to join on 1 Jan 1974, the date that should inaugurate EMU II.'

231. UKNA, PREM 15/1564. Conversation, Chequers, after dinner, 6 October 1973. Pöhl predicted that the Germans would be unlikely to revalue again soon, because – under the impact of recent revaluations – German exports were starting to decline and the economy was slowing. France, he said, was unlikely formally to devalue.

232. UKNA, BT 241/2687. Foreign Office note on Pompidou visit to Heath, 16 and 17 November 1973. 'The PM said he hoped to see the Community starting the second stage of EMU on 1 January.'

233. Giscard radio address, Paris, 19 January 1974. He said the Snake withdrawal would last for six months; in fact, it lasted three times as long.

234. West German government statement, 19 January 1974. Giscard had 'explained to Minister Schmidt the reasons why it would not avail itself of a $3 billion monetary support facility from the Federal Republic.' See also Helmut Schmidt, *Die Deutschen und ihre Nachbarn*, 1990, p. 304. The terms for the credit would presumably have included the pledging of part of France's gold reserves.

235. Giscard, *Macht und Leben*, 1988, p. 122.

236. Three months later, Nixon, too, left office, resigning on 9 August, four days after release of the 'smoking gun' tape revealing covert funding for one of the Watergate burglars. He was replaced by Vice President Gerald Ford.

Chapter 3: Tyranny of the Mark

1. Volcker interview with author, New York, 28 August 2007.
2. Schmidt became chancellor on 16 May 1974. Giscard became president on 27 May.
3. Giscard interview with author, Paris, 28 June 2007.
4. Schmidt interview with author, Hamburg, 4 September 2007.
5. Giscard TV address, 16 October 1978, *Le Monde*, 18 October 1978.
6. Giscard remarks, AMUE dinner, Paris, 1 April 1994.
7. DBA, N2/269. Schmidt speech, transcript, Bundesbank Council, Frankfurt, 30 November 1978.
8. Schmidt, *Die Zeit*, 6 August 1993.
9. Giscard's father headed the finance department of the Allied High Commissioners occupying the Rhineland.
10. Schmidt, *op. cit.*, p. 165. 'I could hardly believe my eyes when I first saw the castle of L'Etoile in Authon, with its beautiful, generously-proportioned park.' Schmidt pointed out that he and his wife Loki lived in a terraced house on an estate built by

the Neue Heimat trade union housing group. Giscard's wife, Anne-Aymone, whose father died in a German concentration camp, was a great-great-great-granddaughter of Louis XIV. During Giscard's presidency, as a result of war-time memories, Anne-Aymone refused to accompany him on trips to Germany apart from his state visit in 1980. Giscard, *op. cit.*, p. 134.

11. Giscard, *op. cit.*, p. 134. Schmidt told Giscard of his Jewish ancestry towards the end of Giscard's state visit to Germany in July 1980. Apart from his wife Loki and his chief aide Manfred Lahnstein, Schmidt had told no one else of this story. Schmidt's grandfather had been a well-off Jewish banker from northern Germany who had an illegitimate child – Schmidt's father – with a young German woman.

12. BNA, PREM 16/799. Callaghan after dinner conversation with Schmidt, Chequers, 10 October 1976. The detailed account of the meeting was prepared by Callaghan immediately afterwards and written by his principal private secretary on 11 October 1976.

13. Schmidt, *Menschen und Mächte*, 1987, p. 459.

14. Giscard, *op. cit.*, p. 114, relating to meeting in Blaesheim, July 1977.

15. Schmidt interview with author, Hamburg, 4 September 2007. 'They have different languages, they have different educations; the memory of Auschwitz still plays an enormous role. There is also the fact that in the view of the French, and also of the Dutch and of the Danes and of the Poles, Germany is a bit too large these days. They are afraid of big Germany.'

16. Giscard, *op. cit.*, 1998, pp. 15–16. The dire state of Pompidou's health was revealed to Giscard and other ministers only in March 1974.

17. Behind Schmidt's legendary high-handedness lay greater sensitivity than many realised. See Callaghan, *Time and Chance*, p. 301: 'His quick intelligence, mastery of economic thinking, practical mind and breadth of outlook meant that every conversation was stimulating. Helmut's bark is worse than his bite, and beneath the hard carapace he is a generous and basically modest man.'

18. UKNA, FCO 33/544, FCO 59/559. Note on Valéry Giscard d'Estaing as minister of economy and finance by H.T. Morgan of West European Department, 1 December 1970.

19. Szász, *The Road to European Monetary Union*, p. 61.

20. UKNA, PREM 1576. Ambassador Nicholas Henderson note, German government dinner for Edward Heath, 29 May 1973, Bonn, 1 June 1973.

21. The general election on 28 February 1974 was inconclusive, with the Heath government failing to win the majority it needed to continue its economic policies, but the Labour party failing to secure an overall majority.

22. AAPD, 1974, Document 157, p. 663. Message from ambassador Braun to Foreign Minister Genscher on talks between Schmidt and Giscard, Paris, 31 May 1974. At their first meeting as government leaders, Schmidt and Giscard said European summit meetings should be cut to a minimum; the most important decisions needed to be taken 'in small committees'.

23. UKNA, PREM 15/1564. Mitchell telegram to 10 Downing Street on conversation with Pöhl, Nairobi, 23 September 1973.

24. According to Manfred Lahnstein, a close associate, 'Schmidt always had a problem with technicians; he admires them but he doesn't want them to stand in his way.' Lahnstein interview with author, Hamburg, 11 June 2007.

25. The referendum took place in June 1975 and resulted in a vote to stay in the Community.

26. UKNA, PREM 16/99. Talks between Wilson and Schmidt, Bonn, 19 June 1974.

27. AAPD 1974, Document 181, p. 780. Talks between Wilson and Schmidt, Bonn, 19 June 1974.

28. UKNA, PREM 16/99. Talks between Wilson and Schmidt, Bonn, 19 June 1974. These remarks were not part of the official record of the meetings – they were excised because of Giscard's domestic political sensitivities with the Gaullists.

29. European politics were overshadowed by preparation for the general election set for October 1974 to resolve the political impasse caused by Wilson's lack of a majority.

30. NYFA, CF/Volcker papers 142546. 'Mr Hayes' notes on European visits, June 10–25 1974.'

31. Schmidt statement as chancellor to Bundestag, Bonn, 17 May 1974. DBA, Letter from Klasen to Schmidt, 16 May 1974. The Bundesbank greeted Schmidt's Bundestag election as chancellor with unusual warmth.

32. AAPD 1974, Document 205, p. 1084. Meeting between Schmidt and Giscard, Paris, 2 September 1974. The note was drawn up by Schmidt. Schmidt explained to Giscard if the Italian government did not follow the right economic policies, it would be unable to repay the credit and would lose roughly one-sixth of its monetary gold to Germany. According to Schmidt, Giscard welcomed the mobilisation of gold and believed it would increase the value of bullion reserves. The facility comprised an 8 per cent six-month revolving credit from the Bundesbank to the Banca d'Italia. DBA, B330/9942. Letter from Klasen to Schmidt, Frankfurt, 29 August 1974. The gold price used as security was $120 per ounce, 80 per cent of the two-monthly average London price.

33. Schmidt, *Die Deutschen und ihre Nachbarn*, p. 304. Schmidt maintained, 'The Bundesbank Law set down no clear rules for competence in this matter.'

34. The Bonn government, backed by the Bundesbank, took a hostile line on multilateral European loan agreements suggested by the Commission.

35. DBA, B330/9942. Letter from Schmidt to Klasen, 25 July 1974 – unusually deploying the familiar 'Du' appellation, 'Such a signal is also necessary in view of the two Land [state] elections in the autumn, which should not be overshadowed by people's uncertainty about jobs.'

36. The Bundesbank made half-point cuts in discount and Lombard rate to 6.per cent and 8.5 per cent on 25 October 1974. The two state elections took place on 27 October.

37. AAPD 1974, Document 162, pp. 687–96. Talks between Schmidt and European Commission president Ortoli, Bonn, 11 June 1974.

38. Szász, *op. cit.*, p. 40.

39. BFA, 1489200205, Box 257. Description of Fourcade Plan, 16 September 1974.

40. AAPD 1974, Document 253, p. 1102. Talks between Schmidt and Giscard, Paris, 2 September 1974. 'The necessary economic policy conditions are not in place for the further development of the [European Monetary Cooperation] Fund into a Central Bank. One cannot put one part of the economic policy instruments on to a Community level (credit policy) and at the same time leave another part (above all, fiscal policy) subject to national sovereignty.'

41. BFA, 1489200205, Box 257. Jean-Yves Haberer statement, European Monetary Committee, 10 October 1974.

42. See BNA, PREM 'Note of talk with Herr Helmut Schmidt on Sunday 1 November 1974' with Wilson's account of Schmidt's insights into Giscard's problems vis-à-vis the Gaullists. 'He said that Giscard was coming under very strong press and other attacks, mainly from the Gaullist papers, and clearly orchestrated by eminent Gaullists. . . . He was dependent upon the Gaullists who were determined to make life hard for him. He had never really been one of them, and his intellectual manner, sometimes appearing arrogant, had offended them.'

43. BFA, 1489200205, Box 273. Extract of transcript of European Monetary Committee meeting, 3 & 4 December 1974, including explanation by Renaud de la Genière of the French plan for a 'flexible' system to allow all European currencies to participate in the Snake. 'Several members of the committee, led by the Dutch and Germans, voiced their fears of seeing the French propositions change current Snake rules.'

44. ECBA. Committee of Governors of EEC Central Banks, Basle, 8 April 1975. While the Dutch, Italian and German central bank governors backed the Swiss move, the French and Belgian representatives made clear their concerns. See also DBA, N2/K741. Emminger letter to Apel, Frankfurt, 9 April 1975. Emminger told the finance minister

about the concerns arising from the previous day's meeting. Fritz Leutzwiler, president of the Swiss National Bank, said he would be speaking further to his government about the French and Belgian concerns and spoke out against 'hasty' action. CAEF, 1A-0000256/1. Fourcade letter to Apel, Paris, 12 May 1975, replying to Apel's letter of 23 April. German finance minister Apel wrote to Paris in April 1975 setting out general support for the proposal. Fourcade replied that the Swiss Franc's entry 'would risk very seriously complicating' the French Franc's planned return to the Snake. Among other conditions, he proposed steps to combat fiscal fraud in Switzerland.

45. CAEF, 1A-0000256/1. 'Note pour le Ministre – Réflexions sur l'avenir de l'union européenne monétaire', by Jacques de Larosière, 2 July 1975. Bureau E3 No. PJ 1 1165 CVD – A briefing paper for finance minister Fourcade and President Giscard d'Estaing.

46. AAPD 1975, Document 348, p. 1642–43. Summit meeting of US, Japan, Germany, France, UK, Italy, Rambouillet, 16 November 1975. Statements by Giscard and Schmidt during talks on trade and monetary issues. Giscard said the developing world and the Eastern bloc saw floating rates as 'a sign of decadence'.

47. AAA, ZA/109.332. German Cabinet papers, Finance Ministers' meeting in Brussels, Bonn, 8 July 1975. To emphasise the Snake's newly-rediscovered Community character, the language for the Snake's deliberations switched back to French.

48. AAA, ZA 105.688. Meeting of European Monetary Committee, Brussels, 11 August 1975. 'The European directors [on the IMF Executive Board] – with the exception of the German representative expressed themselves as very sceptical and partly negative on the French step.'

49. BFA, 1489200205, Box 273. French news agency Agefi reported a reserve loss of FFr 8 billion since 4 March.

50. BFA, 1489200205 Box 273, Ministry of Economy and Finance, Direction du Tresor, 'Note for the Minister', 14 March 1976. Apel told Fourcade, 'France was wrong to enter [the Snake] at an exaggeratedly high rate in July 1975.' At the meeting in Brussels, Fourcade and Apel debated for an hour on whether the Germans might revalue the D-Mark as a contribution to a realignment between the two currencies. Apel offered a revaluation of 2 per cent against a French devaluation of 4 per cent. When Fourcade suggested that France quit the Snake, Apel said that would be worse than a devaluation.

51. Finance ministers and central bank governors of the other Snake members joined the meeting later. Fourcade and Apel presented their ideas for sharing the realignment between Germany and France as a 'purely technical adjustment'. The Danes, Norwegians, Swedes and Belgians opposed any change in their countries' parities, while the Dutch signalled their desire to see France leave the Snake. The evening's wrangling was interrupted by news of losses for government parties in the second round of French regional elections that day. Knowing this would weaken the Franc, in a long telephone call, Giscard ordered Fourcade to leave the Snake.

52. AAPD 1976, Document 90, p. 425. Telephone conversation between Giscard and Schmidt, 16 March 1976.

53. BFA, 1489200205, Box 273. The French embassy in Bonn concluded that the German authorities would always give priority to the exchange rate between the D-Mark and the dollar over European currency relationships. French Embassy, 'The 1976 Monetary Crisis', Bonn, 24 March 1976.

54. AAPD 1976, Document 133, pp. 606–9. German ambassador von Braun message to Foreign Office, Paris, 7 May 1976. 'The criticism of the Chancellor by prime minister Chirac before the National Assembly shows that harmony between Bonn and Paris . . . is somewhat disturbed.'

55. AAPD, Document 337, p. 1531. Ambassador Herbst letter to Foreign Office, Paris, 23 November 1976.

56. AAPD, Document 342, pp. 1547–9. Talks between French foreign minister Louis de Guiringaud and Schmidt, Bonn, 26 November 1976.

57. Callaghan, op. cit., p. 418.

58. Callaghan, *op. cit.*, p. 301.

59. Callaghan, *op. cit.*, p. 431. German assistance would allow the UK to push for a softening of tough US-inspired IMF conditions in areas like public spending cuts. Callaghan saw the need to underpin sterling during a period of weakness, in the expectation that the pound would eventually strengthen as a result of the growing importance of North Sea oil production.

60. AAPD 1976, Document 72, pp. 340–9. Foreign Office ministerial director Lautenschläger paper, analysing the possibility of using the Bundesbank DM80 billion reserves for stabilisation credits, mainly within the European Community.

61. UKNA, PREM 16/881. Telephone conversation between Schmidt and Callaghan, 28 April 1976.

62. UKNA, PREM 16/895. Telephone conversation between Callaghan and Schmidt, 4 October 1976. On 6 October, when the pound dropped to beneath DM4, its lowest ever against the D-Mark, Schmidt's spokesman announced that he had told the German cabinet, 'In our opinion the pound is clearly under valued.'

63. UKNA, PREM 16/799, Callaghan meeting with Schmidt, Chequers, 10 October 1976. Note by Callaghan's Personal Private Secretary, Ken Stowe, on 11 October 1976, based on Callaghan's account. Callaghan said the UK would repay a possible credit in D-Marks. Schmidt said the facility could be funded by Germany 'recalling some of its reserves' from the US. Schmidt saw $5.5 billion being provided by the US, $4.5 billion by Germany and $500 million elsewhere, perhaps Holland. Schmidt promised to send State Secretary Karl Otto Pöhl to London the following week to discuss the issue. UKNA, PREM 16/799. John Hunt handwritten note to Callaghan, 'Secret and Personal', 11 October 1976. 'It is very good news that you were able to make so much progress.' Pöhl never went to London.

64. UKNA, PREM 16/799. John Hunt note to Callaghan, Ref. A02828, reporting meeting in Bonn on 18 October with Pöhl, 19 October 1976. Pöhl warned about the need for IMF conditionality and said that the US Treasury would 'fight to the last against weak conditions'. During the conversation Pöhl telephoned the Bundesbank's Emminger, who relayed the central bank's uncompromising stance that Britain had to agree the IMF loan before any accord on the sterling balances. UKNA, PREM 16/799. Derek Mitchell note to Ken Stowe, Prime Minister's Office, reporting on meeting in Brussels on 2 November 1976 with Pöhl, 3 November 1976. Pöhl said they [the Bundesbank] 'literally own the German reserves'. Pöhl recounted Schmidt's previous fruitless attempts to make political use of the reserves; when Schmidt had wanted to make a loan to Poland, rather than transferring the money from the Bundesbank, Pöhl had been forced to borrow the funds from the Saudi Arabian Monetary Agency 'on very unfavourable terms'. A few days later Healey met Pöhl in Brussels and emphasised the need for the Germans to recognise the political aspects of the British problem. See Douglas Wass, *Decline to Fall*, 2008, p. 248, quoting HMT, BP 98/16/02.

65. UKNA, PREM 16/799. Schmidt letter to Callaghan, 3 November 1976.

66. UKNA, PREM 16/799. John Hunt memo to Callaghan, 4 November 1976.

67. NYFA, CF/Volcker 142577. Notes on BIS meetings of central bank governors by Alan R. Holmes, 13 December 1976. During the discussions, Bernard Clappier of the Banque de France said Britain should abide by its 1972 commitment to reduce the sterling balances.

68. Roy Jenkins, *A Life at the Centre*, 1991, p. 104. He had backed British entry to the Community in the 1960s. 'By the standards of the pioneers, I was a latter day convert [to the European cause], although one well before the bulk of, say, the Foreign Office, City or Conservative Party opinion.'

69. Jenkins caused irritation within the Labour party by leading a minority of Labour MPs in support of the Heath government's policies on joining the European Community in 1971.

70. Peter Ludlow, *The Making of the European Monetary System*, 1982, p. 39.

71. BFA, 1489200205/28. Note from Banque de France foreign directorate, 'Future of the snake,' March 1977.

72. Jenkins speech, European Parliament, 6 July 1977.

73. Ortoli remarks at press conference, 20 October 1977.

74. Jenkins speech, Florence, 27 October 1977.

75. Ludlow, *op. cit.*, p. 57. Jenkins visited Schmidt in Bonn in November 1977 to discuss his proposals.

76. Sparking an abrupt dollar lurch on the foreign exchanges, Carter's Treasury Secretary Michael Blumenthal led a growing Washington campaign for Germany to bolster world growth by reducing its large current account surplus and letting the D-Mark rise. NYFA, CF/Foreign Exchange 260. Note on 'Foreign attitudes towards US exchange rate policy' from Margaret L. Greene to Scott Pardee, New York, 8 July 1977. 'People at the Bundesbank were not happy with Blumenthal's remarks.' Schmidt interviews with author, Cambridge, April 1988, Hamburg, 1991.

77. Szász interview with author, Amsterdam, 23 May 2007.

78. The realignments included devaluations of the Dutch guilder, Belgian and Luxembourg Francs, and the Norwegian, Danish and Swedish crowns as well as the departure of the Swedish crown.

79. AAPD 1977, Document 160, p.832. German–French consultations, 17 June 1977.

80. DBA, B330/843. Statement by finance minister Hans Apel at Bundesbank Council, Frankfurt, 14 July 1977. Apel asked the Council to take Barre's plea seriously. 'That is a very important request from a very important trading partner.'

81. AAPD 1977, Document 231, p. 1141. German ambassador Herbst message to Foreign Office, Paris, 30 August 1977.

82. Jenkins statement, press conference, Brussels, December 1977. Jenkins declared that the idea 'will now be given a fair wind'.

83. BFA, 1489200205, Box 273. 'Les chances de réintégration du franc dans le serpent monétaire européen', Banque de France foreign directorate, February 1978. '[T]he oil crisis, world inflation, the serious recession that accompanies it, the degradation of the international monetary system, the setbacks for the spirit of the Community and the resurgence of protectionist trends.' Confronted by the Mark, the only other currencies within the Snake were those with relatively narrow markets that were forced to follow the Mark's rise and absorb the ensuing financial costs.

84. Schmidt interview with author in Hamburg, 4 September 2007.

85. Pöhl interview with author, Frankfurt, 9 May 2007.

86. DBA, N2/264. Emminger letter to Wolfgang Rieke, head of the Bundesbank's international division, Frankfurt, 9 March 1978. The letter – 'Aufzeichnung über EG-Währungsprobleme für den Bundeskanzler' – was part of a Bundesbank response to technical monetary studies requested by Schmidt at the meeting on 1 March, which was attended by Hans Matthöfer, finance minister, and Otto Lambsdorff, economics minister. This gathering took place a day after Jenkins visited Schmidt in Bonn.

87. The Emminger note criticised an earlier Rieke draft on proposed currency intervention mechanisms as being technically abstruse and missing wider-ranging points. In *D-Mark, Dollar, Währungskrisen*, Emminger does not mention the Bonn meeting and the resultant serious work commissioned from the Bundesbank.

88. DBA, N2/264. 'Personal' Pöhl letter to Schmidt, Frankfurt, 21 March 1978. Exchange rate flexibility. Reflecting on the efforts Schmidt and Pöhl had made in 1973 to try to establish a joint European float, Pöhl wrote, 'It was probably good that our attempt failed . . . Otherwise we would have run the risk of succumbing to a similar [inflationary] development as in Britain, Italy and France.' The copy of the letter in the Bundesbank archive is annotated, mainly with positive comments, in Emminger's handwriting. Pöhl wrote (underlined in Emminger's copy) that this was a 'personal opinion' rather than 'an official statement' and represented an attempt 'to link up with what we have so intensively discussed at the beginning of 1973 [when Pöhl became State Secretary] at a time of the switch to generalised floating rates'.

89. Schmidt, *Die Deutschen und ihre Nachbarn*, 1990, p. 224.
90. Giscard, *op. cit.*, p.127. Schmidt and Callaghan jointly telephoned Giscard to congratulate him on 19 March 1978 – Labour and Social Democratic leaders were the first to applaud victory by a conservative French president.
91. DBA, N2/264. Letter from Emminger to Schmidt, Frankfurt, 30 March 1978. This contained a note 'Monetary policy progress in Europe' summarising options discussed with Clappier, including proposals such as an extension of the Snake (to include the UK as well as France), a pooling of monetary reserves, and the introduction of a parallel currency in the form of the European Unit of Account. In *D-Mark, Dollar, Währungskrisen* Emminger mentions the visit by Clappier but says it was at Giscard's request, failing to note that Pöhl accompanied him. In his letter to Schmidt Emminger said the meeting was held at the chancellor's request and that his former close associate Pöhl also took part.
92. DBA, N2/264. 'The Case for More Intra-European Monetary Cooperation – Summary of comments made at Copenhagen, April 7, 1978.' The document was sent to Emminger by Schmidt's office.
93. DBA, N2/264. Talks between Schmidt and Callaghan, Chequers, 24 April 1978 (German government record). Horst Schulmann sent Emminger the record of the meeting, in a letter from Bonn, 9 May 1978. Emminger attended the meetings (with Gordon Richardson, governor of the Bank of England). This negates Emminger's claim in his memoirs that he was not informed until summer 1978 of the chancellor's EMS plans.
94. See also House of Commons debate on Bremen European meeting, 10 July 1978. Callaghan reminded former prime minister Edward Heath: 'We entered the Snake [in April 1972] at a rate of $2.61 and we had to emerge seven weeks later at $2.45, having lost $2 billion [in reserves]. That is something that is not worth repeating.'
95. Healey interview with author, Alfriston, 10 April 2007. See also Denis Healey, *The Time of My Life*, 1989, p. 438. 'Manfred Lahnstein supported [the EMS] on the grounds of Germany's national interest.' Lahnstein does not dispute that he made this remark. 'I may have mentioned this argument, but rather jokingly and as a casual remark. The main reason why we wanted the EMS was to give the European Community a strong internal market that would be less dependent on the vicissitudes of the dollar.' Lahnstein interview with author, Hamburg, 10 June 2007.
96. Lahnstein interview with author, Hamburg, 10 June 2007.
97. Hurley interview with author, Dublin, 1 October 2007.
98. DBA, B330/9083/I. Emminger letter to Schmidt, Frankfurt, 27 June 1978. This was followed by a meeting of the Bundesbank Council on 28 June.
99. DBA, B330/9083/I. Transcript, Bundesbank Council, Frankfurt, 29 June 1978. Pöhl said that Britain and Italy would want 'symmetry' in the new system, i.e. deficit and surplus countries would be equally obliged to reduce balance of payments disequilibria.
100. Szász, *op. cit.*, p. 58. The suggestion of the Bremen communiqué was that, with the ECU at the 'centre of the system', intervention obligations would be based on the ECU.
101. Schmidt, *Die Deutschen und ihre Nachbarn*, 1990, p. 228. Giscard suggested the use of the word 'Ecu' at the end of June, at a Franco-German meeting in Schmidt's Hamburg home.
102. Under the currency basket idea promoted by France, the D-Mark could reach its upper intervention point in the system without the weakest currency simultaneously hitting the floor, which would be the case under the 'parity grid' system of bilateral intervention 'floors' and 'ceilings' in the Snake. If a large currency such as the Franc weakened on the foreign exchanges, this would simultaneously lower the value of the ECU, so the requirement to maintain a 2.25 per cent fluctuation band against the ECU became much less demanding than the requirement to keep to the same band against the D-Mark. The Bundesbank believed that an ECU system would saddle the Bundesbank with a one-sided intervention obligation and would increase German

inflation.See also DBA, N2/265. 'Erklärung von Dr. O. Emminger zu dem Bremer Währungsplan im Bundeskabinett am 12.2.78', Frankfurt, 12 July 1978. Emminger focused on the risks that the EMS might maintain parities at unrealistic levels; that the planned European Monetary Fund would create undue international liquidity; and that the Bundesbank would lose control of D-Mark creation. DBA, B330/Drs 142 499–522 (1978), including Transcript, Bundesbank Council, Frankfurt, 13 July 1978, attended by Matthöfer and Lahnstein, at which Emminger reported on the previous day's Cabinet meeting. DBA N2/266. Account of status of EMS negotiations submitted by Pöhl to Bundesbank Council, Frankfurt, 4 August 1978.

103. Pöhl interviews with author, Frankfurt, 9 May 2007, and Zurich, 17 August 2007.

104. According to Pöhl, Schmidt's annoyance about Emminger may have cost him the chance of having his mandate renewed for two years as Bundesbank president from the beginning of 1980. Schmidt was toying with the idea of replacing Emminger by Wilfried Guth, spokeman of the management board of Deutsche Bank. Guth however turned down the idea, and would anyway have faced stiff opposition from Germany's other large commercial banks, since he would have been the second Bundesbank president from the Deutsche Bank following Klasen's tenure. Emminger remained in close touch with Schmidt after the Aachen meeting. In a detailed letter, he passed on comments from Gordon Richardson, Governor of the Bank of England, who told him in October that – despite Labour party opposition – the UK remained greatly interested in a possible EMS entry. DBA, N2/267. Emminger letter to Schmidt, Frankfurt, 12 October 1978.

105. Volcker and Gyohten, op. cit., p. 150. According to Paul Volcker, who had become president of the Federal Reserve Bank of New York in 1975, 'To our foreign partners there was special satisfaction that the US had overcome its long-standing aversion to borrowing in foreign currencies in private markets abroad.

106. BFA, 489200205, Box 347. 'Notes on EMS – Need for fixed but adjustable exchange rates', Jean-Yves Haberer, 7 November 1978.

107. DBA, N2/267. Emminger letter to Schmidt, Frankfurt, 16 November 1978, including three appendices. The areas of outstanding agreement also concerned the planned ECU divergence indicator, a temporary transfer via swap agreements of 20 per cent of gold and dollar reserve to the European Monetary Cooperation Fund, and the planned increase in short- and medium-term European credit agreements.

108. Manfred Schüler, Head of Chancellery telex with Schmidt message to Emminger, Bonn, 29 November 1978.

109. For example, Schmidt interview with author, Hamburg, 4 June 1991. 'I made them see they should not over-stretch their independence ... Between the lines, I made them aware that I could go to parliament ... I was very cautious in my wording ... Emminger and Pöhl clearly understood what I was hinting at.' The Bundesbank encouraged the mythology that it was excluded from initial talks on the EMS, See Peter Bernholz, 'The Bundesbank and European Monetary Integration,' in Deutsche Bundesbank, Fifty Years of the Deutsche Mark

110. Szász interview with author, Amsterdam, 23 May 2007. See also Szász, op. cit., p. 59. Legislation in the Bundestag to change the Bundesbank's independence would have been impossible. Schmidt's later bitterness about the role of the Bundesbank in helping to prompt his own departure from office in 1982 contributed to his later exaggerations. During the 1970s Schmidt frequently praised the closeness of cooperation with the Bundesbank. In a speech in 1977 to commemorate the departure of Karl Klasen as Bundesbank president, he said, 'From the Government's point of view, cooperation with the Bundesbank worked so well not despite the autonomy of the Bundesbank, but because of it.' Schmidt speech, Bonn, 11 May 1977.

111. DBA, N2/269. Transcript, Bundesbank Council, Frankfurt, 30 November 1978.

112. DBA, N2/269, Letter from Emminger to Schmidt, Frankfurt, 1 December 1978.

113. Schmidt was accompanied by finance minister Hans Matthöfer and ministerial director Horst Schulmann.

114. DBA, N2/269. Schmidt–Pöhl exchange, transcript, Bundesbank Council, Frankfurt, 30 November 1978, pp. 65–6.

115. DBA, N2/269. Schmidt statement, transcript, Bundesbank Council, Frankfurt, 30 November 1978, pp. 14–15. The author is grateful to Peter Underwood in the Bundesbank's language department for the translation.

116. Schmidt's remarks to the Bundesbank throw doubt on his later statement that, when Mitterrand defeated Giscard in the May 1981 elections, Schmidt had 'no concern about the further development of German–French cooperation'. See Schmidt, *Die Deutschen und ihre Nachbarn*, p. 168.

117. DBA, N2/269. Schmidt–Emminger exchange, transcript, Bundesbank Council, Frankfurt, 30 November 1978, p.59. The German phrase used by Schmidt and Emminger at the Council meeting was 'sachliche Übereinstimmung'. See BArch, B 136/11551 for the original Emminger letter to Schmidt, annotated with 'r' and containing Schmidt's cryptic statement: '*eher fraglich, ob letzte beiden Zeilen schriftlich zu fixieren zweckmäßig ist!?*' – 'It is questionable whether written confirmation of the two last lines [on the Bundesbank's intervention obligations] would be appropriate?' Emminger's account of the Bundesbank's agreement with the chancellor was revealed in *Handelsblatt* on 22 March 1979. This led to an exchange of letters with finance minister Hans Matthöfer in which Matthöfer confirmed Emminger's interpretation of the accord with Schmidt. DBA, N2/264, letters between Matthöfer and Emminger, 4, 6 and 26 April 1979.'

118. Emminger's account of the Bundesbank's agreement with the Chancellor was revealed in *Handelsblatt* on 22 March 1979. This led to an exchange of letters with finance minister Hans Matthöfer in which Matthöfer confirmed Emminger's interpretation of the accord with Schmidt. DBA, N2/264. letters between Matthöfer and Emminger, 4, 6 & 26 April 1979. For the consequences of the 'Emminger letter' see Chapter 5, pp. 155 and 168–9.'

119. DBA, N2/269. Schmidt–Schöllhorn exchange, transcript, Bundesbank Council, Frankfurt, 30 November 1978, pp. 30–1.

120. DBA, N2/269. Schlesinger–Schmidt exchange, transcript, Bundesbank Council, Frankfurt, 30 November 1978, pp. 24–6.

121. DBA, N2/269. Schmidt–Schöllhorn exchange, transcript, Bundesbank Council, Frankfurt, 30 November 1978, pp. 33–4. 'If [the Americans] run a policy to bring their balance of payments into equilibrium, then we might see a D-Mark/dollar rate in quite a different direction in the 1980s.'

122. DBA, N2/269. Schmidt–Irmler exchange, transcript, Bundesbank Council, Frankfurt, 30 November 1978, p. 65.

123. DBA, N2/269. Schmidt–Pöhl exchange, transcript, Bundesbank Council, Frankfurt, 30 November 1978, p. 66.

124. UK Government Green Paper on EMS, London, 25 November 1978.

125. The ERM started operations in March 1979. The delay from the planned January 1979 reflected last-minute wrangling, set off particularly by France, over compensatory payments for farmers. Britain was given 'half-way house' status as a member of the European Monetary System but not of the ERM.

126. Healey interview with author, Alfriston, 19 April 2007.

127. Chirac, *Le Monde*, 15 December 1979.

128. For currency defence ammunition, the Fund could draw on 20 per cent of member countries' gold and foreign exchange reserves, but the transfer was through revolving central bank three monthly 'swap' agreements, and never became a permanent mechanism.

129. Tietmeyer interview with author, Königstein, 10 May 2007.

130. Erik Hoffmeyer, *The International Monetary System*, 1992, p. 131. 'It is generally assumed that the creation of the EMS was indeed a major innovation and that a completely new system was established. This [was an] almost universal misunderstanding.'

131. The Bundesbank action set off a similar interest rate increase in the Netherlands by the Dutch central bank.

132. DBA, N2/K740. De Strycker letter to Emminger, Brussels, 13 July 1979.

133. DBA, N2/K740. Emminger letter to de Strycker, Frankfurt, 26 July 1979. The Bundesbank's interest rates increases represented an adjustment to credit tightening that had already taken place on the capital market – and had not caused any increase in financial market tensions. The Belgian Franc was protected by interest rates 4 to 6 percentage points higher than in Germany.

134. NYFA, CF/Volcker 97654, IMF/IBRD. Confidential memo from Anthony M. Solomon, 'US/German monetary cooperation – Talking Points', Washington, 27 September 1979.

135. Meeting with US and German monetary officials, Hamburg, 29 September 1979. William Miller led the US team, including Volcker, William Miller and Charles Schultze, chairman of the President's Committee of Economic Advisers. The German participants led by Helmut Schmidt included finance minister Matthöfer, Emminger, Pöhl and Lahnstein.

136. Volcker and Gyohten, *op. cit.*, p. 168.

137. D.E. Lindsey, A. Orphanides & R.H. Rasche, 'The Reform of October 1979 – How it happened and why', Federal Reserve Bank of St. Louis, October 2004. 'Volcker returned from the IMF meetings in Belgrade in early October 'with his ears still resonating with strongly stated European recommendations for stern action to stem severe dollar weakness on exchange markets'.

138. William Greider, *Secrets of the Temple*, 1987, p. 121. Charles Schultze, chairman of the President's Committee of Economic Advisers recalled, 'Paul said to us, "It was really a meeting of minds. With Jimmy Carter that gave me the idea. Carter said to me, 'Why don't you control the quantity of credit without raising interest rates?' " Volcker told us that's what gave him the idea to target money supply instead of interest rates.' Volcker's remarks to Schultze were meant to be facetious, explaining Carter's layman ignorance of the fundamentals of economic policy.

139. Volcker and Gyohten, *op. cit.*, p. 172.

140. DBA, CF/Pöhl. Lahnstein letter to Pöhl, 11 February 1981. Lahnstein's letter was an attempt at reconciliation following an earlier critical message to Schmidt from Pöhl. Lahnstein sent Pöhl a report from a closed meeting in Zurich of international monetary officials (including Volcker and the Saudi Arabian finance minister) on 6–7 December 1980. See also FRNA, CF/Volcker, Box 97651.

141. Barre letter to Schmidt, delivered on 3 April 1981 by the French embassy in Bonn.

142. Pöhl and Schlesinger letter to Schmidt, Frankfurt, 15 April 1981. The letter, drafted by Schlesinger, pointed out that until the decision to suspend normal Lombard lending in February, the French authorities had complained that German interest rates were too low. Hans Matthöfer, the German finance minister, had told the Bundesbank Council on 5 March that there was 'no alternative' to recent increases in Bundesbank interest rates. The Bundesbank turned down any suggestion of cutting interest rates to boost the economy, pointing out that Schmidt himself had recently told *Fortune* magazine: 'This "locomotive" theory was wrong from the very beginning.'

143. Joseph B. Treaster, *Paul Volcker: The Making of a Financial Legend*, 2004, p. 171.

144. Late in 1980 interest rates were pushed back up and the funds rate averaged over 19 per cent in June 1981. A new recession began in July, one that saw the unemployment rate reach almost 11 per cent by the end of 1982. By then inflation, which had averaged 14.6 per cent in the year from May 1979 to April 1980, had fallen below 4 per cent.

145. Alan Greenspan, *Age of Turbulence*, 2007, p. 479. Senator Mark Andrew remarks to Volcker, October 1981.

146. Schmidt speech, Bundestag, Bonn, 1 October 1982.

147. IFMS, p. 78. Conversation between Schmidt and Mitterrand associates Regis Debray, Elisabeth Guigou, Hubert Védrine, Hamburg, 5 December 1987. 'There were two

years in which France and the UK were leaders. Then there was a phase of decline with Carter and Brzezinski, then a further decline with Reagan. That man is mad! No in fact he is not really mad, he is a good man, but he is no more capable than Carter.'

Chapter 4: The Coming Trial

1. IFMS, p. 355. Mitterrand statement to Council of Ministers, Paris, 17 August 1988. Attali, *Verbatim III*, 1996, 17 August 1988.
2. Mitterrand's birthplace in Jarnac was 14 km from that of Jean Monnet, the architect of post-war European unity who in 1952 became the first president of the High Authority that fused Europe's coal and steel industries.
3. In his early twenties, when his ambition turned to becoming a writer, the young Mitterrand joined a youth movement linked to an extreme nationalist group, the Croix-de-Feu. Pierre Péan, *Une jeunesse française*, 1994, p.33.
4. François Mitterrand, *Mémoires interrompus*, quoted in Hubert Védrine, *Les mondes de François Mitterrand*, 1996, p. 122.
5. François Mitterrand, 'Pèlerinage en Thuringe', *France, Revue de l'État nouveau*, November 1942, quoted in Péan, *op. cit.*p. 234, Védrine, *op. cit.*, p. 124.
6. At the dinner at which he related the tale, Mitterrand asked his German guests not to recount it elsewhere for fear of spoiling his relations with the Belgrade government.
7. Mitterrand speech, Herrenhausen Castle, 21 October 1987, quoted in Védrine, *op. cit.*, p. 125.
8. Jacques Attali, *C'était François Mitterrand*, 2005, p. 33. Mitterrand said he changed his identity thirty-six times during the war.
9. Péan, *op. cit.*, p. 234. As president, Mitterrand made no secret of his reverence for Pétain's patriotism. His practice of sending a wreath to the Pétain grave on Armistice Day was criticised by many Socialist politicians.
10. Jacques Attali, *C'était François Mitterrand*, p.32.
11. Péan, *op. cit.*, p. 359. Mitterrand flew to Algiers via Gibraltar in a British Douglas aeroplane from an airport in Wales.
12. Brandt, *Erinnerungen*, p. 254. Mitterrand told Brandt that the General's first question was whether he had arrived in a British aeroplane.
13. Mitterrand offered varied accounts of the Algiers meeting with de Gaulle, calibrated to political circumstances. See Péan, *op. cit.*, p. 361. See Helmut Kohl, *Erinnerungen 1982–90*, 2005, p. 36 for Mitterrand's sympathetic description of de Gaulle at their first meeting on 4 October 1982.
14. Catherine Nay, *Le Noir et le Rouge*, 1984, p.84.
15. Brandt, *op. cit.*, p. 491.
16. IFMS, p. 136. Note on meeting between Mitterrand and Schmidt, Latche, 7 October 1981. Attali, *Verbatim I*, 1993, p. 107. Mitterrand said reunification would take time – perhaps a generation – but was 'inscribed in history'. The catalyst would be weakness in the Soviet Union. Schmidt said he would not live to see it.
17. The banking nationalisations were in addition to those of Banque Nationale de Paris, Crédit Lyonnais and Société Générale, which had been nationalised under de Gaulle in 1946.
18. Hervé Hannoun interview with author, Basle, 17 August 2007. Hannoun, an official under Mitterrand's first prime minister, Pierre Mauroy, pointed out that the French current account deficit in 1981 was 3 per cent of GDP and inflation was around 13 per cent.
19. Schmidt, *Die Deutschen und ihre Nachbarn*, p. 203.
20. IFMS, p.194. Note on talks between Mitterrand and Schmidt, Latche, 8 October 1981.
21. Franz-Olivier Giesbert, *Le Président*, p. 164. The summit took place on 5 and 6 June 1982. The second devaluation of the Mitterrand presidency took place on 14 June 1982.

22. IFMS, p. 216. Note on ministerial meeting, 16 June 1982.
23. IFMS, p. 202. Delors note to Mitterrand, 8 November 1982.
24. Védrine interview with author, Paris, 15 June 2007.
25. IFMS, pp. 87–8. Meeting between Mitterrand and Kohl, Paris, 4 October 1982. Kohl told Mitterrand how his uncle died in the First World War and his elder brother in the Second World War.
26. IFMS, p. 135. Note on talks between Kohl and Mitterrand, Bonn, 21 October 1982. BKA-DE, p. 28. Mitterrand said unification would take place 'smoothly . . . perhaps before the end of the century. It will not be a question of generations . . . The Soviet empire will be impaired from within. The countries which have been dominated will recover their liberty. . . . the Germans . . . will recover their opportunities. It is an affair of 20 years, a question of patience.'
27. Until late in the 1980s, Kohl indicated fundamental disquiet about upsetting the status quo in Europe. In Moscow in October 1988, on his first visit to see Mikhail Gorbachev, Kohl said he would not 'experience' German unification. As late as February 1989, he dismissed questioning about *Wiedervereinigung*: 'The difference is that you are a prophet, and I am only the Chancellor.' Kohl interview with author, Bonn, 7 February 1989.
28. IFMS, p. 220. Elysée Palace note on talks between Mitterrand and President José Sarney, Brasilia, 14 October 1985.
29. IFMS, pp. 114–115. Elysée Palace note on talks between Reagan and Mitterrand, Washington, 12 October 1982.
30. IFMS, p. 219. Elysée Palace note on talks between Mitterrand and Kohl, Bonn, 22 October 1982.
31. IFMS, p. 219. Report by Secrétariat Général de la Défense Nationale, *20 years of cooperation between France and Germany*, underlining 'economic and commercial difficulties between Paris and Bonn'.
32. IFMS, p. 220. Hubert Védrine note to Mitterrand, 31 January 1984.
33. Mitterrand speech, Bonn, 20 January 1983.
34. IFMS, p. 203. Christian Sautter note to Mitterrand, 19 January 1983. The bilateral doubled in 1982 to FF38 billion.
35. IFMS, p. 208. Attali note to Mitterrand, 28 February 1983.
36. Védrine interview with author, Paris, 15 June 2007. The process was a '*mise en scène théâtrale*'.
37. Jean Peyrelevade (key adviser to prime minister Pierre Mauroy in 1983) interview with author, Paris, 4 October 2007.
38. Kohl, *Erinnerungen 1982–90*, p. 109. Bianco travelled to Bonn on 14–15 March, 1983 Camdessus on 16 March. Camdessus passed on a letter from Mitterrand. In the evening of 16 March, Pöhl, Genscher and Stoltenberg met Kohl to discuss the threat that France would leave the ERM.
39. Hans Tietmeyer, *Herausforderung Euro*, 2005, p. 87. Stoltenberg travelled to Paris, accompanied by Tietmeyer and Horst Köhler, on 17 March.
40. Gerhard Stoltenberg, *Wendepunkte – Stationen deutscher Geschichte 1947–1990*, 1997, p. 318.
41. Lagayette interview with author, Paris, 28 May 2007. Jacques Attali indicated that France would sell part of its massive gold reserves to support the Franc – an option that Mitterrand and the Treasury never seriously considered.
42. Fabius interview with author, Paris, 29 May 2007.
43. Rocard interview with author, Paris, 30 May 2007.
44. Jacques Delors, *Mémoires*, 2004, p. 196.
45. Kohl, *op. cit.*, 2005, p. 110.
46. IFMS, p. 212. French Cabinet, Paris, 23 March 1983.
47. Szász, *op. cit.*, p. 68.
48. Delors interview with author, Paris, 29 May 2007.

49. Kohl, *Erinnerungen 1992–90*, p. 286. Comment in May 1984.
50. Bérégovoy shot himself in May 1993 shortly after the French Socialists lost legislative elections, following press reports of his shadowy financial dealings with one of Mitterrand's oldest friends.
51. De Grossouvre, a long-established Mitterrand associate with strong contacts with the secret service and African heads of state, killed himself with a hunting rifle in the Elysée Place in April 1994.
52. Delors interview with author, Paris, 29 May 2007.
53. Kimmitt telephone interview with author, Washington, 7 June 2007. Kohl's house was in Oggersheim, in the German Palatinate.
54. Védrine interview with author in Paris, 15 June 2007.
55. Schmidt interview with author, Hamburg, 4 September 2007.
56. Giscard interview with author, Paris, 28 June 2007.
57. Kenneth Dyson and Kevin Weatherstone, *The Road to Maastricht – Negotiating Economic and Monetary Union*, 1999, p. 77.
58. Camdessus interview with author, Paris, 4 October 2007.
59. Fabius interview with author, Paris, 29 May 2007.
60. Pöhl interview with author, Frankfurt, 9 May 2007.
61. Schlesinger interview with author, Oberursel, 2 July 2007.
62. Lamfalussy interview with author, Ohain, 22 May 2007.
63. Sapin interview with author, Paris, 3 October 2007.
64. Genscher interview with author, Bonn, 5 October 2007.
65. Elisabeth Guigou, *Une femme au coeur de l'Etat*, 2000, p. 73.
66. Margaret Thatcher, *The Downing Street Years*, 1993, p. 553. 'I had one overriding positive goal. This was to create a single Common Market.'
67. Young, *op. cit.*, p. 310. Thatcher said the Labour government was 'content to have Britain openly classified as among the poorest and least influential members' of the Community. The UK Conservative manifesto – agreed by Thatcher before she became prime minister – for the June 1979 European elections stated: 'We support the objectives of the new system [EMS] . . . we shall look for ways in which Britain can take her rightful place within it.' Geoffrey Howe, *Conflict of Loyalty*, 1994, p. 111.
68. Thatcher, *op. cit.*, p. 559.
69. IFMS, p. 80. Mitterrand conversation with Kissinger, Paris, 28 June 1984.
70. Nigel Lawson, *The View from No. 11*, 1992, p. 544.
71. Lawson e-mail message to author, 23 June 2007.
72. Gauron interview with author, Paris, 29 May 2007.
73. Hannoun interview with author, Basle, 17 August 2007.
74. Camdessus interview with author, Paris, 4 October 2007.
75. Lawson, *op. cit.*, p. 499.
76. Szász, *op. cit.*, p. 93.
77. Tietmeyer, *op. cit.*, p. 99. Tietmeyer gained British support by insisting that further changes to the Community's monetary arrangements would require full-scale ratification by member governments under Article 236 of the Treaty of Rome, and could not simply be agreed by the Council of Ministers (Article 235) – Delors' original recommendation. Insistence on use of Article 236 led to the independence of the European Central Bank being anchored by treaty rather than an inter-governmental agreement.
78. Lawson, *op. cit.*, p. 500. The visit to Bonn on 7 December 1985 had been arranged before the November ERM Downing Street seminar. The talks with Tietmeyer were with Peter Middleton and Geoffrey Littler, from the Treasury, and Anthony Loehnis, Bank of England director for international affairs.
79. Lawson, *op. cit.*, pp. 655–6. Philip Stephens, *Politics and the Pound*, 1996, pp. 64–5.
80. Lawson interview with author, London, 30 April 2007. In his memoirs, Lawson wrote, 'We would have enjoyed a clear run of five or six years during which the D-Mark

would have served us . . . as a very satisfactory low-inflation anchor.' Lawson, *op. cit.*, p. 504.

81. *New York Times*, 8 May 1995.
82. Camdessus interview with author, Paris, 4 October 2007.
83. NYFA, CF/Volcker papers 07879. Robin Leigh-Pemberton report to Group of Ten governors' meeting, Basle, 7 April 1986. Internal memo by San Cross, New York Federal Reserve Bank.
84. NYFA, CF/Volcker papers 07879.
85. IFMS, p. 221. Marc Boudier note to Mitterrand, 24 October 1986.
86. The West German money stock during 1978 was growing at 7.5 to 8 per cent, roughly double the Bundesbank's 3.5 to 5.5 per cent target.
87. Chirac interview, Radio Europe 1, Paris, 6 January 1987. *Handelsblatt*, 8 January 1997.
88. Stoltenberg, *op. cit.*, p. 327.
89. Balladur paper to European finance ministers, 9 February 1987. *Le Monde*, 11 and 14 February 1987.
90. NYFA, CF/Volcker papers 07879.
91. Lawson, *op. cit.*, pp. 554–5. The Louvre Accord, which set down unpublished bands of between 2.5 and 5 per cent from central rates, proved of only limited effectiveness.
92. Balladur article, *Financial Times*, 17 June 1987.
93. IFMS, p. 352. Jean-Louis Bianco note to Mitterrand, 19 January 1987.
94. IFMS, p. 352. Mitterrand statement to Council of Ministers, 17 February 1987.
95. Attali, *Verbatim II*.
96. Guigou note to Mitterrand, Paris, 7 September 1987.
97. Dyson and Featherstone, *op. cit.*, p. 324.
98. Wilhelm Schönfelder interview with author, Brussels, 22 May 2007.
99. IFMS, p. 355. Mitterrand statement to Council of Ministers, Paris, 17 August 1988. Attali, *Verbatim III*, 17 August 1988.
100. Pöhl Radio Hessen interview, 5 June 1988.
101. IFMS, p. 353. Note on talks between Vogel and Mitterrand, Paris, 9 July 1987.
102. IFMS, p. 237. Note on talks between Vranitzky and Mitterrand, Paris, 5 February 1988.
103. IFMS, p. 354. Note on talks between Gonzalez and Mitterrand, Latche, 25 August 1987.
104. James Baker, the US Treasury Secretary, blamed a mild tightening of the Bundesbank's money market intervention rates for the October 1987 stock market fall.
105. After an argumentative debate, the Bundesbank Council reduced discount rate from 3 per cent to 2.5 per cent with effect on 4 December, when the Copenhagen summit started. However, it left Lombard rate and its money market intervention rate unchanged.
106. Balladur memorandum, Paris, 8 January 1988, Daniel Gros and Niels Thygesen, *European Monetary Integration*, 1992, p. 312. The paper left open a range of crucial questions, including the procedures and powers of a European Central Bank.
107. Schönfelder interview with author, Brussels, 22 May 2007. The paper was based on a text prepared for Genscher for use at an ambassadors' lunch on 24 March 1987. The text was published on 1 April 1987 and Genscher made use of this in numerous speeches in the second half of the year.
108. Genscher memorandum, Bonn, 26 February 1988, written in a personal capacity, rather than as foreign minister, reflecting Stoltenberg's sensitivities on the matter. Schönfelder, who wrote the memorandum, carried out preparatory conversations with Peter-Wilhelm Schlüter, head of the Bundesbank's section on Community monetary policy, who was – exceptionally for a Bundesbank official – in favour of monetary union.
109. Guigou note to Mitterrand, Paris, 11 March 1988.
110. Stoltenberg memorandum, Bonn, 15 March 1988.

111. IFMS, p. 236. Foreign minister Roland Dumas note to Mitterrand, Paris, 30 August 1988, drawing on a conversation with Genscher, who said Pöhl 'contrary to what is said of him is not hostile to the idea of a European [Central] Bank and is better disposed [than Stoltenberg] towards concertation [with France].'

112. Genscher interview with author, Pech, 5 October 2007. 'I verified my approach through informal contacts with the Bundesbank, also using my personal contact with Pöhl.'

113. Eric Aeschimann and Pascal Riché, *La Guerre de Sept Ans*, 1996, pp. 34–5. Bérégovoy letter to de Larosière, 19 May 1988.

114. Kohl speech, European Parliament, Strasbourg, 9 March 1988.

115. Guigou interview with author, Paris, 4 July 2007.

116. Tietmeyer, *op. cit.*, p. 118.

117. Kohl and Mitterrand side-stepped Thatcher's aversion to a European Central Bank by not making this specifically part of the frame of reference for the committee's report, on the grounds that a monetary union would not necessarily entail establishing a unitary central bank.

118. Genscher remarks, Hanover, 27 June 1998.

119. *Financial Times*, 29 June 1998.

120. Aeschimann and Riché, *op. cit.*, p. 49.

121. Aeschimann and Riché, *op. cit.*, p. 41. Bérégovoy letter to Stoltenberg, Paris, 29 June 1988.

122. Pöhl interviews, *Frankfurter Allgemeine Zeitung*, 28 May 1998, Hessischer Rundfunk radio, 5 June 1988.

123. Pöhl interview with author, Zurich, 17 August 2007.

124. Ruding interview with author, Brussels, 22 May 2007.

125. Theo Waigel, *Unsere Zukunft heißt Europa*, 1993, pp. 196–7, 'Der Delors-Bericht und das Statut einer europäischen Zentralbank.'

126. Schmidt interview with author, Hamburg, 4 July 1988.

127. Committee for the Study of Economic and Monetary Union, 'Report on Economic and Monetary Union in the European Community' [Delors Report], April 1989, p. 29. The report was sent to heads of government on 13 April and presented to finance ministers on 17 April. 'Although a monetary union does not necessarily require a single currency, it would be a desirable feature of a monetary union.'

128. Delors Report, pp. 21–2.

129. Delors Report, p. 28.

130. Delors Report, p. 17.

131. Delors Report, pp. 32–3. Further indications of Franco-German divergences were given in detailed appendices to the report, which received little publicity. The main ones were 'The ECU as a parallel currency' by Wim Duisenberg, 'The further development of the European Monetary System' by Karl Otto Pöhl and 'The creation of a European Reserve Fund' by Jacques de Larosière.

132. Saccomanni interview with author, Rome, 26 June 2007.

133. The second *rapporteur*, brought in at the behest of Karl Otto Pöhl, was German economist Gunter Baer from the BIS.

134. Delors interview with author, Paris, 29 May 2007.

135. The other two outside experts were Niels Thygesen, Professor of Economics at the University of Copenhagen, and Miguel Boyer, President, Banco Exterieur de España.

136. Lamfalussy interview with author, Ohain, 22 May 2007.

137. De Larosière interview with author, Paris, 28 June 2007.

138. Pöhl interview with author, Frankfurt, 9 May 2007.

139. Lagayette interview with author, Paris, 28 May 2007.

140. Leigh-Pemberton interview with author, London, 24 April 2007.

141. The dollar rallied towards DM 1.90 in spring 1989 from DM 1.70 in autumn 1988.

142. Talks between Bérégovoy and Pöhl, Paris, 22 February 1989.

143. Germany's UK ambassador Hermann von Richthofen interview with author, Berlin, 19 March 2007. Von Richthofen, along with Britain's Bonn ambassador Christopher Mallaby, was present at the Bundesbank lunch.

144. Pöhl interview with author, Frankfurt, 9 May 2007.

145. Guigou note to Mitterrand, 20 March 1989. Guigou's note detailed the political forces in France for and against monetary union. Figures such as Jacques Delors, Michel Rocard and Jacques de Larosière were in favour. 'They believe that the sole means of escaping from present German monetary hegemony is to organise a decision-making process on monetary and economic policy that take into account the interests of all member states.' French supporters of monetary union, Guigou affirmed, 'consider that France has nothing much to lose by comparison with the present situation where its economic and monetary policy, including interest rates, are very largely dependent on Germany'.

146. IFMS, p. 386. Note on talks between Mitterrand and Italian prime minister Ciriaco de Mita, Taormina, 30 March 1989.

147. Lagayette interview with author, Paris, 28 May 2007. Bérégovoy made his comments to Lagayette during the IMF spring meeting in April 1989 in Washington.

148. Saccomanni interview with author, Rome, 26 June 2007.

149. Thatcher voiced her frustration at Pöhl's inability to stick to an unambiguous position on EMU in an interview with the *Wall Street Journal*, 25 January 1990: 'Let me tell you something about Karl Otto. At some time or another, you will find, he has said everything.'

150. Howe interview with author, London, 18 March 2008.

151. Thatcher, *op. cit.*, p.708. Thatcher's irritation with Pöhl proved short-lived; well after both had retired, Thatcher continued to invite Pöhl (with his wife Ulrike) to discreet private functions in London.

152. Ruding interview with author, Brussels, 22 May 2007. However, see also Szász, *op. cit.*, p. 203. The benefits of the orthodoxy of the Nederlandsche Bank became evident when Dutch money market interest rates fell to around German levels in 1990, and below these levels from 1992 onwards.

153. Howe, *op. cit.*, p. 577. The Chequers meeting took place on 29 April 1989.

154. Lubbers interview with author, Amsterdam, 7 September 2007.

155. Lawson, *op. cit.*, pp. 915–918. 'The economic and political arguments had become an irrelevance. Joining the ERM, as she saw it, had become a battle of wills between her and me; and it had to be her will that prevailed.' The meeting with Thatcher took place on 3 May 1989.

156. The finance ministry had been housed 'provisionally' in the Louvre as a result of a fire in its previous offices in Rue Mont-Thabor. The ministry moved its headquarters to a new complex at Bercy to the east of the city in June 1989.

157. De Larosière interview with author, Paris, 28 June 2007.

158. The Bundesbank announced a 0.5 percentage point increase in discount rate on 20 April.

159. Marc Boudier note to Mitterrand, Paris, 19 April 1989.

160. French cabinet meeting, Paris, 26 April 1992.

161. Védrine, *op. cit.*, p. 419.

162. Guigou note for Mitterrand, Paris, 28 April 1989.

163. Rocard interview with author, Paris, 24 May 2007.

164. Waigel interview with author, Munich, 17 April 2007.

165. The peseta joined on 19 June with a wider fluctuation band of 6 per cent against the ECU, the same as the lira, compared with 2.25 per cent for the other currencies. Following the Spanish decision, of the expanded twelve members of the European Community, only three – the UK, Portugal and Greece – were not in the ERM.

166. Védrine, *op. cit.*, p. 420. Talks between Mitterrand and Kohl at Madrid summit, 26 and 27 June 1989.

167. Lawson, *op. cit.* p. 941. The official was Permanent Secretary Peter Middleton.
168. The competing currencies proposal was the basis of a more formal 'hard ECU' plan proposed the following year.
169. Pöhl interview, *Financial Times*, 1 July 1989.
170. Despite Pohl's verbal efforts, the Germans did not put forward concrete proposals for a D-Mark revaluation against the Franc in 1989. See Aeschimann and Riché, *op. cit.*, pp. 134–7.

Chapter 5: Shock Waves

1. Waigel interview, *EuropaInterview*, December 1991.
2. Mitterrand told the French cabinet on 18 October 1989: 'Regarding the political evolution in Germany, it is clear that our foreign policy has been based up to now on facts that are in the process of changing very quickly. The reunification of Germany is possible . . . It would be vain to think that France could oppose it. In the face of such an eventuality, one can hope that the European Community would be sufficiently attractive to bring in Central Europe.'
3. Estimates based et al. on Bank for International Settlements 1993 Annual Report, p. 188; BIS 1994 Annual Report, p. 169; 'International Capital Markets and Foreign Exchange Markets', Group of Ten Deputies, April 1993.
4. BIS 1993 Annual Report, p. 200.
5. Guigou interview with author, Paris, 4 July 2007. Guigou chaired a European group of foreign and finance ministry officials to try to advance EMU after the Madrid summit.
6. Attali, *C'était François Mitterrand*, p. 302.
7. Guigou interview with author, Paris, 4 July 2007. Talks between Thatcher and Mitterrand, Chequers, 1 September 1989. Guigou was the French note-taker. (British note-taker was Charles Powell.)
8. Guigou, *Une femme au coeur de l'État*, p. 76. The Elysée Palace transcript is a long hand-written note by Guigou which records a remarkably wide-ranging exchange of anecdotes and insights between the two leaders. These included Mitterrand's pithy description of the present and past German chancellors – 'Schmidt always in a bad mood, Kohl always in a good mood', Thatcher's reflection that the Germans had American nuclear weapons on their soil 'because they started the war', and a discussion on the lessons of the emigration of German Jewish scientists in the 1930s that facilitated US production of the atomic bomb.
9. Kohl, *Erinnerungen 1982–1990*, p. 937. 'What I could only guess at then is now proven, with the opening of the archives. Margaret Thatcher wanted to hinder German unity with all possible means.' Kohl appeared to be referring to a record of a conversation between Gorbachev and Thatcher, Moscow, 23 September 1989. Archive of Gorbachev Foundation, Notes of A.S. Chernyaev, National Security Archive, George Washington University, Gelman Library, Washington. Thatcher is quoted as saying: 'We are very concerned about the processes that are under way in East Germany. . . . Britain and Western Europe are not interested in the unification of Germany. The words in the NATO communiqué may sound different, but disregard them. We do not want the unification of Germany.'
10. Guigou, *op. cit.*, p. 77.
11. According to Guigou, Kohl said political and business opposition to EMU was stoking up problems in Bonn. He repeated this to Giulio Andreotti, Italian prime minister, 18 October. BKA-DE, No, 62, p. 452.
12. BKA-DE, No. 70, p. 472. Talks between Kohl and Mitterrand, Bonn, 2 November 1989. During the visit, Mitterrand told a press conference he was 'not afraid' of German reunification. See also IFMS, p. 443, Attali, *Verbatim III*, 3 November 1989.

13. A key milestone in the relationship between Waigel and Bérégovoy came when senior members of the French monetary establishment visited the Germans in Waigel's home state of Bavaria for a meeting of the Franco-German Economic and Finance Council in August 1989.

14. Aeschimann and Riché, *La Guerre de Sept Ans*, p. 137.

15. Attali, *C'était François Mitterrand*, p. 315. *Verbatim III*, 10 November 1989.

16. NYFA, CF/ 93716, BIS/G.10 Notes. Governors' Meeting, Basle, 10 and 11 November 1989, by Margaret L. Greene and Edwin M. Truman.

17. Attali, *Verbatim III*, 14 November 1989.

18. Kohl, *op. cit.*, p. 984. Kohl referred to a NATO summit declaration in 1970, based on Article 7 of the 1955 Germany Treaty.

19. Attali, *Verbatim III*, 18 November 1989. French and German accounts (including Kohl's memoirs, which for the dinner on 18 November seem heavily reliant on the text in Attali's *Verbatim III*), appear to back Thatcher's own various assessments of Mitterrand's thoughts.

20. Attali, *Verbatim III*, 28 November 1989. Attali pointed out that Kohl had written to Mitterrand (underlining caution about EMU) on 27 November, but had said nothing on the 'essential point' of reunification. Attali quoted Mitterrand as saying: 'He [Kohl] told me nothing! Nothing at all! I shall never forget it! Gorbachev will be furious! He will never let it [reunification] happen.' See also Kohl, *op. cit.*, p. 997.

21. Genscher was in the embarrassing position of not having been informed in advance of Kohl's ten-point plan. 'Genscher was beyond suspicion because he could not be suspected of being against the single currency.' Guigou, interview with author, Paris, 4 July 2007. Hans-Dietrich Genscher, *Erinnerungen*, 1995, p. 670.

22. Genscher, *op. cit.*, pp. 677–80.

23. Guigou, *op. cit.*, p. 79. Guigou interview with author, Paris, 4 July 2007.

24. IFMS, p. 464. Interview Theo Schabert with Guigou, Paris, 8 October 2003, reporting on Genscher–Mitterrand talks, 30 November 1989. Genscher quotes Mitterrand saying, 'It is not excluded that we will fall back to the philosophical world of 1913.' Genscher, *op. cit.*, pp. 678. See also Attali, *C'était François Mitterrand*, p.321.

25. Rocard interview with author, Paris, 29 May 2007.

26. BKA-DE, No. 108, p. 596. Bitterlich message to Kohl, Bonn, 2/3 December 1989. 'For Mitterrand, the first and foremost question for the next few years is Economic and Monetary Union. Further steps towards a [political] European Union are secondary.'

27. Attali, *Verbatim III*, 6 December 1989. Védrine, *op. cit.*, p. 442.

28. Mitterrand conversation with Italian prime minister Andreotti, 13 February 1990.

29. Kohl, *op. cit.* p. 1011.

30. Kohl, *op. cit*, p. 1013.

31. Lubbers interview with author, Amsterdam, 7 September 2007.

32. Attali, *Verbatim III*, 8 December 1989. See Stephen Wall, *A Stranger in Europe*, 2008, p. 89. 'He [Mitterrand] told her that the subject matter of the European Council was not what mattered. What mattered was that Germany, a country which had never known its own borders, was on the march again.' Later Thatcher conceded, 'It must be said that his judgment that there was nothing we could do to halt German reunification turned out to be right.' Thatcher, *The Downing Street Years*, p. 798.

33. Thatcher, *op. cit.*, p. 796.

34. Attali, *Verbatim III*, 8 December 1989.

35. BKA-DE, No. 120, p. 638. Talks between Baker and Kohl, West Berlin, 12 December 1989. Kohl voiced understanding for European sensitivities. 'Already now the Federal Republic of Germany is economically No. 1. If 17 million more are added, that will be a nightmare for some. But 17 million are a reality.'

36. Elysée Palace transcript, Mitterrand conversation with Thatcher, Paris, 20 January 1990. The French record is consistent with Thatcher's own account of the meeting: 'The President was clearly irked by German attitudes and behaviour. He accepted

that the Germans had the right to self-determination but they did not have the right to upset the political realities of Europe; nor could he accept that German reunification should take priority over everything else. He complained that the Germans treated any talk of caution as criticism of themselves. Unless you were wholeheartedly for unification, you were treated as an enemy of Germany.' Thatcher, *op. cit.*, p. 797.

37. BKA-DE, No. 158, pp. 753–6. A conversation between Kohl and East German Prime Minister Hans Modrow in Switzerland on 3 February briefly discussed Modrow's proposal for a 'single currency' ['Alleinwährung']. The question came up only at the end of the hour-long meeting. BKA-DE, No. 160, p. 757. In a twenty-minute telephone conversation with Mitterrand on 5 February, Kohl said he would 'do everything to stabilise the situation' in East Germany, which he called 'catastrophic, also from a psychological point of view . . . This migration must be stopped.' However he made no reference to any decision to introduce the D-Mark. BKA-DE, No. 161, p. 759. A preparatory document on 5 February for the Bonn cabinet meeting on 7 February contained no reference to monetary union with Germany; this was inserted only afterwards. Kohl's adviser Horst Teltschik confirmed that the decision on monetary union with the East was taken at a meeting with a small group of advisers at 10 a.m. on 6 February. 'On Monday [5 February] neither Kohl nor Waigel knew anything [about a plan for monetary union].'

38. Pöhl interview, *Die Zeit*, 26 January 1990. Schlesinger interview with author, Frankfurt, 29 January 1990. Waigel statement, Bonn, 19 January 1990. After East Berlin talks on 6 February with Horst Kaminsky, head of the East German State Bank, Pöhl told journalists monetary union was 'premature' – unaware that Kohl was simultaneously meeting aides in Bonn to discuss the D-Mark's introduction.

39. Bank for International Settlements Annual Report 1991, pp. 160–1. 'The 15 per cent increase in the broad money stock which resulted from the introduction of the D-Mark in eastern Germany seemed large in relation to the 10 per cent increase in nominal GNP for the enlarged D-Mark area.'

40. Some of the consequences were eminently foreseeable. See, for instance Robert Z. Lawrence and Warwick J. McKibbin, 'Counting the cost of German unification', *Financial Times*, March 15 1990.

41. Guigou note for Mitterrand, Paris, 7 February 1990. Guigou was partly reporting contacts between the Bundesbank and the French ambassador to Bonn Serge Boidevaix.

42. HMT-FT. 'German Monetary Union Economic Effects', 9 February 1990, in Stephen Davies, 'ERM project paper', 21 December 1993. The paper predicted that the German move would generate upward pressure on inflation and Bundesbank tightening and the D-Mark would probably appreciate. The paper was sent to Thatcher's office on 12 February 1990.

43. DBPO, Series III, Vol. VII, Document 136, Minute from Charles Powell to Thatcher, and *Sunday Correspondent*, 25 February 1990, paraphrasing Thatcher's remarks.

44. The Bundesbank proposed a conversion rate of 2 East Marks per D-Mark. Although current payments such as wages were converted at 1 to 1, the average rate used for savings deposits was 1.8 to 1, close to the Bundesbank's suggestion.

45. Schlesinger interview with author, Frankfurt, 14 February 2007.

46. The key element was the programme of '2 plus 4' talks on an internationally-acceptable legal solution for German division, which formally started in March, linking East and West Germany with the US, Soviet Union, Britain and France.

47. French ambassador Luc de la Barre de Nanteuil message, TD Londres 370 6 DSL Secret, London, 13 March 1990, distribution Elisabeth Guigou.

48. Talks between Thatcher and French prime minister Michel Rocard, March 1990, Wall, *op. cit.*, p. 96.

49. Dyson and Featherstone, *The Road to Maastricht*, pp. 386–7. The Committee of EC Central Bank governors reorganised its working arrangements in January 1990 by

deciding a three-year term for the chairman and strengthening research capacity to prepare for Stage 1 of EMU. Pöhl was formally allotted the task of drafting the statutes for the ECB on 10 April 1990. See also Tietmeyer, *op. cit.*, p. 144.

50. Pöhl interview with author, Frankfurt, 9 May 2007.
51. Thatcher, *op. cit.*, p. 724. Major sent Thatcher a paper in April 1990 pointing out the danger to the UK of a 'two speed Europe'. Thatcher replied: 'What's wrong with that if the other tier is going in the wrong direction?'
52. HMT-FT. Nigel Wicks minute to Major, 13 June 1990, Stephen Davies, ERM Project paper, 21 December 1993. Wicks was reporting on a conversation with Tietmeyer, 'who seemed to be thinking of the effects of German Economic and Monetary Union on the exchange markets as essentially short term . . . He gave as a firm personal view that he would not wish to obstruct UK entry into the wider bands if we were to apply within the next six months or so . . . His advice was to delay entry until the autumn. By then the UK's circumstances would be clearer and GEMU would be out of the way.' Tietmeyer seemed to provide a more welcoming stance on possible UK ERM membership than Pöhl, who had told Britain's ambassador to Germany, Christopher Mallaby, in November 1989 that 'late 1989 would be the wrong time' for the UK to join the ERM. A Treasury document concluded, 'Pöhl's view was clearly the same in September 1990.' When Pöhl visited Major in London in July 1990, he gave the Chancellor of the Exchequer an informal warning not to join the ERM at too high a rate.
53. Major speech to German Industry Forum, London, 21 June 1990. Later, Andrew Turnbull, then a senior Treasury official, concluded: 'It was a diversionary exercise that had no chance of success.' Churchill College-Lombard Street seminar, London, 14 November 2007. See also Wall, *op. cit.*, p. 103: the hard ECU plan was 'a brilliant idea whose time was already past'.
54. Wall, *op. cit.*, p. 103.
55. NYFA, CF/Foreign Exchange 100260. 'Europe 1992: Issues and implications for the US'. President Gerald Corrigan note to board members, 6 September 1992.
56. HMT-FT. Stephen Davies, 'ERM project paper', 21 December 1993, p. 21. 'The Prime Minister had by early September signed up to the argument that interest rate cuts would be hazardous if the UK remained outside the ERM.' [Draft] minute from Major to Thatcher, 3 October 1990. 'It will be vital that there is no fall in the exchange rate . . . I remain convinced that we could not contemplate an interest rate reduction outside the ERM.'
57. Kohl TV address, 3 October 1990.
58. Greenspan, *op. cit.*, pp. 286–7. Greenspan was commenting on talks with Pöhl a few days before unification.
59. Jacques Delors hailed sterling's membership as 'good for the UK and for the Community', although he regretted that the UK had joined only the wide band of the mechanism allowing fluctuations of 6 per cent each side of the currency's central rate.
60. Thatcher statement to House of Commons, 30 October 1990 'This Government has no intention of abolishing the pound sterling . . . This Government believes in the pound sterling.'
61. Hermann von Richthofen interview with author, Berlin, 19 March 2007. The encounter with Thatcher was at a state dinner in late October 1990 for President Cossiga of Italy.
62. HMT-FT. Nigel Wicks, 'Reflections on the UK's membership of the ERM', London, 10 January 1994. Andrew Turnbull wrote, with hindsight, in 1992, 'German policy encountered an external shock which took both its economic cycle, its desired monetary policy and an equilibrium exchange rate out of line of the requirements of its EMS partners.' HMT-FT, 'Should sterling rejoin and when?', 18 September 1992.
63. Before the UK joined, Major (as Chancellor of the Exchequer) had been willing to concede the possibility of realignments, for instance, in an appearance before the House of Commons Treasury and Civil Service Committee, 25 July 1990.

64. Thatcher, *op. cit.*, p. 724. 'I insisted against the Treasury and the Bank on a simultaneous announcement of a 1 per cent cut in interest rates.'

65. Clarke interview with author, London, 11 March 2008. Clarke was Education Secretary at the time of ERM entry.

66. Treasury announcement, 5 October 1990. The headline was: 'UK reduction in interest rates and entry to ERM'.

67. Leigh-Pemberton interview with author, London, 24 April 2007. The governor wrote to Mrs Thatcher immediately after hearing of the decision that interest rates should be cut, saying that 'she should not take the dividend straight away but should wait until she had earned it'.

68. Major interview with author, London, 26 September 2007.

69. According to Major, 'Margaret wanted a slightly higher rate of entry, DM3, for the perfectly good reason that she was obsessed with the rate of inflation and also about the high level of interest rates from which ordinary people were suffering. With a higher entry value for sterling, we would have been able to lower interest rates even more quickly.'

70. Major interview with author, London, 26 September 2007. Major telephoned Karl Otto Pöhl on 5 October to inform the Bundesbank that Britain was joining the ERM. Although Pöhl stated in the past that he criticised the entry rate as too high, Pöhl admitted that the stricture may not have been very clear.

71. Tietmeyer interview with author, Königstein, 10 May 2007. Nigel Wicks, who was at the meeting, said, 'The Bundesbank did not protest too much about the entry rate, though they certainly expressed the view that it was a little on the high side.' HMT-FT, Nigel Wicks, 'Reflections on the UK's membership of the ERM', London, 10 January 1994.

72. The spate of Bundesbank rate tightening became the longest in German history, with the exception of the period up to post-First World War hyper-inflation. Between July 1988 and September 1992, the Bundesbank maintained a tightening cycle that saw the discount rate increased from 2.5 per cent to 8.75 per cent. The Lombard rate also increased on ten separate occasions (not always coinciding with the discount rate increases), from 4.5 per cent to 9.75 per cent. The four-year-two-month credit tightening cycle lasted nine months more than the previous longest cycle in 1979–82 when the Bundesbank increased discount rate from 3 per cent to 7.5 per cent (in five stages) in response to the US credit squeeze.

73. George interview with author, London, 8 April 2008.

74. Although discount and Lombard rate remained unchanged at 6 and 8 per cent respectively during this period, the Bundesbank did gradually raise money market rates through its 'fine-tuning' open market operations (securities repurchase agreements) from an average of 7.3 per cent in November 1989 to 8 per cent in October 1990.

75. NYFA, CF/100260 Foreign Exchange. 'Role of French Intervention in Masking Mark Weakness in EMS.' Foreign exchange paper from Heffernan *et al.* A strong reason for the Bundesbank's hesitancy on interest rates in summer 1990 was to avoid upsetting financial markets, at a time when the D-Mark was relatively weak (and was being intermittently supported by the Banque de France) within the ERM. 'Bundesbank officials have reportedly expressed concerns that a tightening move at present might be seen as substantiating market fears of higher German inflation, thereby heightening rather than allaying inflationary expectations.'

76. Pöhl interview with author, Frankfurt, 9 May 2007.

77. Tietmeyer interview with author, Königstein, 10 May 2007.

78. There were several indications of Bonn–Frankfurt tensions. In November 1990 Pöhl asked Kohl to freeze government spending. In January 1991 Schlesinger unleashed a public warning on the need for ERM realignments. In March 1991 Pöhl made unguarded comments in Brussels on the 'disaster' caused by Kohl's policies on eastern Germany.

79. Schmidt interview with author, Hamburg, 4 September 2007.

80. The Bundesbank had never previously raised rates with such intensity in August, although it did decide 0.5 percentage point increases in discount rate in early to mid-August in 1955 and 1965.

81. Schlesinger interview with author, Frankfurt, 14 February 2007.

82. Bank for International Settlements 1993 Annual Report, p. 183.

83. HMT-FT. Nigel Wicks, 'Reflections on the UK's membership of the ERM', London, 10 January 1994.

84. HMT-FT. Stephen Davies, 'ERM project paper', 21 December 1993: 'Although the Treasury does seem to have played down the relevance of German unification to the prospects for the UK's membership, it cannot be argued that the UK while in the ERM had to cope with domestic interest rates that were higher than expected before ERM entry. In fact, although German interest rates in 1991 and 1992 were higher than forecast when the UK went into the ERM, UK interest rates were actually lower.'

85. In 1991 the French deficit was only 1.7 per cent of GDP. Few foresaw that, as a result of the coming economic slowdown, in the mid-1990s, it would rise to well beyond 3 per cent.

86. Kohl's stipulations on political union followed the line laid down by the Bundesbank and the Bonn Finance and Economics Ministries since the Werner Plan, emphasising the importance of economic policy coordination to accompany a single monetary policy.

87. Maastricht Treaty, Articles 101, 103 and 116.

88. Schlesinger interview with author, Oberursel, 2 July 2007, 'Waigel rang me when the conference was taking place in December 1991. This was to discuss the particular point under which, according to the treaty, the Council of Ministers could give "instructions" to the European Central Bank on the question of the exchange rate.'

89. The cover story for news magazine *Der Spiegel* read '*Angst um die D-Mark*' ('Fear for the D-Mark'). The *Bild-Zeitung* headline was '*Das Ende der Mark*'. Although uncomfortable for Kohl, the headlines helped him toughen his negotiating stance.

90. Von Kyaw conversation with author, Maastricht, 9 December 1991.

91. The wager, agreed with the author at the Maastricht summit, laid down that the winner would receive six bottles of white wine from the loser's country. The author collected three bottles of Meerspinne Riesling and three Biengarten Weißburgunder. Kohl, letter to author, Bonn, 3 February 1997.

92. Aeschimann and Riché, *op. cit.*, p. 105.

93. Hannezo note to Mitterrand, Paris, 18 December 1991.

94. Lubbers letter to Kohl, 15 January 1992. The letter was written in German using the personal 'du' form.

95. Wim Kok interview with author, Amsterdam, 2 October 2007. Szász, *The Road to Monetary Union*, p. 203. 'We [the Nederlandsche Bank] felt we had no choice but to inform the Bundesbank as well as Lubbers that we disagreed.' Szász comments that 'Kohl may have wondered whether the real object of the criticism [in Lubbers' letter] was not once again (as in November–December 1989) his own policy of German reunification.'

96. Lubbers interview with author, Amsterdam, 7 September 2007.

97. The Portuguese escudo, like the Spanish peseta and the British pound, joined with a wider 6 per cent fluctuation band.

98. Bérégovoy took over from another of Mitterrand's later-discarded favourites, the luckless Edith Cresson, who had replaced Michel Rocard in 1991.

99. Bérégovoy address to National Assembly, Paris, 5 May 1992. Later in the campaign to win parliamentary ratification, Bérégovoy said that Europe would risk 'coming apart' if the treaty was not ratified. 'Germany, which is today integrated into Europe . . . could be free to follow its own will', French TV debate, May 1992.

100. German disquiet on the EMU process was particularly marked. The European Commission had to reprint its German language text of the Maastricht Treaty in April 1992 because it referred to 'Ecu' (for European Unit of Account) as a word. The Bonn government insisted that 'ECU' was merely an acronym and not the agreed name for the planned single currency.

101. The Bank of England's Robin Leigh-Pemberton said that, following the 'tremor' of the Danish vote, 'we knew throughout the summer that we were sitting on a grumbling volcano.' Speech, 8 October 1992.

102. Banca d'Italia director general (later Italian prime minister) Lamberto Dini, interview with author, Rome, 26 June 2007.

103. NYFA, CF/Foreign Exchange 100260. Ted Truman (Federal Reserve Board) note to Alan Greenspan, 5 June 1992, reporting on telephone conversations with Wolfgang Rieke and Andrew Crockett on the European Monetary Committee meeting, 3 June 1992. Rieke pointed out to Truman that latest opinion polls in Germany were 90 to 10 against giving up the D-Mark and 80 to 20 against the Maastricht Treaty.

104. Another Monetary Committee member, the Bank of England's Andrew Crockett, saw the vote as 'a major setback' but also 'a useful warning to the "dirigiste types" (the French)'.

105. Major interview with author, London, 26 September 2007.

106. In May 1992 Thatcher wrote that Maastricht 'passes colossal powers from parliamentary governments to a central bureaucracy'. This flatly contradicted Major's statement that Maastricht 'marks the point at which, for the first time, we have begun to reverse that centralising trend'. *Financial Times*, 21 May 1992. As early as January 1992 Thatcher was reported as advocating a devaluation within the Exchange Rate Mechanism. *Guardian*, 7 January 1992. Thatcher's economic adviser Alan Walters and other monetarist economists published a letter in *The Times* on 8 January calling on Britain to pull out of the ERM to allow further cuts in interest rates.

107. For example, Sir Donald McDougall, former government chief economic adviser, wrote, 'I favoured entry into the ERM. But when we did so at DM2.95, I feared we were repeating the mistake of 1925, when we returned to the gold standard at too high a rate. Events since we entered have convinced me I was right, and that we need to devalue.' *Observer*, 22 March 1992.

108. HMT-FT. Stephen Davies, 'ERM Project paper', 21 December 1993. Schlesinger apologised to Christopher Mallaby over a *Financial Times* story on 13 July 1992 in which a 'senior official' of the Bundesbank said 'countries which thought they were suffering from Germany's monetary policies could take the initiative by seeking realignment with in the EMS'. According to the report, the senior officials 'believed market forces might eventually force weaker currencies towards a devaluation'. Schlesinger denied making the reported remarks.

109. Tietmeyer, *Herausforderung Euro*, p. 178. Waigel visit to Bundesbank Council, 17 June 1992.

110. Major, *op. cit.*, p. 316.

111. The Bundesbank rate rise was announced on 16 July. The Banca d'Italia subsequently raised discount rate to 13.75 per cent.

112. French cabinet papers, 22 July 1992.

113. HMT-FT. Stephen Davies, 'ERM project paper', 21 December 1993, p. 81. 'In the Bank's paper of 14 August . . . there was what seemed at the time, and still seems, a very surprising emphasis on the difference that intervention and foreign currency borrowing could make.'

114. Norman Lamont, *In Office*, 1999, p. 228.

115. *Financial Times*, 27 August 1992. Jochimsen's comments, contained in the early release of a speech in Düsseldorf, were later withdrawn – but the damage had been done.

116. French presidential transcript, meeting between Kohl and Mitterrand, Borkum, 26 August 1992.

117. Tietmeyer, interview with author, Königstein, 10 May 2007. Tietmeyer was deputising for Schlesinger, on holiday in Greece. 'I used an expression that was both reasonably clear but also cautiously phrased such as 'I would not exclude such a step (for a D-Mark revaluation).'

118. Lamont interview with author, London, 2 April 2007. See also Lamont, *op. cit.*, p. 228. Lamont records his view of the meeting as 'We tried to put together a statement that German rates would go no higher . . . But Tietmeyer was very difficult and Waigel not helpful.'

119. Major, *op. cit.*, p. 320. Shortly afterwards, Kohl telephoned the Bundesbank to say another Major letter had arrived and that Amato had also written to ask for lower interest rates. Tietmeyer, *op. cit.*, p. 181.

120. Amato telephone interview with author, Rome/London, 28 June 2007.

121. Major letter to Kohl, end-August 1992. Major received a reply a few days later after Downing Street asked Christopher Mallaby, the British ambassador, to intervene. 'Helmut wrote, "The Bundesbank does not intend to further increase interest rates" – which was welcome as far as it went, but ignored the reality that reductions were urgently needed.' Major, *op. cit.*, p. 321–5.

122. Waigel interview with author, Munich, 17 April 2007.

123. Tietmeyer interview with author, Königstein, 10 May 2007.

124. Lamont, *op. cit.*, pp. 233–238. 'I am told that I put my request to Dr. Schlesinger to cut rates four times in all . . . Apparently he later complained that no one had ever spoken to him in his life like that before. Well perhaps he had not lived very fully.'

125. Leigh-Pemberton interview with author, London, 27 April 2007.

126. Kok interview with author, Amsterdam, 2 October 2007.

127. Lamont interview with author, London, 2 April 2007.

128. Clarke interview with author, London, 11 March 2008.

129. Tension affecting the Nordic currencies had started in November 1991 when Finland's foreign exchange reserves were virtually wiped out by capital outflows. This then spilled over to Sweden in December 1991.

130. Banca d'Italia governor Carlo Azeglio Ciampi remarks to parliamentary committee, Rome, 10 September 1992.

131. Bank for International Settlements 1983 Annual Report, p. 188. The Banca d'Italia spent $24 billion defending the lira in September. (This is below the total figure for outflows stated by Lamberto Dini.)

132. The unprecedented meeting took place in the squat 1960s-style Guesthouse in the grounds of the Bundesbank's headquarters.

133. Tietmeyer diary, 4 September 1992. The participants were Kohl, Waigel, finance ministry State Secretary Horst Köhler, head of Finance Ministry international department Gert Haller, head of Chancellor's economic department Johannes Ludewig, as well as Schlesinger and Tietmeyer.

134. Schlesinger said, 'Late on Saturday evening [12 September], when Tietmeyer and Köhler returned from Paris and Rome, and even on Sunday morning [13 September], when Tietmeyer telephoned me at my home, I still believed there would be a monetary committee meeting in Brussels. When Tietmeyer phoned me, I believed he was calling from Brussels; in fact he was telephoning from his home. So a broad realignment did not take place.'

135. Sapin interview with author, Paris, 3 October 2007.

136. Szász interview with author, Amsterdam, 7 September 2007. Szász, *op. cit.*, p. 174. Trichet telephoned Szász towards midnight on Saturday, 12 September to ask him if he could attend a meeting if it took place the next day. 'Next day I was informed that the procedure [for a realignment involving only the lira] would be "by fax and telephone".'

137. Waigel interview with author, Munich, 17 April 2007.

138. Lamberto Dini interview with author, Rome, 26 June 2007.

139. There must be some doubt whether, even if sterling and the lira had taken part in a wider realignment on the weekend of 12 and 13 September, the Bundesbank Council would really have immediately cut interest rates substantially. The events of September 1992 did not lead to a formal wider realignment. However the withdrawal of sterling and the lira from the ERM and the 5 per cent devaluation of the peseta brought about a much larger appreciation of the D-Mark against the weaker currencies than would have been accomplished by the 'wider realignment' the Bundesbank said it wanted on 11 September. None the less, following the September cuts in discount and Lombard rates, the Bundesbank kept interest rates on hold, much to France's disappointment.

140. Major interview with author, London, 26 September 2007.

141. Major, *op. cit.*, p. 327. Amato telephone interview with author, 28 June 2008. At around the same time as the Amato–Major telephone call, officials from the Treasury and Bank of England gathered at the Treasury to discuss the lira crisis. The meeting was told that the Bundesbank had agreed to reduce interest rates by $\frac{1}{4}$–$\frac{1}{2}$ per cent as a result of the Italian devaluation, that Trichet was organising currency changes without a meeting of Monetary Committee, and that the Bundesbank Council was holding an emergency meeting on Monday. The option of whether Britain should join the Italians was briefly mentioned but was not the subject of any discussion. Up until the Amato–Major call, an Italian government aircraft had been kept on standby to take Mario Draghi, the Italian Treasury director, to a Brussels meeting of the European Monetary Committee. Afterwards the aircraft was stood down.

142. Saccomanni interview with author, Rome, 26 June 2007.

143. The lira was lowered 7 per cent against the other ERM currencies. The change (for political reasons) comprised a 3.5 per cent formal devaluation of the lira and a 3.5 per cent revaluation of other currencies.

144. Schlesinger said: 'There was a negative development at around 10 o'clock in the evening on Sunday, 13 September when Theo Waigel announced from the north of Germany that the Bundesbank would cut interest rates tomorrow. Pressure therefore started to rise in the German media, with claims being made that the Bundesbank was somehow under political control and that its independence was lost.'

145. Bérégovoy statement, French cabinet meeting, 16 September 1992.

146. Mitterrand remarks in French TV debate on Maastricht referendum, Paris, 3 September 1992.

147. Budd interview with author, London, 25 September 2007.

148. Schlesinger said: '[The Waigel statement and the aftermath] was the main reason why I agreed to do the interview on Tuesday with the *Wall Street Journal* and *Handelsblatt* [the interview had originally been agreed for Friday, 11 September but this was postponed because of the lira crisis]. The deputy editor of the *Handelsblatt*, whom I knew and had been expecting, did not come to the Bundesbank for the interview, instead it was Werner Benkhoff whom I didn't know, but I could hardly turn him away.'

149. Schlesinger said: 'Terence Roth from the *Wall Street Journal* behaved correctly. He showed me the quotes two hours later. But Benkhoff from the *Handelsblatt* did not. He released an unauthorised text to the news agencies on the evening of the same day.' Manfred Körber, head of the Bundesbank press office, was celebrating his birthday on the outskirts of Frankfurt on Tuesday evening and was out of telephone contact.

150. Bundesbank documentation on ERM crisis, 9 October 1992.

151. Lamont, *op. cit.*, p. 244.

152. The dinner was at the Regents Park residence of US ambassador Raymond Seitz.

153. Lambert interview with author, London, 14 June 2007: 'I went back quickly to the office and we altered the presentation slightly for the next edition.'

154. Leigh-Pemberton interview with author, 27 April 2007

155. Major interview with author, London, 26 September 2007.

156. For some commentators, Wednesday was 'White', because of the ultimately beneficial effect on the British economy. See, for example, Anatole Kaletsky, 'Happy days are

here again', *The Times*, 18 September 1992. 'By this time next year Britain will have the fastest growing economy in Europe ... Interest rates will be down to 6 to 7 per cent and unemployment will be rapidly falling. House prices will be rising at 5 or 6 per cent annually. The balance of payments will have improved by several billion pounds despite the strength of the economic recovery.'

157. HMT-FT. Andrew Holden note to Terry Burns, 'The Cost of Intervention', 10 December 1993. 'At the beginning of August 1992 we had $23 billion net reserves; two months later we had around $16 billion negative net reserves.' In view of disguised forward sterling purchases, as well as heavy borrowing (mainly D-Marks which were then sold) from the European Monetary Cooperation Fund, only a relatively small portion of the reserve losses was ever revealed in official Bank of England and Treasury statements.

158. The talks took place at the prime minister's temporary headquarters of Admiralty House. Downing Street was undergoing refurbishment.

159. Burns interview with author, London, 27 September 2007.

160. Major, *op. cit.*, p. 331. 'If we suspend our membership the pound will fall heavily – and why should anyone [in the markets] believe what we say ever again.'

161. Douglas Hurd, *Memoirs*, 2003, p. 425.

162. Hurd note to author, June 2008. Hurd stressed how at the next cabinet meeting after the ERM departure Lamont still stressed the possibilities of return. 'The idea died quickly; but it was alive that afternoon.'

163. Clarke interview with author, London, 11 March 2008.

164. Budd interview with author, London, 25 September 2007.

165. To counter operations by traders borrowing sterling to sell on the currency markets, the Bank of England organised a liquidity squeeze on 16 September to drive up overnight interest rates to 100 per cent. Because of the foreign exchange markets' view that sterling might fall by as much 5–10 per cent within the next few days, the increase in overnight interest rates would arguably have had to be even greater to deter speculation. Nigel Wicks, the Treasury's senior international official, appeared to discover only relatively late the consequences of the economic principle of 'interest rate parity' – meaning that if the market expects that a currency will be devalued by 10 per cent within the next twenty-four hours, then interest rates need to be 10 per cent *a day* to defend it.

166. Major interview with author, London, 26 September 2007.

167. French cabinet meeting, 16 September 1992.

168. Stephen Wall interview with author, London, 18 June 2007. Kohl rang back Major only after some delay.

169. The formal Cabinet decision was made at 5 pm. Lamont announced the decision from the Treasury steps in Whitehall at 7.30 pm.

170. By early October sterling's fall compared with the ERM central rate had increased to 15 per cent.

171. Tietmeyer, *op. cit.*, p. 188.

172. Lamont interview, BBC *Today* programme, 18 September 1992.

173. Elysée Palace note by Jean Vidal, Paris, 2 November 1992, on ambassador Bertrand Dufourq's conversation on 1 November 1992 with Schlesinger. Schlesinger said the departure of both the lira and the pound had been inevitable as a result of the 'artifical exchange rates' of both currencies.

174. Major interview with author, London, 26 September 2007.

175. On the eve of France's 20 September referendum, Bundesbank deputy president Hans Tietmeyer demonstrated solidarity by telling the official French news agency Agence France Presse (AFP) that the Franc could even be a candidate for revaluation. Tietmeyer interview with AFP, 18 September 1992.

176. Hans Tietmeyer, 'Vertrauliche Aufzeichnung über die Entwicklung und den Verlauf der EWS-Krise im Juli 1993', 3 August 1993. The document was supplied to the

author by a German monetary source who was not present at any of the key meetings during this period.

177. Sapin interview with author, Paris, 3 October 2007. See Aeschimann and Riché, *op. cit.*, pp. 142–57.

178. Two handwritten notes to Mitterrand by European adviser Anne Lauvergnon, 22 September 1992.

179. Elysée Palace transcript of meeting between Mitterrand and Kohl, 22 September 1992 (16.00 to 17.30).

180. Showing the sensitivity of the exchanges with Kohl, Waigel recorded in a personal memo on 22 September that – despite all contrary impressions – the Bundesbank's independence had been formally upheld as Kohl had left all final decisions to the central bank.

181. The account of the Sheraton meeting is taken from a twelve-page summary finalised afterwards by Trichet. 'Compte rendu des entretiens franco-allemands. Mardi après-midi 22 septembre – Washington.' The note – marked 'Secret' – was sent by Trichet to Mitterrand with a covering letter on 31 December 1993. Mitterrand wrote on the note: 'Essential document – to photocopy and keep here.'

182. Before the Sheraton talks started, Sapin spoke to Trichet by telephone, authorising him to remain firm on the Franc's parity and giving him full powers to negotiate a communiqué with the Germans. Sapin was held up at Washington airport for two and a half hours because of a delay in the Concorde flight. During that time he spoke directly to Mitterrand about his talks with Kohl. 'I spoke to François Mitterrand by telephone [on 22 September] while waiting at the departure desk to fly back to France by Concorde from New York. He had Helmut Kohl in front of him in Paris. Kohl was not aware of the gravity of the situation on the foreign exchanges.' Sapin interview with author, Paris, 3 October 2007.

183. Cappenara was head of Banque de France international department.

184. To even up the balance, Trichet asked M. Duquesne, a deputy director from the French Treasury to take part in the meeting after it had started. The resulting Trichet *aide-memoire* was undoubtedly partly based on a note from Cappanera. On the German side, Haller and Rieke both took long notes of the meeting.

185. Trichet letter to Mitterrand, Paris, 31 December 1993. This was a New Year message after Trichet had become governor of the Banque de France. The letter related how Mitterrand had told Trichet at a recent meeting how he had 'pressed' Chancellor Kohl to defend the European Monetary System in September 1992. Trichet sent Mitterrand his twelve-page summary of the ensuing Washington meeting which, Trichet wrote to Mitterrand on 31 December 1993, followed Kohl's 'instruction' to the German delegation on leaving Mitterrand's office.

186. Trichet speech, investiture for Grand Cross 1st Class of Order of Merit from President Horst Köhler, Berlin, 3 April 2008.

187. On German insistence, the text was watered down somewhat from the original French draft.

188. Including spending by the Bank of England and Banca d'Italia, total Bundesbank support for weak ERM currencies would amount to a total DM100 billion of extra liquidity if all the agreed intervention support for France was deployed, Schlesinger said.

189. Schlesinger said the Bundesbank's profits – and hence the annual amount paid to the German Finance Ministry – could be reduced by DM 2 billion if the Franc later devalued, which would reduce in D-Mark terms the value of the automatic ECU lending facility granted to the Banque de France.

190. Tietmeyer, *op. cit.*, p. 192. The statement said the Franc–D-Mark rate 'accurately reflects the underlying situation of the two economies'.

191. Bank for International Settlements 1993 Annual Report, p. 188.

192. Even after the statement was released, the French authorities doubted whether the Bundesbank would supply sufficient credit lines to shore up the Franc; this led

Bérégovoy and his aides to lay contingency plans – which in the event were never used – for the Franc's possible ERM departure.

193. Hannezo note to Mitterrand, Paris, 23 September 1992.

194. Elysée Palace transcript, meeting between Mitterrand and Major, Paris, 30 September 1992.

195. *Financial Times*, 2 October 1992. Lamont said he had received a letter from the German ambassador on 29 September attempting to rebut the criticisms made of the Bundesbank. On 28 September the ambassador called at the Foreign Office and handed over a paper from the Bundesbank with the same message. Lamont, *op. cit.*, pp. 288–9. The affair ended with an unusual Treasury statement attacking perceived Bundesbank misdemeanours and the Foreign Office calling in German ambassador Hermann von Richthofen to tell him of Britain's 'concern'. Von Richthofen speech to Anglo-German Club, Hamburg, 4 March 2008. Stephens, *op. cit.*, p. 274. Major, *op. cit.*, p. 337.

196. Jean Vidal note, Paris, 3 October 1992. Another note said, 'Officially there is no connection between the conversation between Kohl and Mitterrand on 22 September and the communiqué.' Anne Lauvergnon note, 9 October 1992.

197. Transcript of meeting between Amato and Mitterrand, 10 November 1992.

198. Sapin personal letter to Mitterrand (handwritten), Paris, 25 November 1992.

199. Elysée Palace transcript, meeting between Kohl and Mitterrand, Bonn, 3 December 1992.

200. Trichet personal memorandum (handwritten), Paris, 11 December 1992.

201. Bérégovoy letter to Kohl, 16 December 1992.

202. Bundesbank rate reductions were limited between October and February to a fall in securities repurchase rates of about 0.3 percentage points.

203. 'Les attaques contre le franc', Note by Dominique Marcel, 1 April 1993.

204. Balladur interview with author, Paris, 29 May 2007. 'I gave up the idea of a common currency [under which individual European currencies would continue to exist in parallel]. I decided to back the single currency, since I realised these other solutions were too complicated.'

205. Thierry Bert note to Mitterrand, 2 April 1992. Joachim Bitterlich, one of Kohl's principal advisers, visited Paris on 30 March and advised government officials that the start of the legal process on Banque de France independence could encourage a 'conciliatory' Bundesbank statement that would allow France to cut interest rates.

206. Védrine meeting with Balladur, Paris, 31 March 1993.

207. Dominique Marcel note to Mitterrand, Paris, 6 April 1993.

208. A positive outcome to a second Maastricht referendum in Denmark, allowing the ratification process to get back on track, led to generally higher confidence on the financial markets.

209. Dominique Marcel note to Mitterrand, 21 June 1993.

210. Dominique Marcel note to Mitterrand, 9 July 1993. The Elysée Palace note criticised Alphandéry's interview as 'clumsy' since it over-emphasised pressures in France to cut rates.

211. Hans Tietmeyer, 'Vertrauliche Aufzeichnung über die Entwicklung und den Verlauf der EWS-Krise im Juli 1993', 3 August 1993.

212. Védrine note, Paris, 22 July 1993.

213. The French participants were Alphandéry, Trichet, de Larosière and Christian Noyer, Alphandéry's chief of staff, later deputy president of the European Central Bank and governor of the Banque de France. The German participants were Waigel, Schlesinger (from 12.15 am after he was flown in late by a German government plane from his Greek holiday), Tietmeyer, Gert Haller, the new State Secretary at the Finance Ministry, who had taken over from Köhler, and Gerald Grisse, from the Finance Ministry.

214. Tietmeyer paper, p. 5.

215. Note by Dominique Marcel and Thierry Bert to Mitterrand, 29 July 1992.
216. Balladur letter to Kohl, 29 July 1993. See also Aeschimann and Riché, *op. cit.*, p. 224. The letter is referred to in the Tietmeyer account of 3 August.
217. Balladur letter to ERM member prime ministers, 29 July 1992. The letter used the coded formulation to suggest that Germany might leave: 'France is ready to maintain the normal operation of the Exchange Rate Mechanism between its currency and those among its partners who wish it.' The letter was passed on to Bonn by the Dutch government.
218. The French participants were Alphandéry, de Larosière, Trichet and Hannoun. De Larosière did most of the talking on the French side.
219. The lack of limousines in Paris may have represented a *quid pro quo* for the transport shortcomings when the French delegation arrived in Munich for the meeting at the Marriot Hotel on 22 July. No official car awaited them at the airport. The officials were forced to travel by taxi. Aeschimann and Riché, *op. cit.*, p. 216.
220. Tietmeyer Bundesbank paper, 3 August 1993, pp. 6–8.
221. Schlesinger interview with author, Oberursel, 2 July 2007.
222. Tietmeyer paper, p. 15.
223. Tietmeyer paper, pp. 16–17.
224. Tietmeyer, *op. cit.*, pp. 205–12.
225. De Larosière interview with author, Paris, 28 June 2007. 'Finally I said that I would not leave Brussels and I would not reopen the foreign exchange markets until we had agreed much wider bands. This eventually resulted in the agreement on the 30 per cent bands.'
226. Clarke interview with author, London, 11 March 2008. In spite of sterling's withdrawal from the Exchange Rate Mechanism, sterling was still a member of the European Monetary System.
227. Balladur interview with author, Paris, 29 May 2007.
228. French cabinet meeting, Paris, 4 August 1993.

Chapter 6: Europe's Destiny

1. Schlesinger interview with author, Oberursel, 2 July 2007.
2. Von Kyaw interview with author, Berlin, 27 April 2007.
3. Kohl speech, Louvain, 2 February 1996.
4. Schröder interview, *Bild-Zeitung*, 26 March 1998 and API.
5. Inflation in Germany and France fell from 3.1 per cent to 2.5 per cent and 1.7 per cent respectively; in Italy it declined from 5.9 per cent to 3.8 per cent; in the UK it fell most sharply from 6.3 per cent to 2.6 per cent.
6. One of Major's closest aides, Stephen Wall, said: 'Black Wednesday altered the course of UK policies on Europe, and was fundamentally the end of the Major government.' Wall interview with author, London, 18 June 2007.
7. Major speech to Scottish CBI dinner, Glasgow, 10 September 1992.
8. Major interview with author, 26 September 2007. Norman Lamont, who had no influence on the decision to join the ERM but suffered the political opprobrium of leaving, said, 'It was a big political reversal, but it was the moment that inflation in the UK was killed off.' Lamont interview with author, London, 2 April 2007. The Bank of England's Robin-Leigh Pemberton said: 'In hindsight, was [Black Wednesday] so terrible? Inflation came down rather quickly. This was thanks to Lamont. Rather than using indirect targets such as money supply, we targeted inflation directly. It worked. I remember saying: 'Why the hell didn't we have this before rather than messing around with sterling M3?' Leigh-Pemberton interview with author, London, 24 April 2007.
9. Budd Wincott lecture, London, 5 October 2004. A controversial result of Black Wednesday was the wiping out of Britain's foreign exchange reserves, forcing the UK government to rebuild them later at a much higher sterling cost – causing a loss to the

UK Treasury estimated at £3 billion. This sum should be compared with the overall improvement in economic output that followed the ERM departure. Britain's 'extra growth' in 1993–97 compared with France and Germany was worth a cumulative £70 billion in GDP output over the five-year period.

10. Major said: 'On 14 September [at a meeting in Admiralty House in late afternoon] we did discuss the option of leaving the ERM. But if you leave under conditions of such turbulence, there is a clear risk that departure will cause both a falling exchange rate and rising interest rates. My aim was to find the right time to leave the ERM of our own accord . . . For those with eyes to see, this was the implication of the Maastricht opt-out.' Major interview with author, London, 26 September 2007.

11. HMT-FT. Stephen Davies, 'ERM project paper', HM Treasury, 1 December 1993, p. 78. It would be wrong to assume that the market consequences of a voluntary and unforced withdrawal would have been identical to those we actually experienced since Black Wednesday . . . By being forced out as we were, the [UK] authorities did at least demonstrate a determined (and costly) attempt to meet their commitments, and the UK's departure from the ERM occurred after the markets had themselves concluded that this was the optimal course for the UK to take.

12. Hogg interview with author, London, 11 February 2008. Major said in 2007 of his relationship with Kohl, 'I was very fond of Helmut . . . There was empathy in my meetings with him. Given the antipathy to Germany in the British newspapers, this didn't win me many favours.'

13. Major article, *The Economist*, 25 September 1993.

14. The main difference in 1993–95 compared with 1973–75 was that the Bundesbank in the latter period was easing monetary policy.

15. Welteke became president of the Land Central Bank of Hesse in 1995 after the previous incumbent, Horst Schulmann (Helmut Schmidt's former monetary adviser) died in 1994.

16. Welteke interview with author, Frankfurt, 4 April 2007.

17. Balladur interview with author, Paris, 29 May 2007. The meeting took place after the end of the Franco-German Economic and Finance Council that had been postponed from 2 July as a result of the Alphandéry radio gaffe.

18. De Larosière interview with author, Paris, 27 June 2007.

19. The Banque de France announced that the whole of the FFr107 billion it had borrowed through the European Monetary Cooperation fund had been repaid on 14 January 1994, a month ahead of schedule.

20. The figures for debt compared with GDP were: for 1992: 44 per cent in Germany and 42 per cent in the UK; in 1999, 60 per cent in Germany and 45 per cent in the UK.

21. By 1999 French debt rose nearly one-half to 58 per cent. In 2007 total French government borrowings increased further to 65 per cent of GDP (the same figure in Germany and compared with 45 per cent in the UK) – one of the worst performances in the Euro area. OECD Economic Outlook, December 2007 and past issues.

22. *Le Monde*, 29 November 1995.

23. Nicolas Sarkozy, *Ensemble*, 2007, p. 114: 'If France had practised the same monetary policies as England at the beginning of the 1990s, then our public debt would not be much more than theirs.'

24. Sapin interview with author, Paris, 3 October 2007.

25. Guigou interview with author, Paris, 4 July 2007.

26. Noyer interview with author, Paris, 27 June 2007.

27. De Silguy speech, Frankfurt, June 1995.

28. See, for instance, 'Geld stiftet keine Staatlichkeit' ('Money does not provide state-like character'), *Frankfurter Allgemeine Zeitung*, 15 July 1995. The European Union needed 'a financial constitution' that would protect it 'from the dangers that grow from the discrepancies in integration in the monetary field, on the one hand, and in general politics, on the other'.

29. Issing comments at conference, Hamburg, November 2007.
30. Schlesinger article, 'Money is just the start', *The Economist*, 21 September 1996.
31. Previously, Schlesinger had put forward the example of Germany's first unification in 1871, and the foundation of the Reichsbank four years later, as evidence that political union had to come first. Later, he voiced doubts on the aptness of his own analogy. Schlesinger speech at Amsterdam University, 2 April 1997.
32. Schlesinger interview with author, Frankfurt, 14 February 2007.
33. Trichet took over when de Larosière departed to London to take over as the second president of the European Bank for Reconstruction and Development in September 1993 from Jacques Attali, President Mitterrand's former adviser. The Banque de France was made formally independent in August 1993.
34. The independent Monetary Policy Council of the Banque de France convened for the first time in January 1994. As part of the Maastricht process, all European countries that wished to join EMU had to make their central banks formally independent during the 1990s.
35. Trichet, NatWest lecture, London, 16 May 1995. Asked whether France might have benefited if the central bank had been made independent in the mid- to late-1980s, Trichet answered, 'The independence of the central bank gives an additional element of credibility. . . . Independence of the bank would probably, had it been implemented earlier, have delivered something more important.'
36. Balladur interview with author, Paris, 29 May 2007.
37. The Bundesbank suggested that the EMI move into the Messe Tower next to the Frankfurt Industrial Fair complex north of the main railway station. Lamfalussy quickly realised that the Bundesbank was itself a tenant in part of the Messe Tower. Tietmeyer, who made clear that he regarded physical proximity to Bundesbank staff as an advantage for the EMI, was backed by France's Jean-Claude Trichet, who regarded winning the Bundesbank's favour as a vital condition for EMI success. However, Lamfalussy rejected any suggestion of moving in with the Bundesbank, on the grounds that it would compromise the EMI's independence. He was backed by Wim Duisenberg, the Nederlandsche Bank president.
38. Lamfalussy interview with author, Ohain, 22 May 2007.
39. A Christian Democrat discussion paper suggesting a 'core Europe' of France, Germany and the Benelux countries, published in September 1994, caused consternation in Italy and Spain as well as some concern in the UK.
40. Waigel told the Bundestag Finance Committee in September 1995 that Italy would probably not be a member of the first wave of EMU. This sparked a lira fall on the foreign exchanges and a protest letter from Italian prime minister Lamberto Dini.
41. Chirac, radio interview, 13 April 1995. 'The governor of the Banque de France is not there to indicate what type of economic policy the government should follow, nor to tell the social partners what they should do!'
42. Chirac, TV interview, 14 July 1996. In the same interview Chirac attacked the Banque de France for keeping interest rates too high. *Le Monde*, 16 July 1996.
43. Issing, 'Geld stiftet noch keine Staatlichkeit', *Franfurter Allemeine Zeitung*, 15 July 1995.
44. Waigel launched the initiative in a magazine interview on 11 September 1995. He discussed the plan on 14 September with French finance minister Jean Arthuis. Two months later the plan was proposed to European finance ministers in Brussels.
45. *Börsen-Zeitung*, 28 November 1995. A non-interest bearing deposit of ¼ per cent of a country's GDP would be paid for each percentage point that a country's deficit exceeded 3 per cent.
46. Dini statement, Majorca European summit, 23 September 1995.
47. Jacques Attali article, *Börsen-Zeitung*, 21 November 1995. President Mitterrand's former adviser declared, 'From Paris it appears as if Germany no longer wants the common currency.'

48. Wall interview with author, 18 June 2007.
49. Waigel interview, *Financial Times*, 11 December 1995.
50. GDP in the future Euro area grew by 2.6 per cent in 1997 against 1.4 per cent in 1996, according to OECD data.
51. De Silguy, *Le Syndrome du Diploducus, 1996*, quoted in *Sunday Times*, 20 September 1996.
52. Schlesinger interview with author, Frankfurt, 14 February 2007.
53. Prodi interview with author, Rome, 5 June 2007.
54. The lira rejoined the ERM at a relatively competitive rate of 990 lire to the D-Mark. President Chirac, who had repeatedly criticised Italy's benefits from floating, had lobbied for a more expensive rate of 950 lire to make Italian exports less competitive.
55. Tietmeyer speech, Florence, 28 November 1996.
56. Waigel article in *Frankfurter Allgemeine Zeitung*, 21 June 1996.
57. Giscard interview, *Le Monde*, 12 July 1997.
58. Giscard article and interview, *L'Express*, 21 November 1996.
59. *Frankfurter Allgemeine Zeitung*, 9 December 1996.
60. Former Finance Ministry Parliamentary State Secretary Hansgeorg Hauser interview with author, Berlin, 25 January 2008.
61. Lamfalussy revealed in May 1996 that he wished to stand down in 1997 as president of the EMI to allow time for his successor to prepare himself for the job.
62. Schröder interview, *Financial Times*, 17 March 1997. Schröder's jibe sparked an exaggerated riposte from Klaus Kinkel, the German foreign minister: 'This is an irresponsible attempt to frighten the people of Germany.'
63. Richard Lambert interview with author, 14 June 2007. 'As the FT editor, I did the first interview with Gordon Brown after the 1997 election. I sensed something was up because the TV cameras were there.'
64. The idea was raised by Bundesbank deputy president Johann Wilhelm Gaddum who told Waigel the Bundesbank would need to revalue its gold and foreign currency reserves as a prelude to entering EMU.
65. Waigel interview with author, Munich, 17 April 2007.
66. Wellink interview with author, Amsterdam, 7 September 2007. Duisenberg wrote to Prime Minister Wim Kok suggesting that he could become the EMI president but also remain president of the Netherlands Central Bank.
67. *Börsen-Zeitung*, 20 June 1997.
68. Pöhl speech, Rotterdam, 10 June 1997.
69. Trichet interview, *Le Monde*, 25 June 1997.
70. Tietmeyer interview, *Die Woche*, 1 September 1997.
71. 'Declaration expected shortly on UK entry soon after launch', *Financial Times*, 26 September 1997. The *FT* story turned out to be written without the authorisation of the Treasury. A counter-story later initiated by the Treasury, 'Brown rules out single currency for lifetime of this Parliament', *The Times*, 18 October 1997, was also a distortion, since it reflected purely Brown's view and was communicated to the newspaper without the prime minister's knowledge. Alastair Campbell, *The Blair Years*, 2007, p. 253.
72. George speech, Hong Kong, 23 September 1997.
73. Brown statement, House of Commons, 28 October 1997.
74. The central banking operation affecting the securities repurchase intervention rate took place on 10 October 1997. The Belgian, French, German, Luxembourg and Dutch central banks all had rates of 3.3 per cent, with Austria showing a slightly lower rate of 3.2 per cent.
75. *Frankfurter Allgeimene Zeitung*, 15 September 1997.
76. Strauss-Kahn article, *Financial Times*, 27 November 1997.
77. Earlier in the summer Paris had backed for the job Michel Camdessus, the International Monetary Fund managing director and former Banque de France governor. Former Chancellor Helmut Schmidt put forward Valéry Giscard d'Estaing for the job.

78. As a sign of distrust of Trichet's motives, Duisenberg in 1996 – before he took over the EMI job – had obtained from Trichet a declaration of support for his candidature, which he deposited in his personal safe. *Financial Times*, 5 May 1998.

79. McDonough speech, Frankfurt, 17 November 1997.

80. Greenspan comments to Goldman Sachs spring partners' conference, 2006. He added: 'I'm surprised that it worked and didn't think that it would last.'

81. Greenspan, *Ein Leben für die Wirtschaft*, 2007, p. 9. Curiously, the comment appears only in the German edition of Greenspan's *Age of Turbulence*.

82. Friedman article, *The Times*, 19 November 1997.

83. Feldstein article, *Foreign Affairs*, November/December 1997.

84. The lawsuit by Wilhelm Hankel, Wilhelm Nölling, Joachim Starbatty and Karl Albrecht Schachtscheider was launched in January 1998.

85. The professors' petition was launched on 9 February 1998, led by Wim Kosters, Manfred Nauman, Renate Ohr and Roland Vaubel. *Financial Times*, 13 February 1998.

86. *Financial Times*, 13 February 1998.

87. Dahrendorf article, *New Statesman*, 20 February 1998.

88. European Commission and European Monetary Institute Convergence Reports, 25 March 1998. Bundesbank Council statement on convergence, 26 March 1998.

89. Kohl statement to Finance Policy Committee, Bonn, 22 April 1998.

90. Matt Marshall, *The Bank*, 1999, pp. 180–200. This contains a long account of the wrangling over the ECB mandate.

91. German finance minister Theo Waigel regarded favourably Stark's experience in handling foreign exchange market intervention – an attribute the Germans believed might be necessary at the ECB.

92. Issing's well-publicised opposition to revaluing the Bundesbank's gold reserves in May 1997 was interpreted by Kohl as hostility to the Maastricht process. Waigel telephoned Issing on 24 April 1998 to offer him the ECB job, after weeks of discussions about the candidacy.

93. Tietmeyer, *op. cit.*, p. 265.

94. Meeting between Kok, Chirac, Kohl, Blair, Brussels, 2 May 1998. Campbell, *op. cit.*, p. 299.

95. *Financial Times*, 4 May 1998.

96. *Frankfurter Allgemeine Zeitung*, 5 May 1998.

97. Nomination hearings, Brussels, 7 May 1998.

98. The other three board members apart from Issing were Sirka Hämäläinen, the Finnish central bank governor, Tommaso Padoa-Schioppa from the Banca d'Italia and Eugenio Domingo Solans from the Banco d'España.

99. Article 108, EC Treaty. ESCB statute, Article 7.

100. Target stands for Trans-European Automated Real-time Gross Settlement Express Transfer. The UK came out early on in favour of all EU countries to having equal access to Target.

101. Duisenberg interview, *Financial Times*, 7 December 1998.

102. Jospin article, *Le Nouvel Observateur*, 10 September 1998.

103. Fazio interview, *Financial Times*, 10 November 1998.

Chapter 7: Coping with Imbalance

1. Rocard interview with author, Paris, 29 May 2007.

2. Article 2, Constitution of European System of Central Banks (ESCB), 1992. This followed closely the recommendations for the ESCB laid down in the Delors Report, in line with the recommendations of the Bundesbank.

3. McKinsey Global Institute, July 2008. Four main components of private investment groups and sovereign wealth funds – Asian governments, oil exporters, hedge funds

and private equity groups – raised assets under management from $8,800 billion at the end of 2006 to nearly $11,500 billion by the end of 2007.

4. Duisenberg interview, *International Herald Tribune*, 30 October 2000. 'I am direct – some say I am too direct. It is part of my character.'

5. Duisenberg interview, *Financial Times*, 7 December 1998.

6. The ECB's dual decision-making system transposes the Bank deutscher Länder's 1948 model – a six- or seven-strong central Directorate and a Council roughly three times the size including Land central bank presidents. The ECB Council – former politicians, civil servants, economics professors and central bankers – parallels that of the Bundesbank's Council; the average age of ECB Council members at fifty-nine to sixty in 2008 was one or two years lower. The Bundesbank Council had only one woman among its ninety members over fifty years. In 1998–2008, of the thirty-seven people on the ECB Council, two were women, both on the Executive Board.

7. Wellink interview with author, Amsterdam, 7 September 2007.

8. Up to October 2008, the ECB's only other intervention to influence the exchange rate of the Euro against the dollar came in November 2000.

9. Duisenberg interview, *The Times*, 16 October 2000.

10. Muscovici interview, *Der Spiegel*, January 2001.

11. Feldstein, *Wall Street Journal*, 8 February 2000.

12. For example, *Bild-Zeitung* front-page headline, 1 February 2000 '*Euro-Angst*'.

13. ECB Executive Board member Eugenio Domingo Solans speech, Seoul, 13 November 2003.

14. Michael Ehrmann, ECB Working Paper 588, 'Rational inattention, inflation developments and perceptions after the euro cash changeover', February 2006.

15. Juncker interview with author, Luxembourg, 28 January 2008.

16. Prodi interview with author, Rome, 5 June 2007. '[Carlo] Ciampi [the Treasury Minister] and I prepared a very diligent changeover with dual pricing and a system of controls, but this was not enacted by the government [under Silvio Berlusconi] at the time [in 2002].'

17. Duisenberg announcement, 7 February 2002. He said he wished to depart in July 2002.

18. Duisenberg address, farewell dinner, Venice, 29 October 2003.

19. Prodi statement, Brussels, October 2002.

20. *Financial Times*, 26 November 2003.

21. *Financial Times*, 24 December 2007.

22. Trichet interview, *Focus*, 26 February 2007.

23. Trichet remarks, ICCA reception, Frankfurt, 3 July 2007.

24. Trichet Vincent van Gogh Award Lecture, Maastricht, 10 September 2004.

25. Major interview with author, London, 26 September 2007.

26. Lambert interview with author, London, 14 June 2007.

27. Bernanke joined the Federal Reserve Board of Governors in 2002 and took over from Greenspan in 2006, thirteen years after Trichet became governor of the Banque de France. On expiry of his eight-year term to 2011, Trichet would have recorded eighteen consecutive years as a central bank chief – one year less than Greenspan's Federal Reserve tenure.

28. Trichet interview with author, Frankfurt, 14 April 2007.

29. All the members of the Board appointed when Duisenberg took the reins in 1998 reached the end of their contracts by 2006.

30. ECB, *Statistical treatment of the Eurosystem's international reserves*, Frankfurt, October 2000.

31. World central bank reserves totalled $7,000 billion in summer 2008 compared with $2,000 billion at the start of the decade. In the 1990s reserves doubled from $1,000 billion. Behind China, with $1,808 billion, were Japan with $973 billion and Russia with $581 billion. Taiwan, India and South Korea had reserves of $291 billion, $283 billion and $243 billion.

32. IMF data base, April 2008. The figures represent the arithmetical sum of the payments numbers, both surpluses and deficits.

33. America's gross capital imports are much bigger than net capital imports in view of extremely large capital outflows, due to foreign investment, military expenditure and other government and private spending. Between 2003 and 2007 total capital flows into the US reached $7,800 billion. In 2007 total capital imports were $2,100 billion, of which roughly one-third financed the current account deficit and two-thirds funded capital exports. Kristin Forbes, MIT-Sloan School of Management, Euro at 10 conference, Peterson Institute of International Economics, Washington, 10 October 2008.

34. *Financial Times*, August 3 2008

35. Trichet remarks, Davos, January 2007.

36. Trichet interview, *Financial Times*, 14 May 2007.

37. Lamfalussy telephone interview with author, Ohain, 8 May 2008.

38. Steinbrück interview with author, Berlin, 24 January 2008.

39. Sarkozy, *Ensemble*, p. 86.

40. Section 2A, Federal Reserve Act. The Federal Reserve's aims are 'to promote effectively the goals of maximum employment, stable prices, and moderate long-term interest rates'.

41. Fabius interview with author, Paris, 29 May 2007.

42. Balladur interview with author, 30 May 2007.

43. Peyrelevade interview with author, Paris, 4 October 2007.

44. Schröder interview with author, Berlin, 26 April 2007.

45. Delors interview with author, Paris, 29 May 2007.

46. During the first few years' ECB meetings, Trichet – as governor of the Banque de France – insisted on talking in French. But as president he switched to English, lapsing into French only when addressing directly Yves Mersch, the head of the Luxembourg central bank, and Christian Noyer, Trichet's successor as governor of the Banque de France.

47. Bonello, a former official at the United Nations trade and development body UNCTAD, grew up speaking English as well as Maltese and attended Oxford university as a Rhodes scholar.

48. Weber and Draghi took over from Ernst Welteke and Antonio Fazio in 2004 and 2006 respectively. Welteke stepped down after controversy over payment irregularities over a bill at a Berlin hotel used for a Euro launch party. Fazio resigned after accusations of blocking the takeover of an Italian bank by a Dutch institution.

49. Orphanides, born in Czechoslovakia, is the only member of the Governing Council to have attended meetings of the US Federal Open Market Committee.

50. German government representatives had no voting rights at the Bundesbank, but they had the theoretical opportunity to delay Bundesbank interest rate decisions for two weeks under Article 13, Bundesbank Law.

51. Juncker attends about eight or nine meetings a year – normally timing his visits to occur when interest rates are expected to change. Almunia participates in nearly all the ECB meetings.

52. Welteke interview with author, 4 April 2007.

53. For a discussion of ECB transparency issues, see Iain Begg, European Institute, London School of Economics and Political Science, 'Economic policy and institutional transparency: the ECB', August 2005; Jakob De Haan, University of Groningen – Department of Economics, 'A Non-Transparent European Central Bank? Who is to Blame?', April 2003; Jakob de Haan, Sylvester C.W. Eijffinger and Sandra Waller, *The European Central Bank – Credibility, Transparency, and Centralization*, 2005.

54. To meet the challenge of growing membership, the Governing Council drew up a new rotating voting system, to be enacted after the number of national central bank governors exceeded sixteen. 'The adjustment of voting modalities on the governing council', ECB Monthly Bulletin, May 2003.

55. National central bank governors are frequently dependent on the goodwill of their home governments for reconfirmation in their posts at the end of their terms. (The members of the ECB's Executive Board, by contrast, are selected for a non-renewable eight years to reinforce their independence from governments. However, if they are young enough to look for other jobs in the public sector following departure from the ECB, they are still exposed to government pressures.)

56. Papademos speech, New Orleans, 5 January 2008.

57. Trichet speech, European Parliament, Strasbourg, 9 July 2008.

58. Weber interview, *Financial Times*, 29 May 2007.

59. European Parliament 2007 annual report on ECB, April 2007.

60. The ECB's press conferences, unlike those of the Bundesbank, have to be planned well in advance because around 40 per cent of the roughly 120-strong group of economic journalists who follow its deliberations travel to Frankfurt from different parts of Europe. The journalistic community covering the Bundesbank was largely based in Frankfurt, allowing the Bundesbank to convene press conferences at very short notice depending on whether it had decisions to announce. ECB interest rate decisions are made only at its first meeting of the month, since these are the meetings for which press conferences are scheduled.

61. Emphasising Trichet's dominance, vice president Papademos sits alongside Trichet at the press conferences, but rarely says anything. Under the more free-wheeling Duisenberg, Papademos played a more substantial role.

62. ESCB statute, Article 10.1 and 10.2.

63. Hurley interview with author, Dublin, 1 October 2007.

64. Merkel German TV interview, 10 July 2007.

65. Steinbrück and Merkel tried to persuade EMU states to balance their budgets by 2010–12 – a goal that finance ministers earlier set for 2004 but had to abandon in 2002.

66. Eurogroup meeting in Brussels, 9 July 2007.

67. Sarkozy spoke French and Steinbrück German; simultaneous interpretation may have added to the apparent harshness. Steinbrück's State Secretary Thomas Mirow was asked by an enraged Sarkozy to give Steinbrück the message about Franco-German friendship.

68. Trichet's support for independence demonstrates the 'Becket effect', coined by Bundesbank officials who noticed German finance ministry officials became fervent defenders of independence as soon as they joined the central bank, a parallel to Thomas à Becket, Chancellor of Henry II of England, who opposed the King after he was made Archbishop of Canterbury – and was murdered for his change of allegiance.

69. Guigou interview with author, Paris, 4 July 2007.

70. Schmidt interview with author, Hamburg, 4 September 2007.

71. *Le Monde*, 15 September 2007.

72. Elysée Palace press briefing, 1 July 2008. Sarkozy made his remarks ahead of the widely-expected increase in the ECB's lending rates a week later.

73. For most of the first decade of the Euro, yields (running interest rates reflecting the price on bond markets) on government paper issued by Euro members were very close together. Reflecting greater perception of risk, the yield spread between bonds issued by weaker and stronger countries widened in 2008. By 12 December 2008 the differential compared with interest rates on German debt was 2.07 points for Greece, 1.28 points for Italy, 1.42 points for Ireland, 0.91 points for Portugal, 0.75 points for Spain and 0.43 points for France (against only 0.30 points for the UK).

74. Outside the Euro area, other medium-sized European economies displayed broadly similar growth compared with the Euro area. The UK recorded annual average growth of 2.7 per cent in 1999–2008, Sweden 3 per cent, Norway 2.6 per cent, Denmark 2 per cent and Switzerland 1.8 per cent – broadly similar to their performances before 1999.

75. Richard Baldwin, *In or Out: Does It Matter? An Evidence-based Analysis of the Euro's Trade Effects*, Centre for Economic Policy Research, London, 2006.

76. *OECD Economic Outlook No. 83*, June 2008. The figures may overstate other countries' competitiveness losses since they do not take sufficient account of moves into higher-value products that show up in the statistics as higher inflation rather than higher quality. See also 'Current account balances and price competitiveness in the Euro area', Bundesbank Monthly Report, June 2007.

77. World Trade Organisation, 'World Trade 2007', 17 April 2008. German merchandise exports in 2007 were $1,327 billion against $1,218 billion for China, $552 billion for France, $492 billion for Italy, $436 billion for the UK.

78. Trade figures based on OECD data. The buoyancy of Germany's exports outside EMU led to the share of Germany's overall exports ($1,120 billion) channelled to the Euro area falling in 2006 to 42 per cent from 44 per cent in 1999. China made up 3 per cent of German exports in 2006 against 1 per cent in 1999. For France, the EMU share of total exports ($479 billion) fell to 50 per cent in 2006 against 52 per cent in 1999. For Italy, the EMU share of the total ($411 billion) fell to 44 per cent from 49 per cent in 1999.

79. Germany's trade surplus grew to €199 billion in 2007 from €63 billion in 1998. The surplus with the EMU area increased to €109 billion from €28 billion. The trade surplus with France rose to €29 billion from €9 billion; with Italy, to €21 billion from €3 billion; with Spain to €27 billion from €5 billion; with the UK (outside EMU), to €28 billion from €13 billion.

80. IFMS, p. 203. Christian Sautter note to Mitterrand, 19 January 1983. The French trade deficit with West Germany in 1982 was FFr 38 billion (around €6 billion), double the 1981 level.

81. Large European imbalances were not confined to the Euro area – underlined by the significant deficit for the UK and sizeable surpluses in Switzerland and Norway.

82. The overall changes in current account performance over ten years within the Euro area as a percentage of GDP were: Germany +9 per cent, Austria +6 per cent, Netherlands +3 per cent, Finland –3 per cent, Belgium and Italy –4 per cent, France and Portugal –5 per cent, Ireland –6 per cent, Spain –9 per cent, Greece –13 per cent.

83. According to IMF figures for general government debt (central, regional and local government bodies), gross French government debt in 2007 was €1,194 billion compared with €804 billion in 1999 and €333 billion in 1989. The figures for Germany were €1,532 billion, €1,199 billion and €475 billion respectively, for Italy, €1,597 billion, €1,282 billion and €590 billion.

84. In 1989 French government debt as a proportion of GDP was 34 per cent against 41 per cent for Germany and 93 per cent in Italy.

85. Trichet speech, Lausanne, 21 September 2007. 'The financial channel [for smoothing out differences in output among states] can be much more important than the fiscal channel. This is an additional reason for speeding up financial integration in Europe.'

86. In pan-European mergers and acquisitions, the leading investment banks in the first ten years of the Euro were American institutions – Goldman Sachs, Morgan Stanley, Merrill Lynch, JP Morgan and Citibank.

87. According to Bundesbank statistics, German banks raised claims on the rest of the world from €750 billion in January 1999 to €2,400 billion in the first quarter of 2008, mainly through four-fold increase in securities holdings and a tripling of credits. Some of these foreign claims reflected purchases of 'toxic' debt instruments that led to well-publicised difficulties for two leading German banks, Düsseldorf-based IKB Bank and Dresden-based Landesbank Sachsen, in 2007.

88. In October 2008, following the slide in equity market valuations after the exacerbated credit crisis, Banco Santander had an equity market capitalisation of €67 billion, against €59 billion for BNP Paribas, €37 billion for UniCredit and only €26 billion for

Deutsche Bank. The change compared with 1990 – when Deutsche Bank was by far the biggest bank in Europe in terms of equity – was striking. In 1990, Deutsche Bank showed a market capitalisation of $21 billion compared with $5 billion for Banco Santander, $7 billion for Paribas (BNP was denationalised in 1993 and the merger with Paribas took place in 2000) and $3 billion for Credito Italiano (one of the components of UniCredit).

89. Banks outside Germany have been far more successful in mergers within and outside their own countries. German consolidation accelerated only in summer 2008 with the takeover of Dresdner Bank (the long-time No. 2 in Germany) by Commerzbank. The main foreign acquisitions across Europe have been Santander's purchase of UK banks Abbey (2004) and Alliance and Leicester (2008), Uncredit's takeover of Germany's HypoVereinsbank in 2005, and the acquisition of ABN Amro of the Netherlands by a consortium led by Royal Bank of Scotland (RBS) in 2007. The ABN Amro acquisition was, however, one of the factors that led to the near-collapse of RBS as well as of one of the other banks in the consortium, Fortis, in autumn 2008.

90. Pébereau interview with author, Paris, 30 January 2008.

91. Breuer interview with author, 18 October 2007.

92. Profumo interview with author, Milan, 23 July 2007.

93. *Financial Times*, 13 October 2008.

94. Lamfalussy interview with author, Ohain, 22 May 2007.

95. See, for example, 'Is Europe ready for a major banking crisis?', Nicolas Véron, Bruegel Institute, Brussels, August 2007.

Chapter 8: The Reckoning

1. Almunia statement, Euro at 10 conference, Peterson Institute for International Economics, Washington, 10 October 2008.

2. See Edward 'Ted' Truman, Peterson Institute, speech at ECB and Its Watchers conference, Frankfurt, 2 July 2004. 'When I left the Federal Reserve in 1998, when the US current account deficit was 2.3 percent of US GDP, the staff had concluded that deficits on that scale were not sustainable indefinitely. Six years later, the deficit is twice that size and not likely to narrow significantly over the next two years.' According to the OECD, the US current account deficit grew to a peak of 6.2 per cent of GDP in 2006, but declined thereafter to 5.3 per cent in 2007 and 5 per cent in 2008.

3. *OECD Economic Outlook No. 83*, June 2008. Measured by the private consumption deflator, the Euro area recorded consumer price inflation of an average 2.1 per cent between 1999 and 2008, compared with 2.4 per cent for the UK, 1.9 per cent for Norway, 1.6 per cent for Sweden, 0.9 per cent for Switzerland.

4. 'Life without inflation', Lombard Street Research Monthly International Review, April 1998.

5. *OECD Survey on Euro Area*, January 2007, p. 25: 'The evidence suggests that reform intensity has fallen since the advent of EMU while there has been little or no slowdown elsewhere.'

6. Goldman Sachs, *The Euro at Ten: Performance and Challenges for the Next Decade*, June 2008. Overall GDP growth in the Euro area was 2.2 per cent per year on average compared with 2.6 per cent in the US and 1.3 per cent in Japan. However, this was attributable to higher US population growth. Growth per head was 1.8 per cent in the Euro area compared with 1.6 per cent in the US. According to OECD and IMF figures, employment in the Euro area rose by 16.4 million in the Euro area between 1998 and 2007 (to 140.6 million from 124.2 million) against 14.6 million (to 146.1 million from 131.5 million) in the US. The Euro area figures masked large differences between countries. Employment rose over the period by 10 per cent in France, 3 per cent in Germany, 6 per cent in Italy – compared with 13 per cent for the Euro area as a whole and 11 per cent in the US.

7. According to OECD figures, medium-sized to large European economies within and outside the Euro area showed similar employment growth between 1998 and 2008. By far the best performer – accounting for more than one-third of all the jobs created in the Euro area, despite having a GDP share of only 9 per cent – was Spain with employment growth of 5 million.

8. Holger Schmieding, Bank of America, 'Celebrating 10 Years of ECB: The Facts', May 2008.

9. *OECD Economic Survey on European Union*, September 2007, pp. 20–21.

10. Romain Duval and Jorgen Elmeskov, 'The effects of EMU on structural reform in labour and product markets', OECD Economics Department Working Paper, 2005.

11. Pöhl interview with author, Frankfurt, 9 May 2007.

12. Banque de France bulletin, March 2008, Cécilia Lemonnier, 'L'Union monétaire, l'euro et l'opinion publique', March 2008.

13. *Financial Times/*Harris poll, 24 September 2007. When asked whether the European economy should become more like the US, 78 per cent of Germans, 73 per cent of French, 58 per cent of Spanish and 46 per cent of respondents in the UK and Italy said No.

14. Arnauld Miguet, 'France's election year disquiet', *Current History*, March 2007. In an international opinion poll in 2006, France was the only one of around twenty countries, including China, the US and Italy, to give a negative response to the statement, 'The free enterprise system and free market economy is the best system on which to base the future of the world.'

15. Berlin government draft bill, 20 August 2008.

16. Juncker interview with author, Luxembourg, 28 January 2008.

17. Wellink interview with author, Amsterdam, 7 September 2007.

18. Bini Smaghi interview with author, Frankfurt, 17 April 2008.

19. In view of pressure on funding and the 'fiscal federalism' run by the European Union, which has restricted centrally-organised transfers from Brussels to the member states to around 1 per cent of EU GDP, this condition is never likely to be realised.

20. 'Removing Obstacles to Geographic Labour Mobility', *OECD Economic Survey on European Union*, 2007. On average between 2000 and 2005, the internal borders of the EU were crossed by only 0.1 to 0.3 per cent of the working-age population each year, compared with just over 3 per cent of the workforce moving between the fifty states of the US.

21. Weber interview with author, Frankfurt, 21 May 2007.

22. Fernández Ordóñez e-mail interview with author, Madrid/London, 13 June 2008.

23. Simon Tilford, *Will the Eurozone crack?*, Centre for European Reform, September 2006.

24. González-Páramo interview with author, Frankfurt, 16 July 2007.

25. Guth interview with author, Frankfurt, 3 May 2007.

26. Cook speech to Trade Unionists for Europe, 6 July 2000.

27. Lambert interview with author, London, 14 June, 2007.

28. Lawson interview with author, London, 3 April 2007.

29. Hogg interview with author, London, 11 February 2008.

30. Müller interview with author, Frankfurt, 3 May 2007.

31. De Silguy interview with author, Paris, 2 April 2007.

32. French GDP in 1989 was 72.6 per cent of German GDP, the same as 2007–08. IMF data base, April 2008.

33. Wilhelm Nölling, *Monetary Policy after Maastricht*, 1993, p. 161: 'It is quite conceivable that the stronger countries will become even stronger and increase their share of Community markets.'

34. Rocard interview with author, Paris, 29 May 2007.

35. Strauss-Kahn reply to question from author, The Euro at 10 conference, Peterson Institute for International Economics, Washington, 10 October 2008.

36. Alphandéry interview with author, Paris, 30 May 2007.

37. Fabius interview with author, Paris, 29 May 2007.

38. Prodi interview with author, Rome, 5 June 2007.

39. Profumo interview with author, Milan, 23 July 2007.

40. Eichel interview with author, Berlin, 25 April 2007.

41. Healey interview with author, Alfriston, 10 April 2007.

42. Major interview with author, London, 26 September 2007.

43. Eurostat population projections, August 2008. The EU old age dependency ratio – the population aged 65 years and older divided by the working age population – is projected to increase from 25 per cent in 2008 to 53 per cent in 2060. The ratio will increase in France from 25 per cent to 45 percent; in Germany from 30 to 59 per cent; in Italy from 31 per cent to 59 per cent; in Spain from 24 per cent to 59 per cent; in the UK from 24 per cent to 42 per cent. By 2060 the UK is projected to become the most populous member of the EU with 77 million people against 72 million for France, 71 million for Germany and 59 million for Italy.

44. Noyer interview with author, 27 June 2007.

45. Schmidt interview with author, 4 September 2007.

46. For a discussion of possible circumstances under which Germany might seek to leave EMU, see Goldman Sachs, *The Euro at Ten: Performance and Challenges for the Next Decade*, June 2008, p. 92.

47. Moves to increase flows of information on the ECB's decision-making procedures, without reference to individual names or countries, would be in line with recommendations in European Parliament, Annual Report on ECB, June 2008.

48. Sarkozy conspicuously avoided similar tactics to President Jacques Chirac in January 1997, who nominated to the Monetary Policy Committee of the Banque de France two members with close links to him as a means of putting Governor Trichet under pressure.

49. IMF Currency Composition of Official Foreign Exchange Reserves, first quarter 2008. The data provide an increasingly incomplete picture of total world holdings as they do not include the official holdings of many developing and emerging economies, as well as the increasingly important sovereign wealth funds.

50. For a review of the international security policy considerations behind the dollar's long-lasting reserve role, see Adam Posen, 'Why the Euro will not Rival the Dollar', *International Finance*, 11:1, 2008, pp. 75–100.

SOURCES AND BIBLIOGRAPHY

Archives

European Union
European Central Bank Archives, Frankfurt (ECBA)

Germany
Deutsche Bundesbank (Historisches Archiv) (DBA), including Correspondence Files (CF)
Federal Archive (Bundesarchiv), Koblenz (BArch-K)
Federal Archive (Bundesarchiv), Potsdam (BArch-P)
Federal Chancellery (Bundeskanzleramt), *Dokumente zur Deutschlandpolitik: Deutsche Einheit – Sonderedition aus den Akten des Bundeskanzleramtes 1989/90*, R. Oldenbourg Verlag, eds, Hans Jürgen Küsters and Daniel Hofmann, Munich (BKA-DE)
Federal Ministry of Foreign Affairs (Auswärtiges Amt) Archives, Berlin (AAA)
Federal Ministry of Foreign Affairs (Auswärtiges Amt), Akten zur Außenpolitik der Bundesrepublik Deutschland, Institut für Zeitgeschichte, Berlin (AAPD)
Schleswig-Holstein Parliament Archives, Kiel (SHA)

France
Banque de France Archives, France (BFA)
Institut François Mitterrand, *Mitterrand et la réunification allemande – Une histoire secrète (1981–1995*, Thilo Schabert, Paris (IFMS)
Ministry of Economics and Finance Archives, Centre des archives économiques et financières, Savigny-le-Temple (CAEF)

Switzerland
Bank for International Settlements Archives, Basle (BISA)

UK
Bank of England Archives, London (BEA)
Documents on British Policy Overseas, Foreign and Commonwealth Office, London (DBPO)
HM Treasury, Freedom of Information Act, *Financial Times* documents 2005 (HMT-FT)
National Archives, Kew (UKNA)

US

Federal Reserve Bank of New York Archives, New York (NYFA)
International Monetary Fund Archives, Washington (IMFA)
National Archives, Washington (USNA)
National Records Center, Washington (NRC)
The author has also made use of various private sources.

Books

Aeschimann, Éric and Riché, Pascal, *La Guerre de Sept Ans: Histoire secrète du franc fort 1989–1996* (Paris: Calman-Lévy, 1996)
Albert, Michel, *Capitalime contre Capitalisme* (Paris: Éditions du Seuil, 1991)
Aldrich, Richard J., *The Hidden Hand: Britain, America and Cold War secret intelligence* (Woodstock and New York: Overlook Press, 2002)
Allinson, A.R., *The War Diary of the Emperor Frederick III 1870–71* (Westport: Greenwood Press. 1971 – originally published 1926)
Aron, Raymond, *In Defence of Decadent Europe* (New York: University Press of America, 1979)
Arthuis, Jean, *Mondialisation: la France à contre-emploi* (Paris: Calman-Lévy, 2007)
Attali, Jacques, *Verbatim I 1981–86* (Paris: Fayard, 1993)
—— , *Verbatim II 1986–88* (Paris: Fayard, 1995)
—— , *Verbatim III, Première partie 1988–89* (Paris: Fayard, 1996)
—— , *Verbatim III, Deuxième partie 1990–91* (Paris: Fayard, 1996)
—— , *C'était François Mitterrand* (Paris: Fayard, 2005)
Bakker, Age, Boot, Henk, Skijen, Olaf and Vanthoor, Wim (eds), *Monetary Stability through International Cooperation: Essays in honour of André Szász* (Dordrecht: Kluwer, 1994)
Baldwin, Richard, *Towards an Integrated Europe* (London: Centre for European Policy Research, 2004)
Bank for International Settlements, *The Bank for International Settlements and the Basle Meetings* (Basle: Bank for International Settlements, 1980)
Baring, Arnulf, *Scheitert Deutschland?* (Stuttgart: Deutsche Verlags-Anstalt, 1997)
Barucci, Piero, *L'Isola Italiana del Tesoro* (Milan: Rizzoli, 1995)
Bini Smaghi, Lorenzo, *Il Paradosso dell'Euro* (Milan: Rizzoli, 2008)
Bizouarne, Léon, *La Haute Banque: Son rôle dans la libération du territoire Français en 1871–72 et 1873* (Paris: P. Dupont, 1892)
Blessing, Karl, *Im Kampf um gutes Geld* (Frankfurt: Fritz Knapp, 1966)
Bordo, Michael D. and Schwarz, Anna J. (eds), *A Retrospective on the Classical Gold Standard, 1821–1931* (Chicago: University of Chicago, 1984)
Bower, Tom, *Gordon Brown* (London: Harper Collins, 2004)
Brandt, Willy, *Erinnerungen* (Frankfurt: Propyläen, 1989)
Brawand, Leo, *Wohin steuert die deutsche Wirtschaft?* (Munich: Desch, 1971)
Brown, Brendan, *Euro on Trial* (London: Palgrave Macmillan, 2004)
Buchan, David, *Europe: The Strange Superpower* (Dartmouth: Aldershot, 1993)
Callaghan, James, *Time and Chance* (London: William Collins, 1987)
Camdessus, Michel, *Le Soursaut: Vers une nouvelle croissance pour la France* (Paris: La documentation Française, 2004)
Campbell, Alastair, *The Blair Years* (London, Hutchinson, 2007)
Chabot, Christian, *Understanding the Euro: The clear and concise guide to the new trans-European currency* (New York: McGraw Hill, 1999)
Ciampi, Carlo Azeglio, *Dalla Crisi al Risanamento* (Rome: Treves Editore, 2005)
Cobham, David and Zis, George (eds) *From EMS to EMU, 1979 to 1999 and Beyond* (London: Macmillan, 1999)
Cohen, Benjamin J. *The Future of Sterling as an International Currency* (London, New York: Macmillan/St Martin's Press, 1971)
Colchester, Nicholas and Buchan, David, *Europe Relaunched: Truths and illusions on the way to 1992* (London: Hutchinson, 1990)

Cole, Alistair, *François Mitterrand: A study in political leadership* (London: Routledge, 1994)

Collignon, Stefan, *Europe's Monetary Future* (London: Pinter Publishers, 1994)

Congdon, Tim, *Keynes, the Keynesians and Monetarism* (Cheltenham: Edward Elgar, 2007)

Connolly, Bernard, *The Rotten Heart of Europe* (London: Faber and Faber, 1995)

Coombs, Charles, *The Arena of International Finance* (New York: John Wiley, 1976)

Cottrell, Philip, Notaras, Gérassimos and Tortella, Gabriel (eds), *From the Athenian Tetradrachm to the Euro: Studies in European Monetary Integration* (Aldershot: Ashgate, 2007)

Cottrell, Philip, Lange, Even and Olsson, Ulf (eds), *Centres and Peripheries in Banking: The historical development of financial markets* (Aldershot: Ashgate, 2007)

Crockett, Andrew, *International Money* (London: Thomas Nelson, 1977)

Davies, Glyn, *A History of Money From Ancient Times to the Present Day* (Cardiff: University of Wales Press, 2002)

Deane, Marjorie and Pringle, Robert, *The Central Banks* (London: Hamish Hamilton, 1994).

Debré, Michel, *Mémoires: Gouverner autrement 1962–70* (Paris: Albin Michel, 1993)

Delors, Jacques. *Mémoires* (Plon: Paris, 2004)

—— , *L'Europe Tragique et Magnifique: Les grands enjeux européens* (Paris, Éditions Saint-Simon, 2006)

Deutsche Bundesbank (ed.) *Währung und Wirtschaft in Europa 1875–1975* (Frankfurt: Fritz Knapp, 1976)

—— , *Hans Tietmeyer: Währungsstabilität für Europa* (Baden-Baden: Nomos Verlag, 1996)

—— , *Fünfzig Jahre Deutsche Mark: Notenbank und Währung in Deutschland seit 1948* (Munich: C.H. Beck, 1998) [also published as *Fifty Years of the Deutsche Mark: Central Bank and the Currency in Germany since 1948* (Oxford/New York: Oxford University Press, 1999)]

Driffill, John and Beber, Massimo (eds), *A Currency for Europe: The currency as an element of division or of union in Europe* (London: Lothian Foundation Press, 1991)

Duchêne, François, *Jean Monnet: The first statesman of interdependence* (London, New York: W.W. Norton, 1994)

Dyson, Kenneth and Featherstone, Kevin, *The Road to Maastricht: Negotiating Economic and Monetary Union* (Oxford: Oxford University Press, 1999).

Eichengreen, Barry, *Golden Fetters: The Gold Standard and the Great Depression, 1919–1939* (New York, Oxford: Oxford University Press, 1992)

—— , *The European Economy since 1945* (Princeton: Princeton University Press, 2007)

Eltis, Walter, *Britain, Europe and EMU* (London: Macmillan, 2000)

Emminger, Otmar, *Währungspolitik im Wandel der Zeit* (Frankfurt: Fritz Knapp, 1966)

—— , *D-Mark, Dollar, Währungskrisen* (Stuttgart: Deutsche Verlags-Anstalt, 1986)

European Central Bank, *Monetary Policy: A journey from theory to practice* (Frankfurt: European Central Bank, 2006)

European Commission, *EMU@10: Successes and challenges after ten years of Economic and Monetary Union* (Brussels: European Communities, 2008)

Feldman, Gerald D., *The Great Disorder: Politics, economics and society in the German Inflation, 1914–1924* (New York/Oxford: Oxford University Press, 1993)

Ferguson, Niall, *The War of the World* (London, Allen Lane, 2006)

Funk, Walther, *Wirtschaftliche Neuordnung Europas* (Berlin: M. Müller und Sohn, 1940)

Gaddis, John Lewis, *The Cold War* (London: Penguin, 2005)

Galbraith, J.K., *Money, Whence It Came, Where It Went* (Boston: Houghton Mifflin, 1975)

Garton Ash, Timothy, *In Europe's Name: Germany and the Divided Continent* (London: Jonathan Cape, 1993)

de Gaulle, Charles, *Mémoires de l'Espoir, L'Effort 1962–1971* (Paris: Plon, 1971)

Gauron, André, *European Misunderstanding* (New York: Algora, 2000)

Gayer, Arthur D., *Monetary Policy and Economic Stabilisation: A study of the Gold Standard* (A. and C. Black: London, 1935)

Genscher, Hans-Dietrich, *Erinnerungen* (Berlin: Siedler, 1995)

George, Stephen, *An Awkward Partner: Britain in the European Community* (Oxford: Oxford University Press, 1990)

Giersch, Herbert, Paque, Karl-Heinz, and Schmieding, Holger, *The Fading Miracle: Four Decades of Market Economy in Germany* (Cambridge: Cambridge University Press, 1992)

Giesbert, Franz-Olivier, *Jacques Chirac* (Paris: Éditions du Seuil, 1987)

——— , *Le Président* (Paris: Éditions du Seuil, 1990)

Gilbert, Milton, *Quest for World Monetary Order: The Gold-Dollar system and its aftermath* (New York: John Wiley, 1980)

Giordano, Francesco, *Storia del Sistema Banacario Italiano* (Rome: Donzelli, 2007)

Giscard D'Estaing, Valéry, *Macht und Leben, Erinnerungen* (Ullstein: Berlin, 1988) [originally published as *Le Pouvoir et la Vie* (Paris: Compagnie 12, 1988)]

Grant, Charles, *Delors: Inside the house that Jacques built* (London: Nicholas Brealey, 1994)

Greenspan, Alan, *The Age of Turbulence: Adventures in a new world* (London, New York: Penguin, 2007)

Greider, William, *Secrets of the Temple: How the Federal Reserve runs the country* (New York: Simon and Schuster, 1987)

Gretschmann, Klaus (ed.), *Economic and Monetary Union: Implications for national policymakers* (Maastricht: European Institute of Public Administration, 1993)

von der Groeben, Hans and Mestmäcker, Ernst-Joachim (eds), *Ziele und Methoden der europäischen Integration* (Frankfurt: Athenäum, 1972)

Gros, Daniel and Thygesen, Niels, *European Monetary Integration* (London: Longman, 1992)

Grubel, Herbert G., *The International Monetary System* (London: Penguin, 1969)

Guigou, Elisabeth, *Une Femme au Coeur de l'État* (Paris: Fayard, 2000)

Hankel, Wilhelm, Schachtschneider, Karl Albrecht and Starbatty, Joachim (eds), *Der Ökonom als Politiker: Europa, Geld und die soziale Frage: Festschrift für Wilhelm Nölling* (Stuttgart: Lucius and Lucius, 2003)

Harding, Rebecca and Paterson, William E. (eds), *The Future of the German Economy: An end to the miracle?* (Manchester: Manchester University Press, 2000)

Healey, Denis, *The Time of My Life* (London: Michael Joseph, 1989)

Heath, Edward, *The Course of My Life* (London: Hodder and Stoughton, 1998)

Helfferich, Karl, *Das Geld* (Leipzig: C.L. Hirschfeld, 1903/1923) [also published as *Money* (London: Ernst Benn, 1927)]

Henderson, Nicholas, *Mandarin: The diaries of an ambassador* (London: Weidenfeld and Nicholson, 1994)

Hennessy, Peter, *The Prime Minister: The office and its holders since 1945* (London: Penguin, 2000)

Hoffmeyer, Erik, *The International Monetary System* (Amsterdam: Elsevier Science Publishers, 1992)

Hogg, Sarah and Hill, Jonathan *Too Close to Call* (London: Little, Brown, 1995)

Horne, Alistair, *Harold Macmillan, Volume II 1956–1986*, (London/New York: Penguin, 1989)

Howe, Geoffrey, *Conflict of Loyalty* (London: Macmillan, 1994)

Hüfner, Martin, *Europa: Die Macht von Morgen* (Munich: Hanser Verlag, 2006)

——— , *Comeback für Deutschland* (Munich: Hanser Verlag, 2007)

Hurd, Douglas, *Memoirs* (London: Little, Brown, 2003)

Issing, Otmar, *Der Euro: Geburt, Erfolg, Zukunft* (Munich: Franz Vahlen, 2008).

James, Harold, *International Monetary Cooperation since Bretton Woods* (New York, Oxford: Oxford University Press, 1996)

——— , *The End of Globalization: Lessons from the Great Depression* (Cambridge: Harvard University Press, 2001)

——— , *The Roman Predicament: How the rules of international order create the politics of Empire* (Princeton: Princeton University Press, 2006)

——— , *Family Capitalism* (Cambridge, Mass., London: Belknap Press, 2006)

Jenkins, Roy, *The Chancellors* (London: Macmillan, 1998)

Johnson, Christopher and Collignon, Stefan (eds), *The Monetary Economics of Europe: Causes of the EMS Crisis* (London: Pinter Publishers, 1994)

Jörges, Hans-Ulrich (ed.) *Der Kampf um den Euro: Wie riskant ist die Währungsunion?* (Hamburg: Hoffmann and Campe, 1998)

Judt, Tony, *Postwar: A history of Europe since 1945* (London: Heinemann, 2005)

Keegan, Victor and Kettle, Martin (eds), *The New Europe* (London: Fourth Estate, 1993)

Keegan, William, *The Prudence of Mr Gordon Brown* (Chichester: John Wiley, 2003)

Kenen, Peter B., *Economic and Monetary Union in Europe: Moving beyond Maastricht* (Cambridge, New York: Cambridge University Press, 1995)

Kennedy, Ellen *The Bundesbank: Germany's Central Bank in the International Monetary System* (London: Pinter Publishers, 1991)

Keynes, John Maynard, *The Economic Consequences of the Peace* (London: Macmillan, 1919)

—— , *Monetary Reform* (London: Macmillan, 1923)

—— , *A Treatise on Money* (London: Macmillan, 1930)

Kissinger, Henry, *Diplomacy* (New York: Simon and Schuster, 1994)

—— , *The White House Years* (Boston: Little, Brown, 1979)

Koerfer, Daniel, *Kampf ums Kanzleramt: Erhard und Adenauer* (Stuttgart: Deutsche Verlags-Antalt, 1988)

Kohl, Helmut, *Ich wollte Deutschlands Einheit* (Berlin: Propyläen, 1996)

—— , *Erinnerungen 1982–1990* (Droemer: Munich, 2005)

—— , *Erinnerungen 1990–1994* (Droemer: Munich, 2007)

Krause, Axel, *Inside the New Europe* (New York: Cornelia and Michael Bessie Books, 1991)

Küsters, Hans Jürgen and Hofmann, Daniel (eds), *Dokumente zur Deutschlandpolitik Deutsche Einheit: Sonderedition aus den Akten des Bundeskanzleramtes 1989/90* (Munich: R. Oldenbourg, 1998)

Lamont, Norman, *In Office.* (Little, Brown: London, 1999)

Lawson, Nigel, *The View from No. 11: Memoirs of a Tory radical* (Bantam Press, 1992)

Leach, Rodney, *Europe: A Concise Encyclopedia of the European Union* (London: Profile Books, 1998)

Ledwidge, Bernard, *De Gaulle* (London: Weidenfeld and Nicolson, 1982)

Ludlow, Peter, *The Making of the European Monetary System* (London: Butterworth, 1982)

Macmillan, Harold, *Riding the Storm 1956–1959* (London: Macmillan, 1971)

—— , *Pointing the Way 1959–1961* (London: Macmillan, 1972)

—— , *At the End of the Day 1961–1963* (London: Macmillan, 1973)

Major, John, *The Autobiography* (London: Harper Collins, 1999)

Marshall, Matt, *The Bank: The birth of Europe's Central Bank and the rebirth of Europe's power* (London: Random House, 1999)

Markwell, Donald, *John Maynard Keynes and International Relations: Economic paths to war and peace* (Oxford: Oxford University Press, 2006)

Marsh, David, *The Germans: Rich, bothered and divided* (London: Hutchinson, 1989)

—— , *The Bundesbank: The Bank that Rules Europe* (London: Heinemann, 1992)

—— , *The Crisis of Unity* (London: Heinemann, 1994)

Meisner, H.O., *Denkwürdigkeiten des General-Feldmarschalls Alfred Grafen von Waldersee* (Stuttgart, Berlin: Deutsche Verlags-Anstalt, 1922)

Mitterrand, François, *Réflexions sur la Politique Extérieure de la France* (Fayard: Paris, 1986)

—— , *De l'Allemagne, de la France* (Paris: Odile Jacob, 1996)

—— , *Mémoires interrompues* (Paris: Odile Jacob, 1996)

Moravcsik, Andrew, *The Choice for Europe* (Itaca: Cornell University Press, 1998)

Morgan, Kenneth O., *Callaghan: A Life* (Oxford: Oxford University Press, 1997)

Naudin, Francois, *The European Central Bank, A bank for the 21st century* (London: Kogan Page, 2000)

Naughtie, James, *The Rivals: The intimate story of a political marriage* (London: Fourth Estate, 2001)

Nay, Catherine, *Le Noir et le Rouge* (Paris: Grasset, 1984)

Newhouse, John, *De Gaulle and the Anglo-Saxons* (London: André Deutsch, 1970)

Nölling, Wilhelm, *Unser Geld: Der Kampf um die Stabilität der Währungen in Europa* (Berlin, Frankfurt: Ullstein 1993)

Nölling, Wilhelm, Schachtschneider, Karl Albrecht and Starbatty, Joachim (eds), *Währungsunion und Wirtschaft: Festschrift für Wilhelm Hankel* (Stuttgart: Lucius and Lucius, 1999)

Norman, Peter, *Plumbers and Visionaries: Securities settlement and Europe's financial market* (New York: John Wiley, 2008)

Péan, Pierre, *Une Jeunesse Française* (Paris: Fayard:, 1994)

Peston, Robert, *Brown's Britain* (London: Short Books, 2005)

Posen, Adam (ed.), *The Euro at Five: Ready for a global role?* (Washington: Institute for International Economics, 2005)

Rawnsley, Andrew, *Servants of the People: The inside story of New Labour* (London: Hamish Hamilton, 2000)

Reading, Brian, *The Fourth Reich* (London: Weidenfeld and Nicolson, 1995)

Ridley, Nicholas, *My Style of Government: The Thatcher years* (London: Hutchinson, 1991)

Roberts, Richard and Kynaston, David, *The Bank of England: Money, power and influence 1694–1884* (London, 1994)

de Rougemont., Denis, *The Meaning of Europe* (London: Sidgwick and Jackson, 1965)

Sandbrook, Dominic, *Never Had It So Good: A History of Britain from Suez to the Beatles* (London: Little, Brown, 2005)

Sarkozy, Nicolas, *Ensemble* (Paris: XO Éditions, 2007)

Schabert, Tilo, *Mitterrand et la Réunification Allemande: Une histoire secrète (1981–1995)* (Grasset, Paris, 2005)

Scheller, Hanspeter K., *The European Central Bank: History, role and functions* (Frankfurt: European Central Bank, 2004)

Schiller, Karl, *Der schwierige Weg in die offene Gesellschaft: Kritische Anmerkungen zur deutschen Wiedervereinigung* (Berlin: Siedler, 1994)

Schönfelder, Wilhelm and Thiel, Elke (eds), *Ein Markt, Eine Währung: Die Verhandlungen zur Wirtschafts- und Wähungsunion* (Baden-Baden: Nomos, 1994)

Schmidt, Helmut, *Menschen und Mächte* (Berlin: Siedler, 1987)

——, *Die Deutschen und ihre Nachbarn*, (Berlin: Siedler, 1990)

Sédillot, René, *Histoire Morale et Immorale de la Monnaie* (Paris: Bordas, 1999)

de Silguy, Yves-Thibault, *L'Économie, Fil d'Ariane de l'Europe* (Paris: Presses de Sciences Po, 2000)

Sinn, Hans-Werner, *Ist Deutschland noch zu retten?* (Munich: Econ Verlag, 2003)

Smyser, W.R., *The Economy of United Germany: Colussus at the Crossroads* (London: C. Hurst, 1992)

Snyckers, Alexander, *La Reichsbank et la Banque de France: Leur Politique* (Paris: Arthur Rousseau, 1908)

Solomon, Stephen, *The Confidence Game: How unelected central bankers are governing the changed world economy* (New York: Simon and Schuster, 1995)

Soros, George, *Open Society: Reforming global capitalism* (New York: Public Affairs, 1998)

——, *The New Paradigm for Financial Markets: The credit crash of 2008 and what it means* (New York: Public Affairs, 2008)

Spierenburg, Dirk and Poidevin, Raymond, *The History of the High Authority of the European Coal and Steel Community: Supranationality in operation* (London: Weidenfeld and Nicolson, 1994)

Stephens, Philip, *Politics and the Pound* (London: Macmillan, 1996)

Stern, Fritz, *Gold and Iron, Bismarck, Bleichröder and the building of the German Empire* (London: George Allen and Unwin, 1977)

Stoltenberg, Gerhard, *Wendepunkt: Stationen deutscher Geschichte 1947–1990* (Berlin: Siedler, 1997)

Strauss, Franz-Josef, *Die Erinnerungen* (Berlin: Siedler, 1989)

Stürmer, Michael, *The German Empire 1871–76* (London: Weidenfeld and Nicolson, 2000)

Stürmer, Michael, Teichmann, Gabriele and Treue, Wilhelm, *Wagen und Wägen* (Munich: Piper Verlag, 1989)

Szász, André, *The Road to Monetary Union* (London: Macmillan, 1999)

Teltschik, Horst, *329 Tage: Innenansichten der Einigung* (Berlin: Siedler, 1991)
Temperton, Paul (ed.), *The Euro* (John Wiley: New York, 1997)
——, *The European Currency Crisis: What chance now for a single European currency?* (Cambridge, Chicago: Probus, 1993)
Thatcher, Margaret, *The Downing Street Years* (London: Harper Collins, 1993)
Tietmeyer, Hans, *Herausforderung Euro* (Munich/Vienna: Hanser, 2005)
Tilford, Simon, *Will the Eurozone Crack?* (London: Centre for European Reform, 2006)
Toniolo, Gianni (with the assistance of Clement, Piet) *Central Bank Cooperation at the Bank for International Settlements 1930–1973* (Cambridge, New York: Cambridge University Press, 2005)
Treaster, Joseph B., *Paul Volcker: The making of a financial legend* (New York: John Wiley, 2004)
Trotsky, Léon, *Où Va la France?* (Paris: Librairie du Travail, 1936)
Tsoukalis, Loukas, *The New European Economy: The politics and economics of integration* (Oxford: Oxford University Press, 1991)
Van Dormel, Armand, *Bretton Woods: Birth of a monetary system* (London: Macmillan, 1978)
Védrine, Hubert, *Les Mondes de François Mitterrand* (Paris: Fayard, 1996)
Volcker, Paul and Gyohten, Toyoo, *Changing Fortunes: The world's money and the threat to American leadership* (New York: Times Books, 1992)
Waigel, Theo (ed.), *Unser Zukunft heißt Europa: Der Weg zur Wirtschafts- und Währungsunion* (Düsseldorf: EconVerlag, 1996)
Waigel, Theo and Schell, Manfred (eds), *Tage, die Deutschland und die Welt veränderten: Vom Mauerfall zum Kaukasus – Die deutsche Währungsunion* (Munich: Ferenczy, 1994)
Wall, Stephen, *A Stranger in Europe: Britain and the EU from Thatcher to Blair* (Oxford, New York: Oxford University Press, 2008)
Wass, Douglas, *Decline to Fall: The making of British macro-economic policy and the 1976 IMF crisis* (Oxford, New York: Oxford University Press, 2008)
Weber, Adolf, *Spekulationsbanken und Depositenbanken* (Leipzig: Duncker and Humblot, 1902)
Weber, Manfred (ed.), *Europe auf dem Weg zur Währungsunion* (Darmstadt: Wissenschaftliche Buchgesellschaft, 1991)
Williams, Charles, *The Last Great Frenchman: A Life of General de Gaulle* (London: Little, Brown, 1993)
Young, Hugo, *One of Us* (London: Macmillan, 1989)
——, *This Blessed Plot* (London, Macmillan, 1998)
Zelikow, Philip and Rice, Condoleezza, *Germany Reunited and Europe Transformed* (Cambridge: Harvard University Press, 1995)

Main Author Interviews, with Interview Dates

Amato, Giuliano Prime Minister, Italy (1992–93 and 2000–01); Interior Minister (2006–08): London/Rome, 29 June 2008*
Alphandéry, Edmond Finance Minister, France (1993–95): Paris, 30 May 2007
Autheman, Marc-Antoine Chief of Staff to Finance Minister Pierre Bérégovoy (later Prime Minister): Paris, 30 January 2008
Balladur, Edouard Prime Minister, France (1993–95); Finance Minister, (1986–88): Paris, 30 May 2007
Barucci, Piero Finance Minister, Italy (1992–93): London/Rome, 6 August and 11 October 2007†
Bini Smaghi, Lorenzo Member, Executive Board, European Central Bank (2005–); Director General for International Financial Relations, Finance Ministry, Italy (1998–2005): Frankfurt, 16 April 2007
Bonello, Michael Governor, Central Bank of Malta (1999–): Valetta/London, 11 July 2008*
Breuer, Rolf Chairman, Supervisory Board, Deutsche Bank (2002–06); Speaker, Management Board (1995–2002): Frankfurt, 18 October 2007
Budd, Sir Alan Member, Bank of England Monetary Policy Committee (1997–99); Chief Economic Adviser, HM Treasury (1991–97): London, 25 September 2007

Burns, Lord Terence Permanent Secretary, HM Treasury (1991–98); Chief Economic Adviser (1980–1991): London, 27 September 2007

Camdessus, Michel Director, Treasury, France (1982–84); Governor, Banque de France (1984–87); Managing Director, International Monetary Fund (1987–2000): Paris, 15 June and 4 October 2007

Chevènement, Jean-Pierre Interior Minister, France (1997–2000); Defence Minister (1988–91); Education Minister (1984–86): Paris, 4 July 2007

Clarke, Kenneth Chancellor of the Exchequer, UK (1993–1997): London, 11 March 2008

Crockett, Sir Andrew General Manager, Bank for International Settlements (1994–2003); Executive Director, Bank of England (1989–93): New York/London, 26 February 2008*

Dini, Lamberto Foreign Minister, Italy (1996–2001); Prime Minister (1995–96); Finance Minister (1994); Director General, Banca d'Italia (1979–94): Rome, 26 June 2007

Delors, Jacques President, European Commission (1985–94); Finance Minister, France (1981–84): Paris, 29 May 2007

Eichel, Hans Finance Minister, Germany (1999–2005): Berlin, 25 April 2007

Fabius, Laurent Finance Minister, France (2000–02); Prime Minister (1984–86); Industry and Research Minister (1983–84); Budget Minister (1981–83): Paris, 29 May 2007

Fernández Ordóñez, Miguel Ángel Governor, Banco de España (2006–); Secretary of State for Economy; Secretary of State for Commerce: Madrid/London, 13 June 2008†

Gauron, André Adviser to Finance Minister, later Prime Minister Pierre Bérégovoy: Paris, 29 May 2007

Genscher, Hans-Dietrich Foreign Minister, Germany (1974–93): Pech, 5 October 2007

George, Edward Lord Governor, Bank of England (1993–2003); Deputy Governor (1990–93); Executive Director, (1982–90): London, 8 April 2008

Giscard d'Estaing, Valéry President, France (1974–81); Finance Minister (1962–66, 1969–74): Paris, 28 June 2007

González-Páramo, José Manuel Member, Executive Board, European Central Bank (2004–); Member, Executive Board, Banco de España (1998–2004): Frankfurt, 16 July 2007

Guaino, Henri Adviser to President Nicolas Sarkozy (2007–): Paris, 30 January 2008

Guigou, Elisabeth Employment Minister, France (2000–02); Justice Minister (1997–2000); Europe Minister (1990–93), Adviser to President François Mitterrand (1982–90): Paris, 4 July 2007

Guth, Wilfried Chairman, Supervisory Board, Deutsche Bank (1985–90); Speaker, Management Board (1976–85): Frankfurt, 3 May 2007

Hannoun, Hervé Deputy General Manager, Bank for International Settlements (2006–); Deputy Governor, Banque de France (1993–2005): Basle, 17 August 2007

Hauser, Hansgeorg Parliamentary State Secretary, Finance Ministry, Germany (1995–98): Berlin, 25 January 2008

Healey, Denis Lord Chancellor of the Exchequer, UK (1974–1979); Defence Secretary (1964–70): Alfriston, 10 April 2007

Henderson, Sir Nicholas UK Ambassador to the US (1979–82); Ambassador to Paris (1975–79); Ambassador to West Germany (1972–75): London, 14 May 2008

Hogg, Sarah Baroness Chairman, 3i plc (2002–); Head of Prime Minister John Major's Policy Unit (1990–95): London, 11 February 2008

Howe, Geoffrey Lord Chancellor of the Exchequer (1979–83); Foreign Secretary (1983–87): London, 18 March 2008

Hurd, Douglas Lord Foreign Secretary, UK (1989–95): London, 18 June 2008

Hurley, John Governor, Central Bank and Financial Services Authority, Ireland (2002–09): Dublin, 1 October 2007

Issing, Otmar Member, Executive Board, European Central Bank (1998–2006); Member, Directorate, Deutsche Bundesbank (1990–98); Frankfurt, 27 April 2007: Hamburg, 16 October 2007

Juncker, Jean-Claude Prime Minister, Luxembourg (1995–); Finance Minister (1989–): Luxembourg, 28 January 2008

Kohl, Helmut Chancellor, Germany (1982–98): Bonn, 7 February 1989

Kok, Wim Prime Minister, Netherlands (1994–2002); Finance Minister (1989–2004): Amsterdam, 2 October 2007

von Kyaw, Dietrich Permanent Representative, Germany, European Union (1993–99): Berlin, 26 April 2007

Lagayette, Philippe Chief Executive, Caisse des Dépôts et des Consignations (1992–97); Deputy Governor, Banque de France (1984–92); Chief of Staff to Finance Minister Jacques Delors (1982–84): Paris, 28 May 2007

Lahnstein, Manfred Finance Minister, Germany (1982); State Secretary, Finance Ministry (1977–82): Hamburg, 16 June 2007

Lambert, Richard Director General, Confederation of British Industry (2007–): London, 14 June 2007

Lamfalussy, Alexandre President, European Monetary Institute (1994–97); General Manager, Bank for International Settlements (1985–93): Ohain, 22 May 2007

Lamont, Norman Chancellor of the Exchequer, UK (1990–93): London, 2 April 2007

de Larosière, Jacques President, European Bank for Reconstruction and Development (1993–98); Governor, Banque de France (1987–93); Managing Director, International Monetary Fund (1978–87); Director, Treasury (1974–78): Paris, 28 June 2007

Lawson, Nigel Lord Chancellor of the Exchequer, UK (1983–89): London, 30 April 2007

Leigh-Pemberton, Robin (Lord Kingsdown) Governor, Bank of England (1983–93): London, 24 April 2007

Lemierre, Jean, President, European Bank for Reconstruction and Development (2000–08); Director, Treasury, France (1995–2000): London, 8 May 2007

Lipsky, John First Deputy Managing Director, International Monetary Fund (2006–): Washington, 9 March 2007

Loehnis, Anthony International Director, Bank of England (1980–89): London, 26 March 2008

Lubbers, Ruud Prime Minister, Netherlands (1982–94): Amsterdam, 7 September 2007

Kimmitt, Robert Deputy Secretary, US Treasury (2005–08); Ambassador to Germany (1991–93): Washington/London, 7 June 2007*

MacShane, Denis Minister for Europe, UK (2002–05): London, 13 May 2008

Major, Sir John Prime Minister, UK (1990–97); Chancellor of the Exchequer (1989–90); Foreign Secretary (1989): London, 26 September 2007

Müller, Klaus-Peter Chairman, Supervisory Board, Commerzbank (2008–); Chief Executive, (2001–08): Frankfurt, 3 May 2007

Noyer, Christian Governor, Banque de France (2003); Deputy President, European Central Bank (1998–2003); Director, Treasury, France (2003); Chief of Staff to Finance Ministers Jean Arthuis (1995–97) and Edmond Alphandéry (1993–95): Paris, 27 June 2007

Orphanides, Athanasios Governor, Central Bank of Cyprus (2007–): Nicosia/London, 11 July 2008*

Padoa-Schioppa, Tommaso Finance Minister, Italy (2006–08); Member, Executive Board, European Central Bank (1998–2005); Deputy Director General, Banca d'Italia (1984–97): Rome, 24 July 2007

Papademos, Lucas Deputy President, European Central Bank (2002–); Governor, Bank of Greece (1994–2002); Deputy Governor (1993–94): Frankfurt, 16 April 2007

Pébereau, Michel Chairman (1993–), BNP Paribas (to 2003, BNP); Chief Executive (1993–2003); Chairman and Chief Executive Crédit Commercial de France (1987–93); Chief of Staff to Finance Minister René Monory (1978–81): Paris, 30 January 2008

Peyrelevade, Jean Chairman, Crédit Lyonnais (1993–2003); Chairman, UAP (1988–93); Chairman, Compagnie de Suez (1983–85); Deputy Chief of Staff to Prime Minister Pierre Mauroy (1981–84): Paris, 4 October 2007

Pöhl, Karl Otto President, Deutsche Bundesbank (1980–91); Deputy President (1977–79); State Secretary, Finance Ministry, Germany (1972–77): Frankfurt, 9 May 2007 and Zurich, 17 August 2007

Prodi, Romano Prime Minister, Italy (1995–98 and 2006–08); President, European Commission (1999–2004): Rome, 5 June 2007

Profumo, Alessandro Chief Executive, Unicredit (1998–): Milan, 23 July 2007

von Richthofen, Hermann German Ambassador to the UK (1989–93): Berlin, 19 March 2007

Rocard, Michel Prime Minister, France (1988–91); Agriculture Minister (1983–85); Planning Minister (1981–83): Paris, 29 May 2007

Ruding, Onno Finance Minister, Netherlands (1982–89): Brussels, 22 May 2007

Saccomanni, Fabrizio Director General, Banca d'Italia (2006–); Vice President, European Bank for Reconstruction and Development (2003–06): Rome, 26 June 2007

Sapin, Michel Finance Minister, France (1991–93): Paris, 3 October 2007

Schlesinger, Helmut President, Deutsche Bundesbank (1991–93); Deputy President (1980–91): Frankfurt, 14 February 2007; Oberursel 2 July 2007

Schmidt, Helmut Chancellor, Germany (1974–82); Finance Minister (1972–74); Defence Minister (1969–72): Hamburg, 4 September 2007

Schönfelder, Wilhelm Permanent Representative, Germany, European Union (2003–07): Brussels, 22 May 2007

Schröder, Gerhard Chancellor, Germany (1998–2005): Berlin, 26 April 2007

de Silguy, Yves-Thibault Member, European Commission (1995–99): Paris, 15 June 2007

Simon, David Lord Minister for Trade and Competitiveness, UK (1997–99); Chairman BP plc (1995–97); Chief Executive; (1992–95): London, 22 January 2008

Stark, Dr Jürgen Member, Executive Board, European Central Bank (2006–); Deputy President, Deutsche Bundesbank (1998–2006); State Secretary, Finance Ministry (1995–98): Frankfurt, 14 April 2007

Steinbrück, Peer Finance Minister, Germany (2005–09): Berlin, 24 January 2008

Szász, André Member, Executive Board, Nederlandsche Bank (1973–94): Amsterdam, 23 May 2007

Tietmeyer, Hans President, Deutsche Bundesbank (1993–99); Deputy President (1991–93); Member of the Directorate (1990–91); State Secretary, Finance Ministry (1982–90): Königstein, 10 May 2007 and 17 April 2008

Trichet, Jean-Claude President, European Central Bank (2003–); Governor, Banque de France (1993–2003); Director, Treasury, France (1987–93): Frankfurt, 14 April 2007

Tumpel-Gugerell, Gertrude Board Member, Executive Board, European Central Bank (2003–); Deputy Governor, Österreichische Nationalbank (1998–2003): Frankfurt, 16 July 2007

Védrine, Hubert Foreign Minister, France (1997–2002); Adviser to President François Mitterrand (1981–91) Paris, 15 June 2007

Viermetz, Kurt Chairman, Supervisory Board, Deutsche Börse (2005–) and Hypo Real Estate (2003–): London, 27 November 2007

Volcker, Paul Chairman, Federal Reserve Board (1979–87); President, Federal Reserve Bank of New York (1975–79); Under Secretary for International Monetary Affairs, US Treasury (1969–74): New York, 28 August 2007

Waigel, Theo Finance Minister, Germany (1989–98): Munich, 17 April 2007

Walker, Peter Lord Secretary of State for Energy, UK (1983–87); Secretary of State for Trade and Industry (1972–74); Secretary of State for the Environment (1970–72): London, 17 January 2008

Wall, Sir Stephen Head, European Secretariat, Cabinet Office, UK (2000–04); Permanent Representative, UK, European Union (1995–2000): London, 18 June 2007

Weber, Axel President, Deutsche Bundesbank (2004–): Frankfurt, 21 May 2007

Wellink, Nout Member, Governing Board, Nederlandsche Bank (1982–); President (1997–): Amsterdam, 7 September 2007

Welteke, Ernst President, Deutsche Bundesbank (1999–2004): Frankfurt, 4 April 2007

All interviews in personal meetings except where stated: * Telephone; † E-mail

INDEX